SHADOWLAND
STREET HEROES

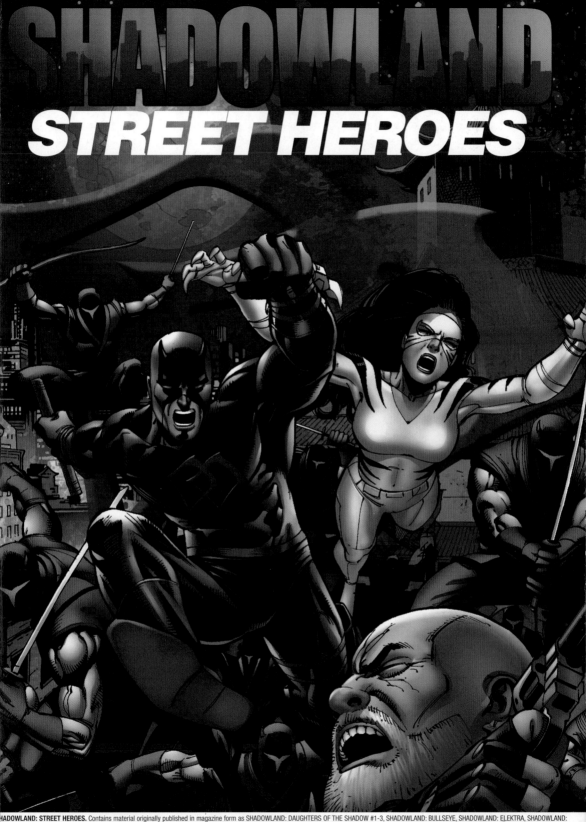

SHADOWLAND: STREET HEROES. Contains material originally published in magazine form as SHADOWLAND: DAUGHTERS OF THE SHADOW #1-3, SHADOWLAND: BULLSEYE, SHADOWLAND: ELEKTRA, SHADOWLAND: GHOST RIDER and SHADOWLAND: SPIDER-MAN. First printing 2011. ISBN# 978-0-7851-4887-6. Published by MARVEL WORLDWIDE, INC., a subsidiary of MARVEL ENTERTAINMENT, LLC. OFFICE OF PUBLICATION: 135 West 50th Street, New York, NY 10020. Copyright © 2010 and 2011 Marvel Characters, Inc. All rights reserved. $24.99 per copy in the U.S. and $27.99 in Canada (GST #R127032852); Canadian Agreement #40668537. All characters featured in this issue and the distinctive names and likenesses thereof, and all related indicia are trademarks of Marvel Characters, Inc. No similarity between any of the names, characters, persons, and/or institutions in this magazine with those of any living or dead person or institution is intended, and any such similarity which may exist is purely coincidental. **Printed in the U.S.A.** ALAN FINE, EVP - Office of the President, Marvel Worldwide, Inc. and EVP & CMO Marvel Characters B.V.; DAN BUCKLEY, Chief Executive Officer and Publisher - Print, Animation & Digital Media; JIM SOKOLOWSKI, Chief Operating Officer; DAVID GABRIEL, SVP of Publishing Sales & Circulation; DAVID BOGART, SVP of Business Affairs & Talent Management; MICHAEL PASCIULLO, VP Merchandising & Communications; JIM O'KEEFE, VP of Operations & Logistics; DAN CARR, Executive Director of Publishing Technology; JUSTIN F. GABRIE, Director of Publishing & Editorial Operations; SUSAN CRESPI, Editorial Operations Manager; ALEX MORALES, Publishing Operations Manager; STAN LEE, Chairman Emeritus. For information regarding advertising in Marvel Comics or on Marvel.com, please contact Ron Stern, VP of Business Development, at rstern@marvel.com. For Marvel subscription inquiries, please call 800-217-9158. **Manufactured between 1/10/2011 and 2/7/2011 by R.R. DONNELLEY, INC., SALEM, VA, USA.**

10 9 8 7 6 5 4 3 2 1

SHADOWLAND
STREET HEROES

SHADOWLAND: BULLSEYE
WRITER: **JOHN LAYMAN**
PENCILER: **SEAN CHEN**
INKER: **SANDU FLOREA**
COLORIST: **GURU eFX**
LETTERER: **VC'S JOE CARAMAGNA**
COVER ARTIST: **JOHN CHRISTOPHER TYLER**
ASSISTANT EDITOR: **TOM BRENNAN**
EDITOR: **STEPHEN WACKER**

SHADOWLAND: ELEKTRA
WRITER: **ZEB WELLS**
ARTIST: **EMMA RIOS**
COLORIST: **FABIO D'AURIA**
LETTERER: **VC'S JOE CARAMAGNA**
COVER ARTIST: **SANA TAKEDA**
ASSISTANT EDITOR: **ALEJANDRO ARBONA**
EDITOR: **STEPHEN WACKER**

SHADOWLAND: GHOST RIDER
WRITER: **ROB WILLIAMS**
ARTIST: **CLAYTON CRAIN**
LETTERER: **VC'S JOE CARAMAGNA**
COVER ARTIST: **CLAYTON CRAIN**
ASSISTANT EDITOR: **ALEJANDRO ARBONA**
EDITOR: **STEPHEN WACKER**

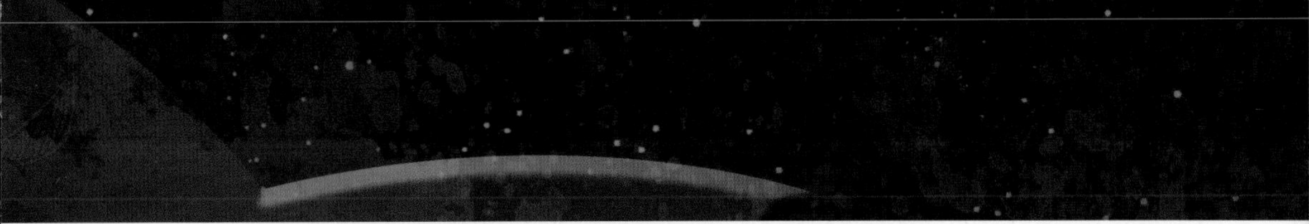

SHADOWLAND: DAUGHTERS OF THE SHADOW #1-3
WRITER: **JASON HENDERSON**
ARTIST: **IVAN RODRIGUEZ**
COLORIST: **JORGE MAESE**
LETTERER: **DAVE SHARPE**
COVER ARTIST: **JEAN-BAPTISTE ANDRENE**
ASSISTANT EDITOR: **MICHAEL HORWITZ**
EDITOR: **MARK PANICCIA**

SHADOWLAND: SPIDER-MAN
WRITER: **DAN SLOTT**
PENCILER: **PAULO SIQUEIRA**
INKERS: **AMILTON SANTOS, ROLAND PARIS**
& **PAULO SIQUEIRA**
COLORIST: **FABIO D'AURIA**
LETTERER: **VC'S JOE SABINO**
COVER ARTIST: **STEPHANIE HANS**
ASSISTANT EDITOR: **TOM BRENNAN**
EDITOR: **STEPHEN WACKER**
EXECUTIVE EDITOR: **TOM BREVOORT**

COLLECTION EDITOR & DESIGN: **CORY LEVINE**
EDITORIAL ASSISTANTS: **JAMES EMMETT** & **JOE HOCHSTEIN**
ASSISTANT EDITORS: **MATT MASDEU, ALEX STARBUCK** & **NELSON RIBEIRO**
EDITORS, SPECIAL PROJECTS: **JENNIFER GRÜNWALD** & **MARK D. BEAZLEY**
SENIOR EDITOR, SPECIAL PROJECTS: **JEFF YOUNGQUIST**
SENIOR VICE PRESIDENT OF SALES: **DAVID GABRIEL**

EDITOR IN CHIEF: **JOE QUESADA**
PUBLISHER: **DAN BUCKLEY**
EXECUTIVE PRODUCER: **ALAN FINE**

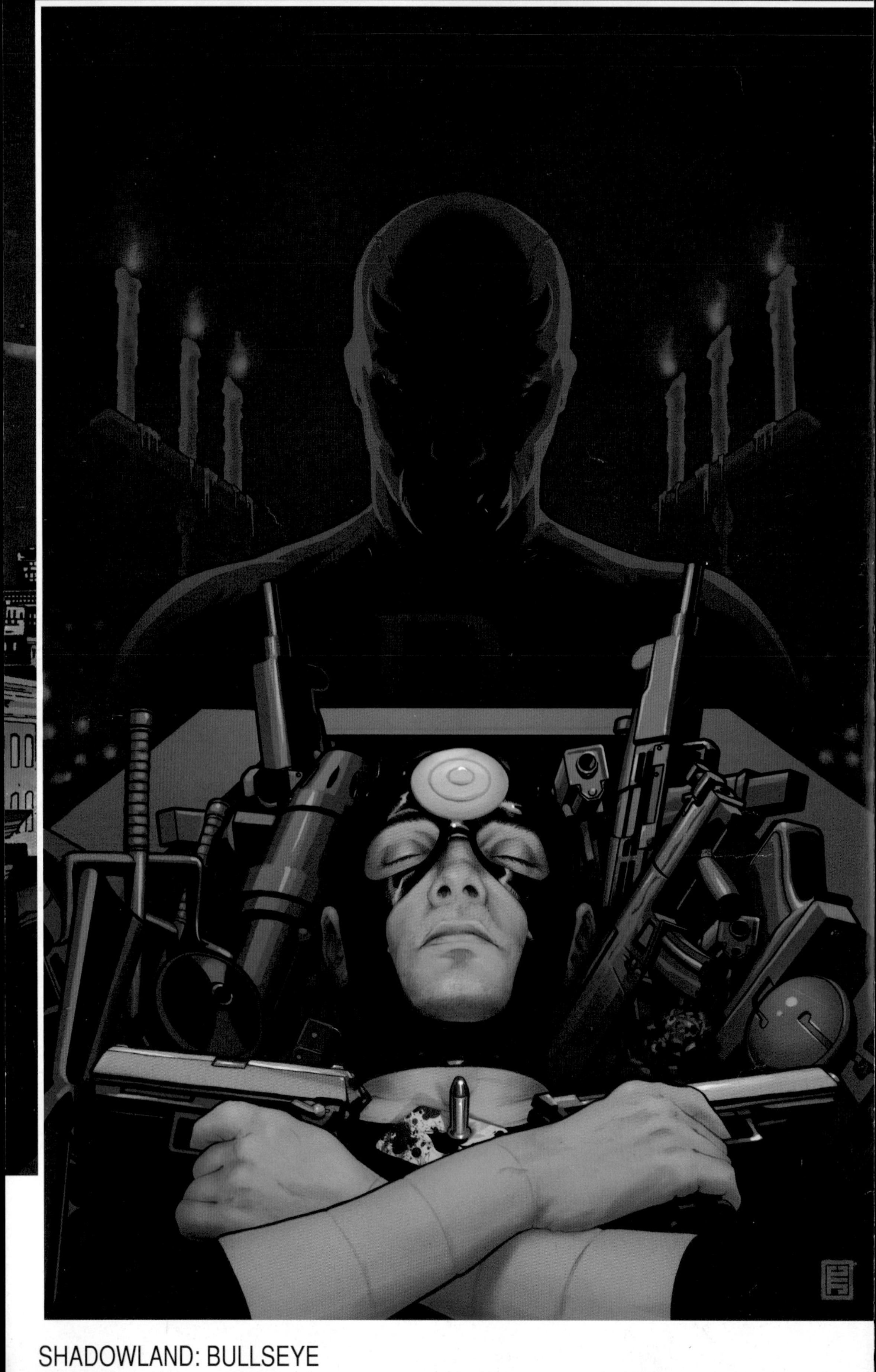

SHADOWLAND: BULLSEYE

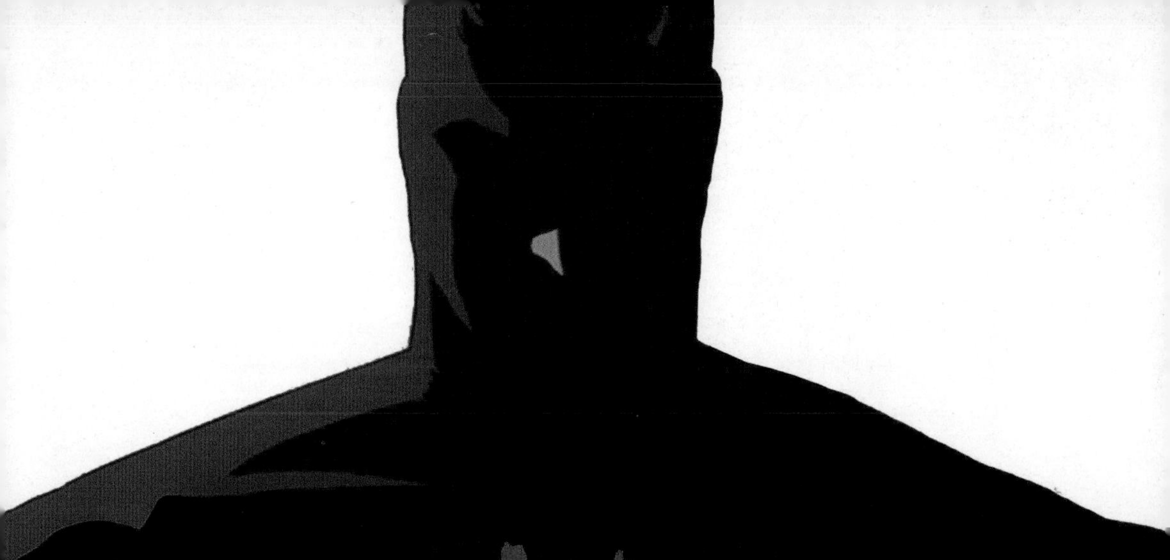

MATT MURDOCK DARED EVIL, AND LOST.

FOR YEARS, BULLSEYE, THE SUPERHUMAN ASSASSIN WHOSE LETHAL PRECISION CAN TURN ANY OB-
JECT INTO A WEAPON, HAS BEEN CONSIDERED ONE OF THE DEADLIEST KILLERS ON THE PLANET. WHEN
HIS ARCH-ENEMY, DAREDEVIL, TOOK LEADERSHIP OF THE HAND, BULLSEYE WAS SENT BY THEN-TOP
COP NORMAN OSBORN TO KILL
THE MAN WITHOUT FEAR.

BULLSEYE FAILED IN KILLING MURDOCK, BUT DID BLOW UP AN ENTIRE CITY BLOCK, KILLING 107
PEOPLE IN THE PROCESS. THESE DEATHS PUSHED DAREDEVIL OVER THE EDGE. HE TURNED THE HAND
INTO A VERITABLE ARMY, ONE THAT DEFENDED THE CITY STREETS WITH BRUTAL FORCE. AND ON THE
SITE OF THE BUILDING BULLSEYE
DEMOLISHED, DAREDEVIL BUILT SHADOWLAND, A FORTRESS FOR HIS FOLLOWERS...
AND A PRISON FOR HIS ENEMIES

BULLSEYE BROKE INTO SHADOWLAND, LOOKING FOR A FIGHT WITH DAREDEVIL...AND HE GOT ONE.
DAREDEVIL BRUTALIZED BULLSEYE, BREAKING BOTH HIS ARMS BEFORE KILLING BULLSEYE IN COLD
BLOOD.

SHADOWLAND
BULLSEYE

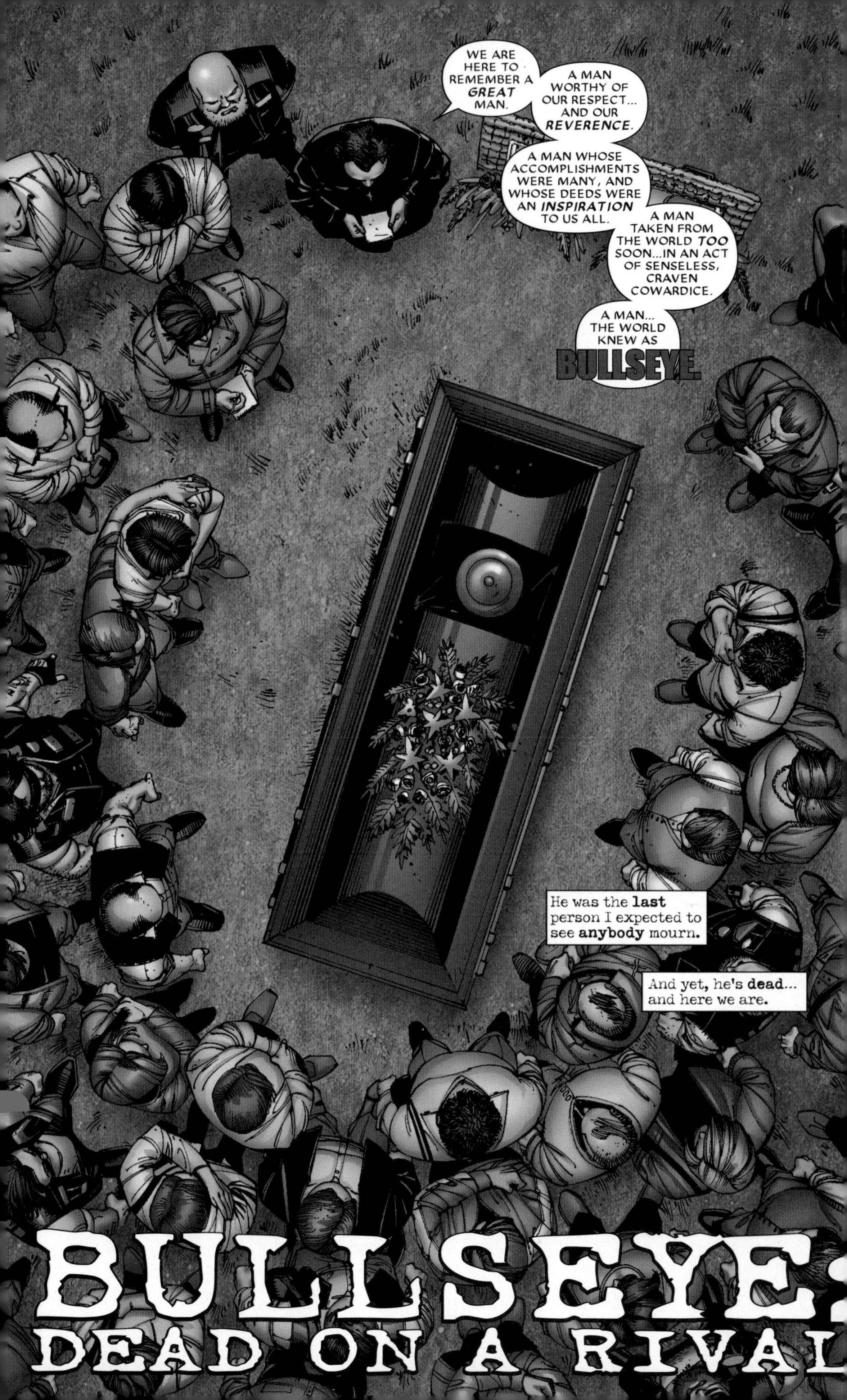
WE ARE HERE TO REMEMBER A GREAT MAN.
A MAN WORTHY OF OUR RESPECT... AND OUR REVERENCE.
A MAN WHOSE ACCOMPLISHMENTS WERE MANY, AND WHOSE DEEDS WERE AN INSPIRATION TO US ALL.
A MAN TAKEN FROM THE WORLD TOO SOON...IN AN ACT OF SENSELESS, CRAVEN COWARDICE.
A MAN... THE WORLD KNEW AS BULLSEYE.
He was the last person I expected to see anybody mourn.
And yet, he's dead... and here we are.
BULLSEYE:
DEAD ON A RIVAL

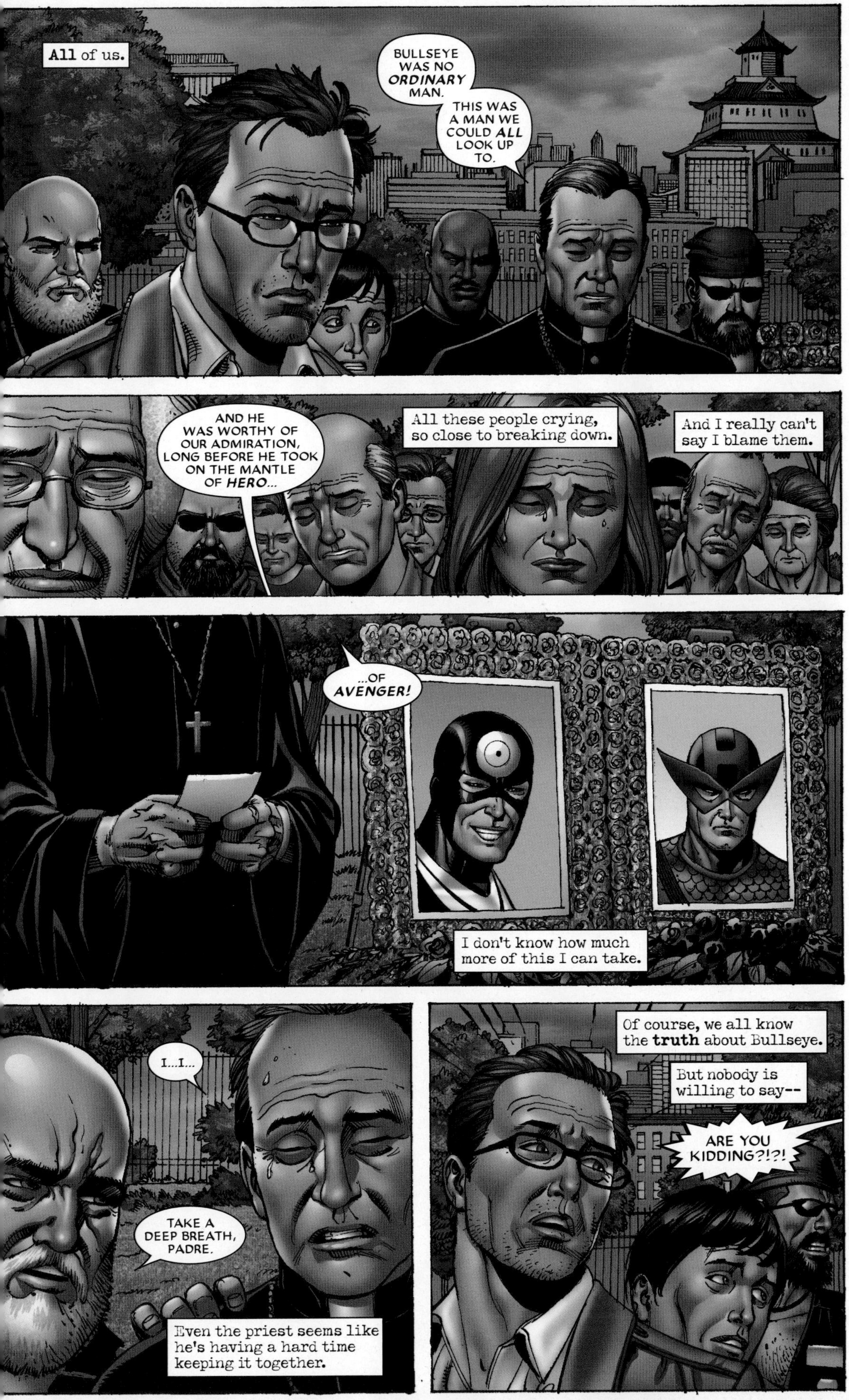

All of us.
BULLSEYE WAS NO ORDINARY MAN.
THIS WAS A MAN WE COULD ALL LOOK UP TO.
AND HE WAS WORTHY OF OUR ADMIRATION, LONG BEFORE HE TOOK ON THE MANTLE OF HERO...
All these people crying, so close to breaking down.
And I really can't say I blame them.
...OF AVENGER!
I don't know how much more of this I can take.
I...I...
TAKE A DEEP BREATH, PADRE.
Even the priest seems like he's having a hard time keeping it together.
Of course, we all know the truth about Bullseye.
But nobody is willing to say--
ARE YOU KIDDING?!?!

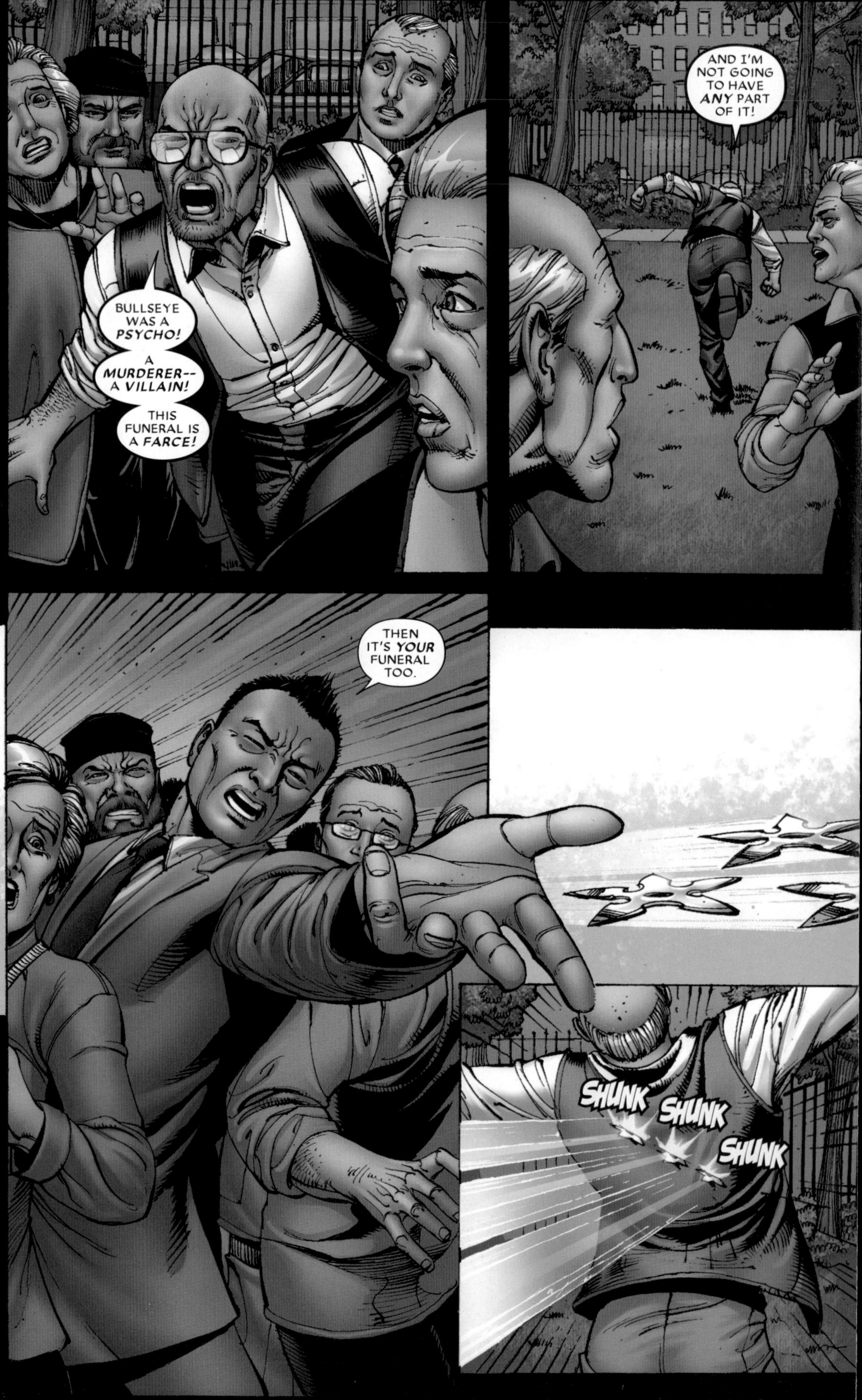
BULLSEYE WAS A PSYCHO!
A MURDERER-- A VILLAIN!
THIS FUNERAL IS A FARCE!
AND I'M NOT GOING TO HAVE ANY PART OF IT!
THEN IT'S YOUR FUNERAL TOO.
SHUNK
SHUNK
SHUNK

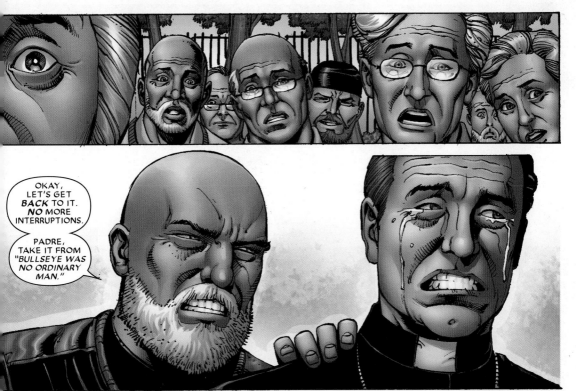

OKAY, LET'S GET *BACK* TO IT. *NO* MORE INTERRUPTIONS.

PADRE, TAKE IT FROM *"BULLSEYE WAS NO ORDINARY MAN."*

AND YOU-- *REPORTER* GUY--

BEN URICH.

WHATEVER-- WHEN YOU WRITE YOUR STORY, YOU CAN JUST *SKIP OVER* THAT LAST PART...

...OR *YOU'LL* BE NEXT.

B-BULLSEYE WAS N-N-NO *ORDINARY* MAN.

T-THIS WAS A MAN WE COULD *ALL* L-LOOK UP TO.

PSST. MR. URICH.

HE'S *BACK.*

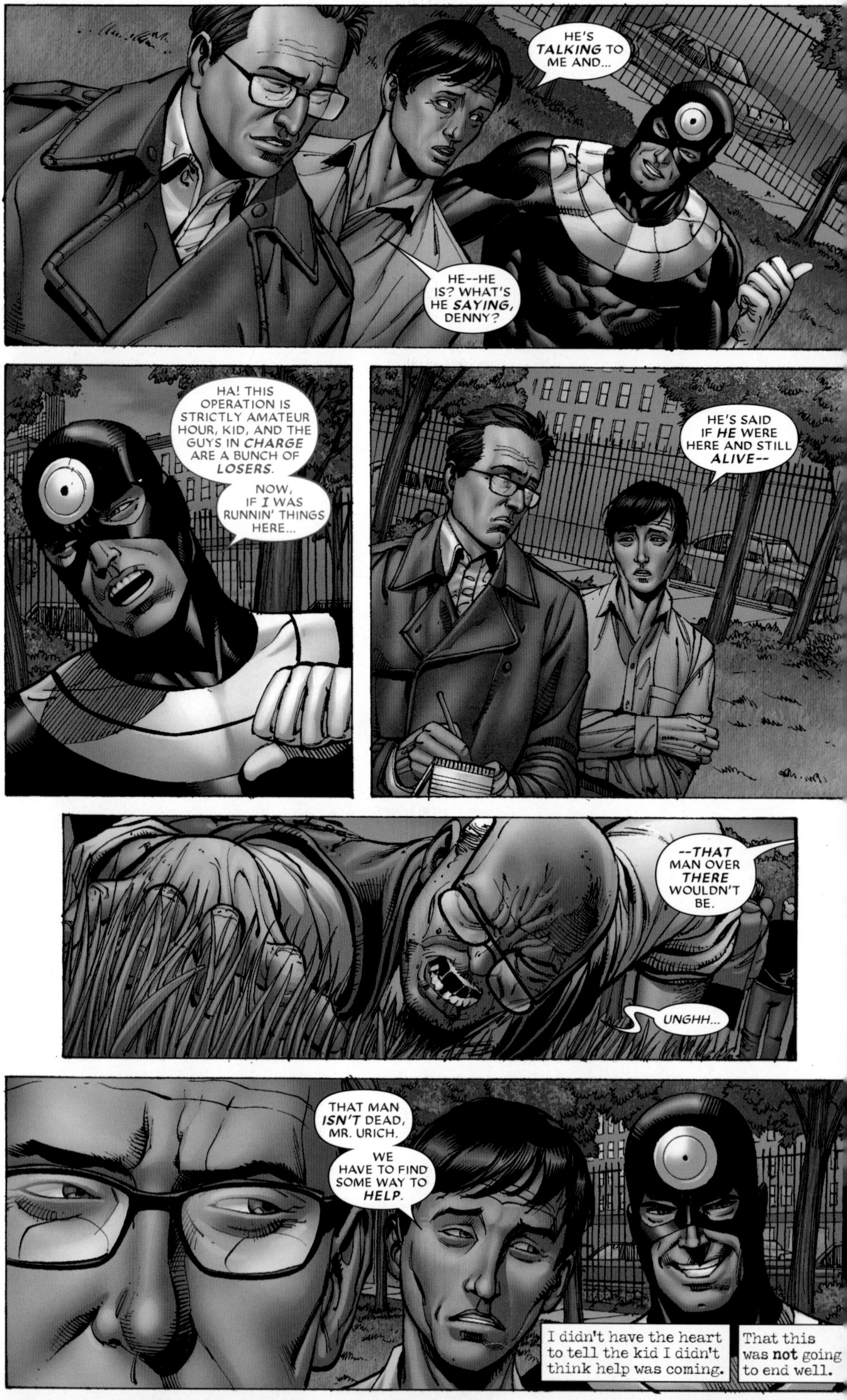
HE'S TALKING TO ME AND...
HE--HE IS? WHAT'S HE SAYING, DENNY?
HA! THIS OPERATION IS STRICTLY AMATEUR HOUR, KID, AND THE GUYS IN CHARGE ARE A BUNCH OF LOSERS.
NOW, IF I WAS RUNNIN' THINGS HERE...
HE'S SAID IF HE WERE HERE AND STILL ALIVE--
--THAT MAN OVER THERE WOULDN'T BE.
UNGHH...
THAT MAN ISN'T DEAD, MR. URICH.
WE HAVE TO FIND SOME WAY TO HELP.
I didn't have the heart to tell the kid I didn't think help was coming.
That this was not going to end well.

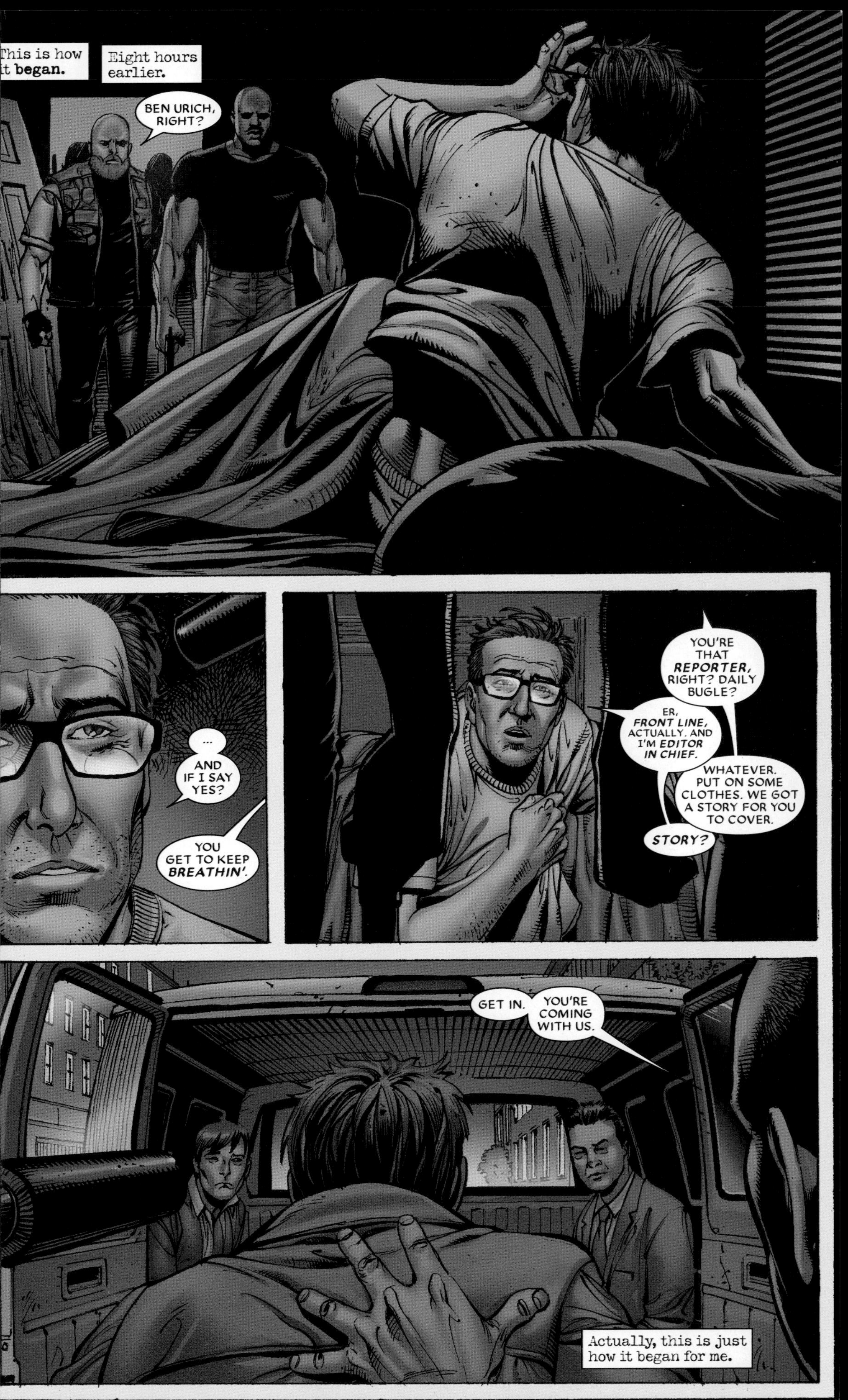
This is how it began.
Eight hours earlier.
BEN URICH, RIGHT?
...AND IF I SAY YES?
YOU GET TO KEEP BREATHIN'.
YOU'RE THAT REPORTER, RIGHT? DAILY BUGLE?
ER, FRONT LINE, ACTUALLY. AND I'M EDITOR IN CHIEF.
WHATEVER. PUT ON SOME CLOTHES. WE GOT A STORY FOR YOU TO COVER.
STORY?
GET IN.
YOU'RE COMING WITH US.
Actually, this is just how it began for me.

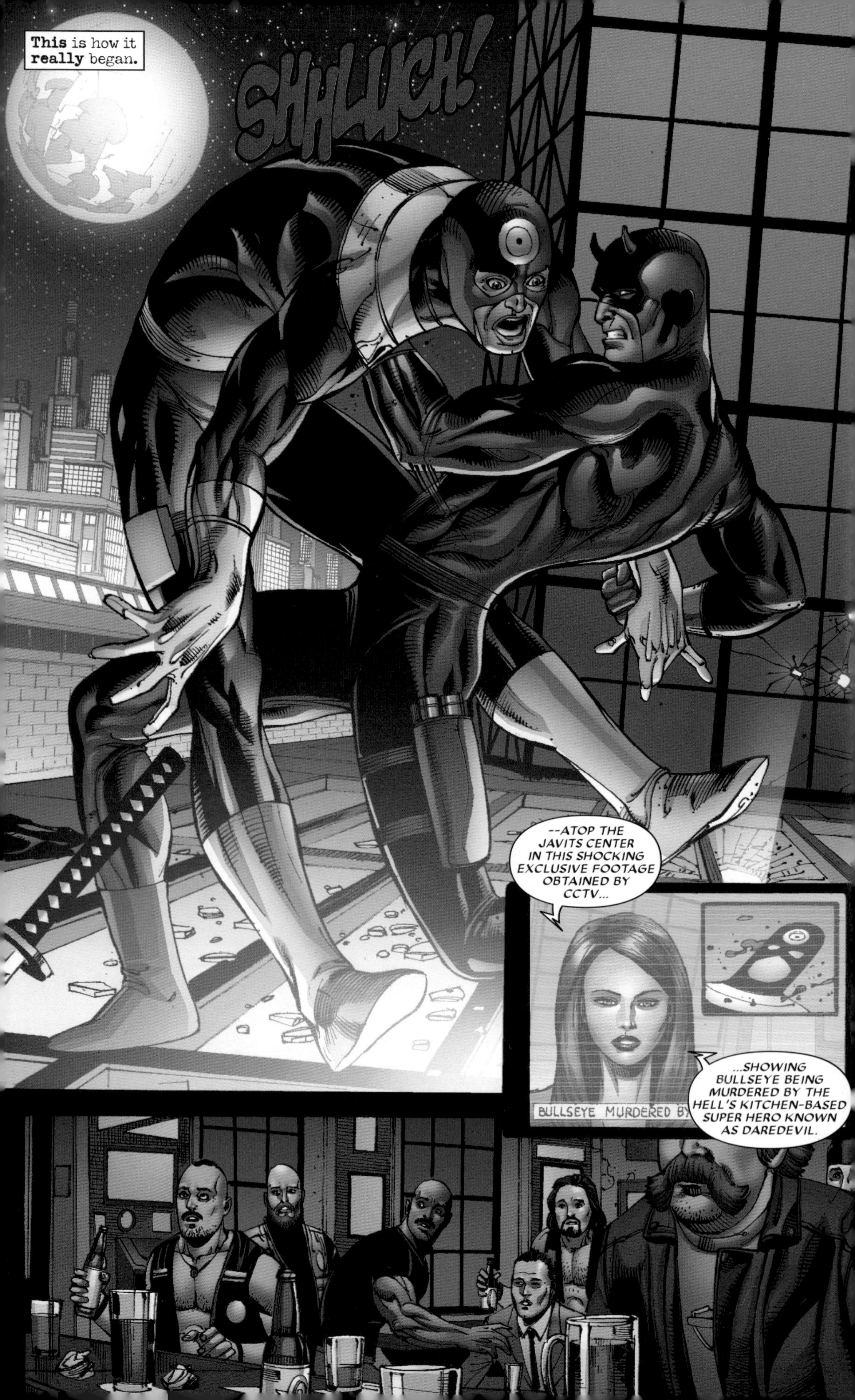

This is how it really began.
SHHLUCH!
--ATOP THE JAVITS CENTER IN THIS SHOCKING EXCLUSIVE FOOTAGE OBTAINED BY CCTV...
BULLSEYE MURDERED BY
...SHOWING BULLSEYE BEING MURDERED BY THE HELL'S KITCHEN-BASED SUPER HERO KNOWN AS DAREDEVIL.

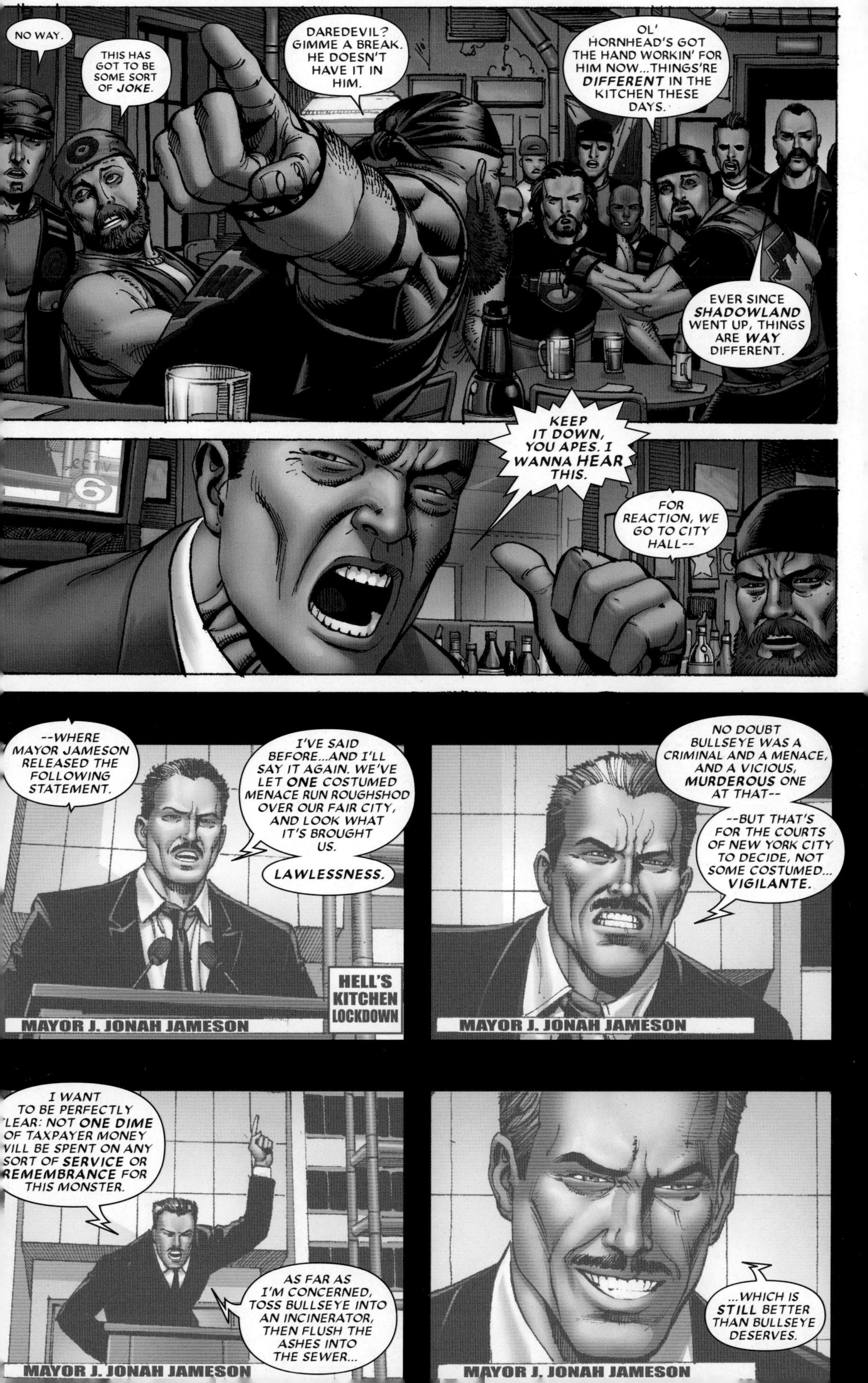
NO WAY.
THIS HAS GOT TO BE SOME SORT OF JOKE.
DAREDEVIL? GIMME A BREAK. HE DOESN'T HAVE IT IN HIM.
OL' HORNHEAD'S GOT THE HAND WORKIN' FOR HIM NOW...THINGS'RE DIFFERENT IN THE KITCHEN THESE DAYS.
EVER SINCE SHADOWLAND WENT UP, THINGS ARE WAY DIFFERENT.
KEEP IT DOWN, YOU APES. I WANNA HEAR THIS.
FOR REACTION, WE GO TO CITY HALL--
--WHERE MAYOR JAMESON RELEASED THE FOLLOWING STATEMENT.
I'VE SAID BEFORE...AND I'LL SAY IT AGAIN. WE'VE LET ONE COSTUMED MENACE RUN ROUGHSHOD OVER OUR FAIR CITY, AND LOOK WHAT IT'S BROUGHT US.
LAWLESSNESS.
HELL'S KITCHEN LOCKDOWN
MAYOR J. JONAH JAMESON
NO DOUBT BULLSEYE WAS A CRIMINAL AND A MENACE, AND A VICIOUS, MURDEROUS ONE AT THAT--
--BUT THAT'S FOR THE COURTS OF NEW YORK CITY TO DECIDE, NOT SOME COSTUMED... VIGILANTE.
MAYOR J. JONAH JAMESON
I WANT TO BE PERFECTLY 'LEAR: NOT ONE DIME OF TAXPAYER MONEY VILL BE SPENT ON ANY SORT OF SERVICE OR REMEMBRANCE FOR THIS MONSTER.
AS FAR AS I'M CONCERNED, TOSS BULLSEYE INTO AN INCINERATOR, THEN FLUSH THE ASHES INTO THE SEWER...
MAYOR J. JONAH JAMESON
...WHICH IS STILL BETTER THAN BULLSEYE DESERVES.
MAYOR J. JONAH JAMESON

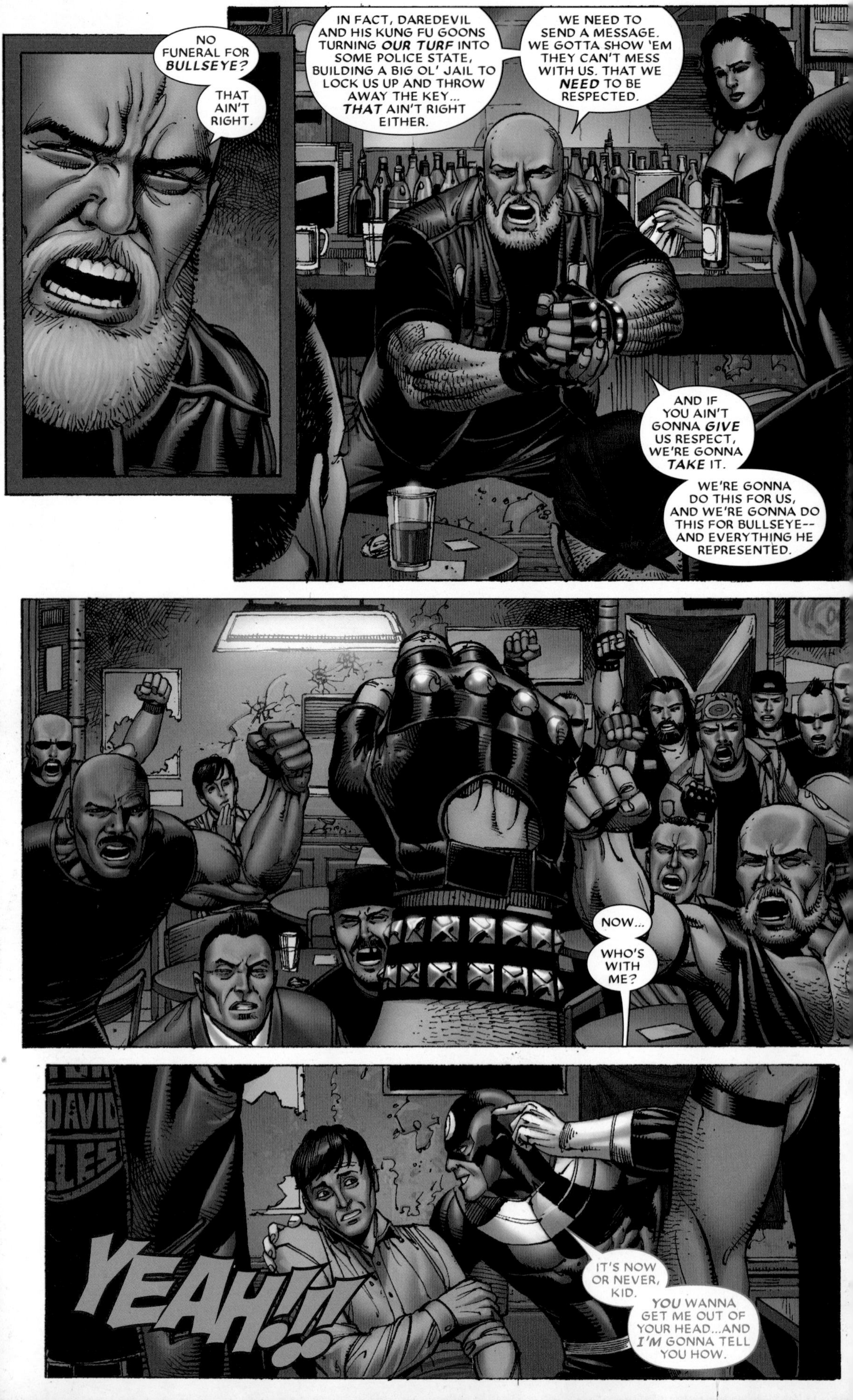

NO FUNERAL FOR BULLSEYE?
THAT AIN'T RIGHT.
IN FACT, DAREDEVIL AND HIS KUNG FU GOONS TURNING OUR TURF INTO SOME POLICE STATE, BUILDING A BIG OL' JAIL TO LOCK US UP AND THROW AWAY THE KEY... THAT AIN'T RIGHT EITHER.
WE NEED TO SEND A MESSAGE. WE GOTTA SHOW 'EM THEY CAN'T MESS WITH US. THAT WE NEED TO BE RESPECTED.
AND IF YOU AIN'T GONNA GIVE US RESPECT, WE'RE GONNA TAKE IT.
WE'RE GONNA DO THIS FOR US, AND WE'RE GONNA DO THIS FOR BULLSEYE-- AND EVERYTHING HE REPRESENTED.
NOW...
WHO'S WITH ME?
YEAH!!!!
IT'S NOW OR NEVER, KID.
YOU WANNA GET ME OUT OF YOUR HEAD...AND I'M GONNA TELL YOU HOW.

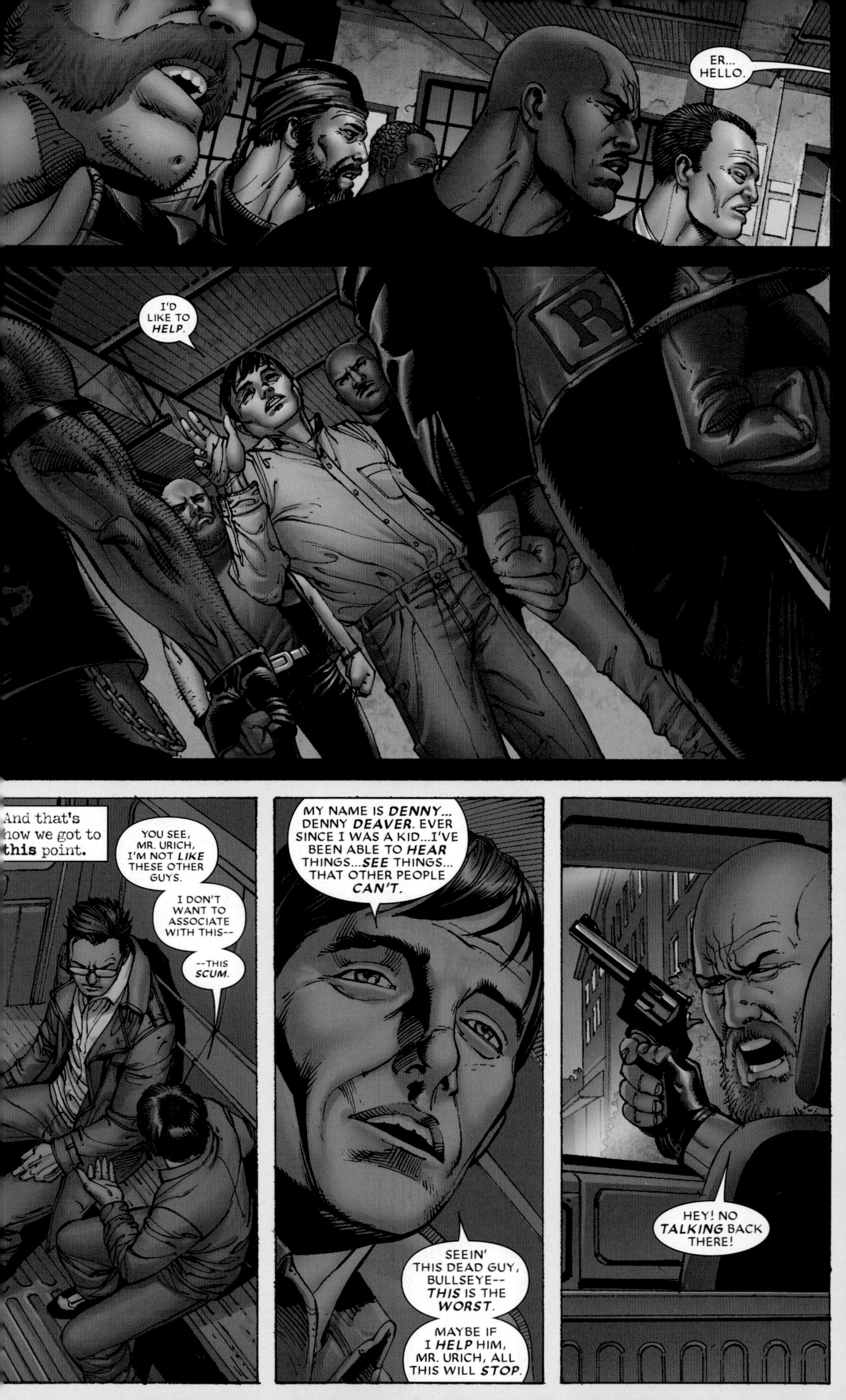
ER... HELLO.
I'D LIKE TO HELP.
And that's how we got to this point.
YOU SEE, MR. URICH, I'M NOT LIKE THESE OTHER GUYS.
I DON'T WANT TO ASSOCIATE WITH THIS--
--THIS SCUM.
MY NAME IS DENNY... DENNY DEAVER. EVER SINCE I WAS A KID...I'VE BEEN ABLE TO HEAR THINGS...SEE THINGS... THAT OTHER PEOPLE CAN'T.
SEEIN' THIS DEAD GUY, BULLSEYE-- THIS IS THE WORST.
MAYBE IF I HELP HIM, MR. URICH, ALL THIS WILL STOP.
HEY! NO TALKING BACK THERE!

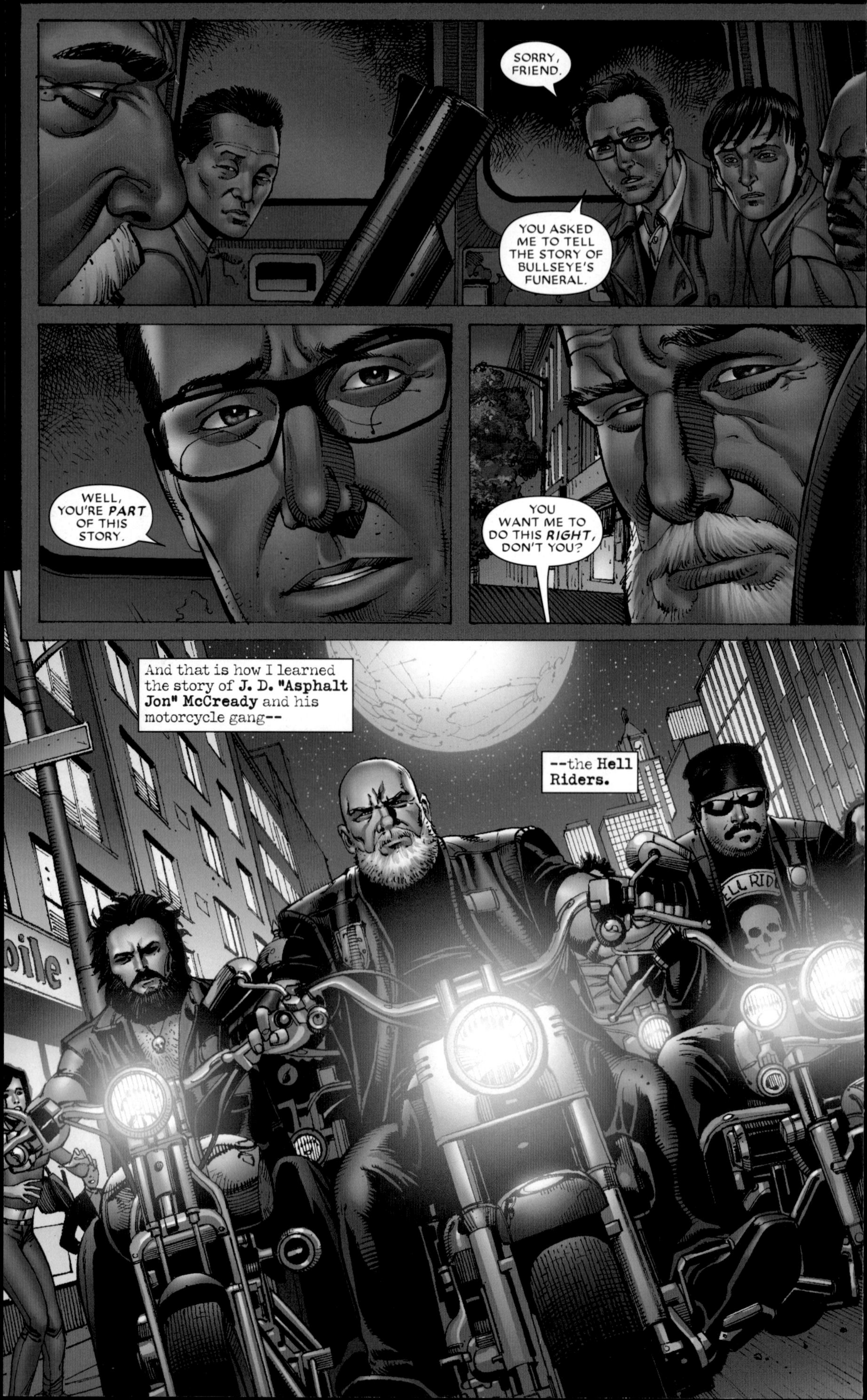
SORRY, FRIEND.
YOU ASKED ME TO TELL THE STORY OF BULLSEYE'S FUNERAL.
WELL, YOU'RE *PART* OF THIS STORY.
YOU WANT ME TO DO THIS *RIGHT*, DON'T YOU?
And that is how I learned the story of **J. D. "Asphalt Jon" McCready** and his motorcycle gang--
--the **Hell Riders.**

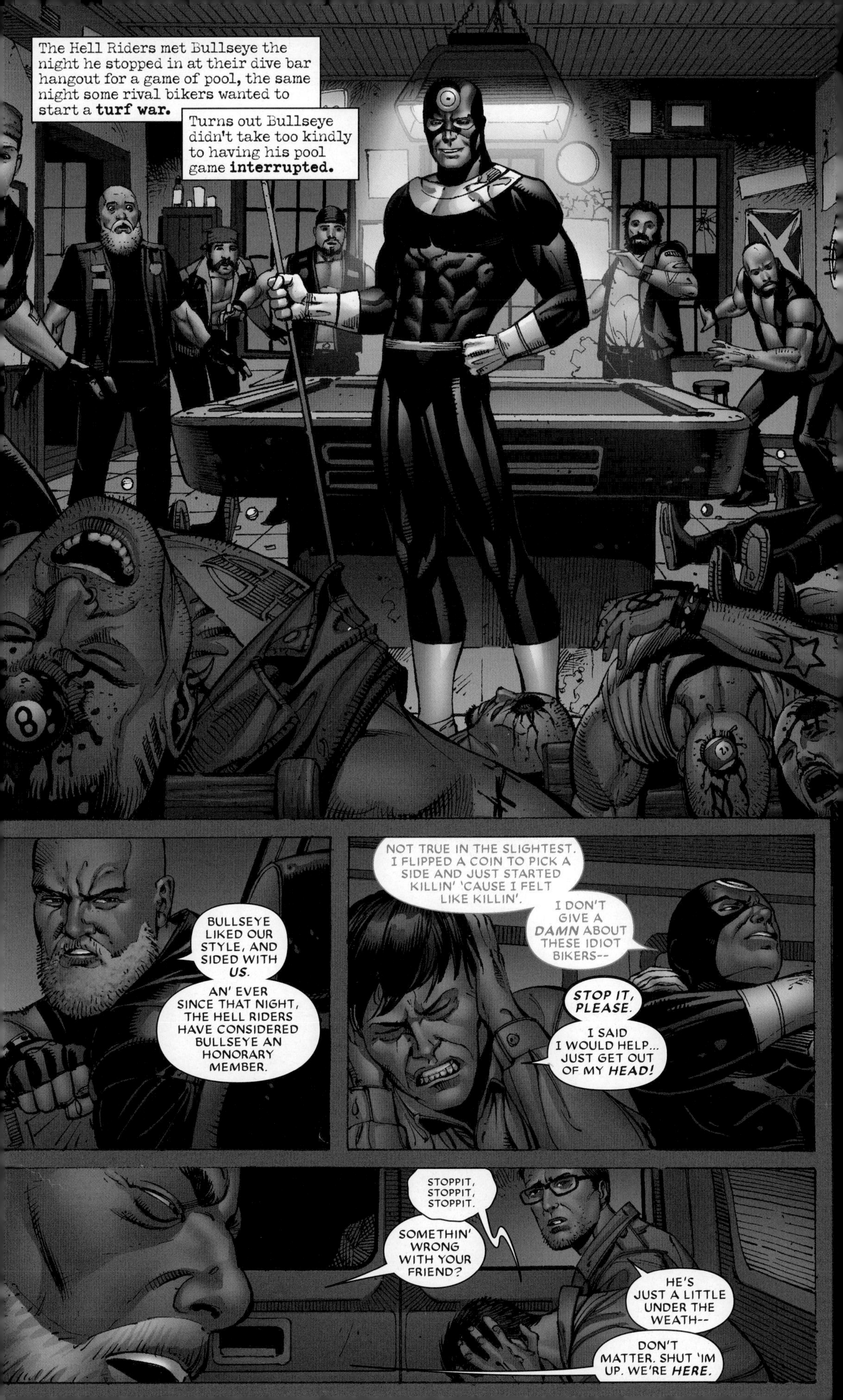
The Hell Riders met Bullseye the night he stopped in at their dive bar hangout for a game of pool, the same night some rival bikers wanted to start a **turf war.**
Turns out Bullseye didn't take too kindly to having his pool game **interrupted.**
BULLSEYE LIKED OUR STYLE, AND SIDED WITH *US*.
AN' EVER SINCE THAT NIGHT, THE HELL RIDERS HAVE CONSIDERED BULLSEYE AN HONORARY MEMBER.
NOT TRUE IN THE SLIGHTEST. I FLIPPED A COIN TO PICK A SIDE AND JUST STARTED KILLIN' 'CAUSE I FELT LIKE KILLIN'.
I DON'T GIVE A *DAMN* ABOUT THESE IDIOT BIKERS--
STOP IT, PLEASE.
I SAID I WOULD HELP... JUST GET OUT OF MY *HEAD!*
STOPPIT, STOPPIT, STOPPIT.
SOMETHIN' WRONG WITH YOUR FRIEND?
HE'S JUST A LITTLE UNDER THE WEATH--
DON'T MATTER. SHUT 'IM UP. WE'RE *HERE.*

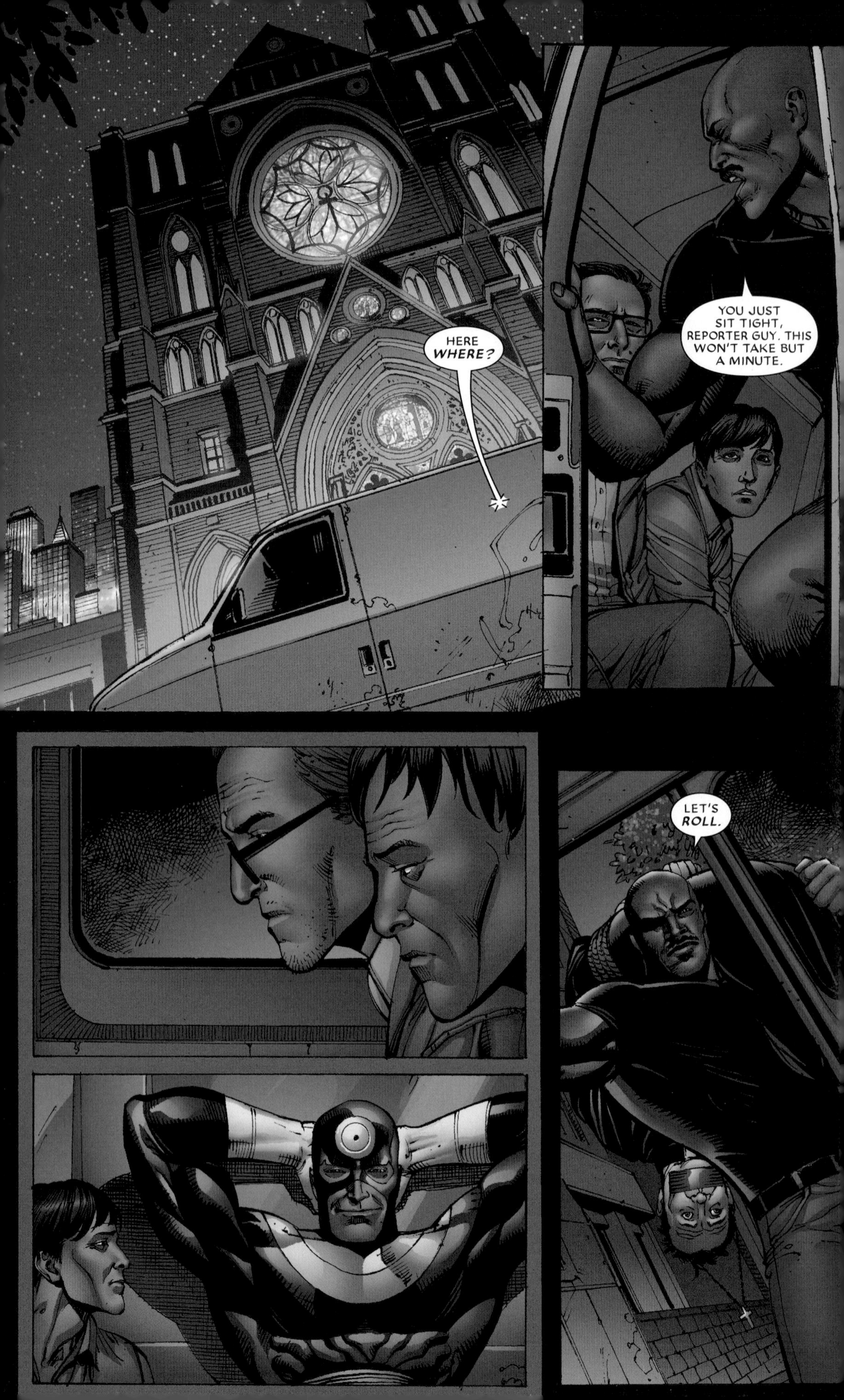
HERE *WHERE?*
YOU JUST SIT TIGHT, REPORTER GUY. THIS WON'T TAKE BUT A MINUTE.
LET'S *ROLL.*

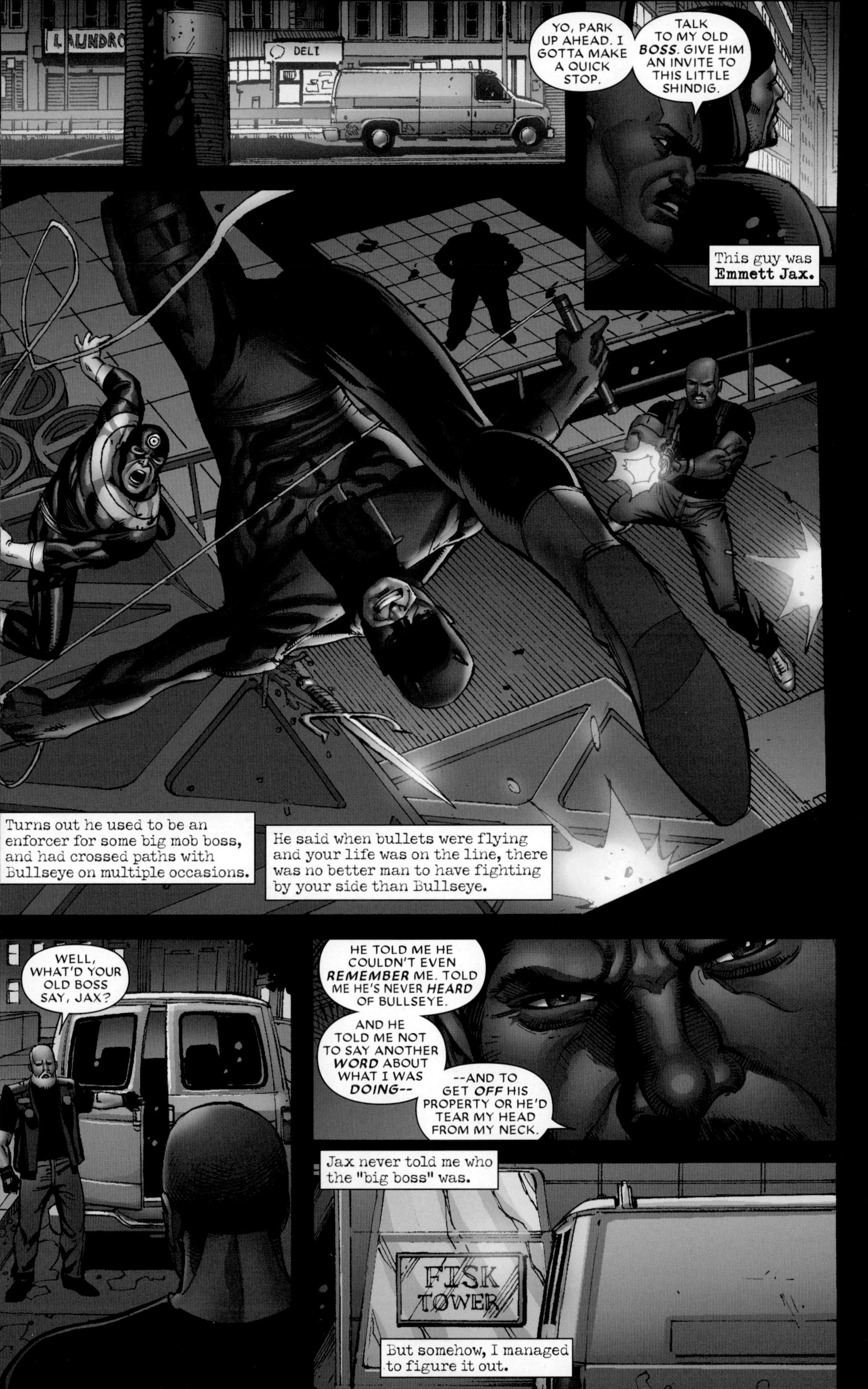

LAUNDRO
DELI
YO, PARK UP AHEAD. I GOTTA MAKE A QUICK STOP.
TALK TO MY OLD BOSS. GIVE HIM AN INVITE TO THIS LITTLE SHINDIG.
This guy was Emmett Jax.
Turns out he used to be an enforcer for some big mob boss, and had crossed paths with Bullseye on multiple occasions.
He said when bullets were flying and your life was on the line, there was no better man to have fighting by your side than Bullseye.
WELL, WHAT'D YOUR OLD BOSS SAY, JAX?
HE TOLD ME HE COULDN'T EVEN REMEMBER ME. TOLD ME HE'S NEVER HEARD OF BULLSEYE.
AND HE TOLD ME NOT TO SAY ANOTHER WORD ABOUT WHAT I WAS DOING--
--AND TO GET OFF HIS PROPERTY OR HE'D TEAR MY HEAD FROM MY NECK.
Jax never told me who the "big boss" was.
FISK TOWER
But somehow, I managed to figure it out.

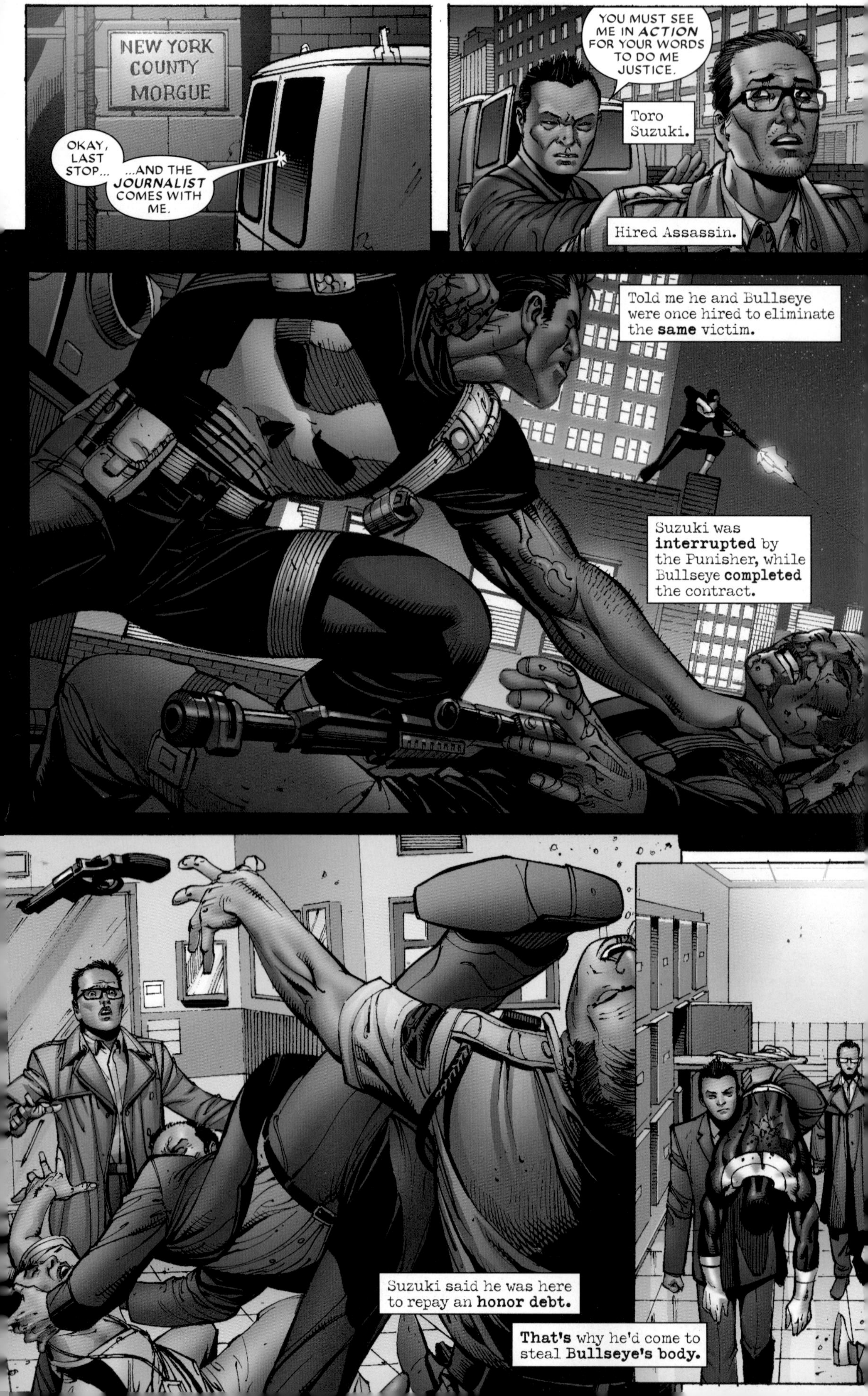
NEW YORK COUNTY MORGUE
OKAY, LAST STOP...
...AND THE JOURNALIST COMES WITH ME.
YOU MUST SEE ME IN ACTION FOR YOUR WORDS TO DO ME JUSTICE.
Toro Suzuki.
Hired Assassin.
Told me he and Bullseye were once hired to eliminate the same victim.
Suzuki was interrupted by the Punisher, while Bullseye completed the contract.
Suzuki said he was here to repay an honor debt.
That's why he'd come to steal Bullseye's body.

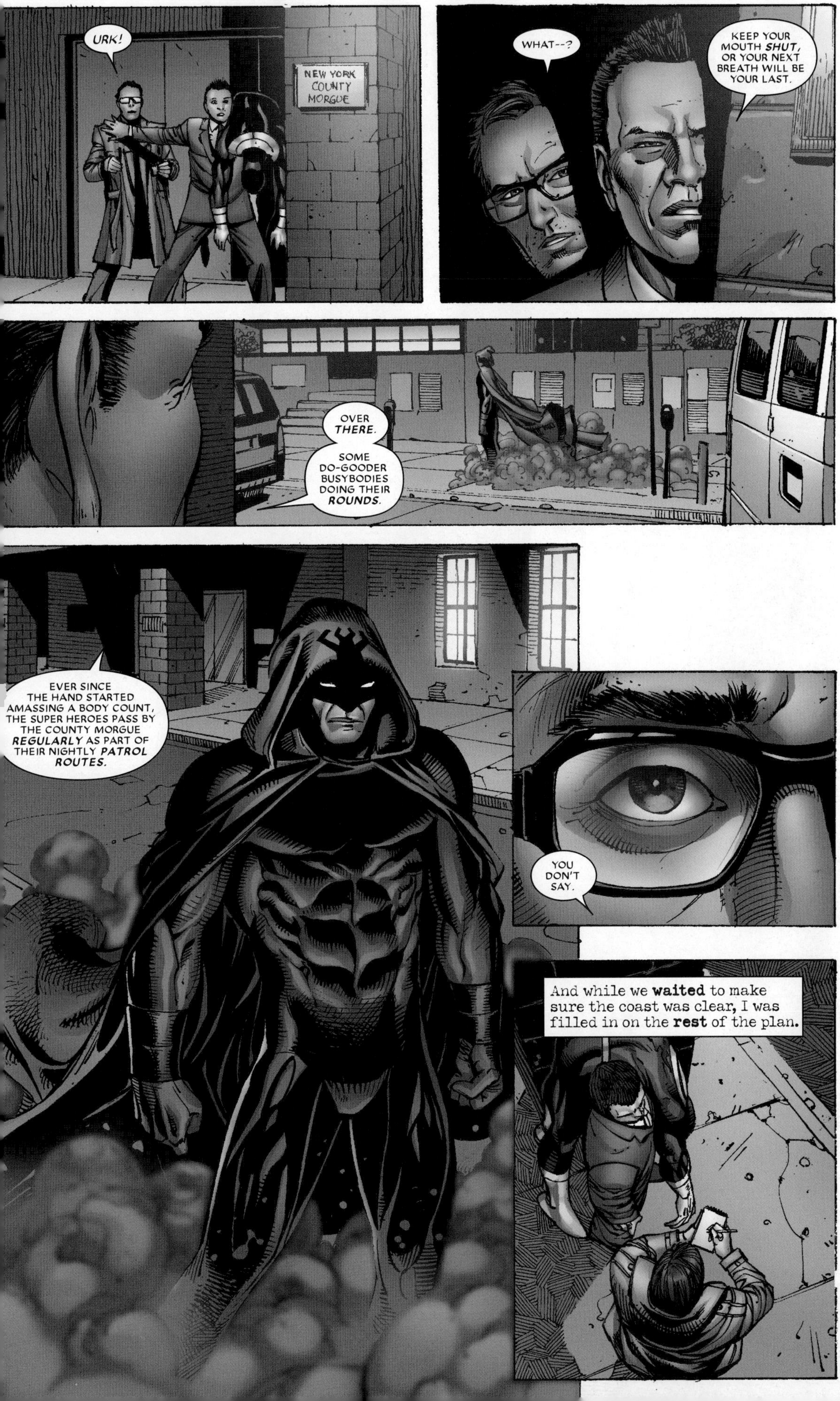
URK!
NEW YORK COUNTY MORGUE
WHAT--?
KEEP YOUR MOUTH *SHUT*, OR YOUR NEXT BREATH WILL BE YOUR LAST.
OVER *THERE*.
SOME DO-GOODER BUSYBODIES DOING THEIR *ROUNDS*.
EVER SINCE THE HAND STARTED AMASSING A BODY COUNT, THE SUPER HEROES PASS BY THE COUNTY MORGUE *REGULARLY* AS PART OF THEIR NIGHTLY *PATROL ROUTES*.
YOU DON'T SAY.
And while we **waited** to make sure the coast was clear, I was filled in on the **rest** of the plan.

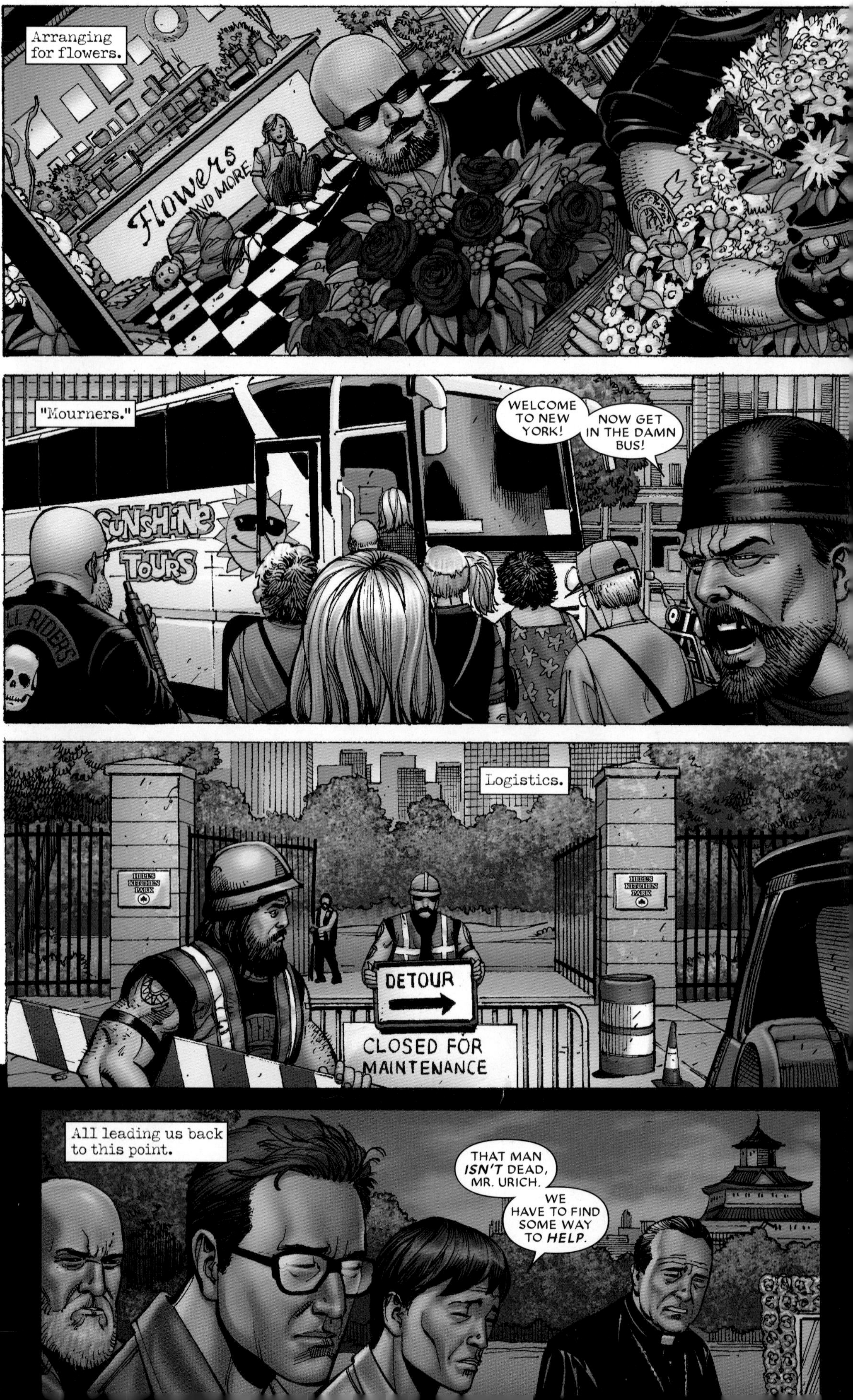
Arranging for flowers.
Flowers AND MORE
"Mourners."
WELCOME TO NEW YORK!
NOW GET IN THE DAMN BUS!
SUNSHINE TOURS
Logistics.
HELL'S KITCHEN PARK
DETOUR
CLOSED FOR MAINTENANCE
All leading us back to this point.
THAT MAN *ISN'T* DEAD, MR. URICH.
WE HAVE TO FIND SOME WAY TO *HELP*.

Of course, the most crucial component of their part of the plan hinged on them being able to complete the service before anybody figured out what was going on.

WE NOW COMMIT THE BODY OF THIS GREAT, GREAT MAN TO THE GROUND, ASHES TO ASHES, DUST TO DUST, THOUGH HE WILL LIVE ON FOREVER IN OUR MEMORY.

YOU'RE GETTIN' ALL THIS, AIN'TCHA, LOU GRANT?

So tipping somebody off was my only shot.

HEY--WHAT THE??!! THIS NOTEBOOK IS *BLANK!*

First rule of reporting.

Something every rookie learns, sometimes the hard way, the first week on the job.

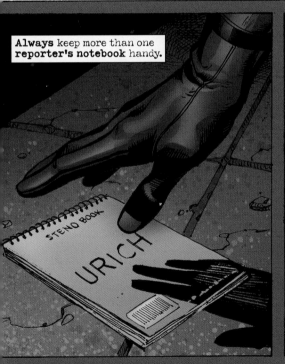

Always keep more than one **reporter's notebook** handy.

STENO BOOK

URICH

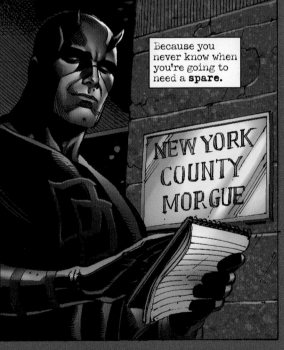

Because you never know when you're going to need a **spare.**

NEW YORK COUNTY MORGUE

WHY YOU *SNEAKY* SON OF A--

And just like that...

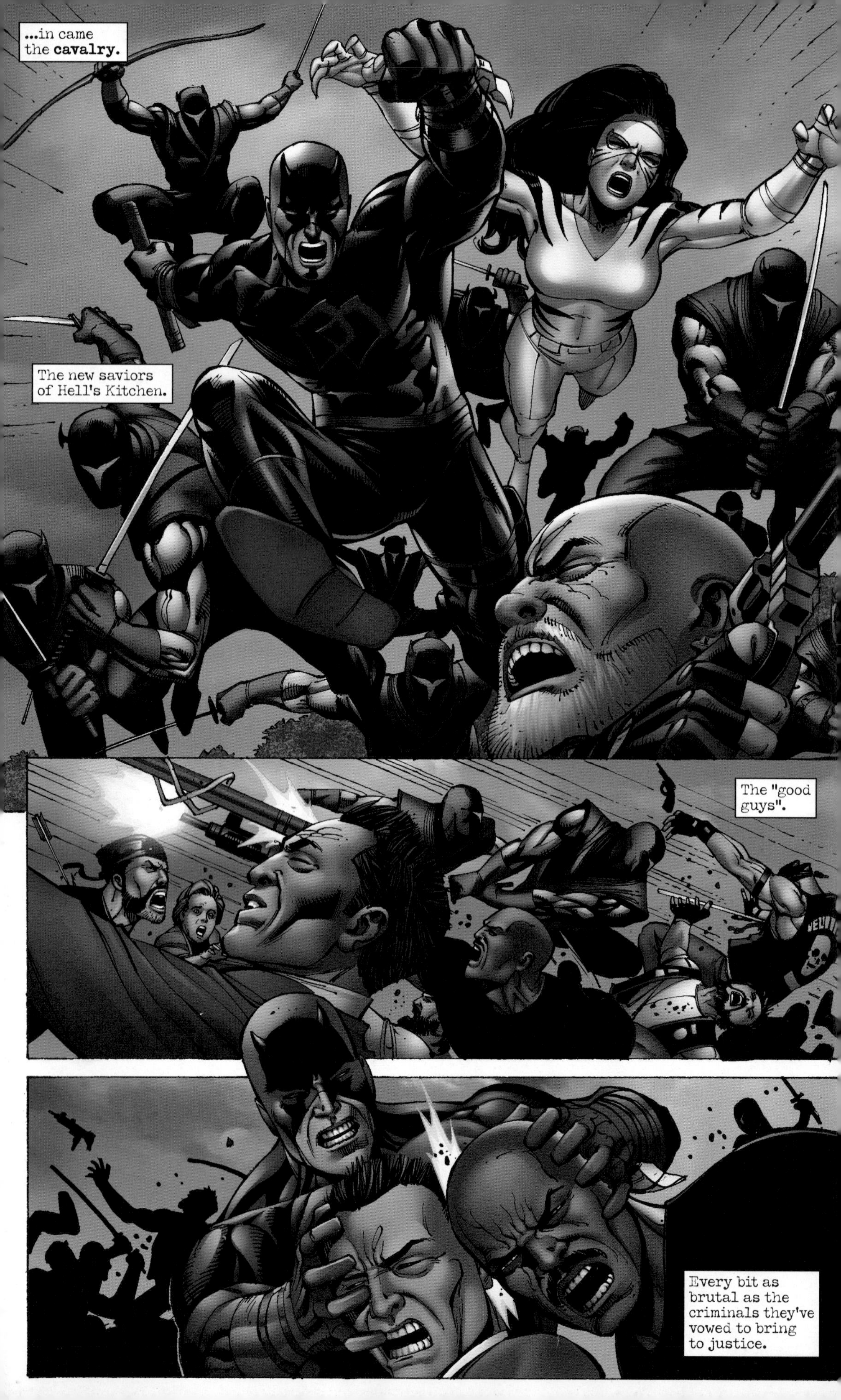
...in came the **cavalry.**
The new saviors of Hell's Kitchen.
The "good guys".
Every bit as brutal as the criminals they've vowed to bring to justice.

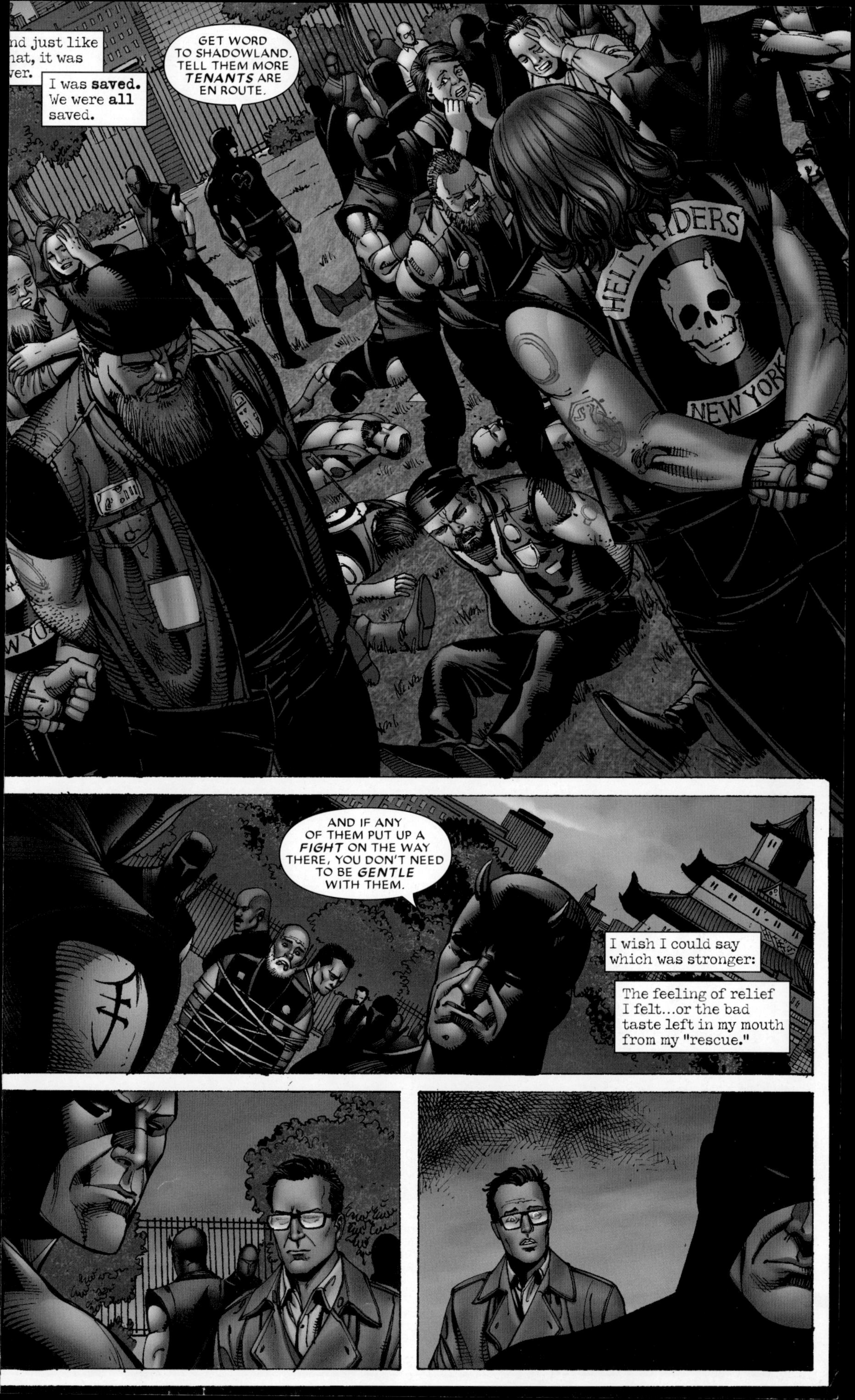

nd just like
nat, it was
ver.
I was **saved.** We were **all** saved.
GET WORD TO SHADOWLAND. TELL THEM MORE *TENANTS* ARE EN ROUTE.
HELL RIDERS
NEW YORK
AND IF ANY OF THEM PUT UP A *FIGHT* ON THE WAY THERE, YOU DON'T NEED TO BE *GENTLE* WITH THEM.
I wish I could say which was stronger:
The feeling of relief I felt...or the bad taste left in my mouth from my "rescue."

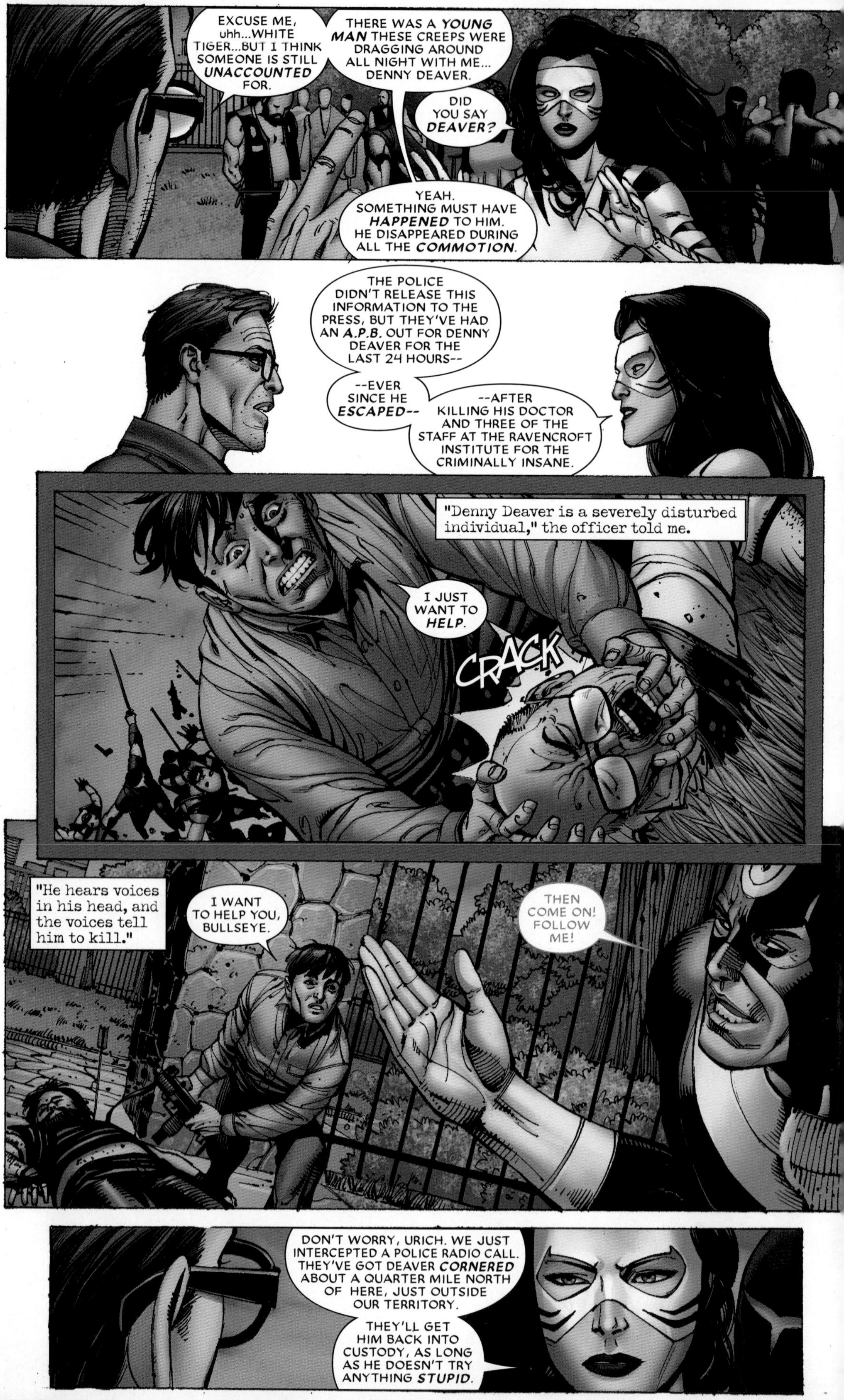

EXCUSE ME, uhh...WHITE TIGER...BUT I THINK SOMEONE IS STILL UNACCOUNTED FOR.
THERE WAS A YOUNG MAN THESE CREEPS WERE DRAGGING AROUND ALL NIGHT WITH ME... DENNY DEAVER.
DID YOU SAY DEAVER?
YEAH. SOMETHING MUST HAVE HAPPENED TO HIM. HE DISAPPEARED DURING ALL THE COMMOTION.
THE POLICE DIDN'T RELEASE THIS INFORMATION TO THE PRESS, BUT THEY'VE HAD AN A.P.B. OUT FOR DENNY DEAVER FOR THE LAST 24 HOURS--
--EVER SINCE HE ESCAPED--
--AFTER KILLING HIS DOCTOR AND THREE OF THE STAFF AT THE RAVENCROFT INSTITUTE FOR THE CRIMINALLY INSANE.
"Denny Deaver is a severely disturbed individual," the officer told me.
I JUST WANT TO HELP.
CRACK
"He hears voices in his head, and the voices tell him to kill."
I WANT TO HELP YOU, BULLSEYE.
THEN COME ON! FOLLOW ME!
DON'T WORRY, URICH. WE JUST INTERCEPTED A POLICE RADIO CALL. THEY'VE GOT DEAVER CORNERED ABOUT A QUARTER MILE NORTH OF HERE, JUST OUTSIDE OUR TERRITORY.
THEY'LL GET HIM BACK INTO CUSTODY, AS LONG AS HE DOESN'T TRY ANYTHING STUPID.

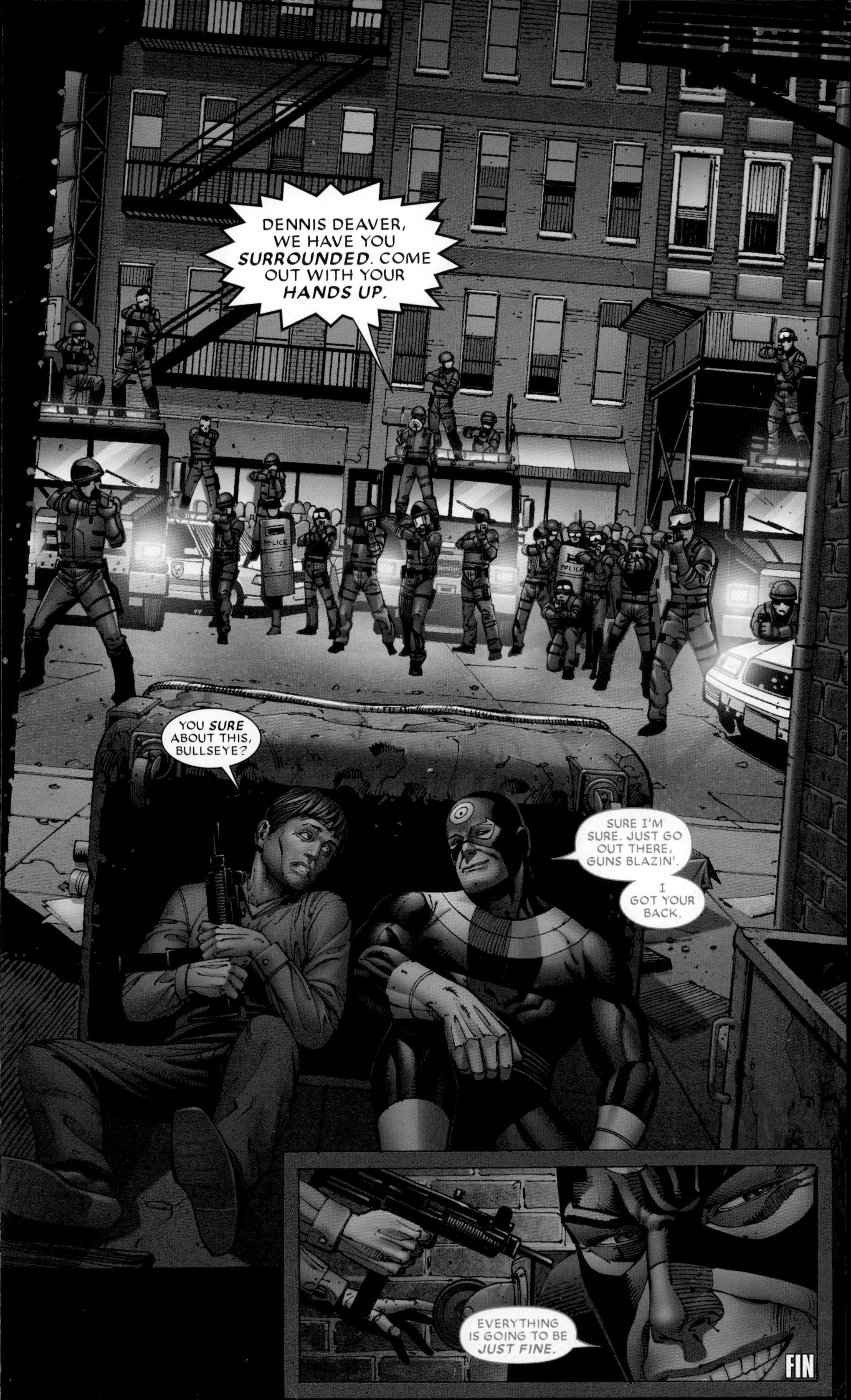
DENNIS DEAVER, WE HAVE YOU *SURROUNDED*. COME OUT WITH YOUR *HANDS UP.*
YOU *SURE* ABOUT THIS, BULLSEYE?
SURE I'M SURE. JUST GO OUT THERE, GUNS BLAZIN'.
I GOT YOUR BACK.
EVERYTHING IS GOING TO BE *JUST FINE.*
FIN

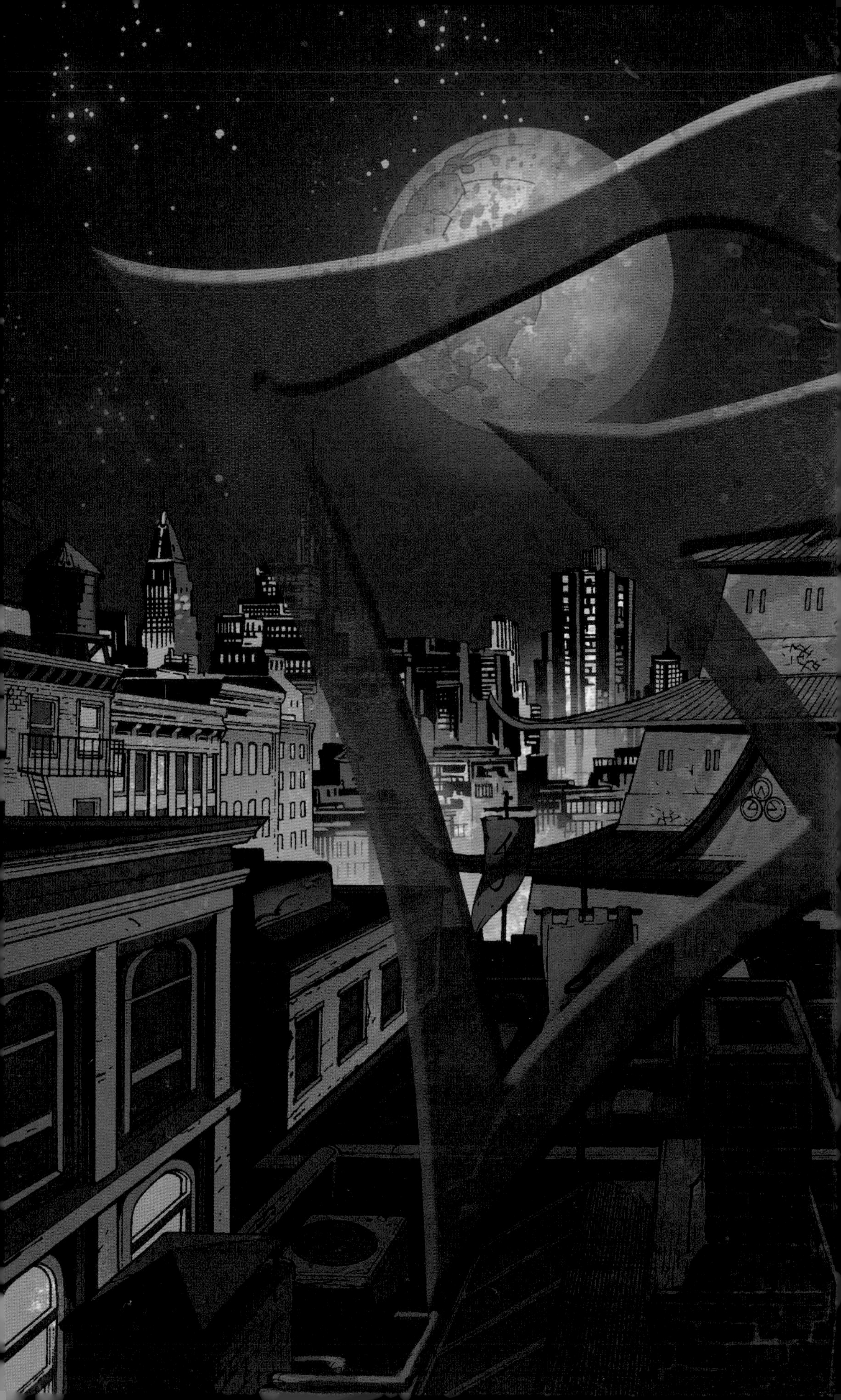

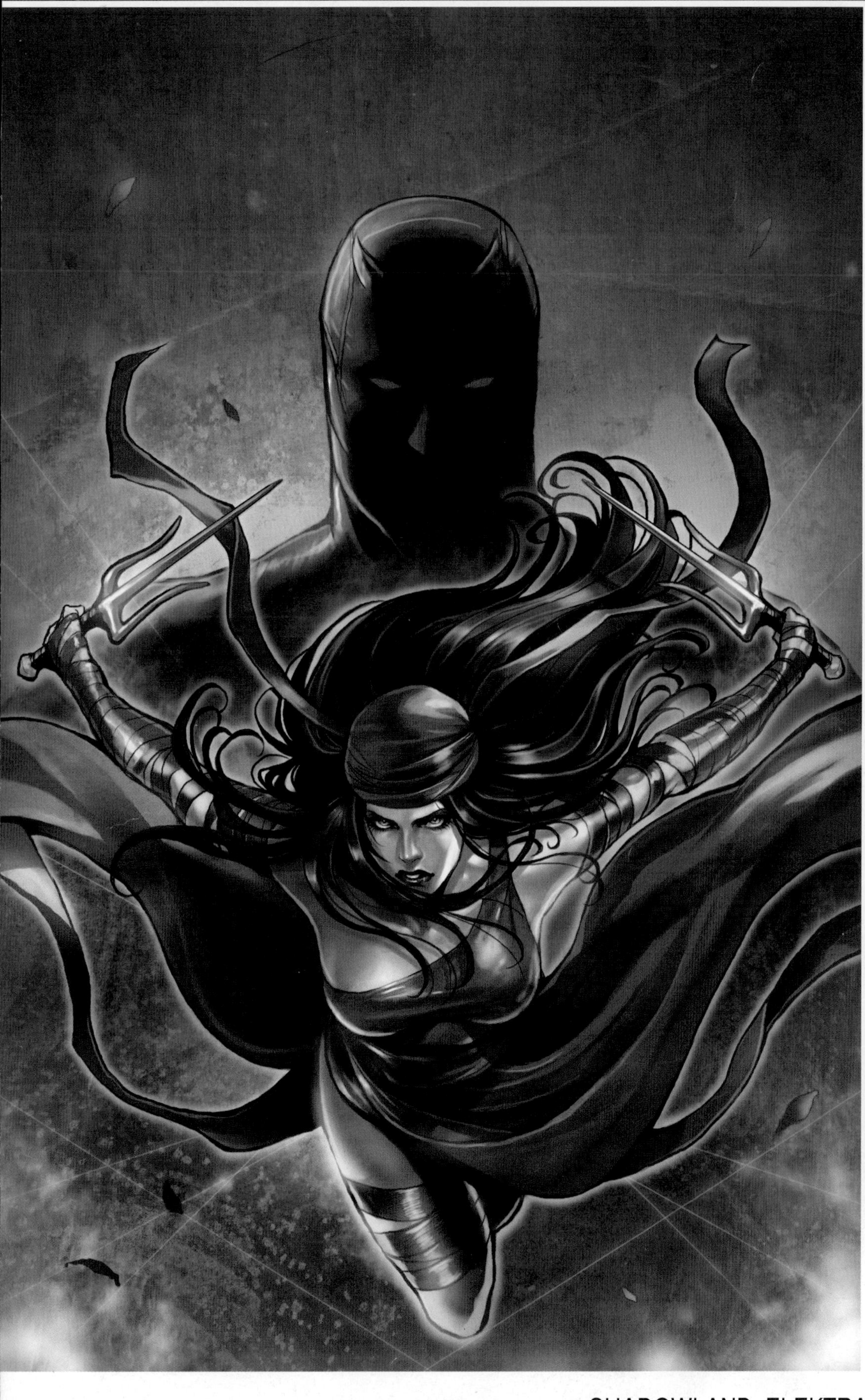

SHADOWLAND: ELEKTRA

THEY WERE CALLED THE HAND — AN ORGANIZATION OF NINJA, THIEVES AND ASSASSINS. ORIGINALLY BANDING TOGETHER 800 YEARS AGO TO FIGHT THE OPPRESSIVE SYSTEM OF FEUDAL JAPAN, THE HAND TURNED TO CORRUPTION AND DARKNESS WHEN MUTINOUS FACTIONS SEIZED POWER.

OVER THE CENTURIES, THE HAND FREQUENTLY TURNED TO ADEPTS OF THE MARTIAL ARTS, SUCH AS THE MASTER ASSASSIN ELEKTRA, TO SERVE AS THEIR AGENTS AND FIGUREHEADS. TODAY, WITH A BASE OF OPERATIONS IN NEW YORK CITY, THE HAND RECRUITED A NEW LEADER: MATT MURDOCK, A.K.A. THE COSTUMED HERO DAREDEVIL, AND A FORMER LOVER OF ELEKTRA.

TO DRAW MURDOCK IN, THEY DESTROYED EVERYTHING HE LIVED FOR — BUT MATT STILL HOPED TO TURN THE STRENGTH AND RESOURCES OF THE HAND TO NOBLE ENDS. THEN THE SOCIOPATHIC ASSASSIN BULLSEYE, AN ARCH-ENEMY OF BOTH DAREDEVIL AND ELEKTRA, DESTROYED AN ENTIRE CITY BLOCK IN MATT'S NEIGHBORHOOD OF HELL'S KITCHEN, KILLING OVER A HUNDRED PEOPLE.

MURDOCK ERECTED A FORBIDDING HEADQUARTERS CALLED SHADOWLAND ON THE SITE OF THE DESTROYED BUILDING, AND DECLARED HELL'S KITCHEN A NO-MAN'S LAND UNDER THE CONTROL OF THE HAND.

SHADOWLAND
ELEKTRA

THIS STORY TAKES PLACE BEFORE **SHADOWLAND #3**

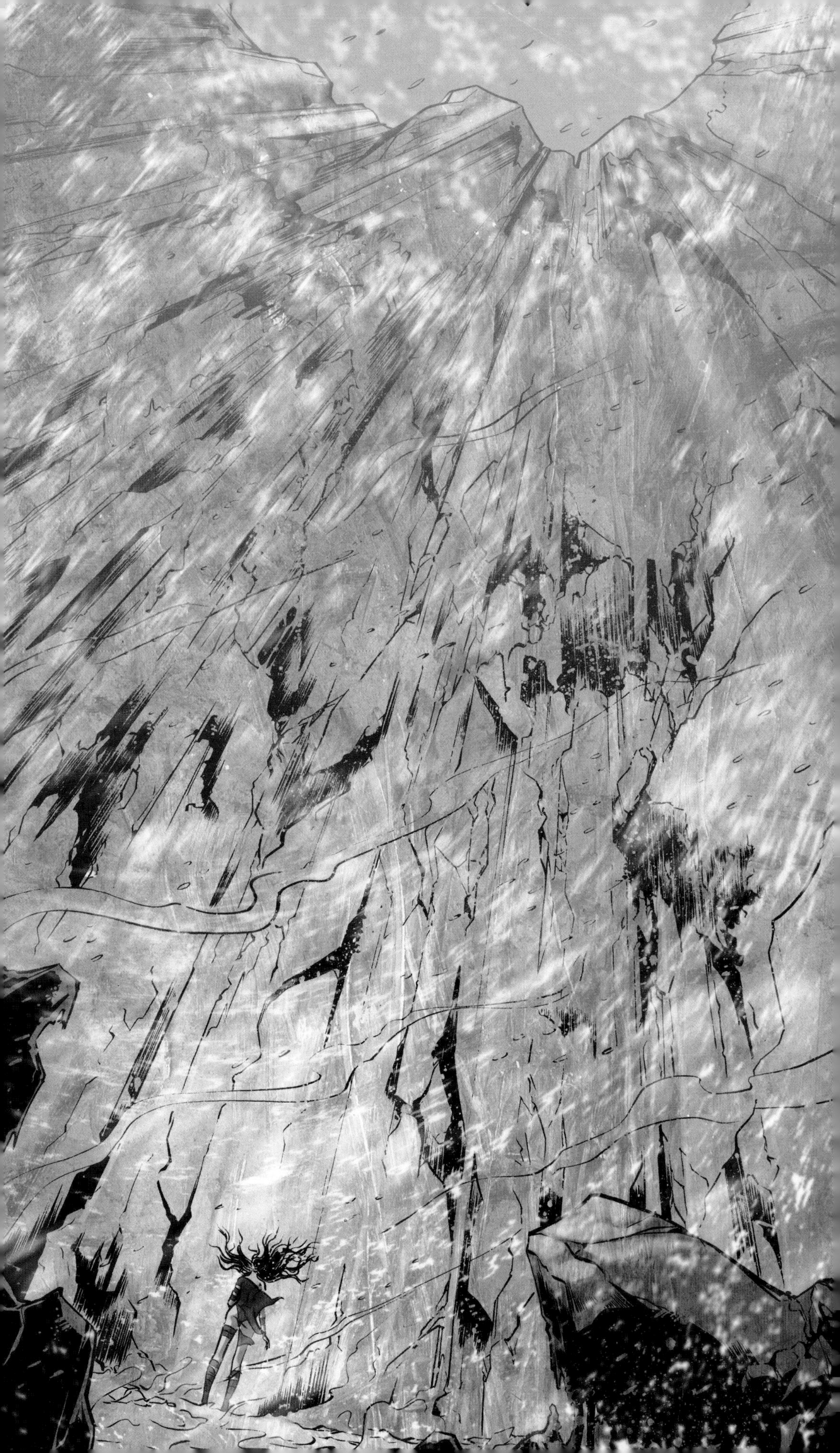

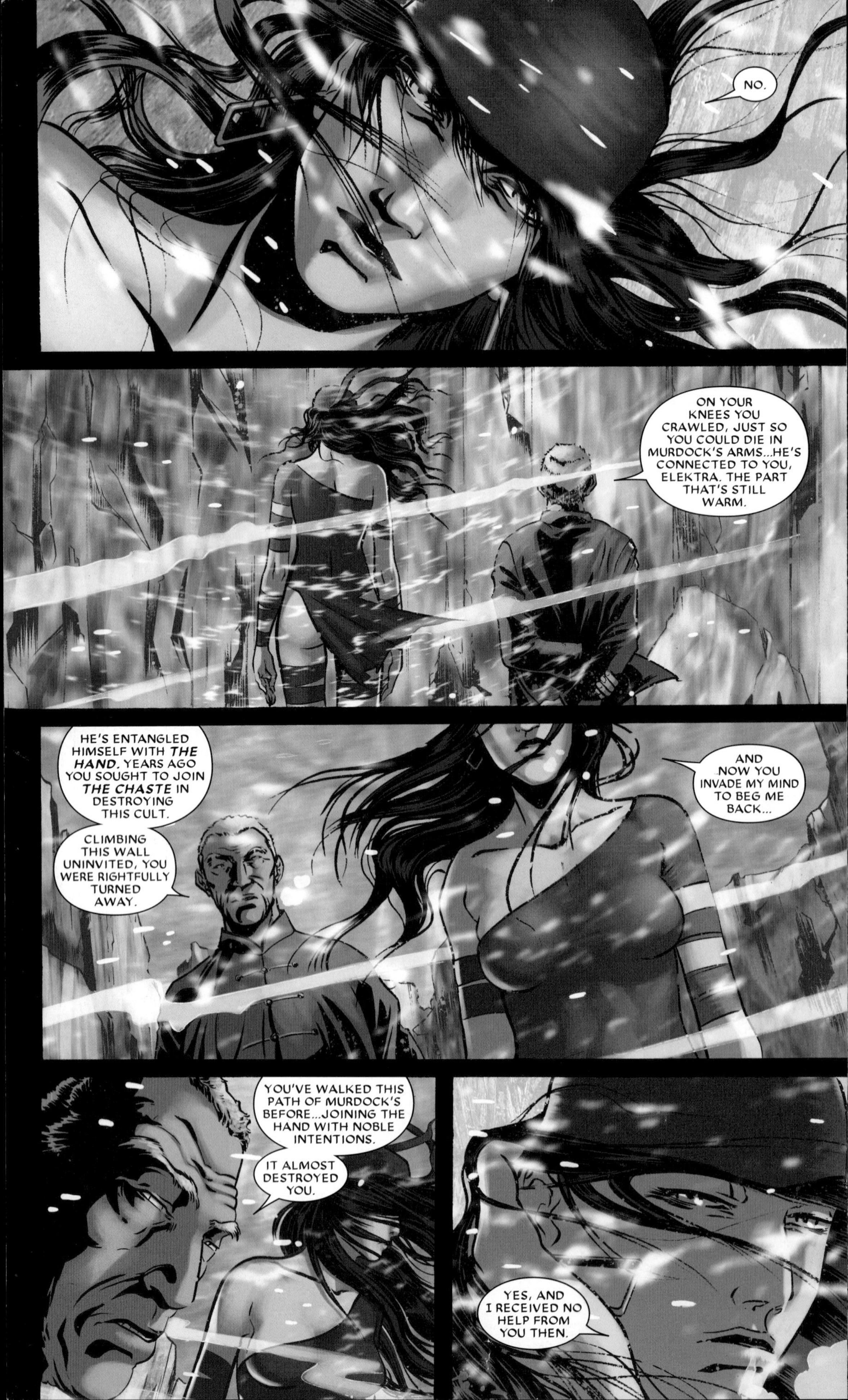

NO.
ON YOUR KNEES YOU CRAWLED, JUST SO YOU COULD DIE IN MURDOCK'S ARMS...HE'S CONNECTED TO YOU, ELEKTRA. THE PART THAT'S STILL WARM.
HE'S ENTANGLED HIMSELF WITH THE HAND. YEARS AGO YOU SOUGHT TO JOIN THE CHASTE IN DESTROYING THIS CULT.
CLIMBING THIS WALL UNINVITED, YOU WERE RIGHTFULLY TURNED AWAY.
AND NOW YOU INVADE MY MIND TO BEG ME BACK...
YOU'VE WALKED THIS PATH OF MURDOCK'S BEFORE...JOINING THE HAND WITH NOBLE INTENTIONS.
IT ALMOST DESTROYED YOU.
YES, AND I RECEIVED NO HELP FROM YOU THEN.

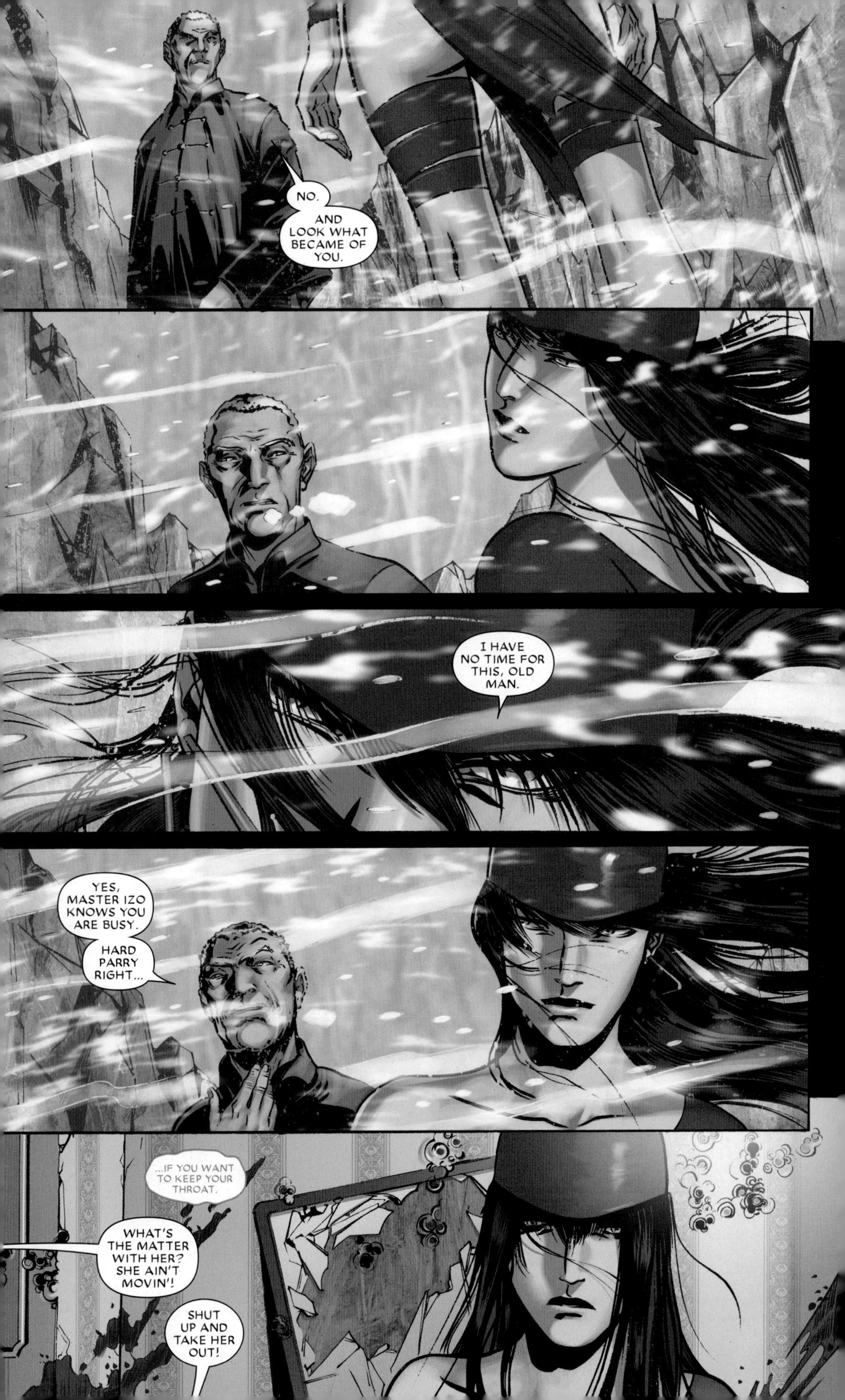
NO.
AND LOOK WHAT BECAME OF YOU.
I HAVE NO TIME FOR THIS, OLD MAN.
YES, MASTER IZO KNOWS YOU ARE BUSY.
HARD PARRY RIGHT...
...IF YOU WANT TO KEEP YOUR THROAT.
WHAT'S THE MATTER WITH HER? SHE AIN'T MOVIN'!
SHUT UP AND TAKE HER OUT!

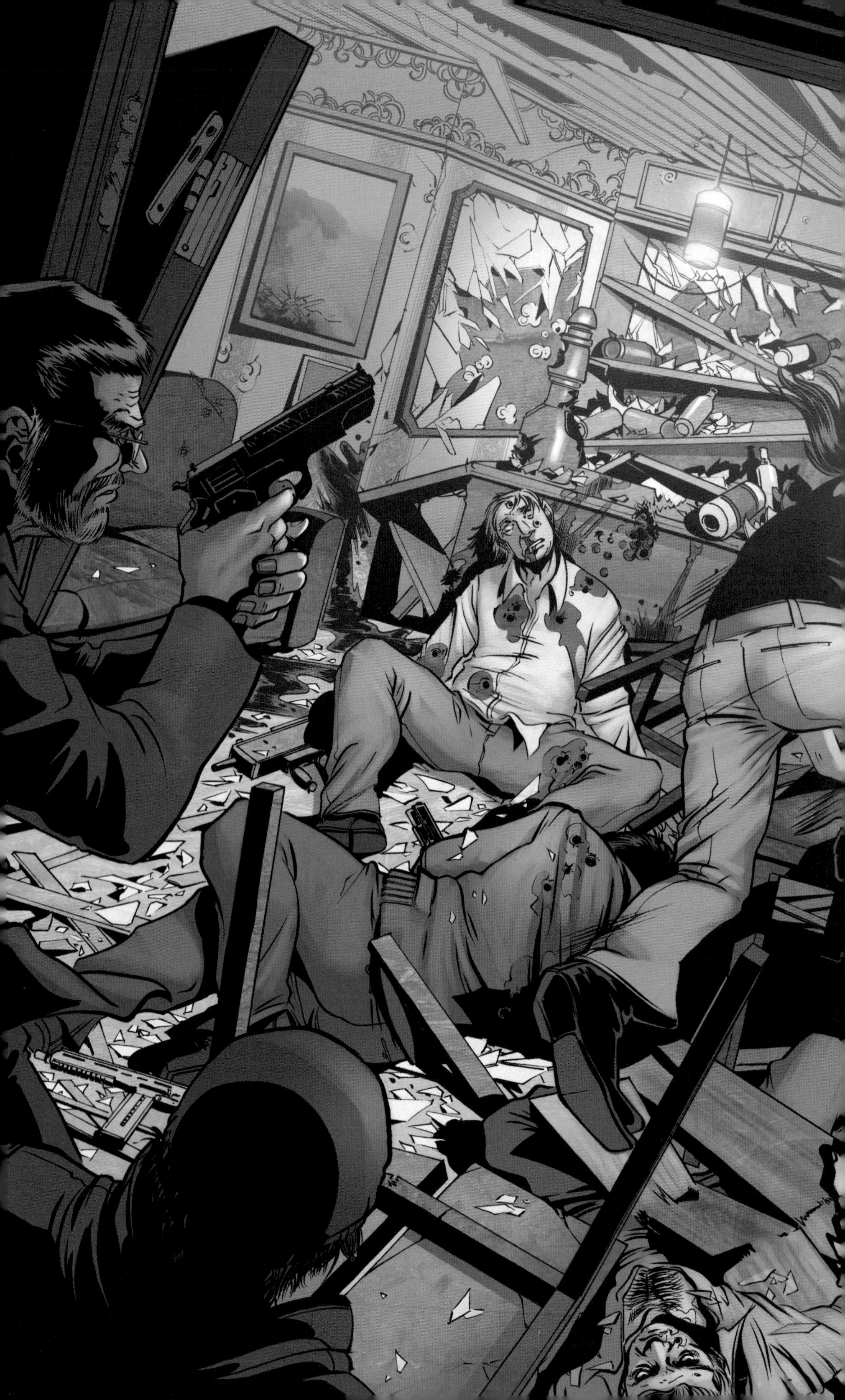

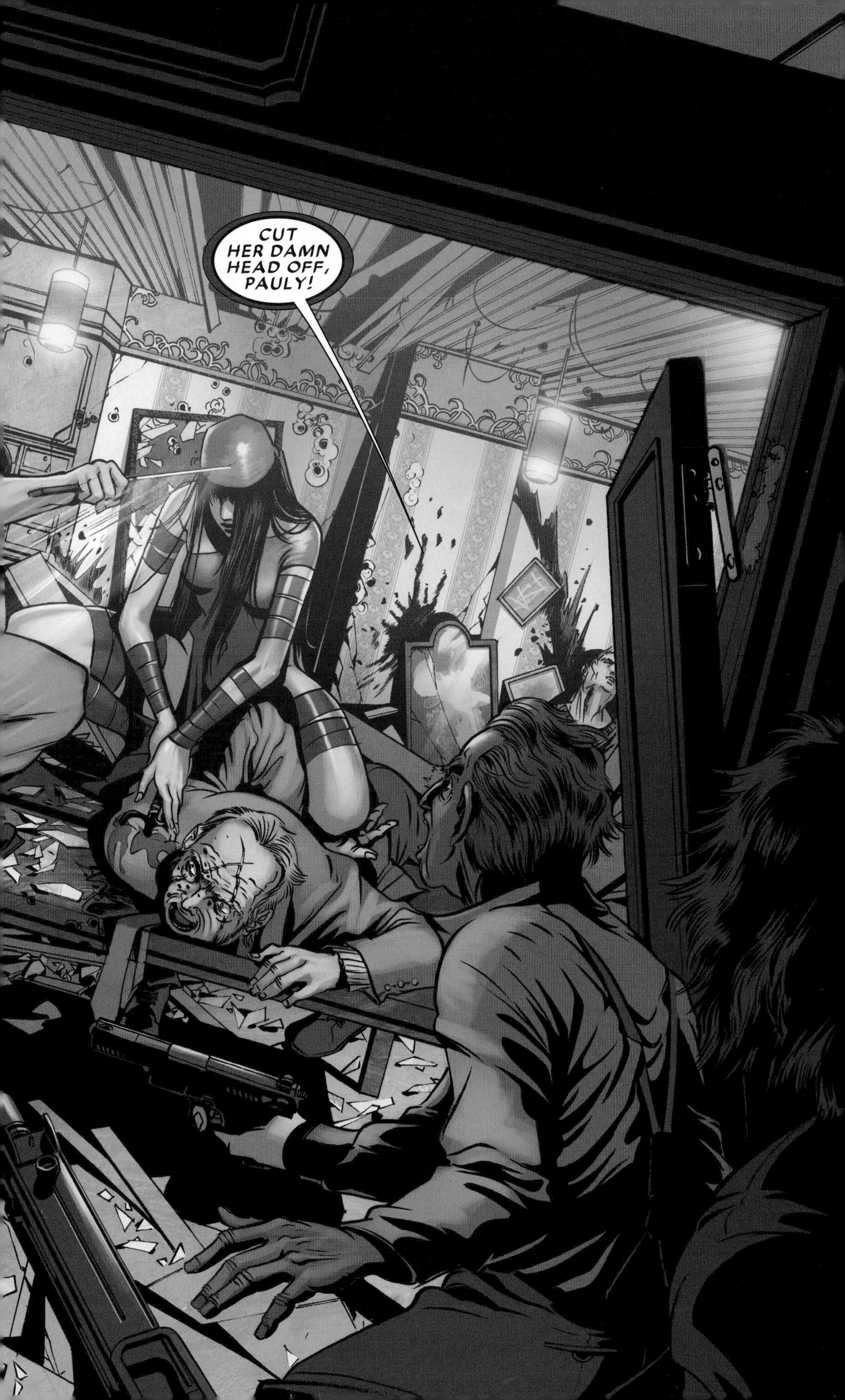
CUT HER DAMN HEAD OFF, PAULY!

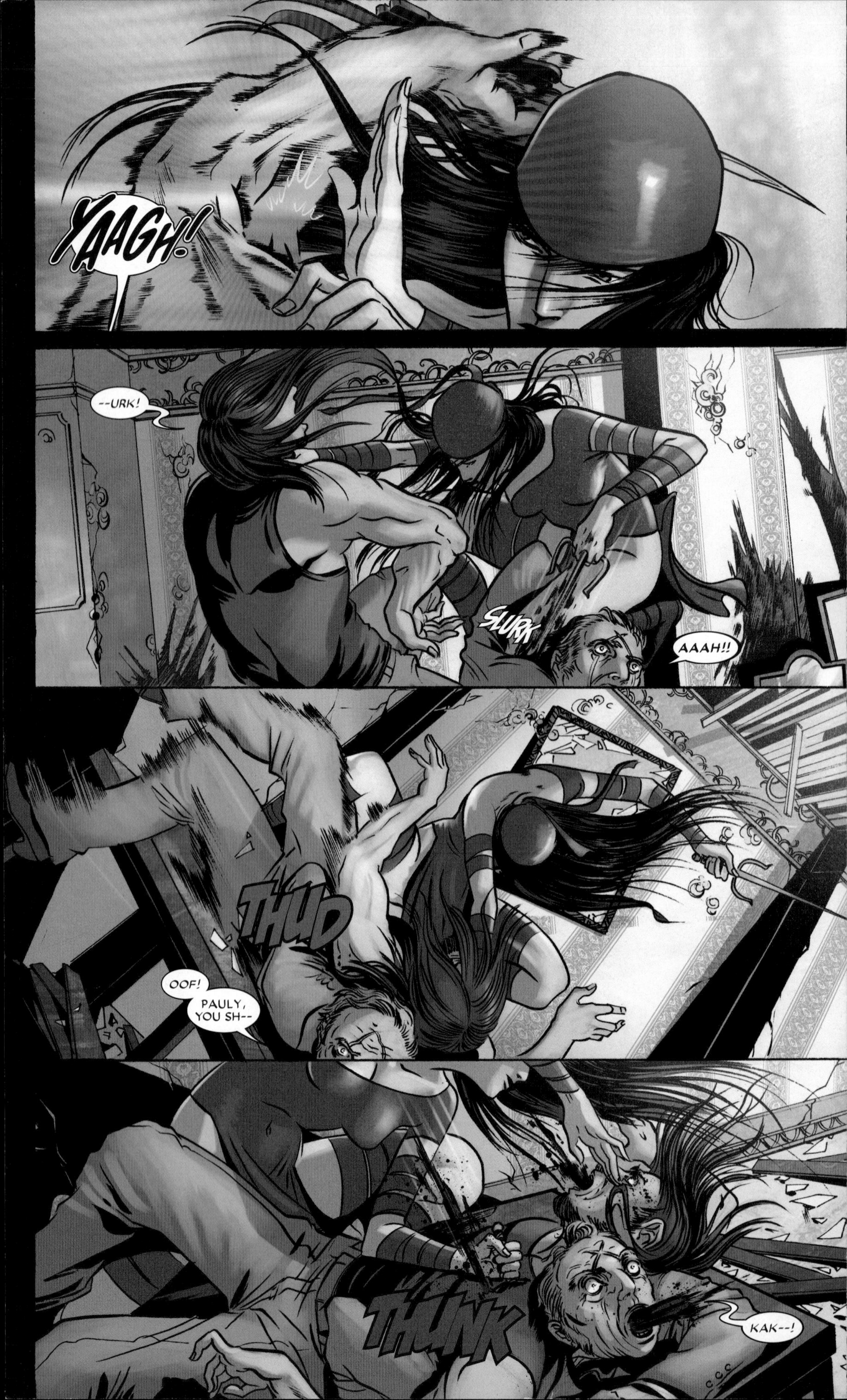
YAAGH!!
--URK!
SLURK
AAAH!!
THUD
OOF!
PAULY, YOU SH--
THUNK
KAK--!

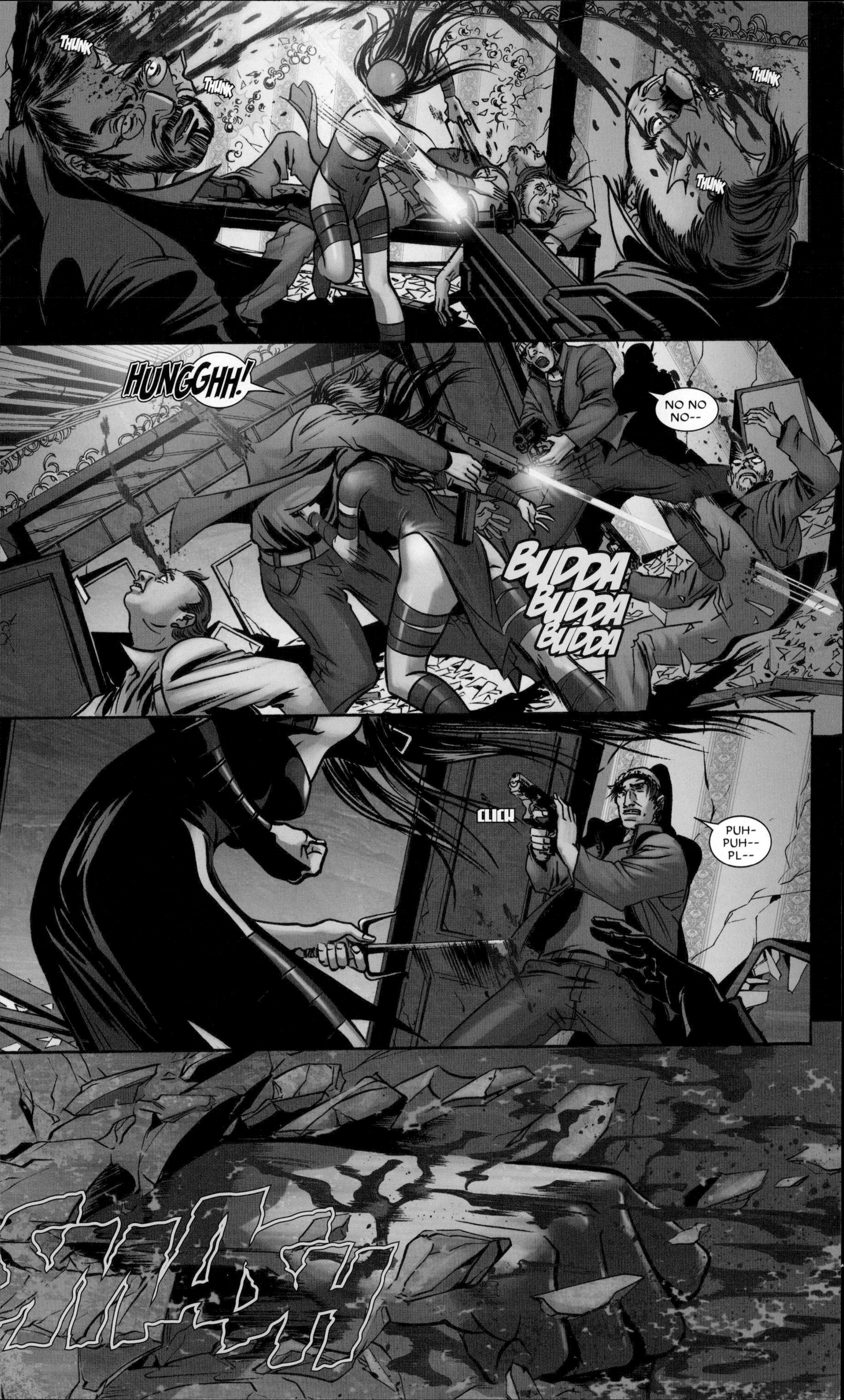
THUNK
THUNK
THUNK
THUNK
HUNGGHH!
NO NO NO--
BUDDA BUDDA BUDDA
CLICK
PUH-PUH--PL--

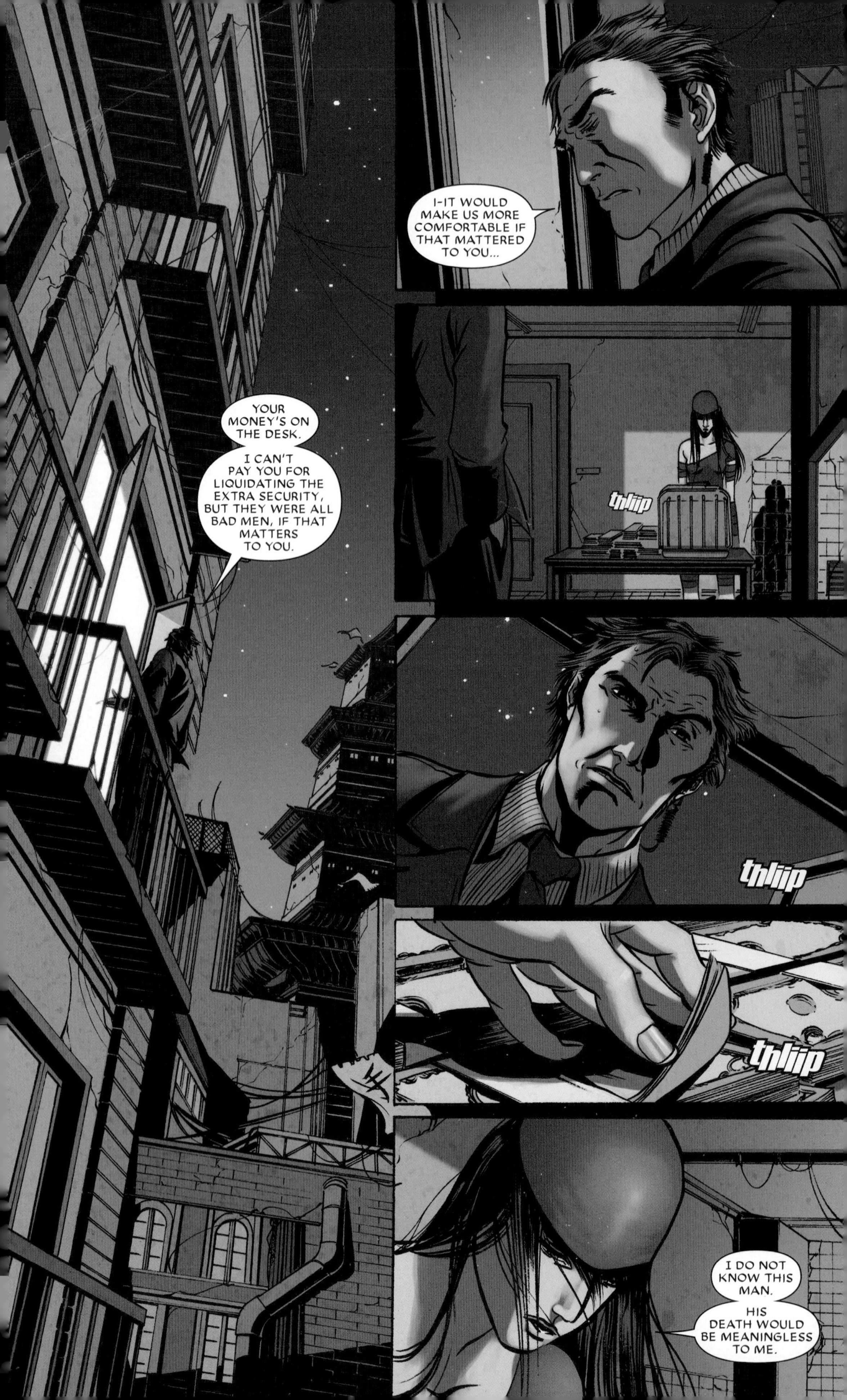
YOUR MONEY'S ON THE DESK.
I CAN'T PAY YOU FOR LIQUIDATING THE EXTRA SECURITY, BUT THEY WERE ALL BAD MEN, IF THAT MATTERS TO YOU.
I-IT WOULD MAKE US MORE COMFORTABLE IF THAT MATTERED TO YOU...
thliip
thliip
thliip
I DO NOT KNOW THIS MAN.
HIS DEATH WOULD BE MEANINGLESS TO ME.

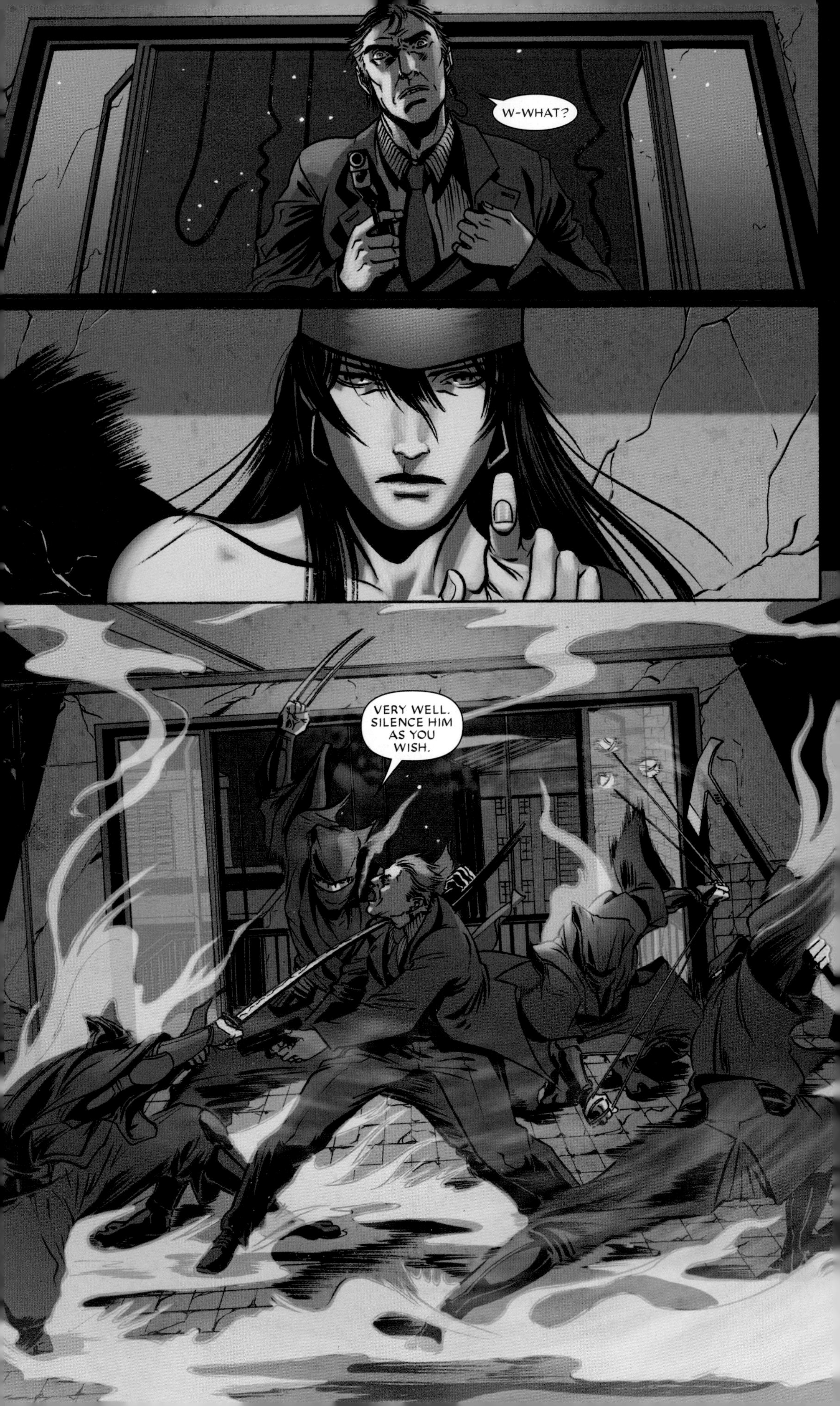
W-WHAT?
VERY WELL. SILENCE HIM AS YOU WISH.

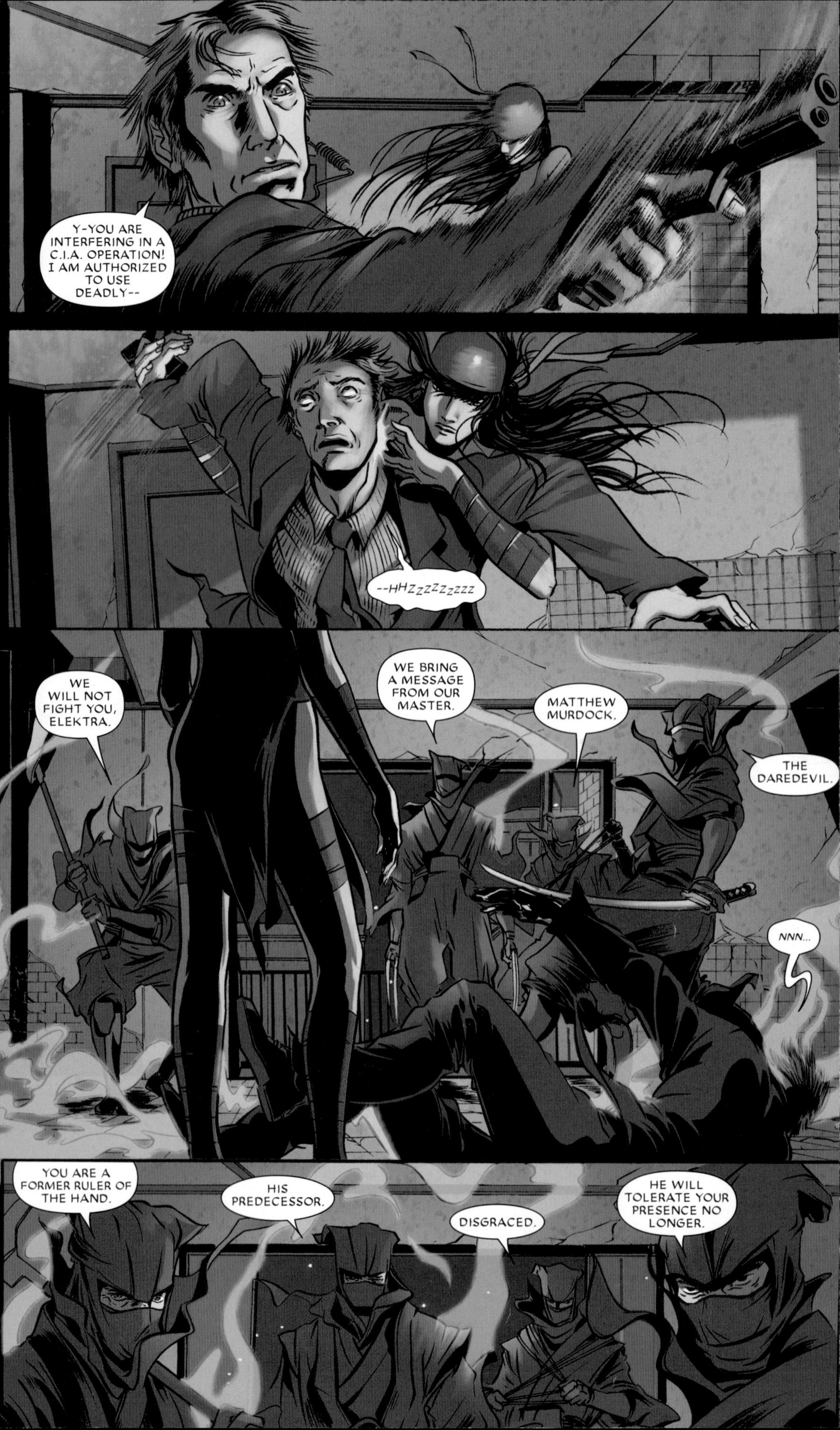
Y-YOU ARE INTERFERING IN A C.I.A. OPERATION! I AM AUTHORIZED TO USE DEADLY--
--HHZZZZZZZZZ
WE WILL NOT FIGHT YOU, ELEKTRA.
WE BRING A MESSAGE FROM OUR MASTER.
MATTHEW MURDOCK.
THE DAREDEVIL.
NNN...
YOU ARE A FORMER RULER OF THE HAND.
HIS PREDECESSOR.
DISGRACED.
HE WILL TOLERATE YOUR PRESENCE NO LONGER.

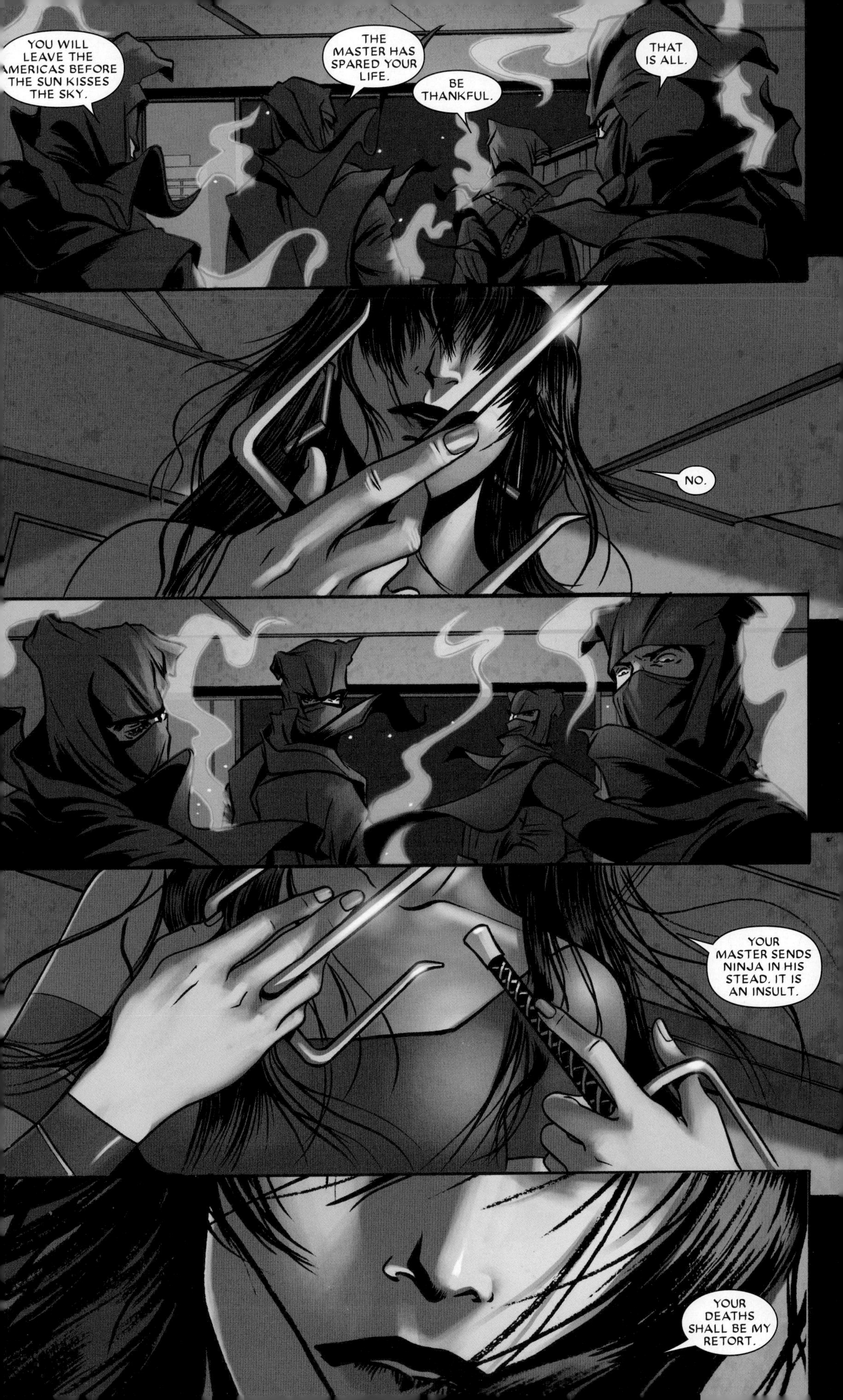

YOU WILL LEAVE THE AMERICAS BEFORE THE SUN KISSES THE SKY.
THE MASTER HAS SPARED YOUR LIFE.
BE THANKFUL.
THAT IS ALL.
NO.
YOUR MASTER SENDS NINJA IN HIS STEAD. IT IS AN INSULT.
YOUR DEATHS SHALL BE MY RETORT.

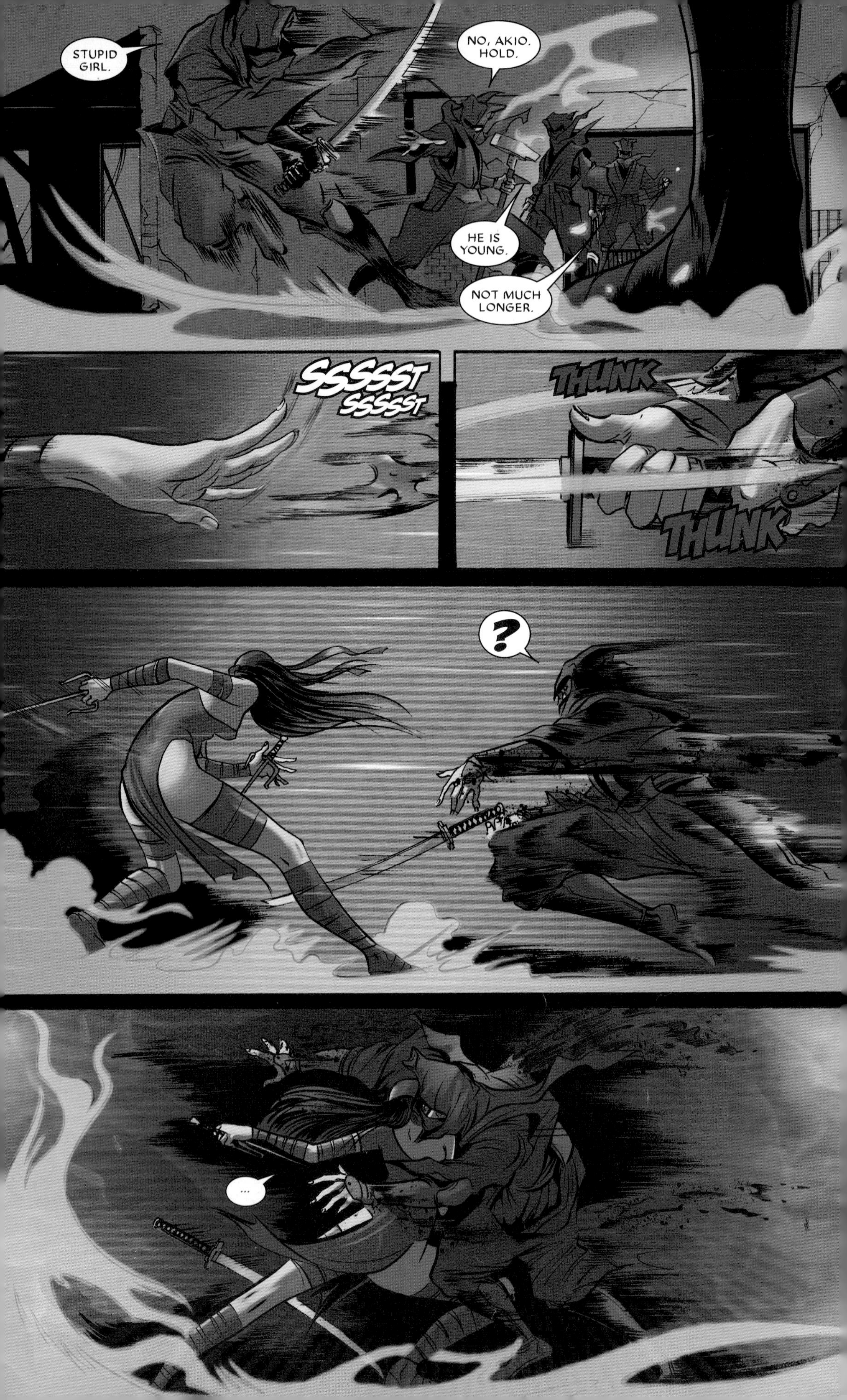
STUPID GIRL.
NO, AKIO. HOLD.
HE IS YOUNG.
NOT MUCH LONGER.
SSSSST SSSSST
THUNK
THUNK
?
...

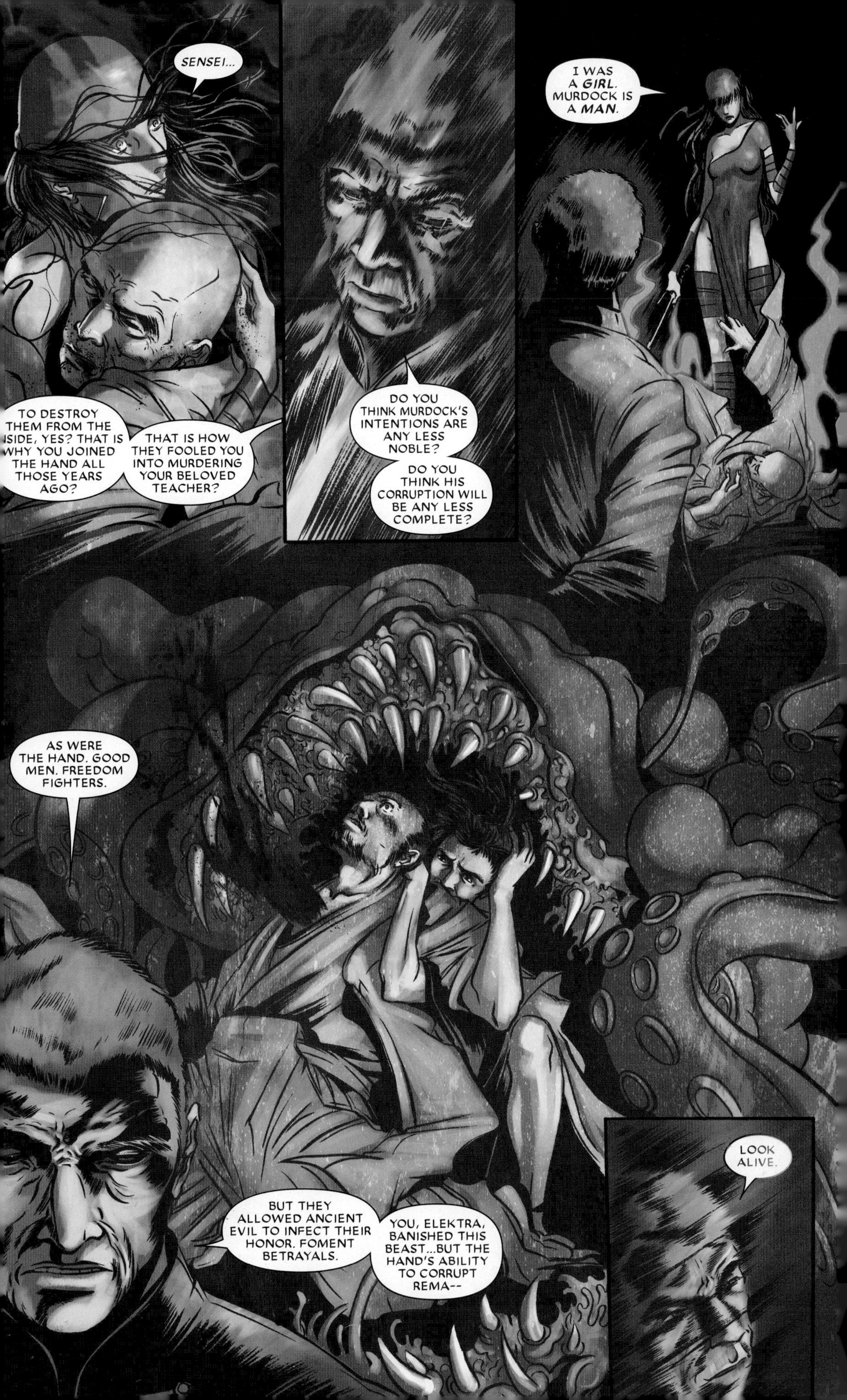
SENSEI...
TO DESTROY THEM FROM THE INSIDE, YES? THAT IS WHY YOU JOINED THE HAND ALL THOSE YEARS AGO?
THAT IS HOW THEY FOOLED YOU INTO MURDERING YOUR BELOVED TEACHER?
DO YOU THINK MURDOCK'S INTENTIONS ARE ANY LESS NOBLE?
DO YOU THINK HIS CORRUPTION WILL BE ANY LESS COMPLETE?
I WAS A GIRL. MURDOCK IS A MAN.
AS WERE THE HAND. GOOD MEN. FREEDOM FIGHTERS.
BUT THEY ALLOWED ANCIENT EVIL TO INFECT THEIR HONOR. FOMENT BETRAYALS.
YOU, ELEKTRA, BANISHED THIS BEAST...BUT THE HAND'S ABILITY TO CORRUPT REMA--
LOOK ALIVE.

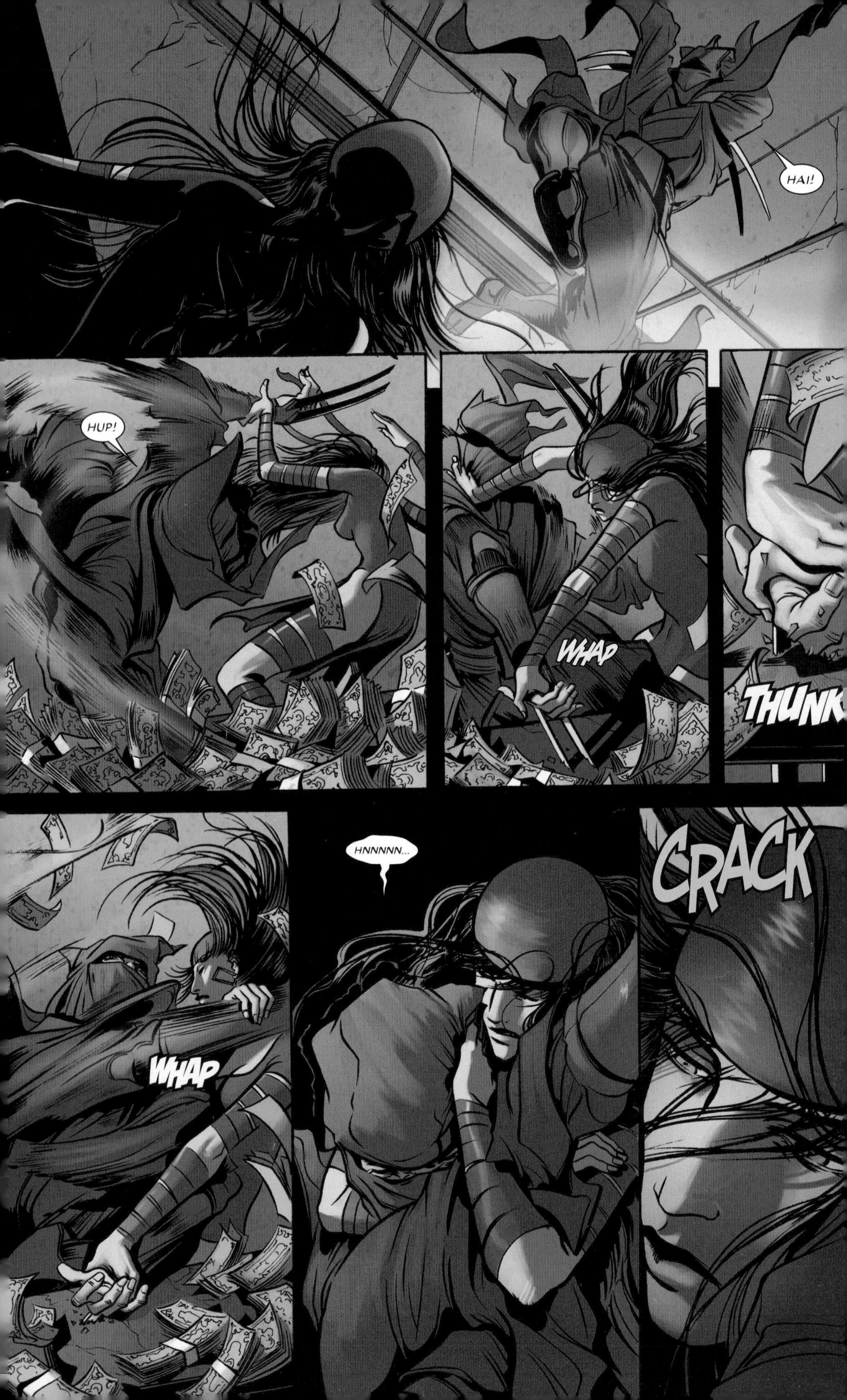
HAI!
HUP!
WHAP
THUNK
WHAP
HNNNNN...
CRACK

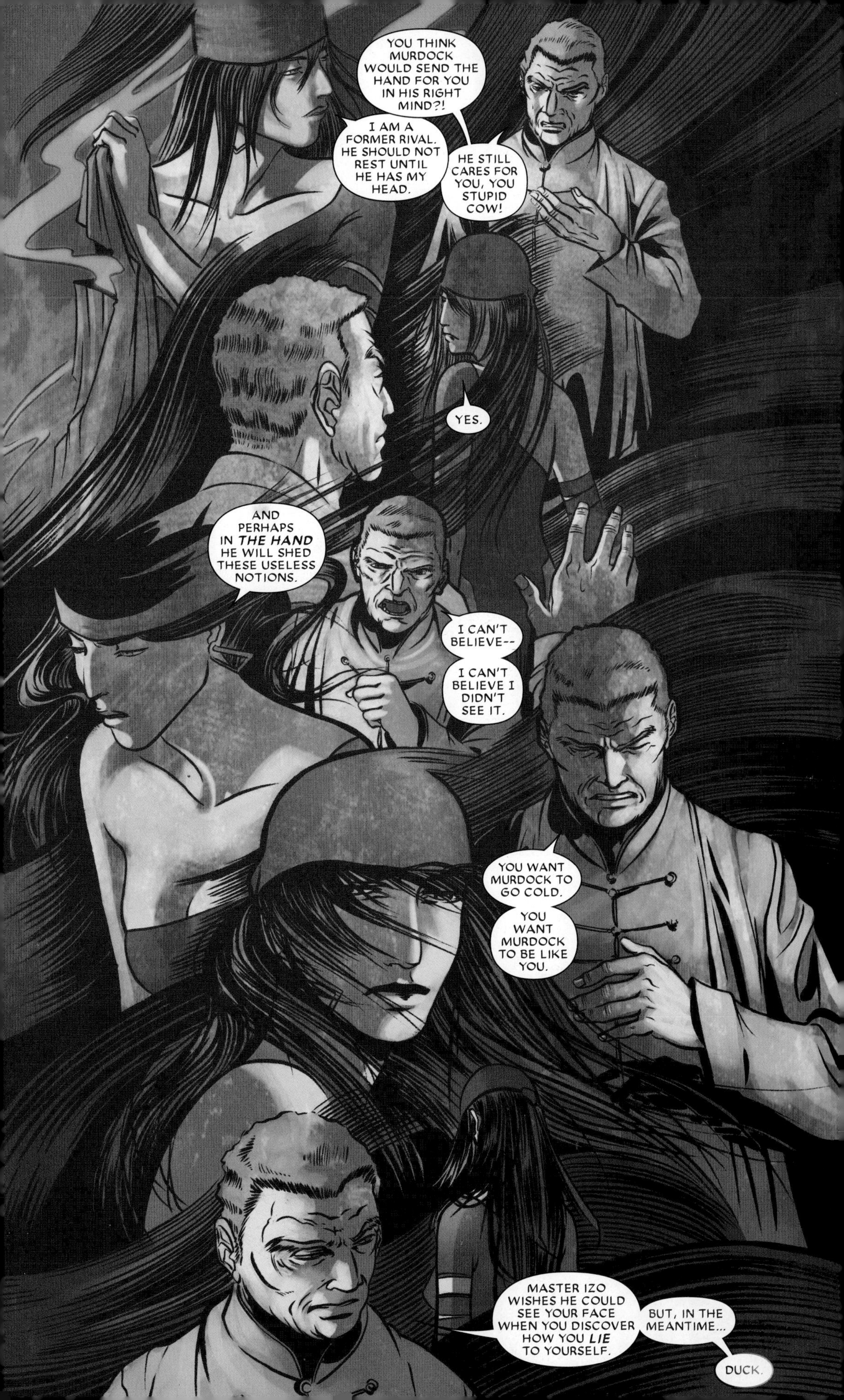
YOU THINK MURDOCK WOULD SEND THE HAND FOR YOU IN HIS RIGHT MIND?!
I AM A FORMER RIVAL. HE SHOULD NOT REST UNTIL HE HAS MY HEAD.
HE STILL CARES FOR YOU, YOU STUPID COW!
YES.
AND PERHAPS IN THE HAND HE WILL SHED THESE USELESS NOTIONS.
I CAN'T BELIEVE--
I CAN'T BELIEVE I DIDN'T SEE IT.
YOU WANT MURDOCK TO GO COLD.
YOU WANT MURDOCK TO BE LIKE YOU.
MASTER IZO WISHES HE COULD SEE YOUR FACE WHEN YOU DISCOVER HOW YOU LIE TO YOURSELF.
BUT, IN THE MEANTIME...
DUCK.

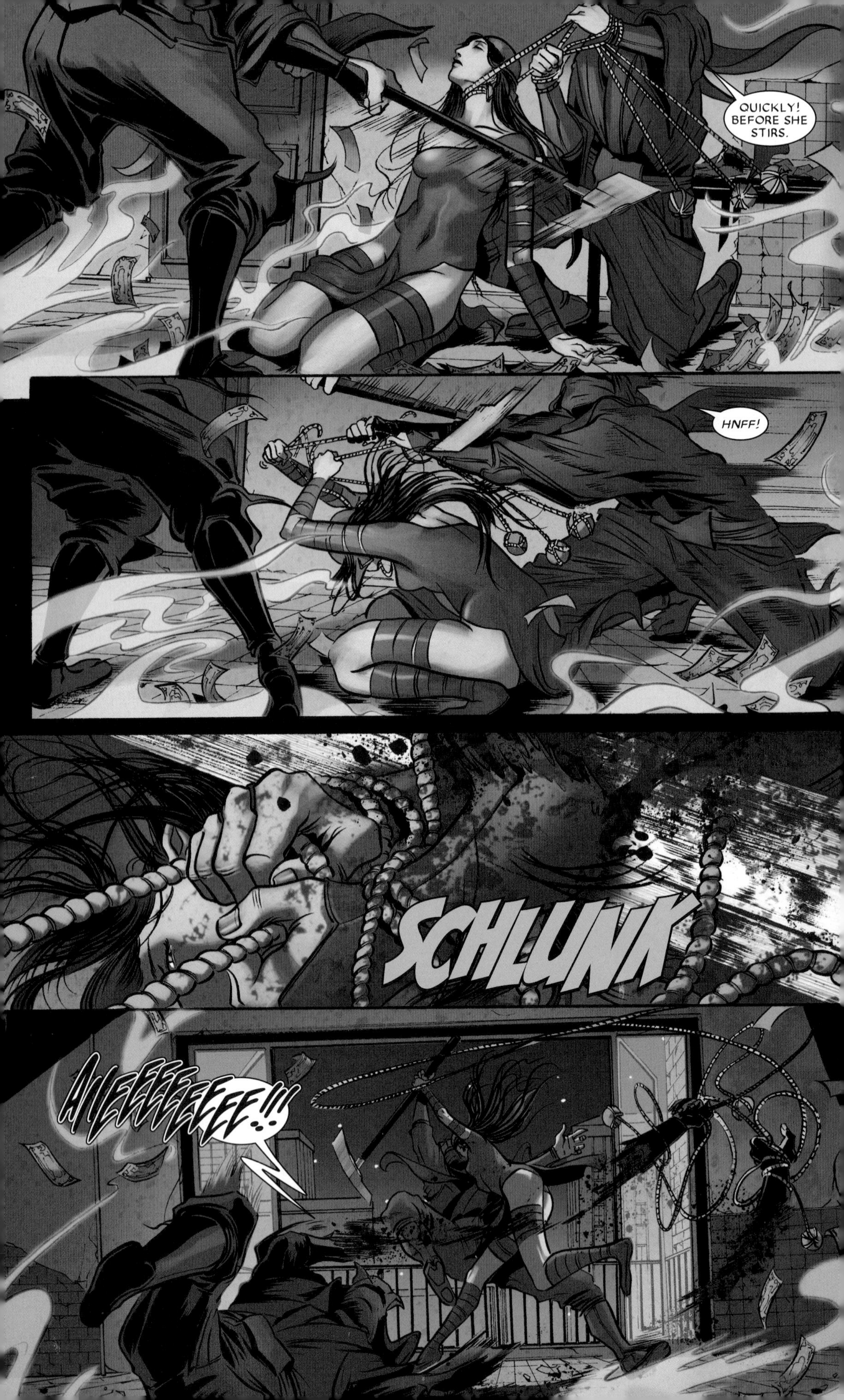
QUICKLY! BEFORE SHE STIRS.
HNFF!
SCHLUNK
AIIEEEEEEEEE!!!

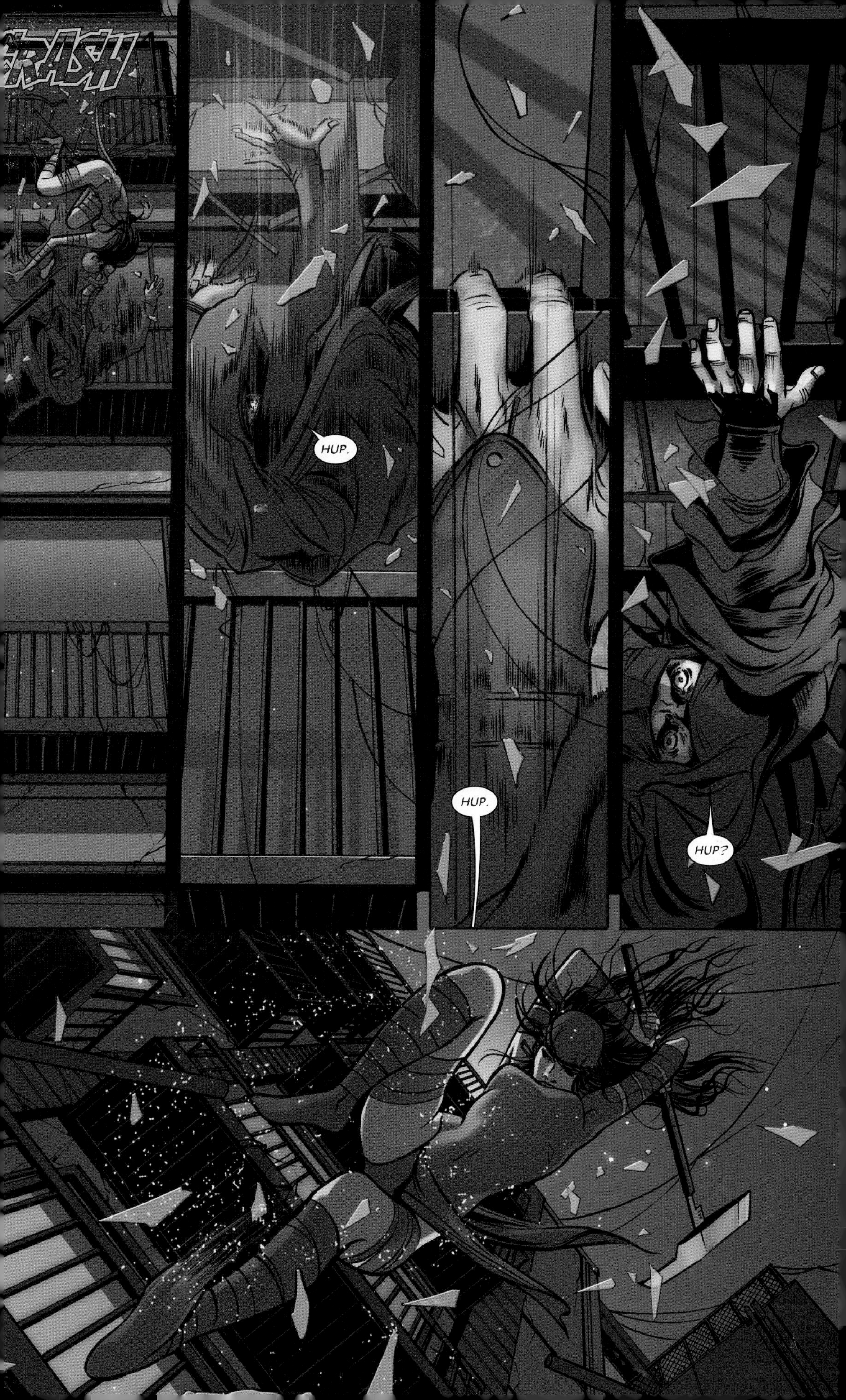
RASH
HUP.
HUP.
HUP?

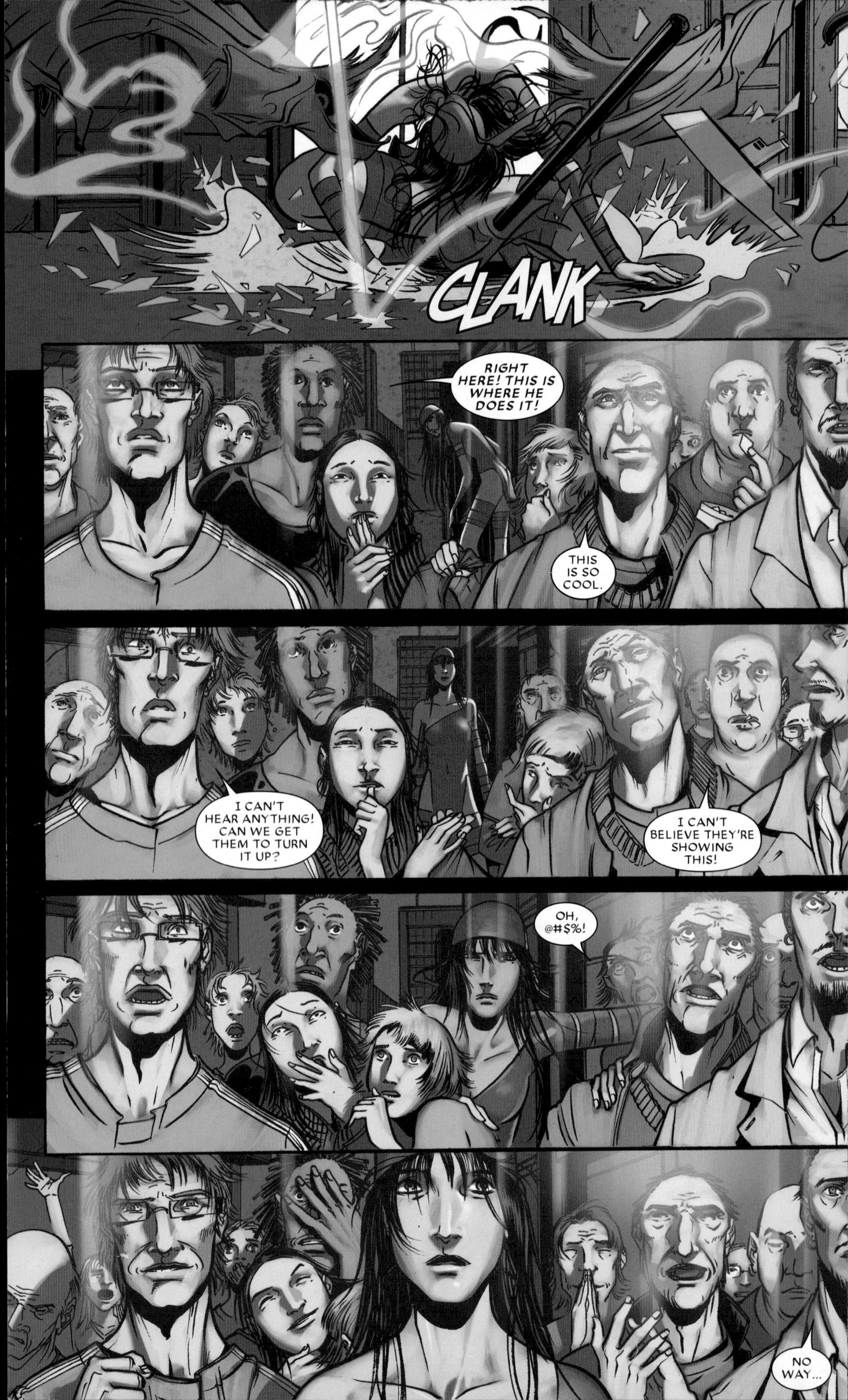
CLANK
RIGHT HERE! THIS IS WHERE HE DOES IT!
THIS IS SO COOL.
I CAN'T HEAR ANYTHING! CAN WE GET THEM TO TURN IT UP?
I CAN'T BELIEVE THEY'RE SHOWING THIS!
OH, @#$%!
NO WAY...

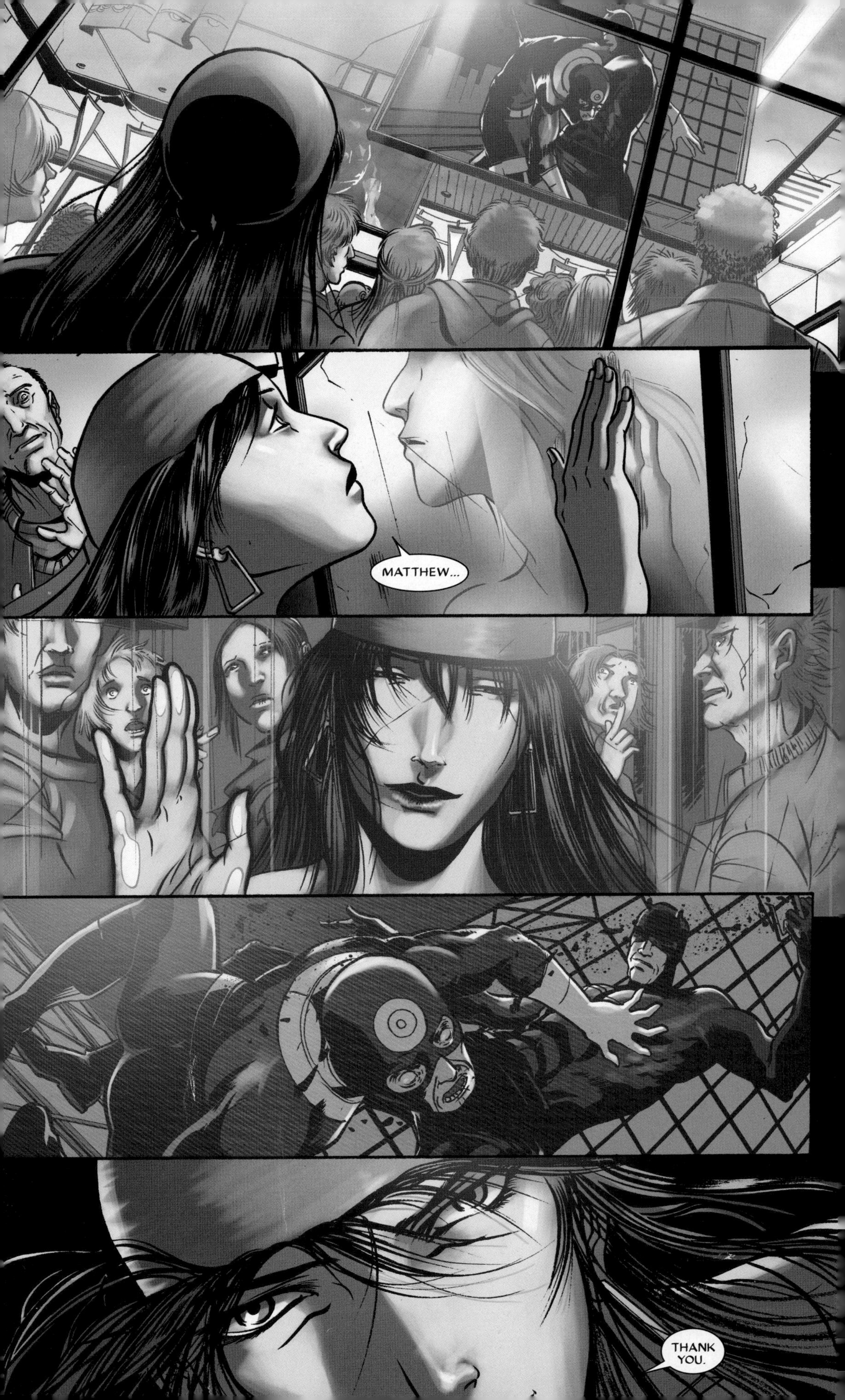
MATTHEW...
THANK YOU.

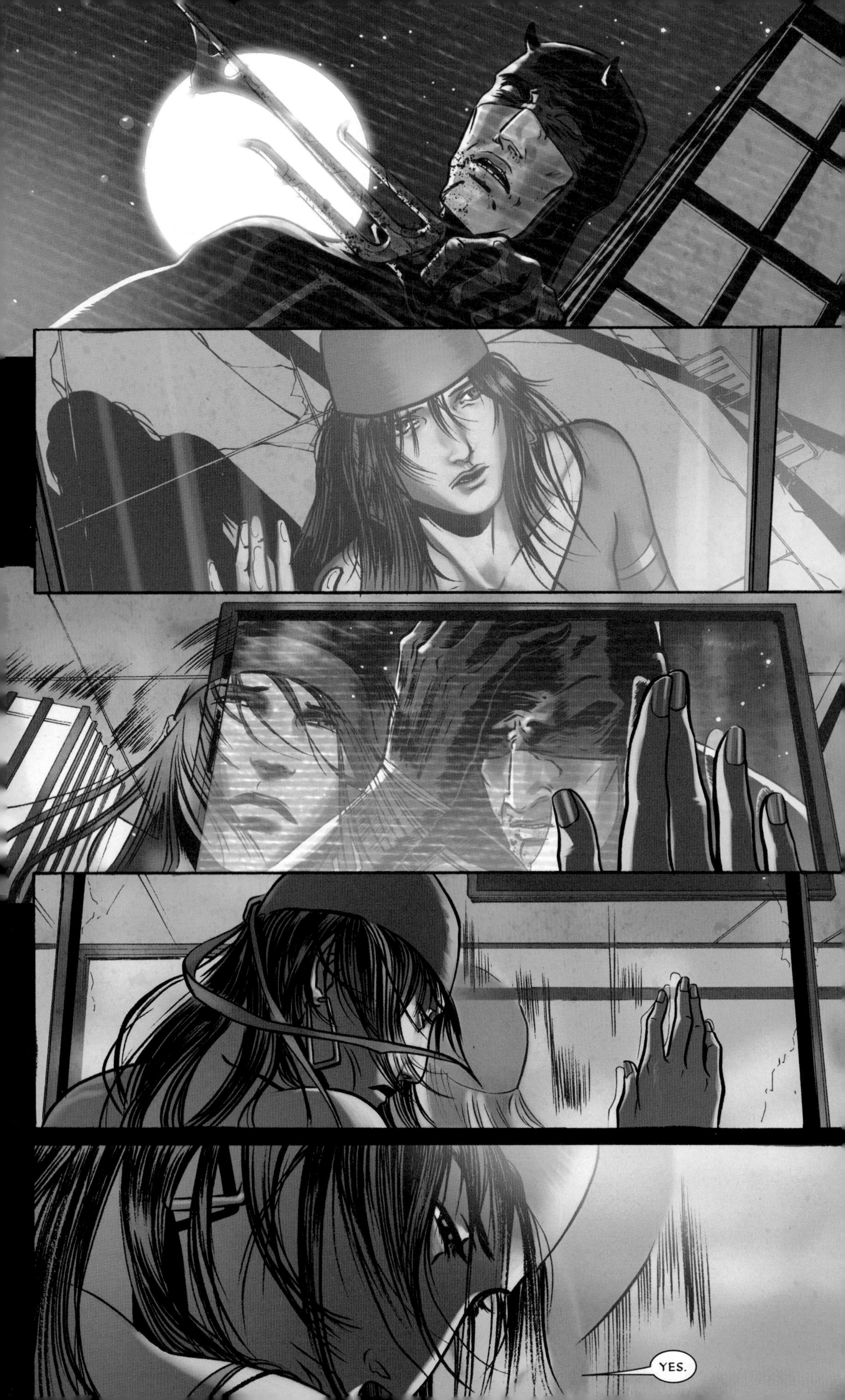
YES.

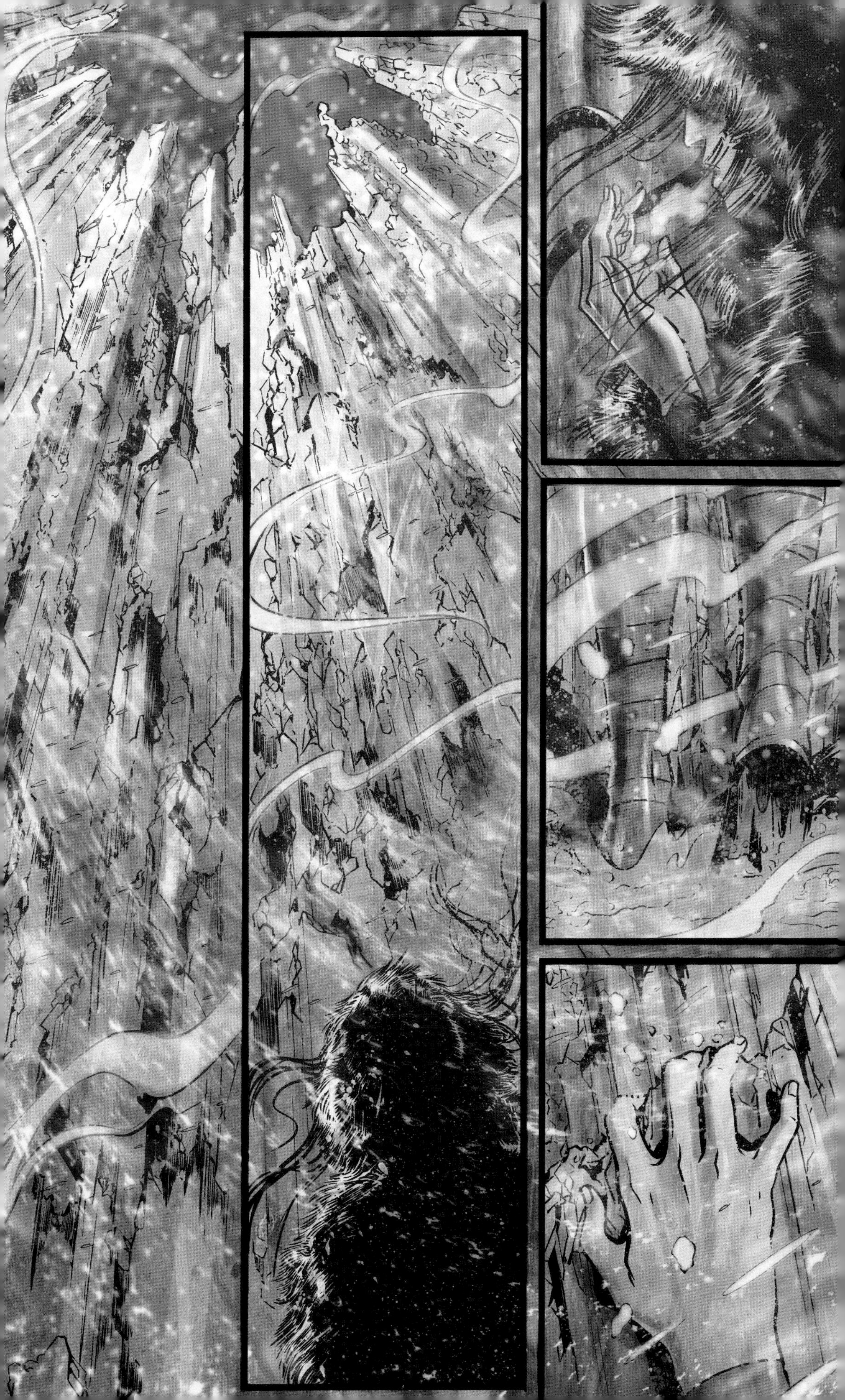

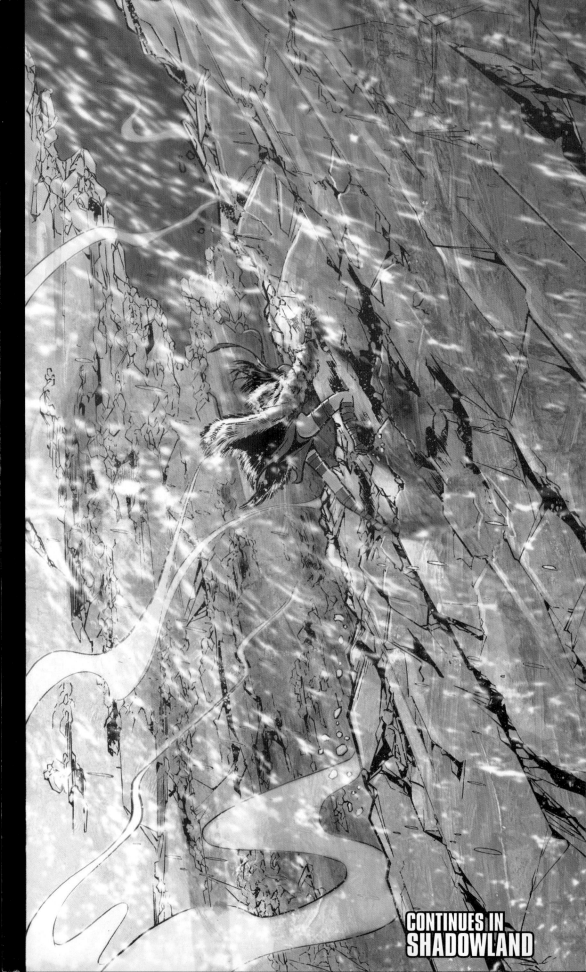

CONTINUES IN SHADOWLAND

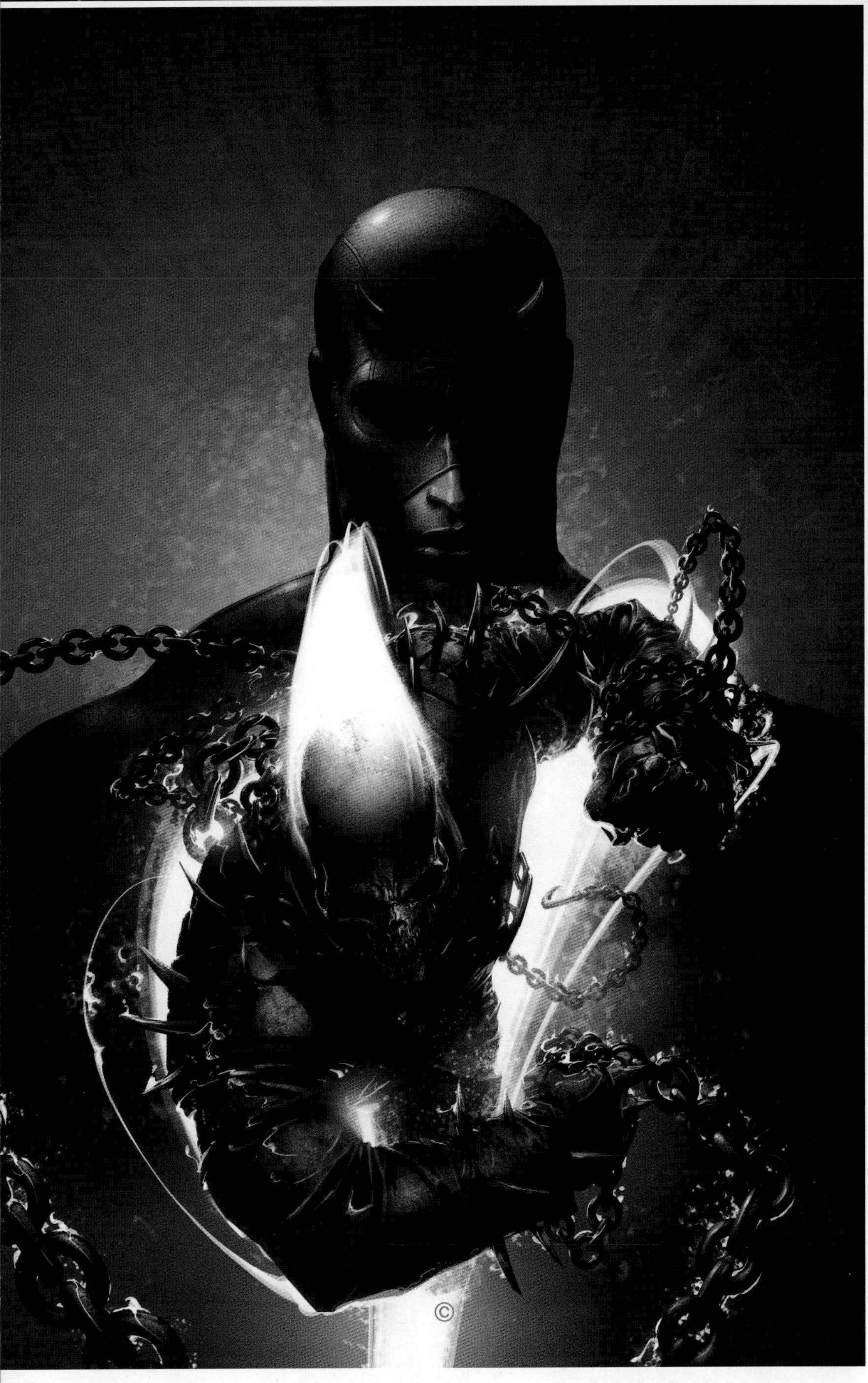

SHADOWLAND: GHOST RIDER

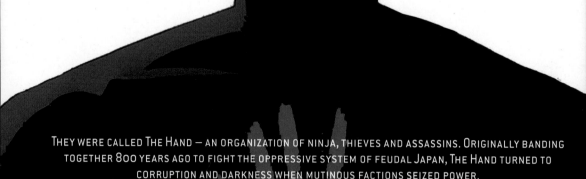

THEY WERE CALLED THE HAND — AN ORGANIZATION OF NINJA, THIEVES AND ASSASSINS. ORIGINALLY BANDING TOGETHER 800 YEARS AGO TO FIGHT THE OPPRESSIVE SYSTEM OF FEUDAL JAPAN, THE HAND TURNED TO CORRUPTION AND DARKNESS WHEN MUTINOUS FACTIONS SEIZED POWER.

OVER THE CENTURIES, THE HAND FREQUENTLY TURNED TO OUTSIDERS TO SERVE AS THEIR AGENTS AND FIGUREHEADS. TODAY, WITH A BASE OF OPERATIONS IN NEW YORK CITY, THE HAND RECRUITED A NEW LEADER: MATT MURDOCK, A.K.A. THE COSTUMED HERO DAREDEVIL. TO DRAW MURDOCK IN, THEY DESTROYED EVERYTHING HE LIVED FOR — BUT MATT STILL HOPED TO TURN THE STRENGTH AND RESOURCES OF THE HAND TO NOBLE ENDS. HOWEVER, WHEN MURDOCK ACCEPTED THE JOB, HE THWARTED THE AMBITIONS TO CONTROL THE HAND OF THE CRIME LORD OF HELL'S KITCHEN, WILSON FISK — A.K.A. THE KINGPIN — AND CORRUPTED HIS OWN SOUL IN THE PROCESS. UNBEKNOWNST TO MATT, THE HAND IS SECRETLY CONTROLLED BY THE TREACHEROUS SNAKEROOT CLAN IN JAPAN, PULLING HIS STRINGS AND LEADING HIM TO EVIL.

SEEKING TO DECAPITATE THE LEADERSHIP OF THE HAND AND TAKE ITS NINJA ARMY FOR HIMSELF, FISK TURNED TO POWERFUL JAPANESE MAGIC TO SUMMON FORTH AN ANCIENT ENEMY OF THE CULT — AN EMBODIMENT OF THE SPIRIT OF VENGEANCE ITSELF...

SHADOWLAND

GHOST RIDER

THIS STORY TAKES PLACE BEFORE **SHADOWLAND #3**

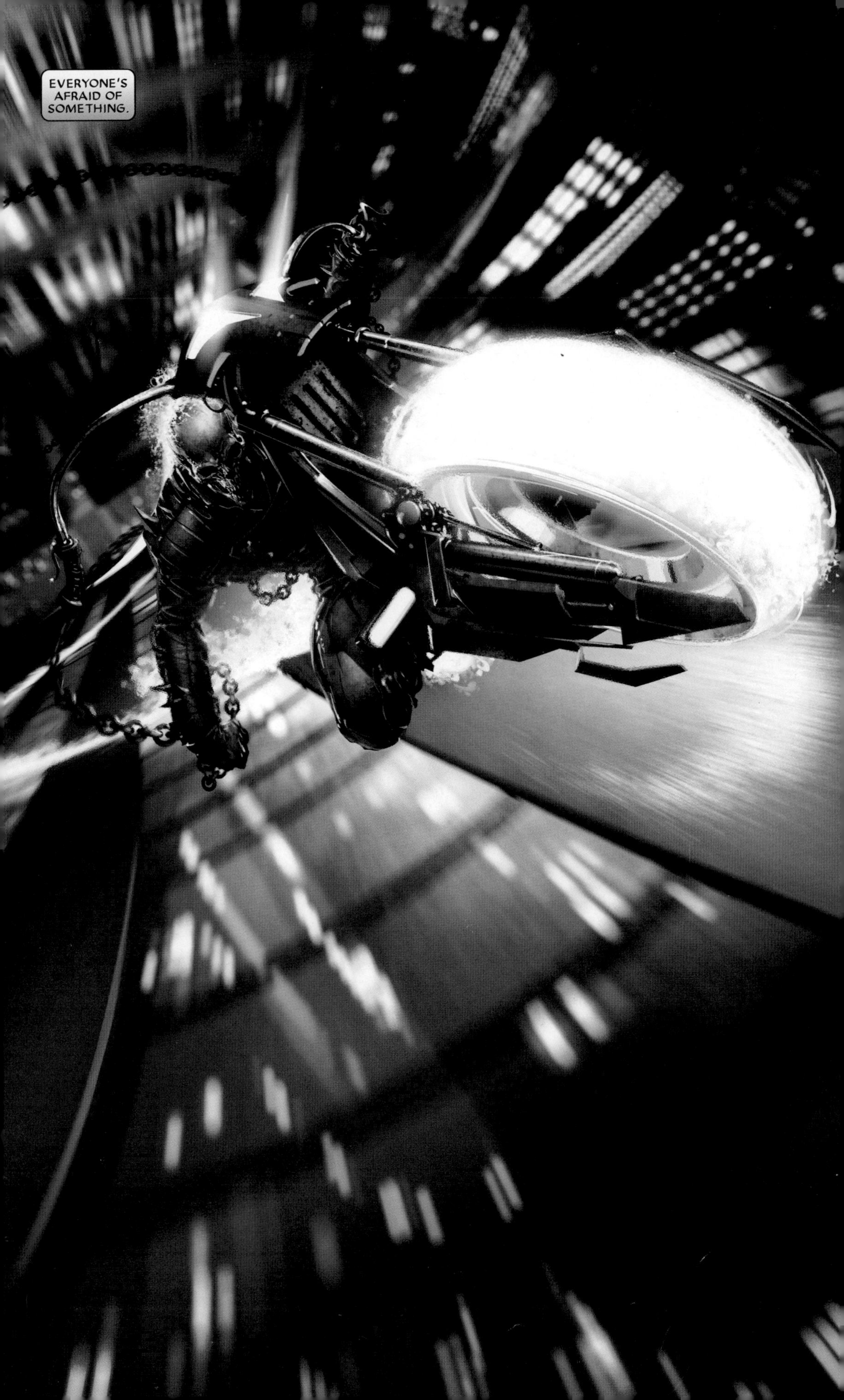
EVERYONE'S AFRAID OF SOMETHING.

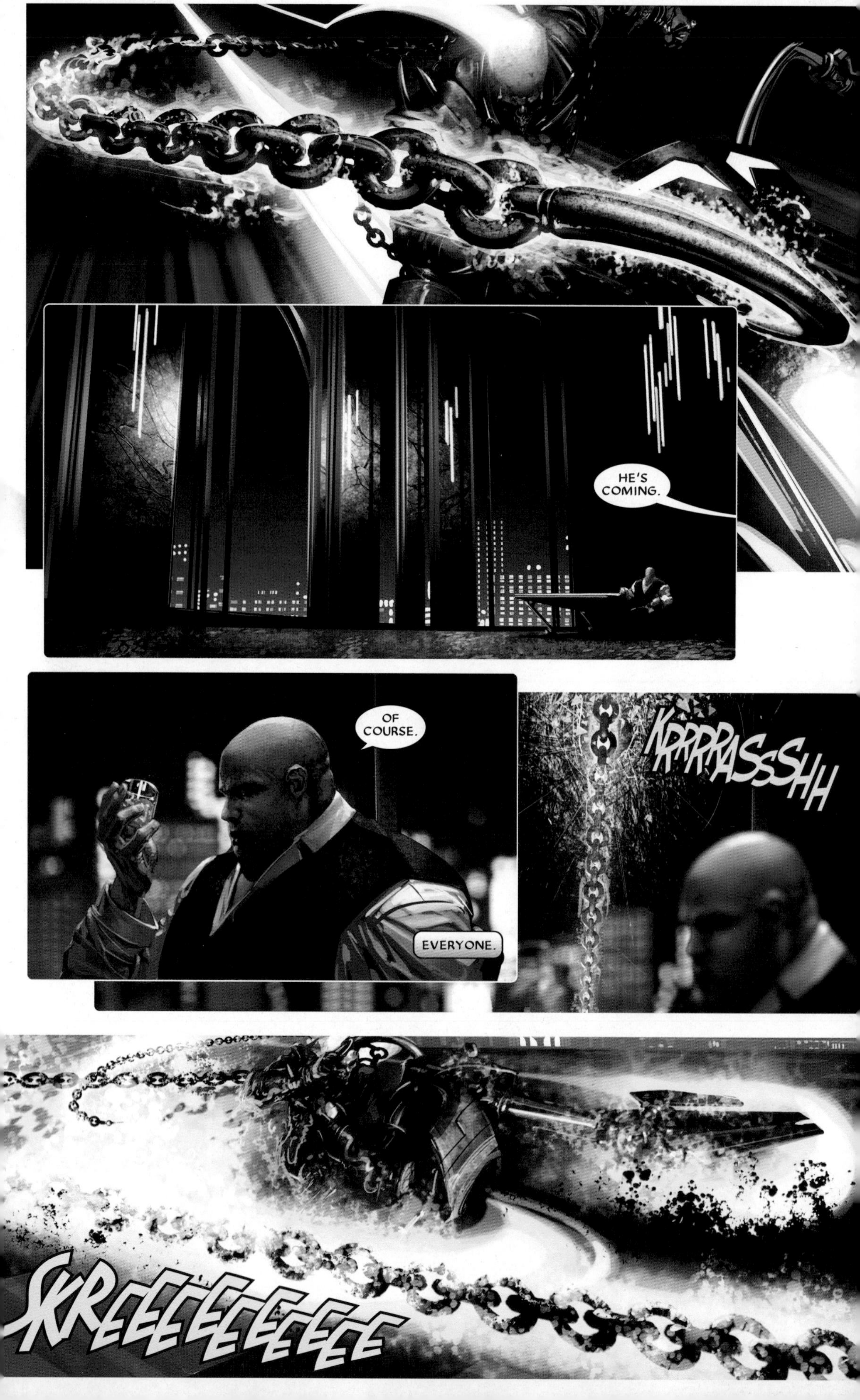

HE'S COMING.
OF COURSE.
EVERYONE.
KRRRRASSSHH
SKREEEEEEEEEEE

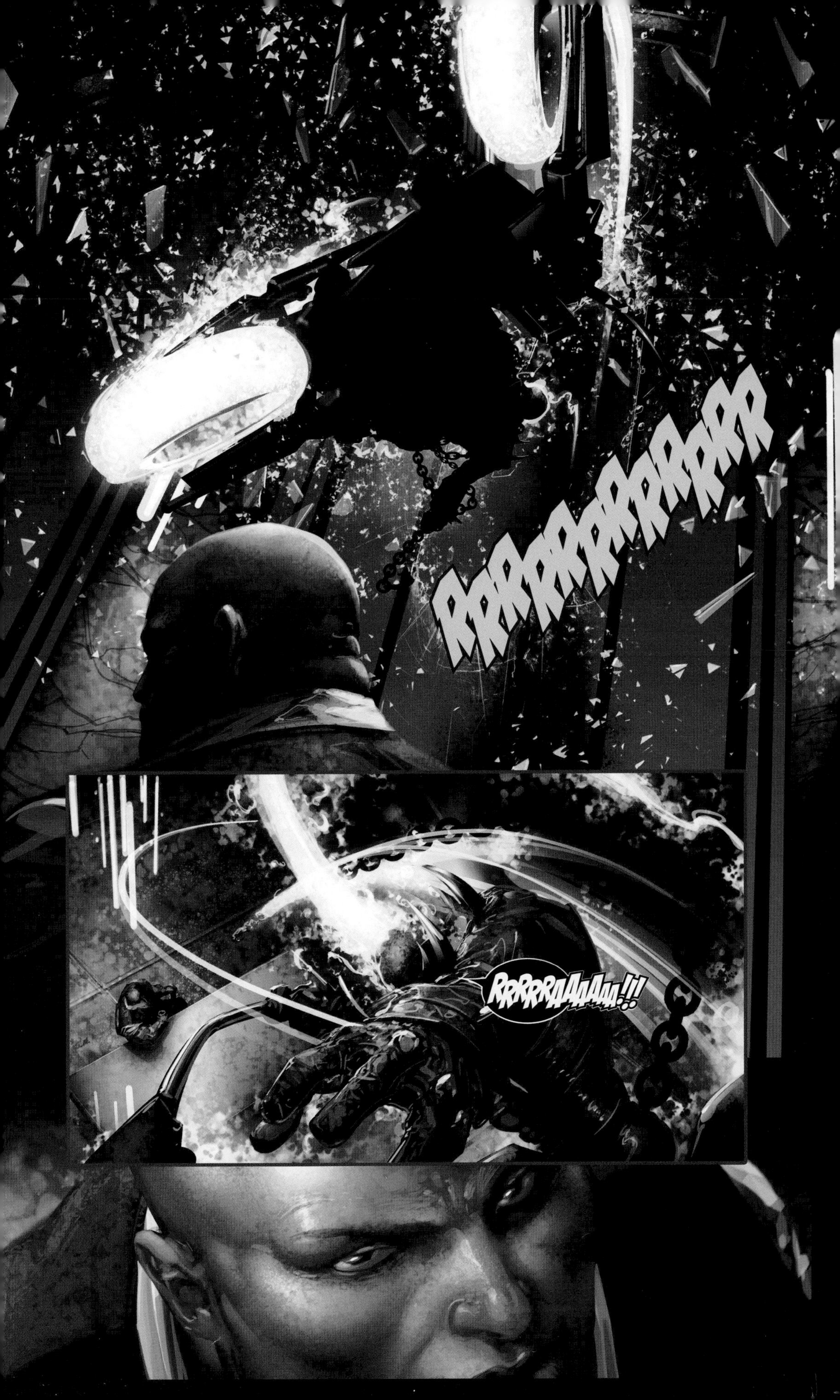

RRRRRRRRRRRR
RRRRRAAAAAA!!!

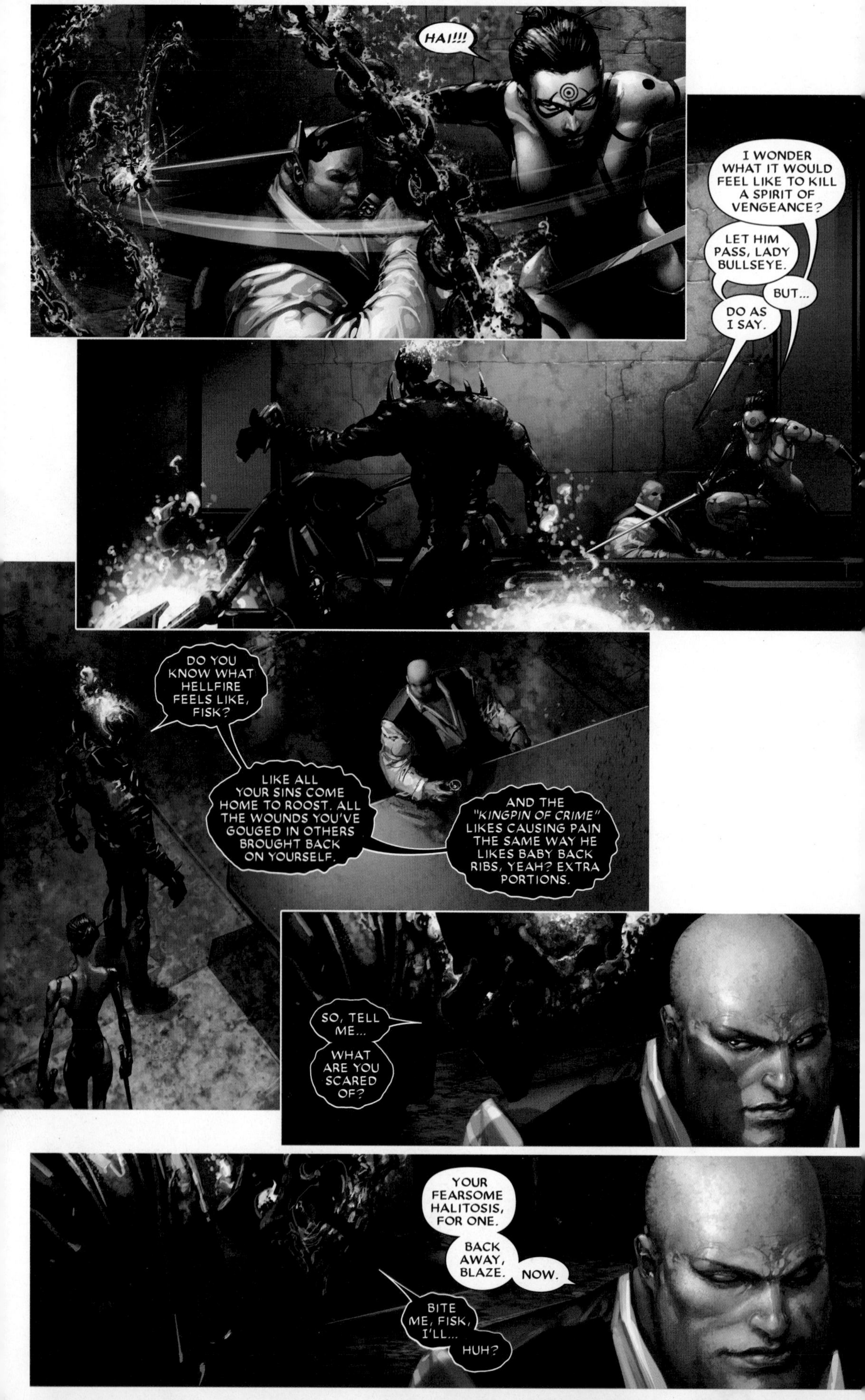
HAI!!!
I WONDER WHAT IT WOULD FEEL LIKE TO KILL A SPIRIT OF VENGEANCE?
LET HIM PASS, LADY BULLSEYE.
BUT...
DO AS I SAY.
DO YOU KNOW WHAT HELLFIRE FEELS LIKE, FISK?
LIKE ALL YOUR SINS COME HOME TO ROOST. ALL THE WOUNDS YOU'VE GOUGED IN OTHERS BROUGHT BACK ON YOURSELF.
AND THE *"KINGPIN OF CRIME"* LIKES CAUSING PAIN THE SAME WAY HE LIKES BABY BACK RIBS, YEAH? EXTRA PORTIONS.
SO, TELL ME...
WHAT ARE YOU SCARED OF?
YOUR FEARSOME HALITOSIS, FOR ONE.
BACK AWAY, BLAZE.
NOW.
BITE ME, FISK, I'LL...
HUH?

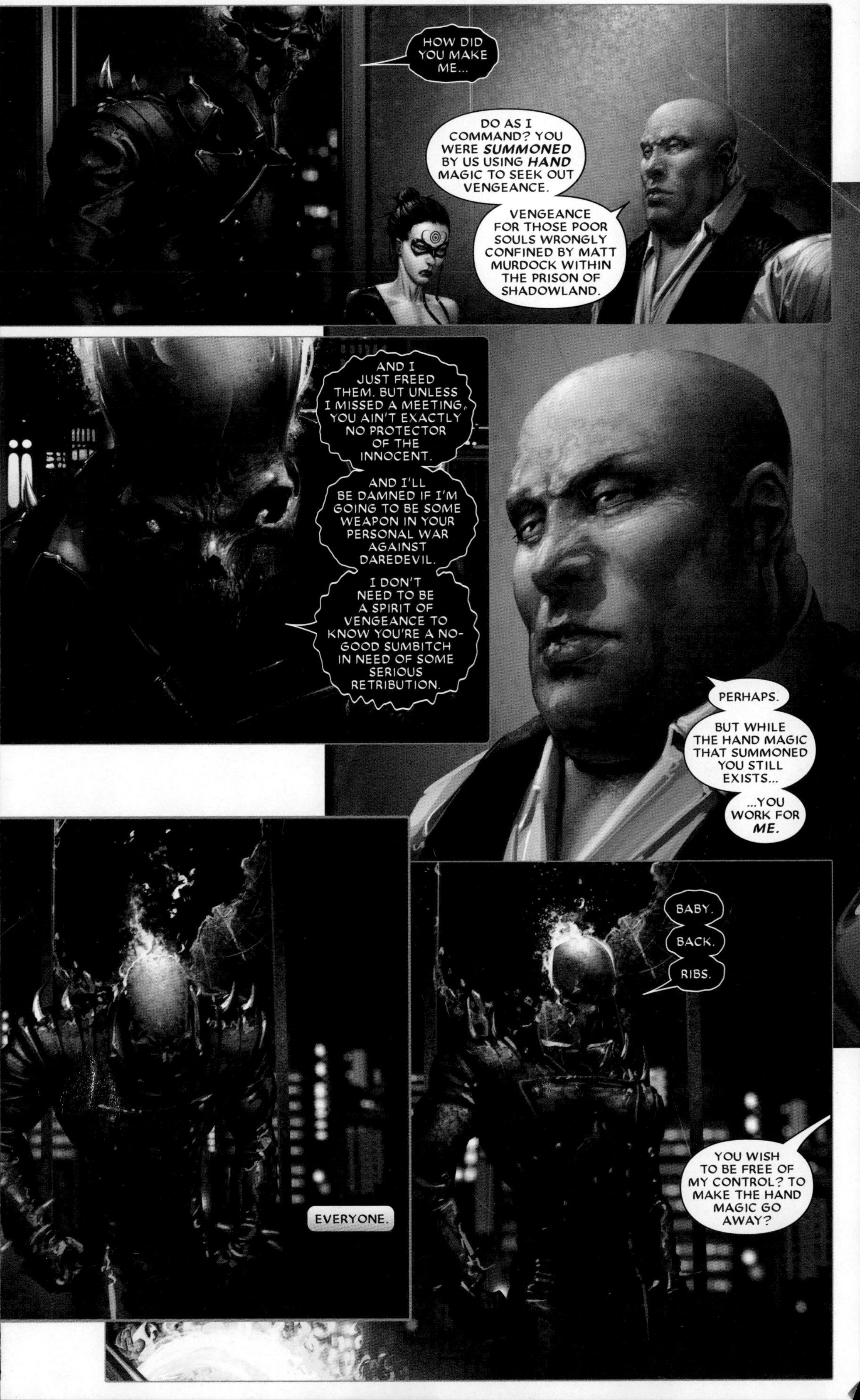
HOW DID YOU MAKE ME...
DO AS I COMMAND? YOU WERE SUMMONED BY US USING HAND MAGIC TO SEEK OUT VENGEANCE.
VENGEANCE FOR THOSE POOR SOULS WRONGLY CONFINED BY MATT MURDOCK WITHIN THE PRISON OF SHADOWLAND.
AND I JUST FREED THEM. BUT UNLESS I MISSED A MEETING, YOU AIN'T EXACTLY NO PROTECTOR OF THE INNOCENT.
AND I'LL BE DAMNED IF I'M GOING TO BE SOME WEAPON IN YOUR PERSONAL WAR AGAINST DAREDEVIL.
I DON'T NEED TO BE A SPIRIT OF VENGEANCE TO KNOW YOU'RE A NO-GOOD SUMBITCH IN NEED OF SOME SERIOUS RETRIBUTION.
PERHAPS.
BUT WHILE THE HAND MAGIC THAT SUMMONED YOU STILL EXISTS...
...YOU WORK FOR ME.
EVERYONE.
BABY.
BACK.
RIBS.
YOU WISH TO BE FREE OF MY CONTROL? TO MAKE THE HAND MAGIC GO AWAY?

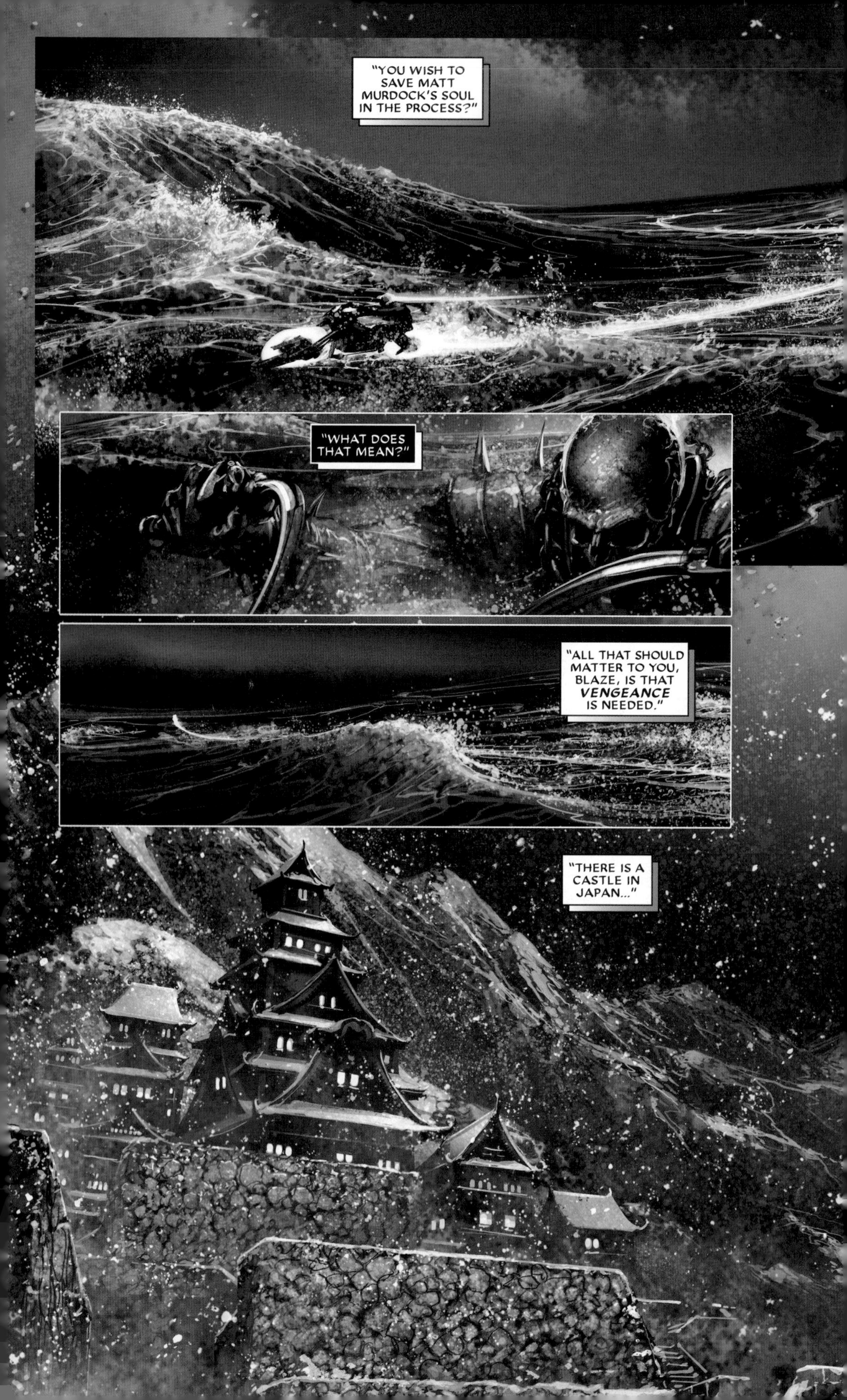
"YOU WISH TO SAVE MATT MURDOCK'S SOUL IN THE PROCESS?"
"WHAT DOES THAT MEAN?"
"ALL THAT SHOULD MATTER TO YOU, BLAZE, IS THAT *VENGEANCE* IS NEEDED."
"THERE IS A CASTLE IN JAPAN..."

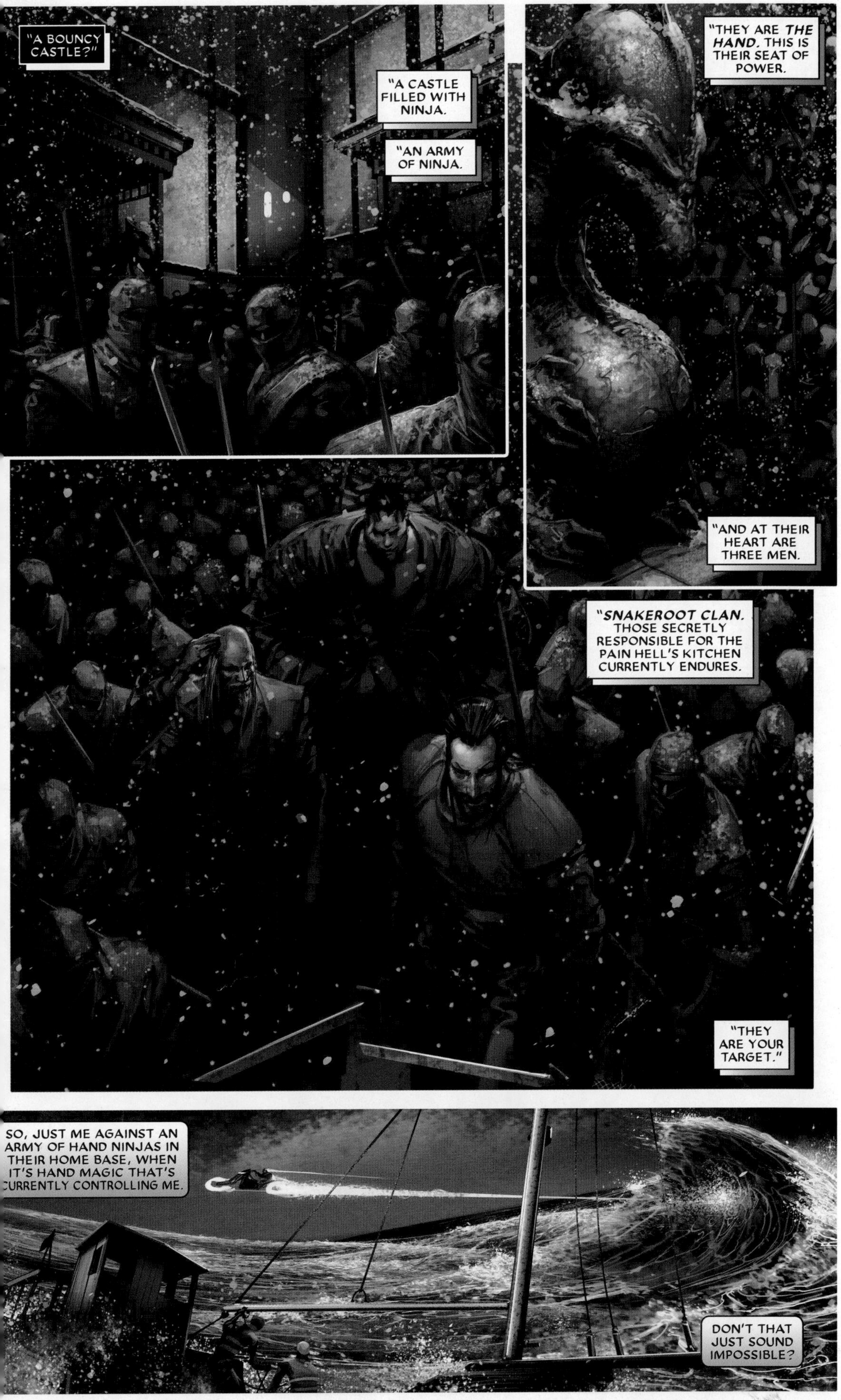
"A BOUNCY CASTLE?"
"A CASTLE FILLED WITH NINJA.
"AN ARMY OF NINJA.
"THEY ARE *THE HAND.* THIS IS THEIR SEAT OF POWER.
"AND AT THEIR HEART ARE THREE MEN.
"*SNAKEROOT CLAN.* THOSE SECRETLY RESPONSIBLE FOR THE PAIN HELL'S KITCHEN CURRENTLY ENDURES.
"THEY ARE YOUR TARGET."
SO, JUST ME AGAINST AN ARMY OF HAND NINJAS IN THEIR HOME BASE, WHEN IT'S HAND MAGIC THAT'S CURRENTLY CONTROLLING ME.
DON'T THAT JUST SOUND IMPOSSIBLE?

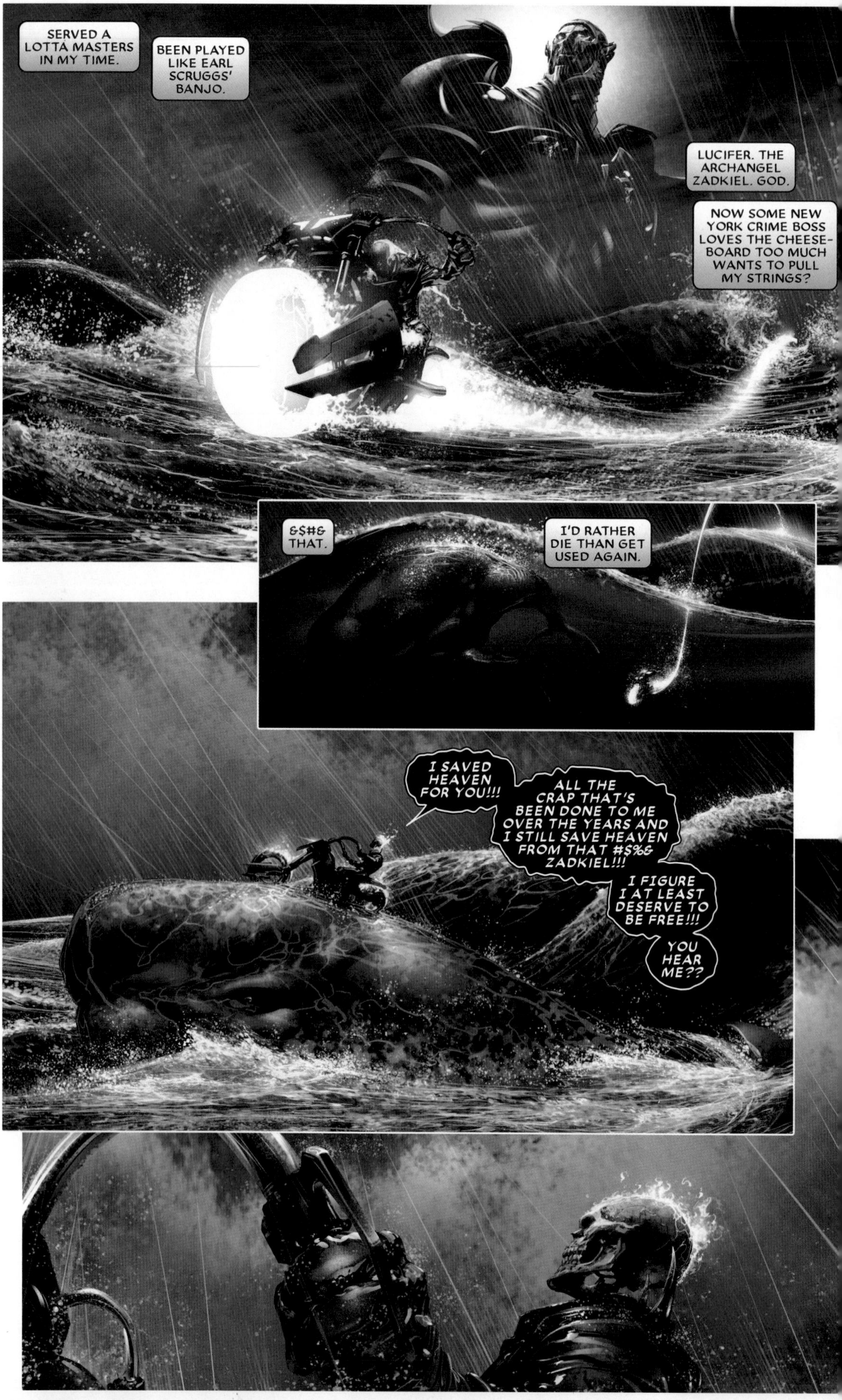
SERVED A LOTTA MASTERS IN MY TIME.
BEEN PLAYED LIKE EARL SCRUGGS' BANJO.
LUCIFER. THE ARCHANGEL ZADKIEL. GOD.
NOW SOME NEW YORK CRIME BOSS LOVES THE CHEESE-BOARD TOO MUCH WANTS TO PULL MY STRINGS?
&$#& THAT.
I'D RATHER DIE THAN GET USED AGAIN.
I SAVED HEAVEN FOR YOU!!!
ALL THE CRAP THAT'S BEEN DONE TO ME OVER THE YEARS AND I STILL SAVE HEAVEN FROM THAT #$%& ZADKIEL!!!
I FIGURE I AT LEAST DESERVE TO BE FREE!!!
YOU HEAR ME??

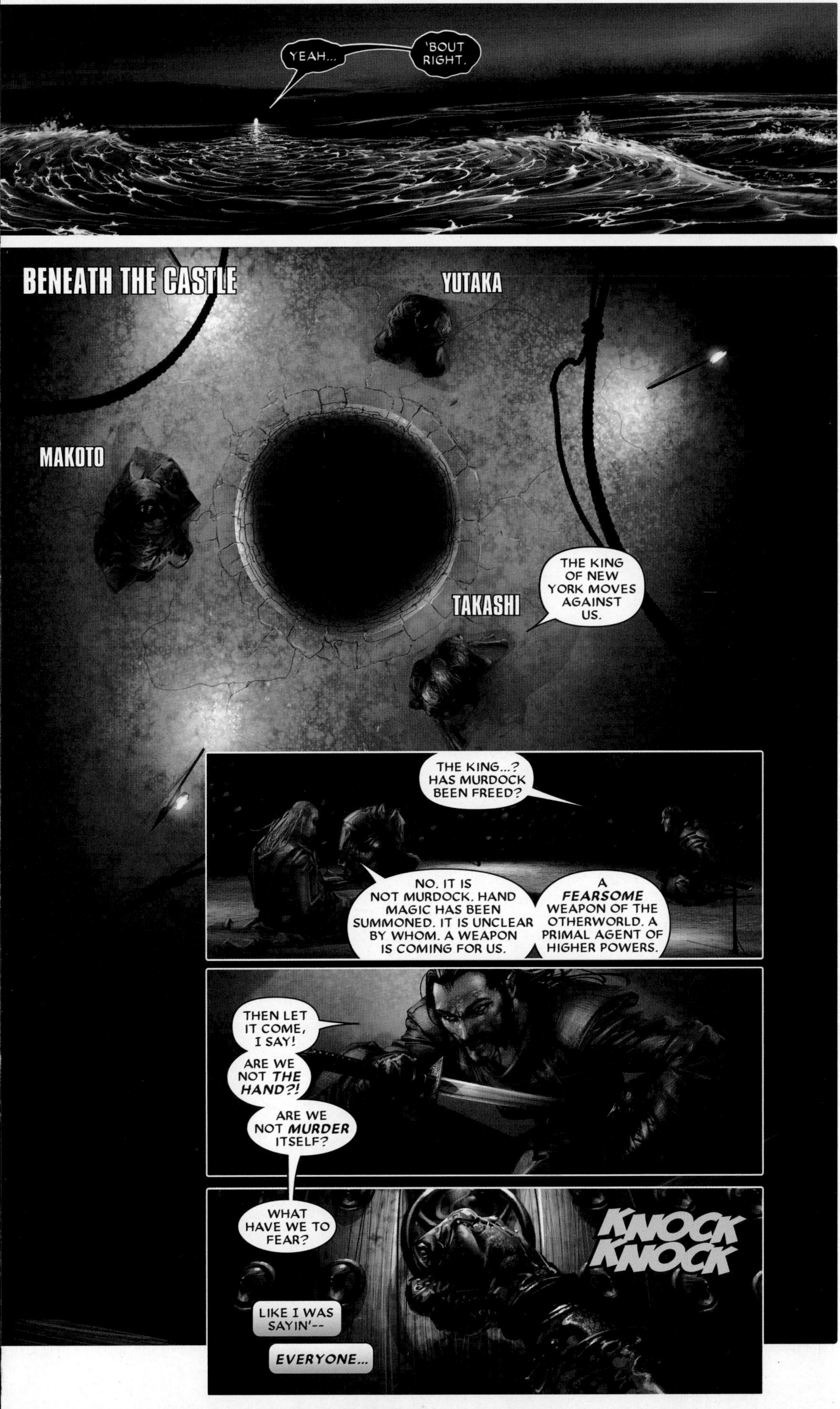

YEAH...
'BOUT RIGHT.
BENEATH THE CASTLE
YUTAKA
MAKOTO
TAKASHI
THE KING OF NEW YORK MOVES AGAINST US.
THE KING...? HAS MURDOCK BEEN FREED?
NO. IT IS NOT MURDOCK. HAND MAGIC HAS BEEN SUMMONED. IT IS UNCLEAR BY WHOM. A WEAPON IS COMING FOR US.
A FEARSOME WEAPON OF THE OTHERWORLD. A PRIMAL AGENT OF HIGHER POWERS.
THEN LET IT COME, I SAY!
ARE WE NOT THE HAND?!
ARE WE NOT MURDER ITSELF?
WHAT HAVE WE TO FEAR?
KNOCK KNOCK
LIKE I WAS SAYIN'--
EVERYONE...

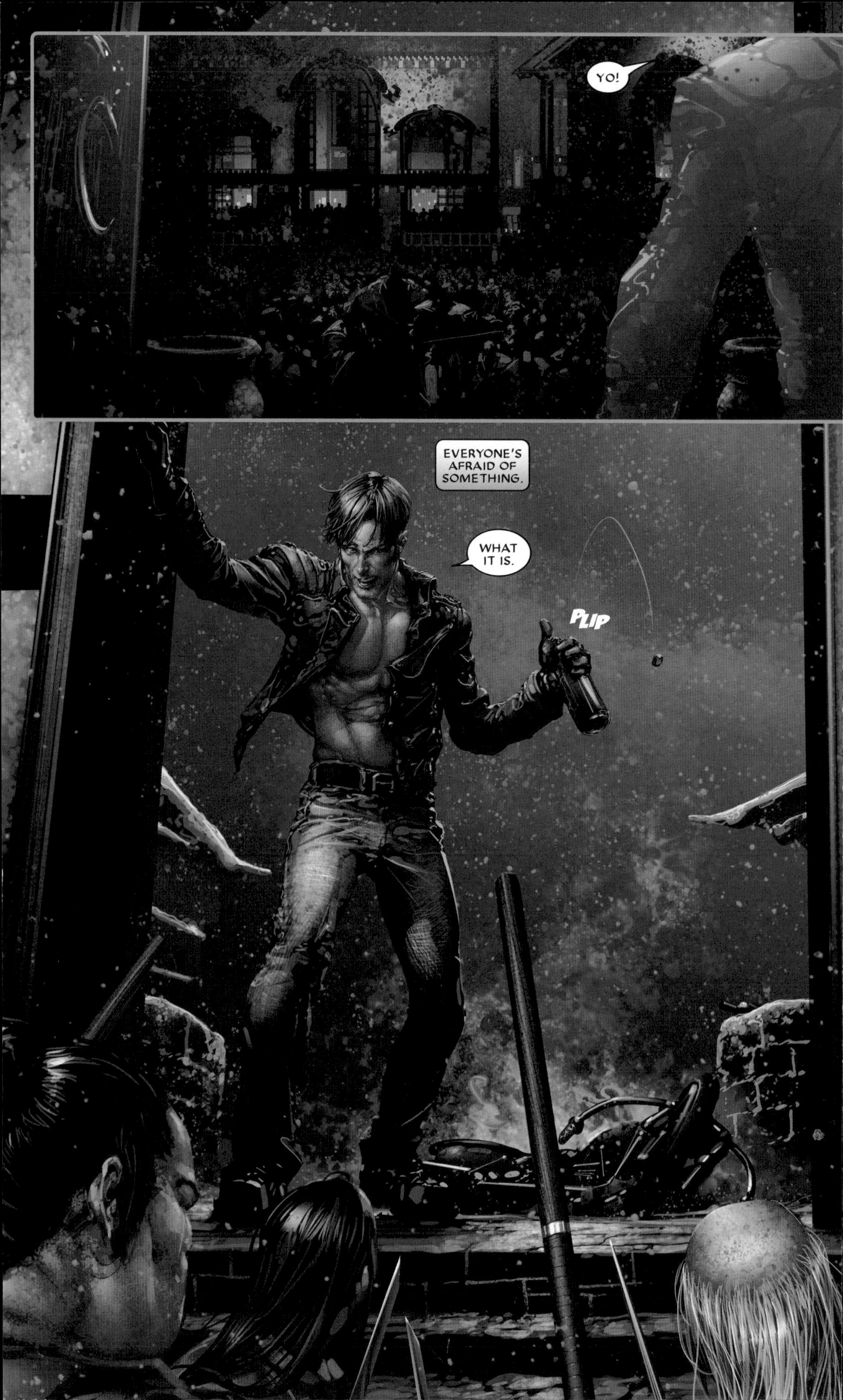
YO!
EVERYONE'S AFRAID OF SOMETHING.
WHAT IT IS.
PLIP

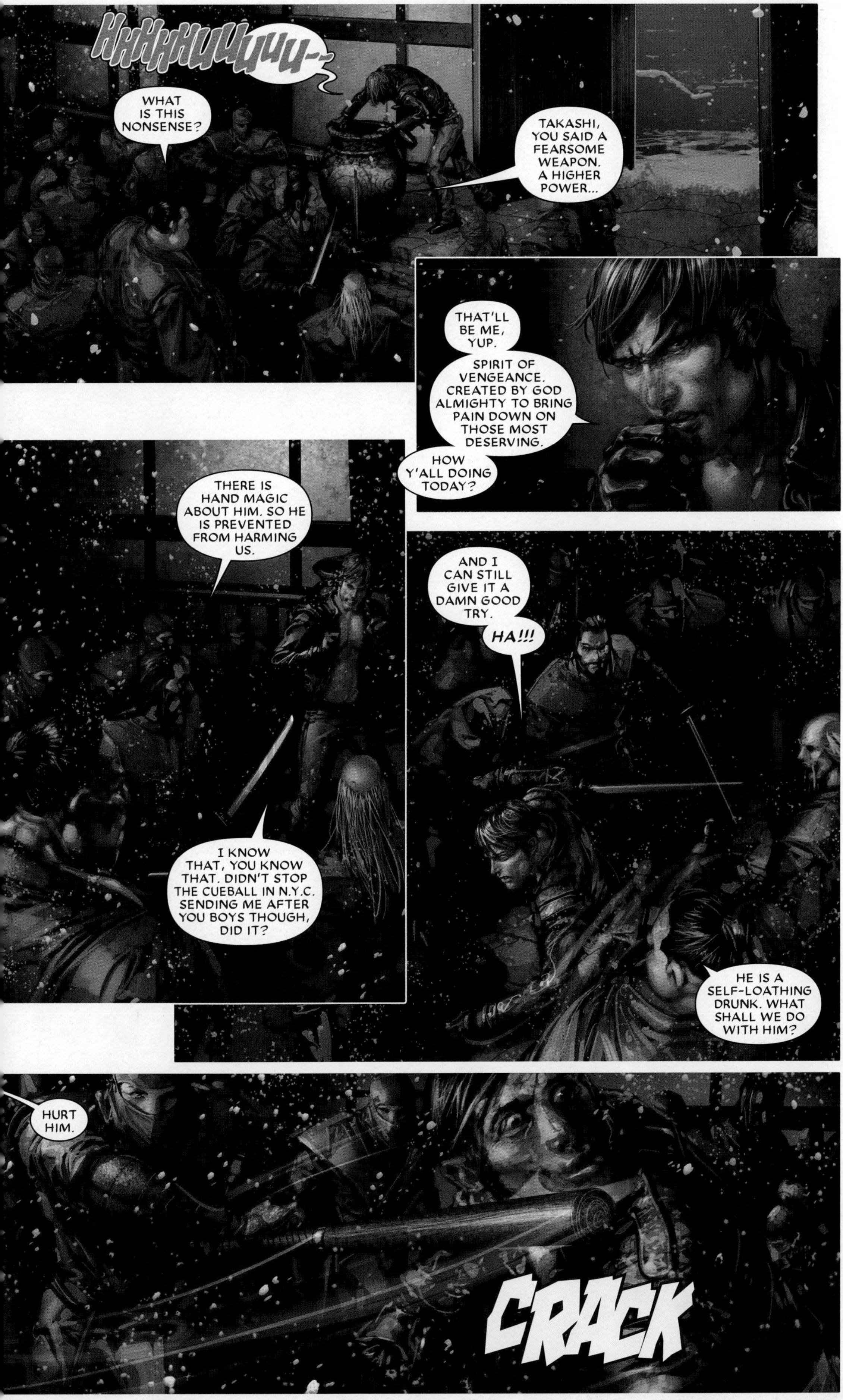
HHHHHUUUUUU--
WHAT IS THIS NONSENSE?
TAKASHI, YOU SAID A FEARSOME WEAPON. A HIGHER POWER...
THAT'LL BE ME, YUP.
SPIRIT OF VENGEANCE. CREATED BY GOD ALMIGHTY TO BRING PAIN DOWN ON THOSE MOST DESERVING.
HOW Y'ALL DOING TODAY?
THERE IS HAND MAGIC ABOUT HIM. SO HE IS PREVENTED FROM HARMING US.
I KNOW THAT, YOU KNOW THAT. DIDN'T STOP THE CUEBALL IN N.Y.C. SENDING ME AFTER YOU BOYS THOUGH, DID IT?
AND I CAN STILL GIVE IT A DAMN GOOD TRY.
HA!!!
HE IS A SELF-LOATHING DRUNK. WHAT SHALL WE DO WITH HIM?
HURT HIM.
CRACK

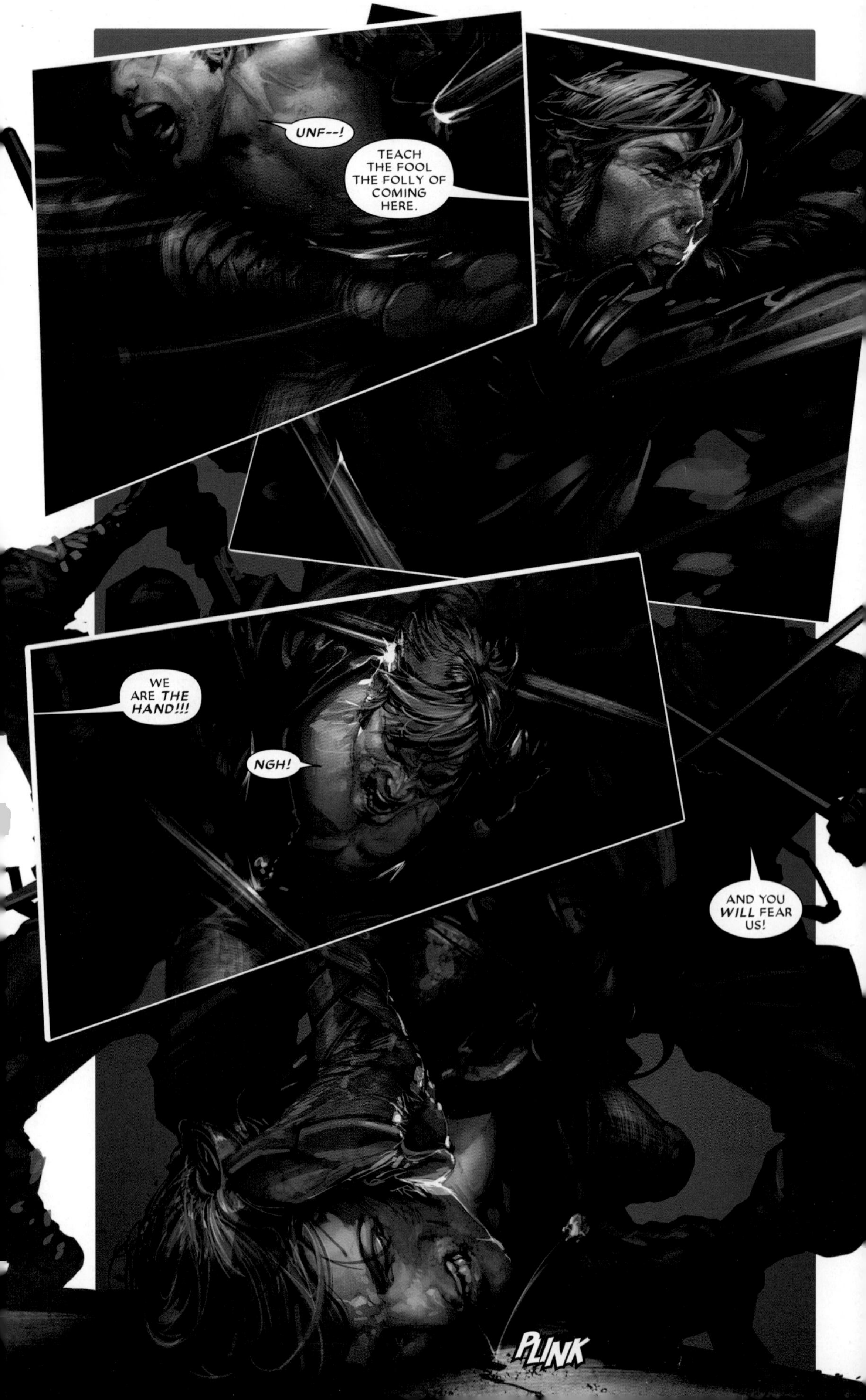
UNF--!
TEACH THE FOOL THE FOLLY OF COMING HERE.
WE ARE *THE HAND!!!*
NGH!
AND YOU *WILL* FEAR US!
PLINK

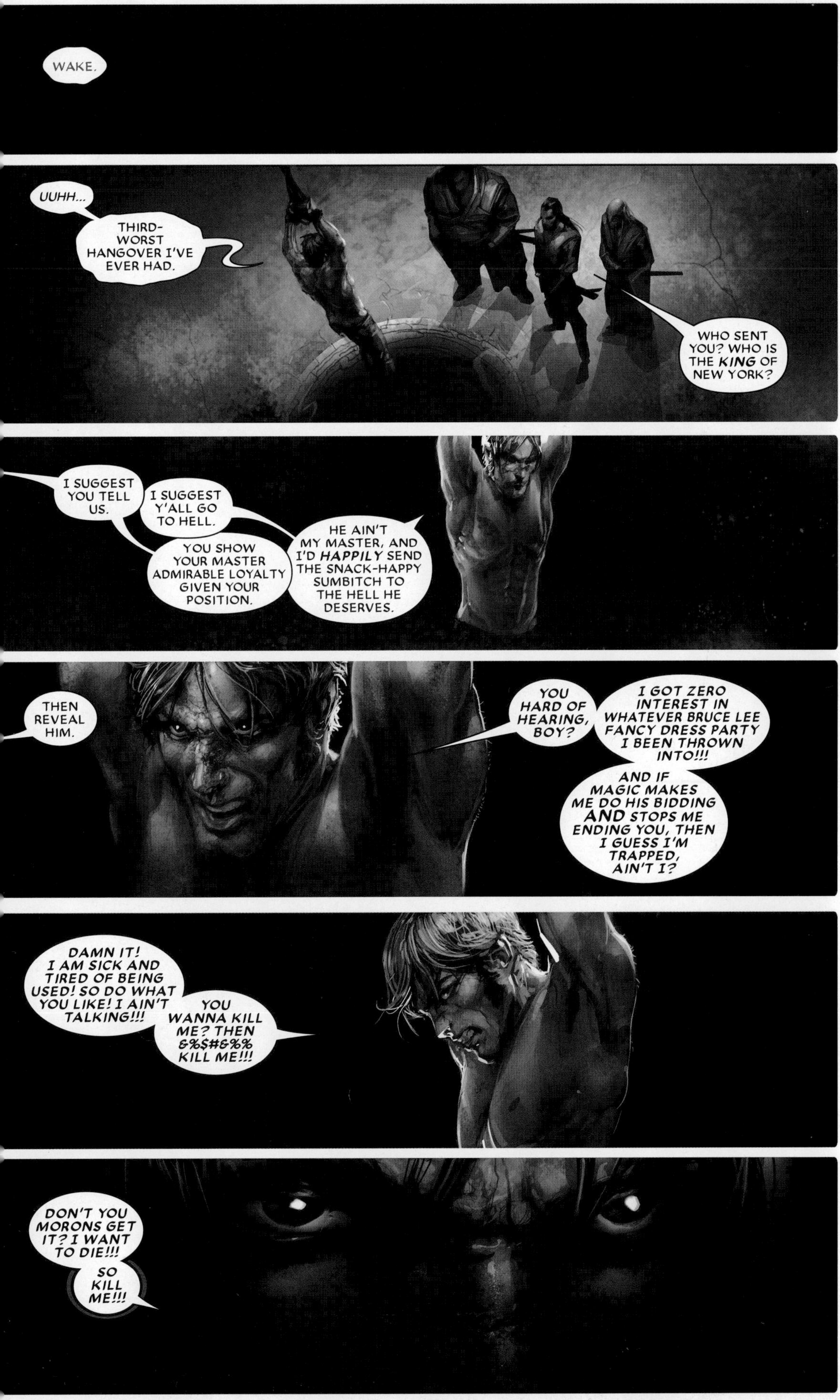
WAKE.
UUHH...
THIRD-WORST HANGOVER I'VE EVER HAD.
WHO SENT YOU? WHO IS THE KING OF NEW YORK?
I SUGGEST YOU TELL US.
I SUGGEST Y'ALL GO TO HELL.
YOU SHOW YOUR MASTER ADMIRABLE LOYALTY GIVEN YOUR POSITION.
HE AIN'T MY MASTER, AND I'D HAPPILY SEND THE SNACK-HAPPY SUMBITCH TO THE HELL HE DESERVES.
THEN REVEAL HIM.
YOU HARD OF HEARING, BOY?
I GOT ZERO INTEREST IN WHATEVER BRUCE LEE FANCY DRESS PARTY I BEEN THROWN INTO!!!
AND IF MAGIC MAKES ME DO HIS BIDDING AND STOPS ME ENDING YOU, THEN I GUESS I'M TRAPPED, AIN'T I?
DAMN IT! I AM SICK AND TIRED OF BEING USED! SO DO WHAT YOU LIKE! I AIN'T TALKING!!!
YOU WANNA KILL ME? THEN &%$#&% KILL ME!!!
DON'T YOU MORONS GET IT? I WANT TO DIE!!!
SO KILL ME!!!

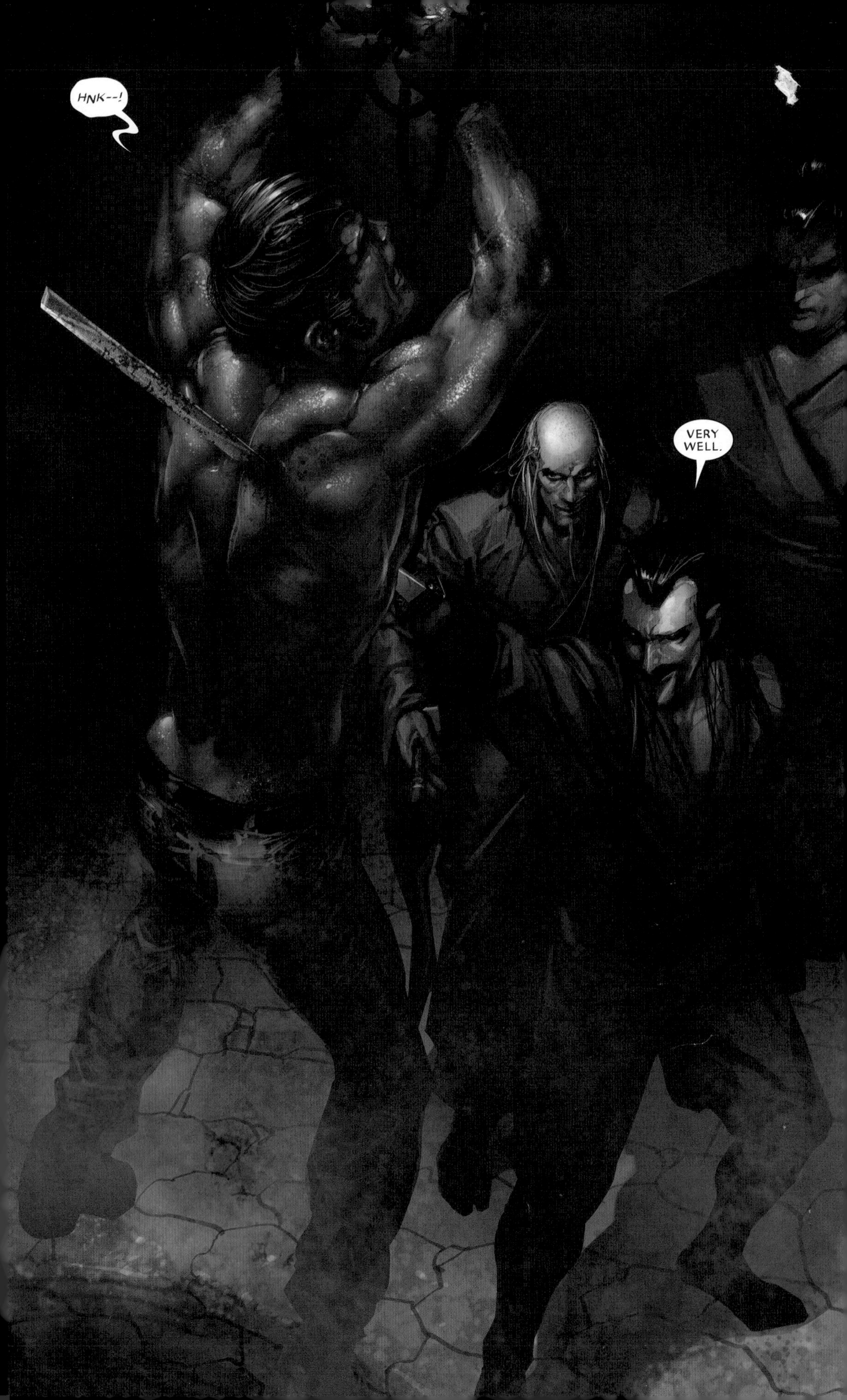
HNK--!
VERY WELL.

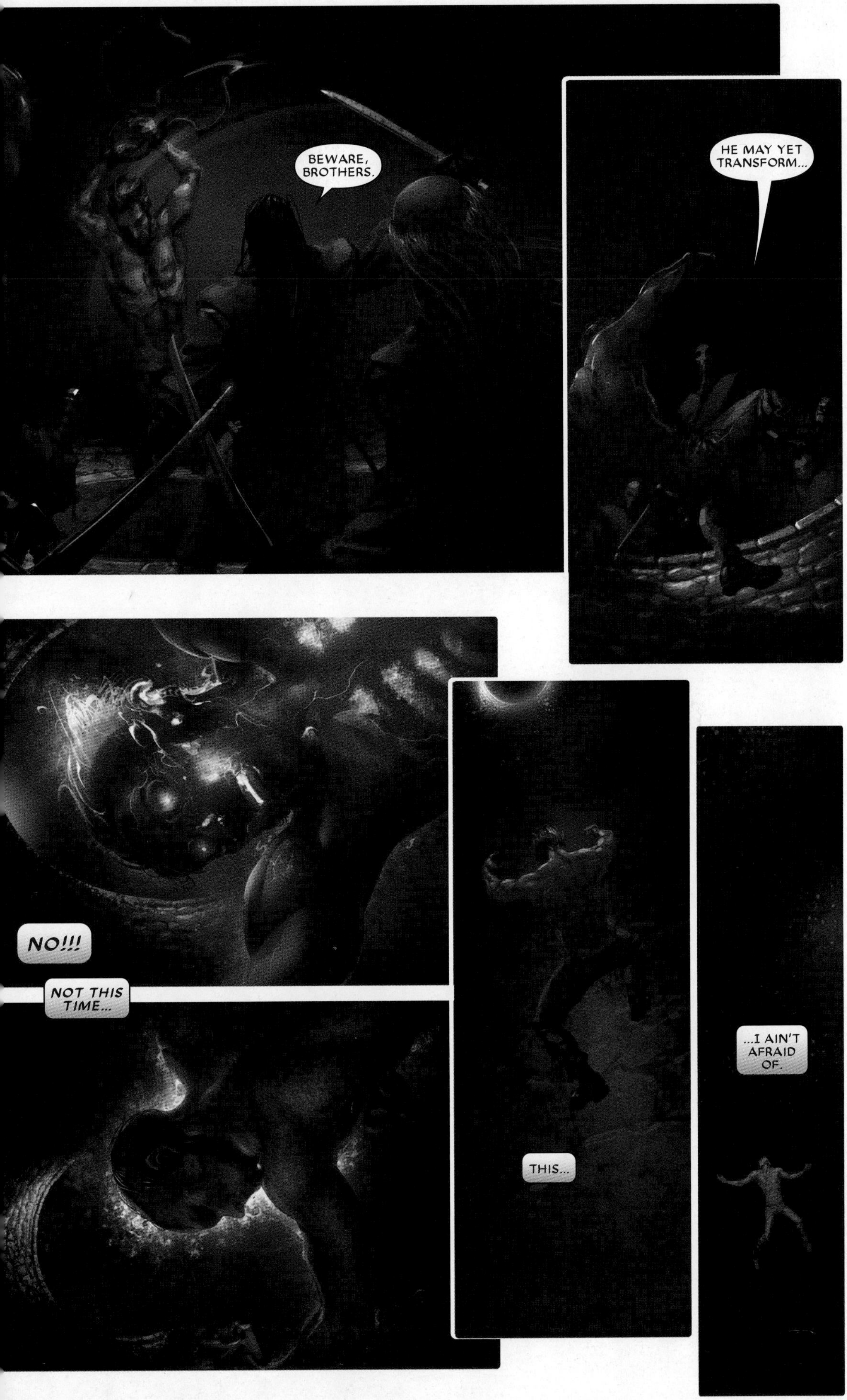

BEWARE, BROTHERS.
HE MAY YET TRANSFORM...
NO!!!
NOT THIS TIME...
THIS...
...I AIN'T AFRAID OF.

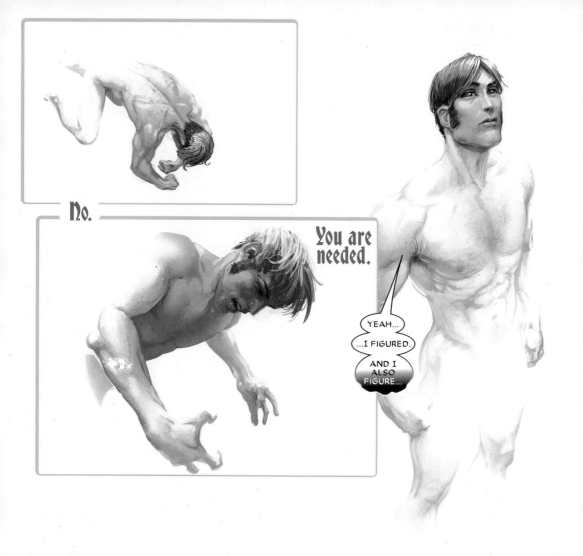

No.

You are
needed.

YEAH...

...I FIGURED.

AND I
ALSO
FIGURE...

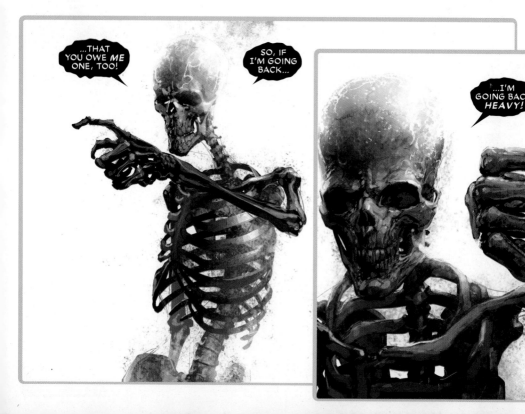

...THAT
YOU OWE ME
ONE, TOO!

SO, IF
I'M GOING
BACK...

...I'M
GOING BACK
HEAVY!

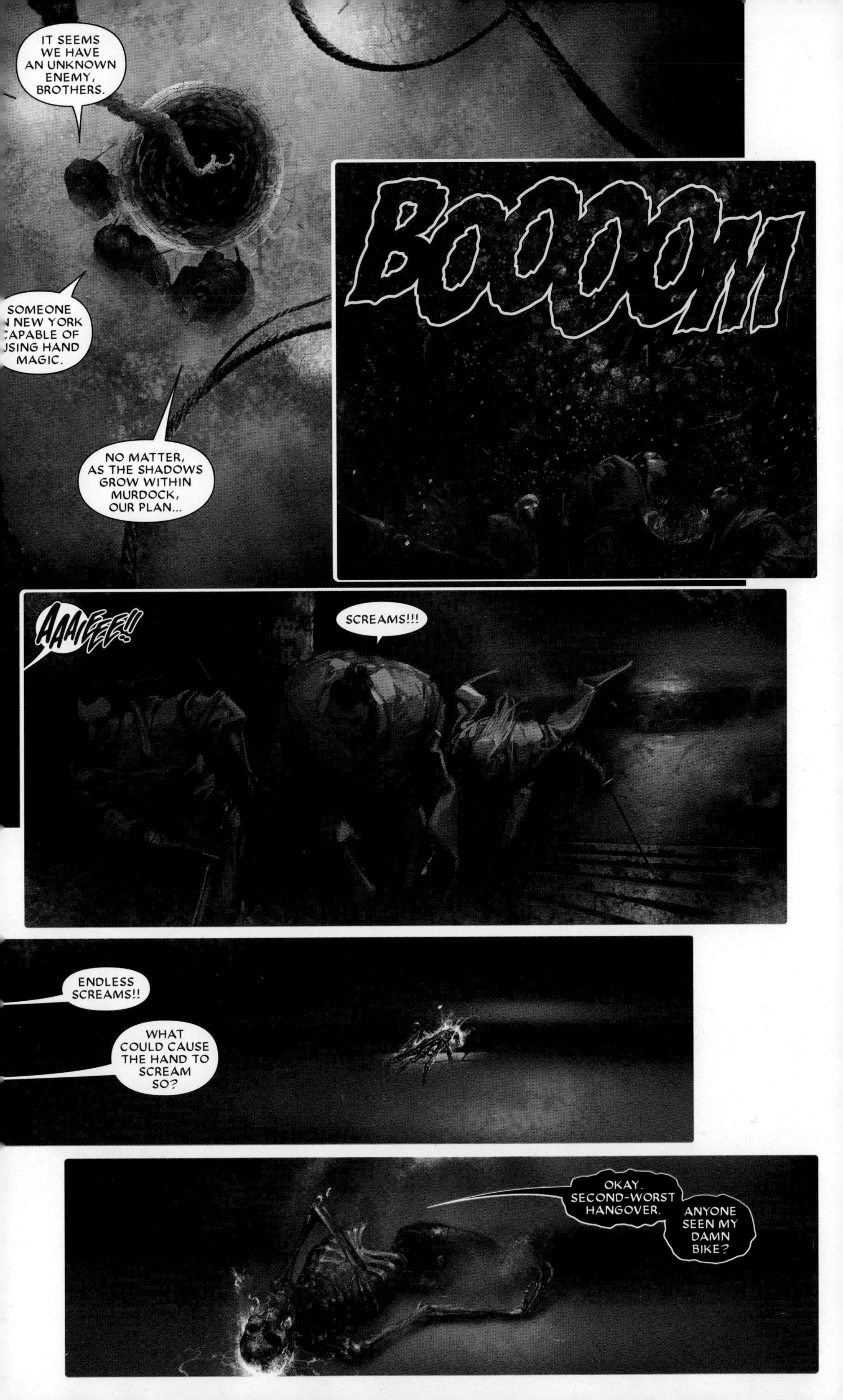
IT SEEMS WE HAVE AN UNKNOWN ENEMY, BROTHERS.
SOMEONE IN NEW YORK CAPABLE OF USING HAND MAGIC.
NO MATTER, AS THE SHADOWS GROW WITHIN MURDOCK, OUR PLAN...
BOOOOM
AAAIEEE!!
SCREAMS!!!
ENDLESS SCREAMS!!
WHAT COULD CAUSE THE HAND TO SCREAM SO?
OKAY. SECOND-WORST HANGOVER.
ANYONE SEEN MY DAMN BIKE?

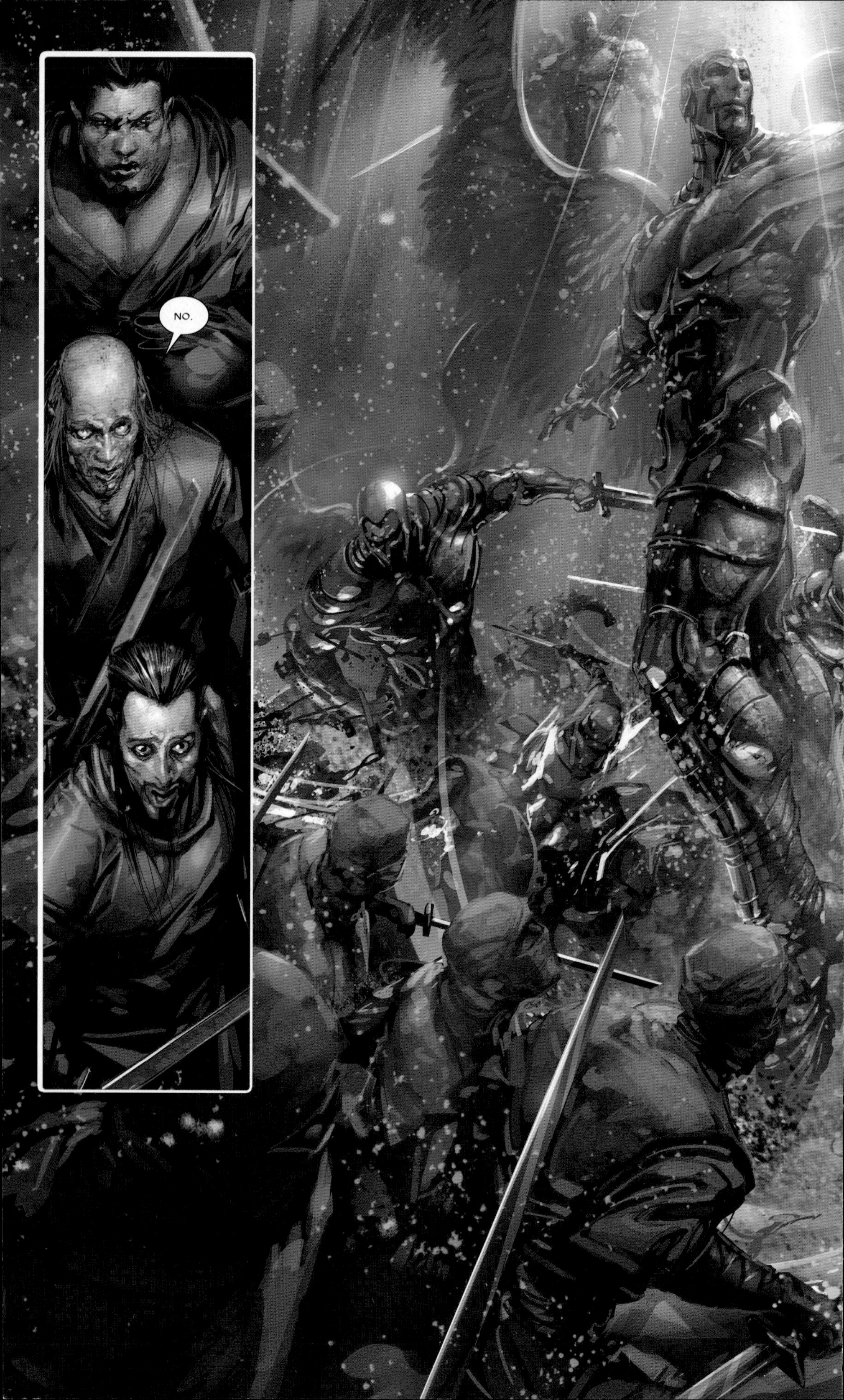
NO.

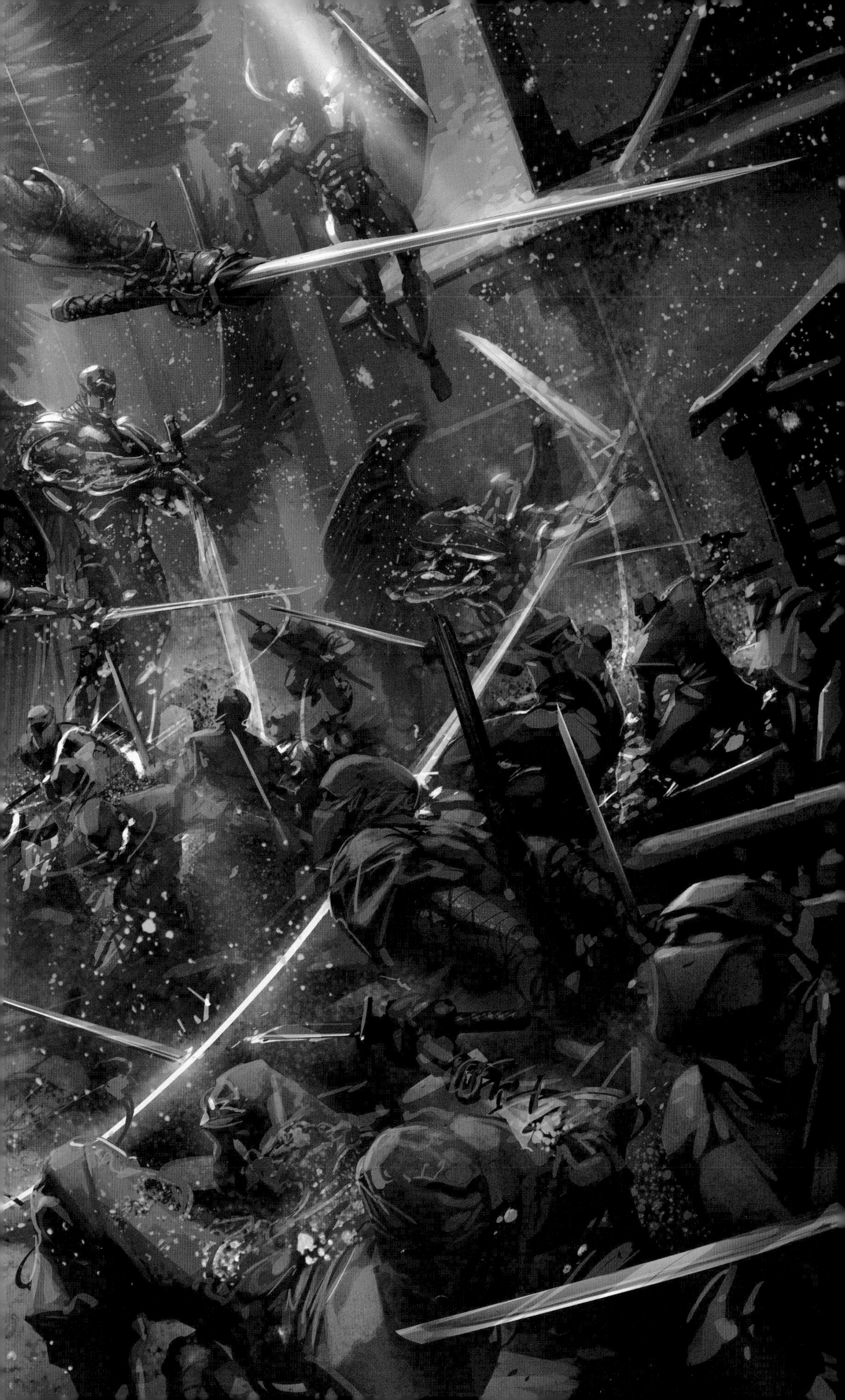

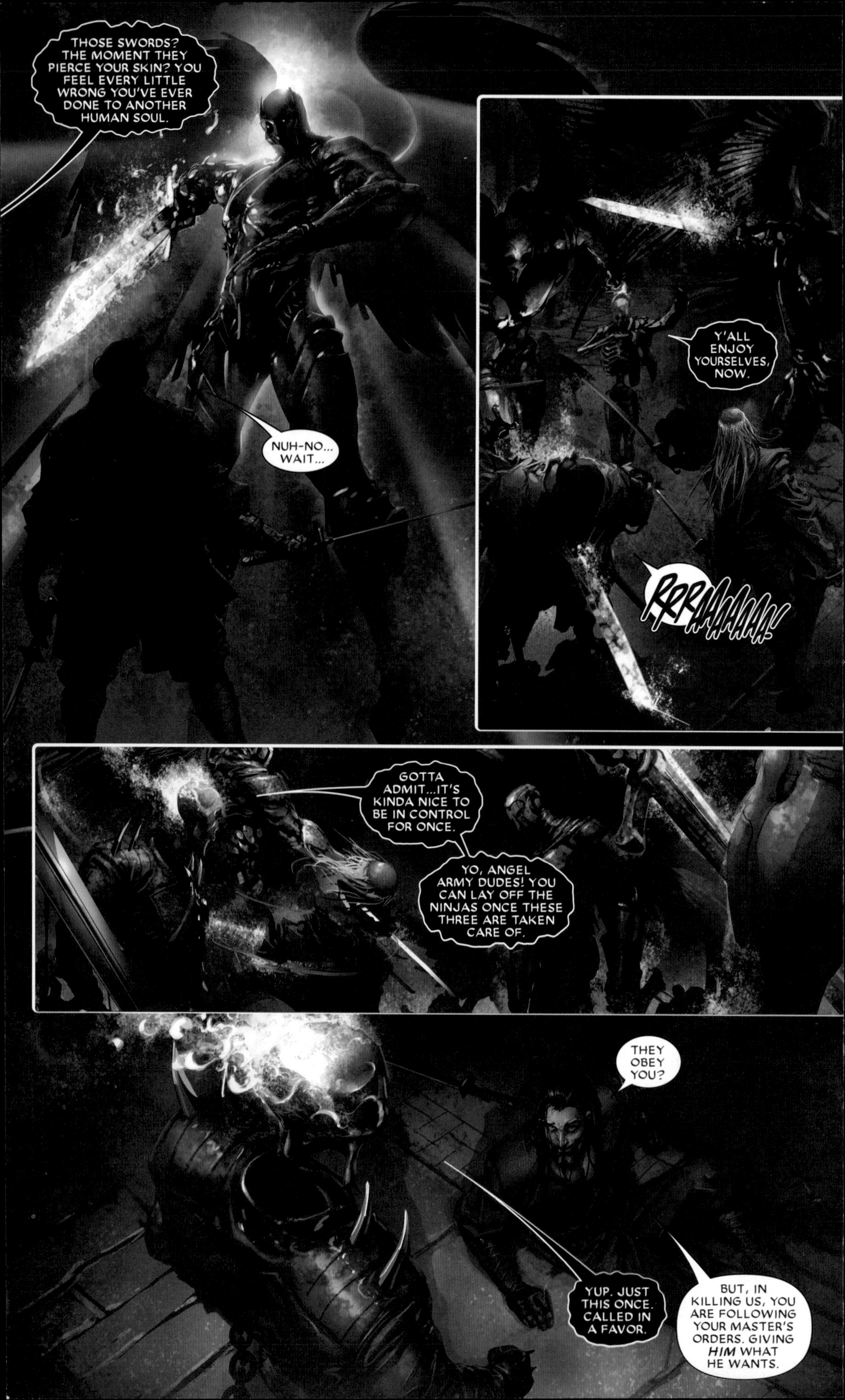
THOSE SWORDS? THE MOMENT THEY PIERCE YOUR SKIN? YOU FEEL EVERY LITTLE WRONG YOU'VE EVER DONE TO ANOTHER HUMAN SOUL.
NUH-NO... WAIT...
Y'ALL ENJOY YOURSELVES, NOW.
RRRAAAAAAA!
GOTTA ADMIT...IT'S KINDA NICE TO BE IN CONTROL FOR ONCE.
YO, ANGEL ARMY DUDES! YOU CAN LAY OFF THE NINJAS ONCE THESE THREE ARE TAKEN CARE OF.
THEY OBEY YOU?
YUP. JUST THIS ONCE. CALLED IN A FAVOR.
BUT, IN KILLING US, YOU ARE FOLLOWING YOUR MASTER'S ORDERS. GIVING HIM WHAT HE WANTS.

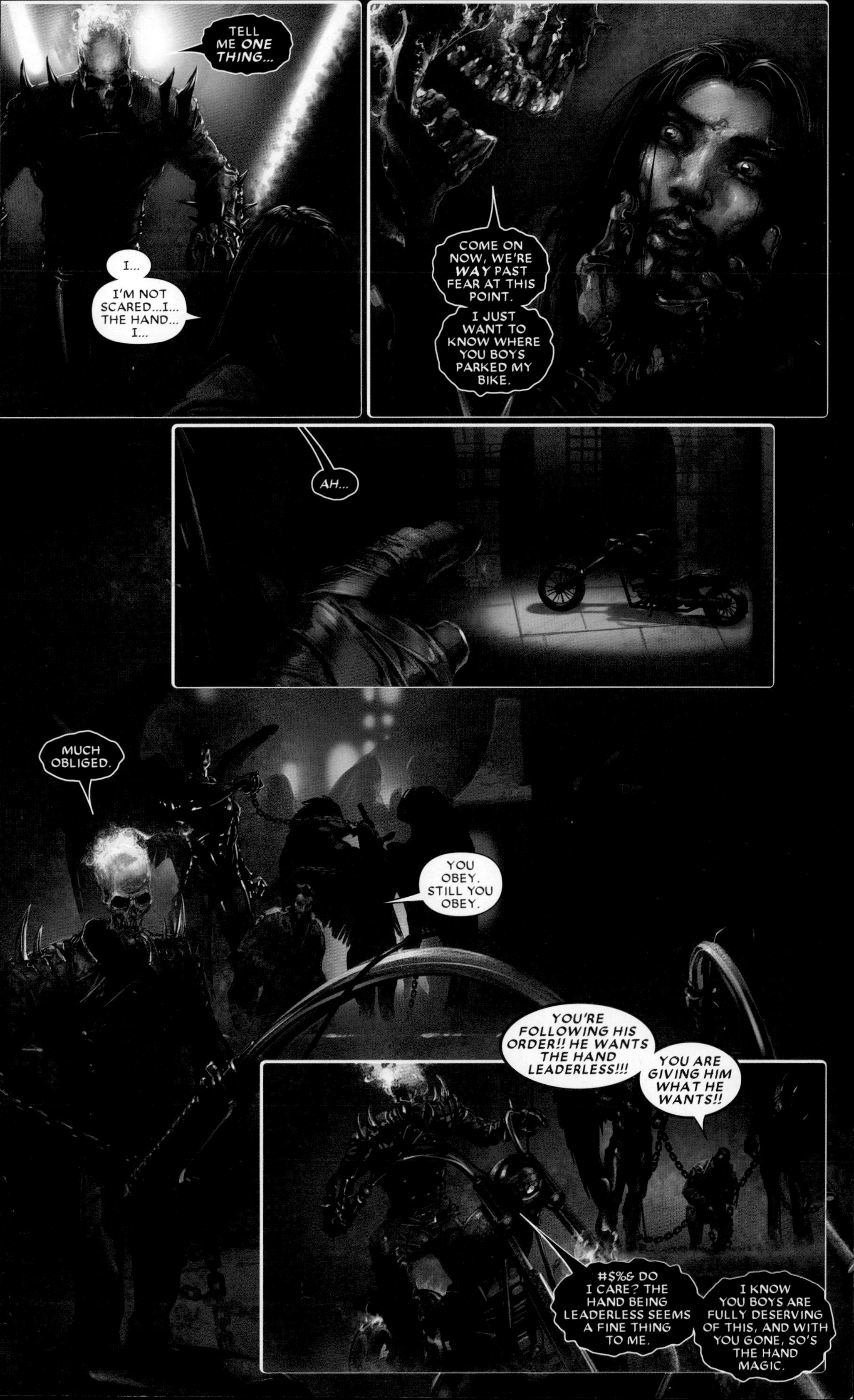
TELL ME *ONE* THING...
I...
I'M NOT SCARED...I... THE HAND... I...
COME ON NOW, WE'RE *WAY* PAST FEAR AT THIS POINT.
I JUST WANT TO KNOW WHERE YOU BOYS PARKED MY BIKE.
AH...
MUCH OBLIGED.
YOU OBEY. STILL YOU OBEY.
YOU'RE FOLLOWING HIS ORDER!! HE WANTS THE HAND LEADERLESS!!!
YOU ARE GIVING HIM WHAT HE WANTS!!
#$%& DO I CARE? THE HAND BEING LEADERLESS SEEMS A FINE THING TO ME.
I KNOW YOU BOYS ARE FULLY DESERVING OF THIS, AND WITH YOU GONE, SO'S THE HAND MAGIC.

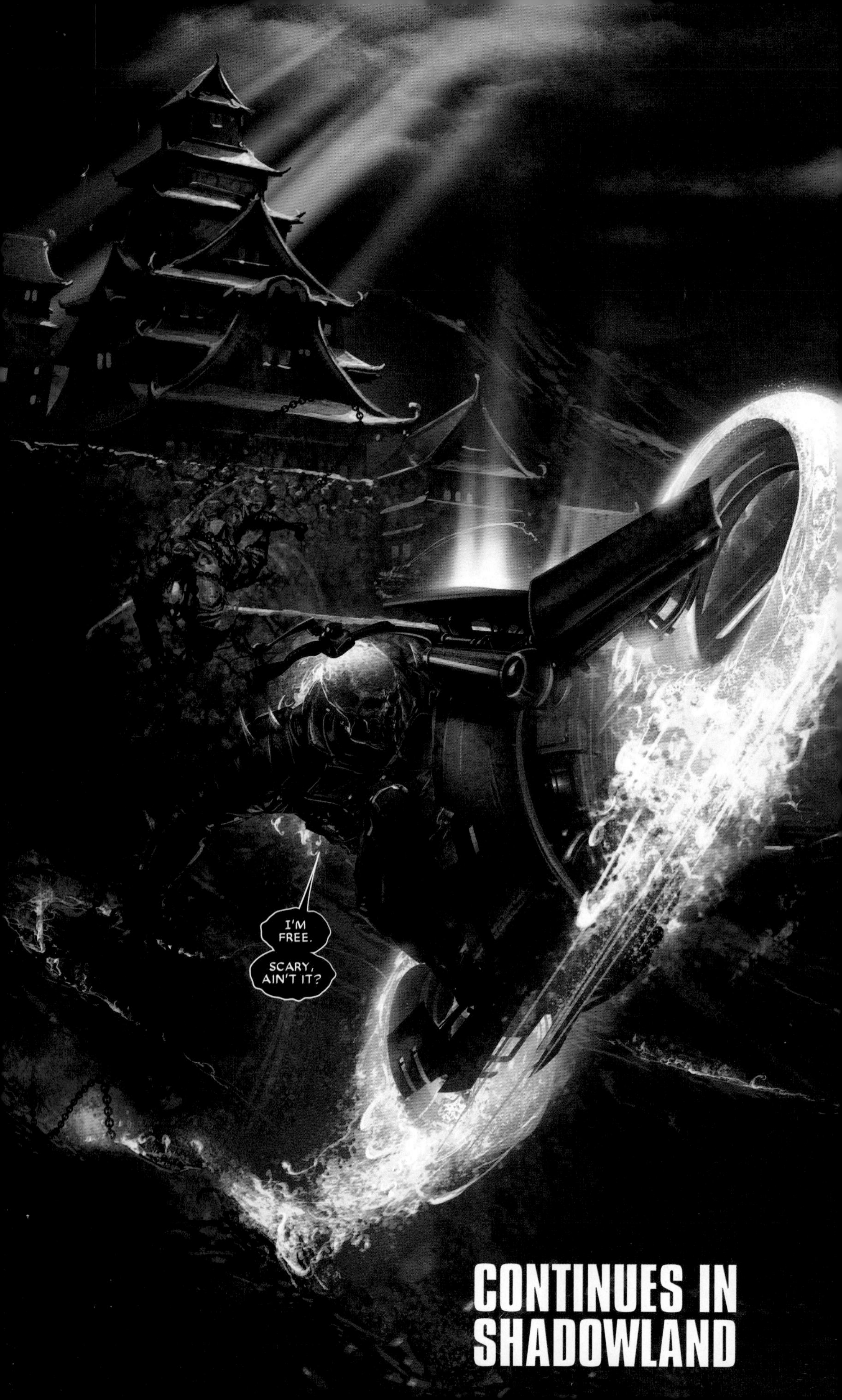
I'M FREE.
SCARY, AIN'T IT?
CONTINUES IN SHADOWLAND

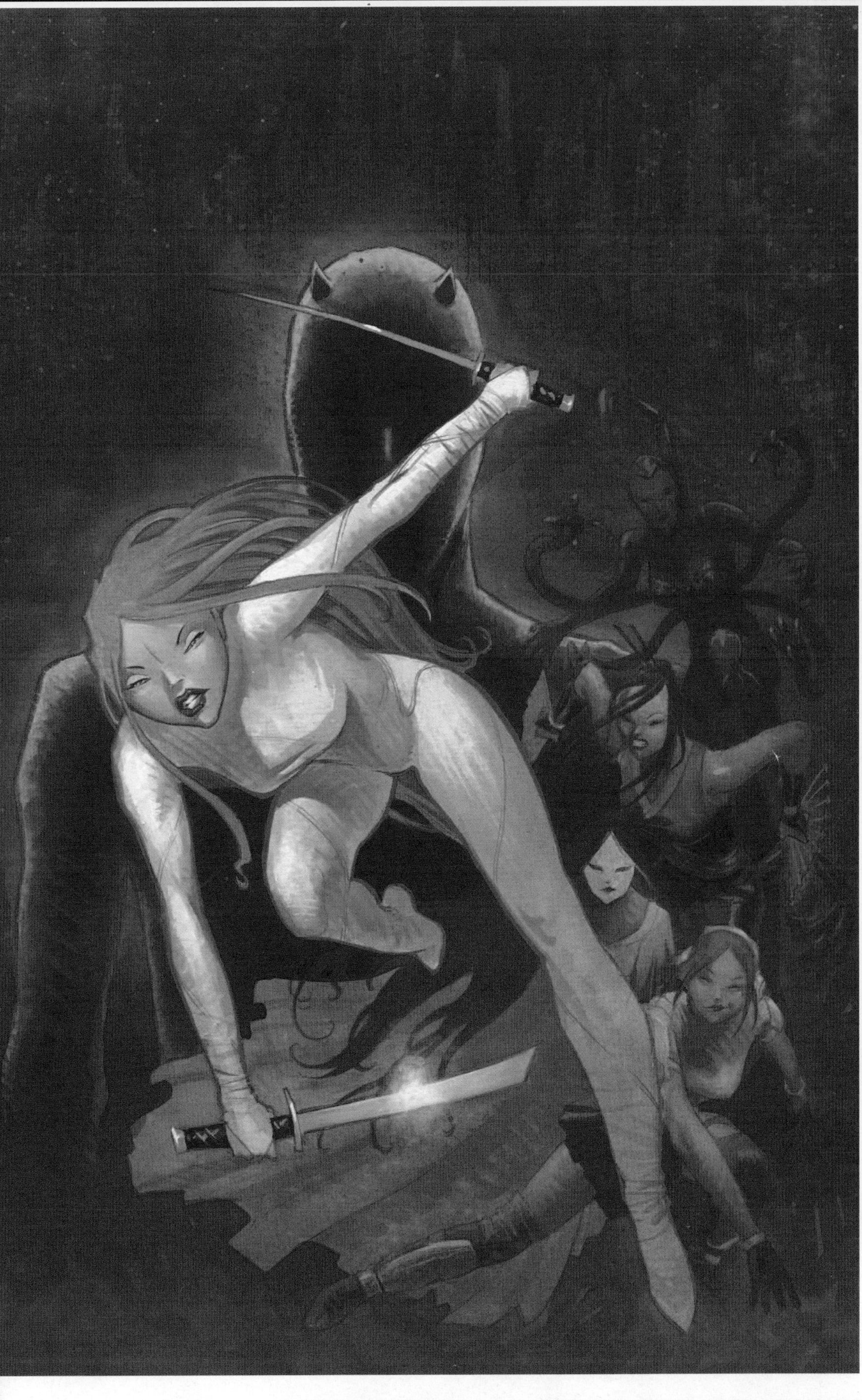

SHADOWLAND: DAUGHTERS OF THE SHADOW #1

THEY ARE CALLED THE HAND—A CADRE OF NINJAS, THIEVES AND ASSASSINS. ORIGINALLY BANDING TOGETHER 800 YEARS AGO TO FIGHT THE OPPRESSIVE SYSTEM OF FEUDAL JAPAN, THE HAND TURNED TO CORRUPTION AND DARKNESS WHEN THE MUTINOUS SNAKEROOT CLAN SEIZED POWER.

WHEN THE HAND SOUGHT DAREDEVIL OUT TO BECOME THEIR NEW LEADER, HE PLOTTED TO USE THE ORGANIZATION AS A FORCE FOR GOOD. WHEN HIS ARCHENEMY BULLSEYE DESTROYED A CITY BLOCK—AND 107 PEOPLE IN THE PROCESS—MURDOCK WAS PUSHED OVER THE EDGE AND TURNED THE HAND INTO AN ARMY OF PROTECTORS. ON THE SITE OF THE DECIMATED CITY BLOCK, HE BUILT HIS FORTRESS, SHADOWLAND.

AFTER WATCHING DAREDEVIL CROSS THE LINE AND MURDER BULLSEYE IN COLD BLOOD, A HANDFUL OF HIS OLDEST FRIENDS, INCLUDING PRIVATE DETECTIVES-TURNED-BOUNTY HUNTERS COLLEEN WING AND MISTY KNIGHT, ATTEMPTED TO APPEAL TO WHATEVER HUMANITY MIGHT REMAIN IN THE FORMER VIGILANTE. BUT THIS EFFORT FAILED, LEADING TO A VIOLENT BATTLE BETWEEN THE HAND'S FORCES AND THE STREET-LEVEL HEROES.

REALIZING THAT MATT IS BEYOND SALVATION, MISTY HAS LEFT TO PURSUE OTHER MEANS OF ENDING MURDOCK'S REIGN OF MADNESS...LEAVING COLLEEN ON HER OWN TO PICK UP THE PIECES OF NIGHTWING INVESTIGATIONS...

SHADOWLAND

DAUGHTERS OF THE SHADOW

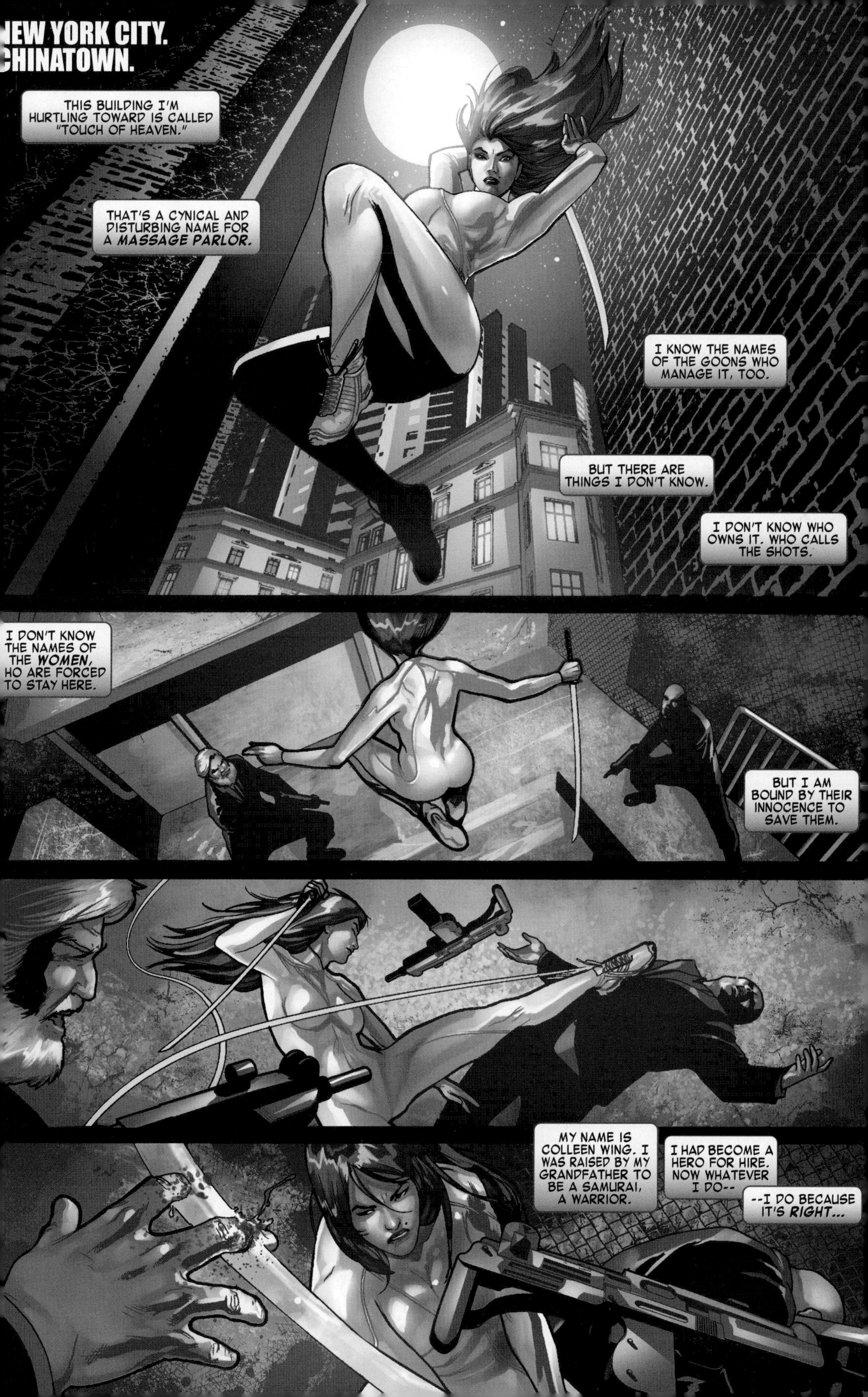

EW YORK CITY.
HINATOWN.
THIS BUILDING I'M HURTLING TOWARD IS CALLED "TOUCH OF HEAVEN."
THAT'S A CYNICAL AND DISTURBING NAME FOR A MASSAGE PARLOR.
I KNOW THE NAMES OF THE GOONS WHO MANAGE IT, TOO.
BUT THERE ARE THINGS I DON'T KNOW.
I DON'T KNOW WHO OWNS IT. WHO CALLS THE SHOTS.
I DON'T KNOW THE NAMES OF THE WOMEN, HO ARE FORCED TO STAY HERE.
BUT I AM BOUND BY THEIR INNOCENCE TO SAVE THEM.
MY NAME IS COLLEEN WING. I WAS RAISED BY MY GRANDFATHER TO BE A SAMURAI, A WARRIOR.
I HAD BECOME A HERO FOR HIRE. NOW WHATEVER I DO--
--I DO BECAUSE IT'S RIGHT...

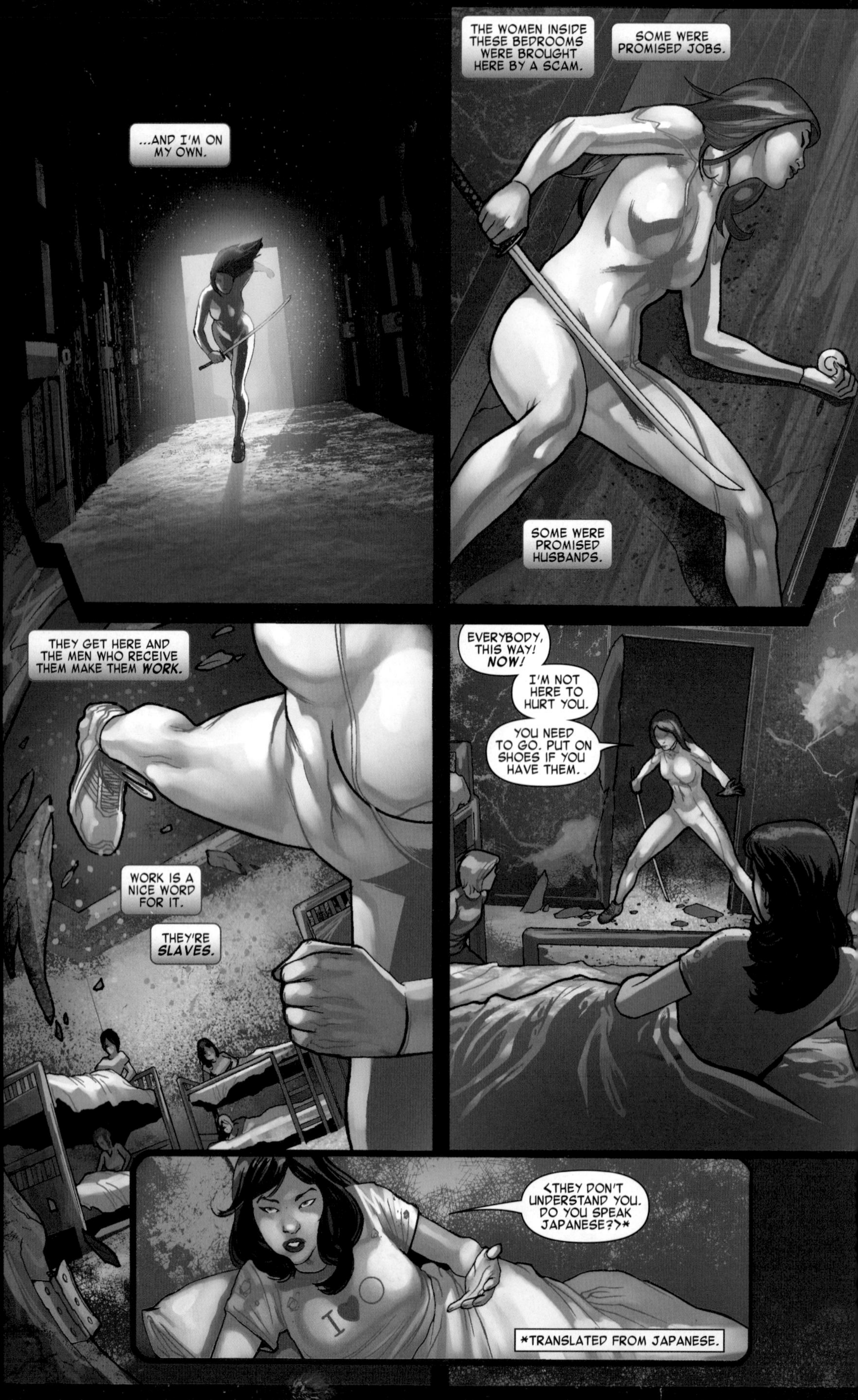
...AND I'M ON MY OWN.
THE WOMEN INSIDE THESE BEDROOMS WERE BROUGHT HERE BY A SCAM.
SOME WERE PROMISED JOBS.
SOME WERE PROMISED HUSBANDS.
THEY GET HERE AND THE MEN WHO RECEIVE THEM MAKE THEM WORK.
WORK IS A NICE WORD FOR IT.
THEY'RE SLAVES.
EVERYBODY, THIS WAY! NOW!
I'M NOT HERE TO HURT YOU.
YOU NEED TO GO. PUT ON SHOES IF YOU HAVE THEM.
<THEY DON'T UNDERSTAND YOU. DO YOU SPEAK JAPANESE?>*
*TRANSLATED FROM JAPANESE.

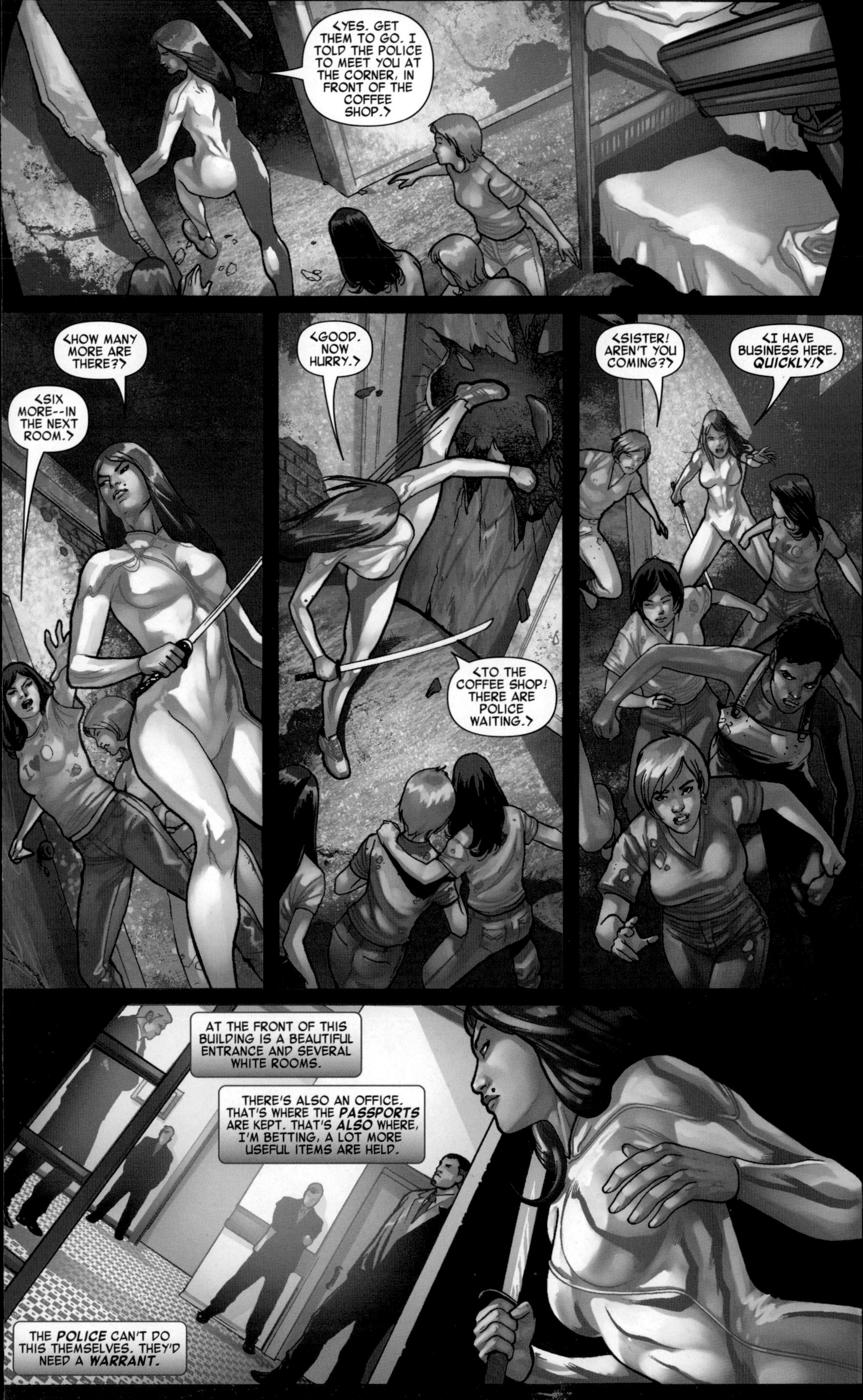
<YES. GET THEM TO GO. I TOLD THE POLICE TO MEET YOU AT THE CORNER, IN FRONT OF THE COFFEE SHOP.>
<HOW MANY MORE ARE THERE?>
<SIX MORE--IN THE NEXT ROOM.>
<GOOD. NOW HURRY.>
<TO THE COFFEE SHOP! THERE ARE POLICE WAITING.>
<SISTER! AREN'T YOU COMING?>
<I HAVE BUSINESS HERE. QUICKLY!>
AT THE FRONT OF THIS BUILDING IS A BEAUTIFUL ENTRANCE AND SEVERAL WHITE ROOMS.
THERE'S ALSO AN OFFICE. THAT'S WHERE THE PASSPORTS ARE KEPT. THAT'S ALSO WHERE, I'M BETTING, A LOT MORE USEFUL ITEMS ARE HELD.
THE POLICE CAN'T DO THIS THEMSELVES. THEY'D NEED A WARRANT.

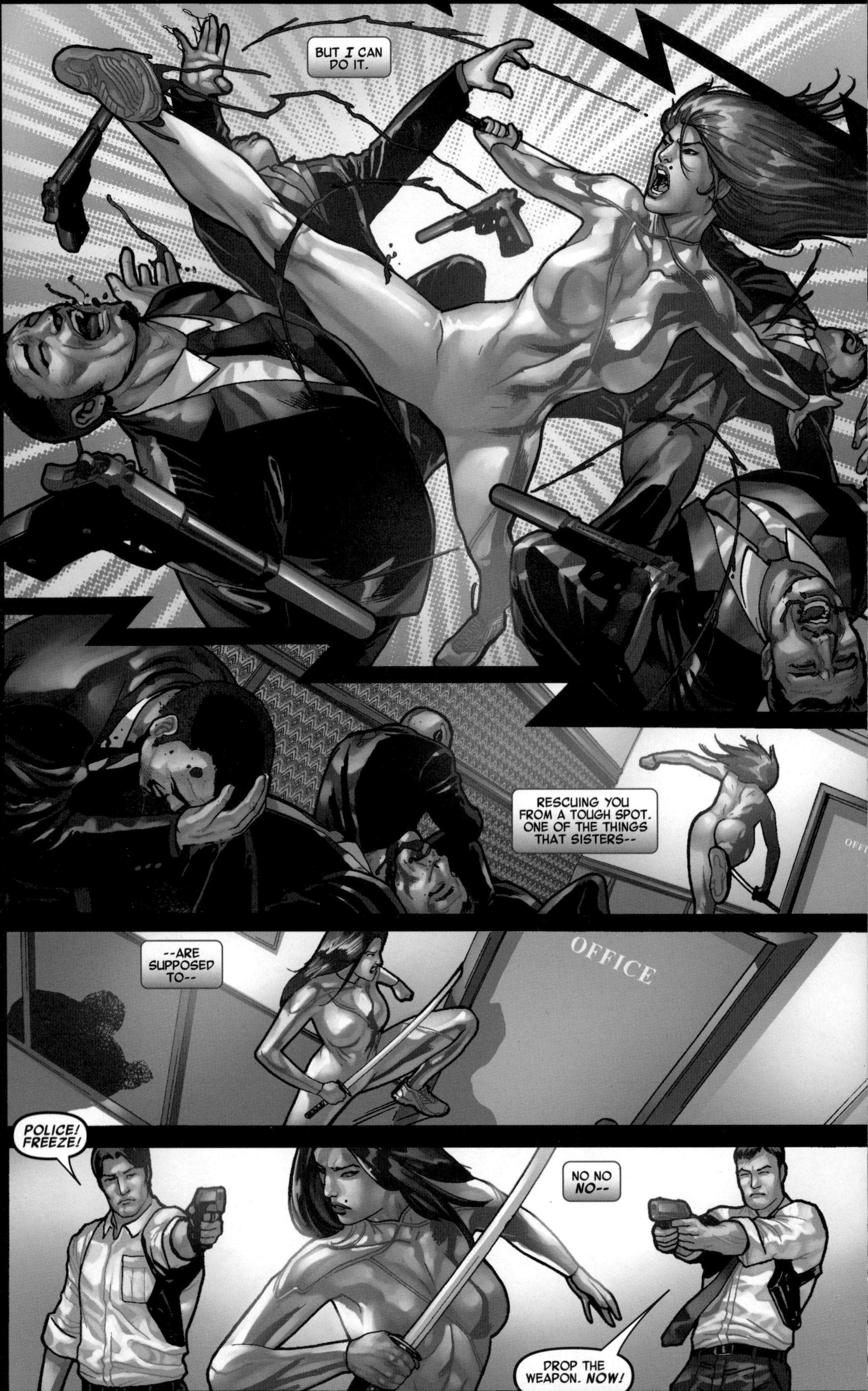
BUT I CAN DO IT.
RESCUING YOU FROM A TOUGH SPOT. ONE OF THE THINGS THAT SISTERS--
OFFICE
--ARE SUPPOSED TO--
POLICE! FREEZE!
NO NO NO--
DROP THE WEAPON. NOW!

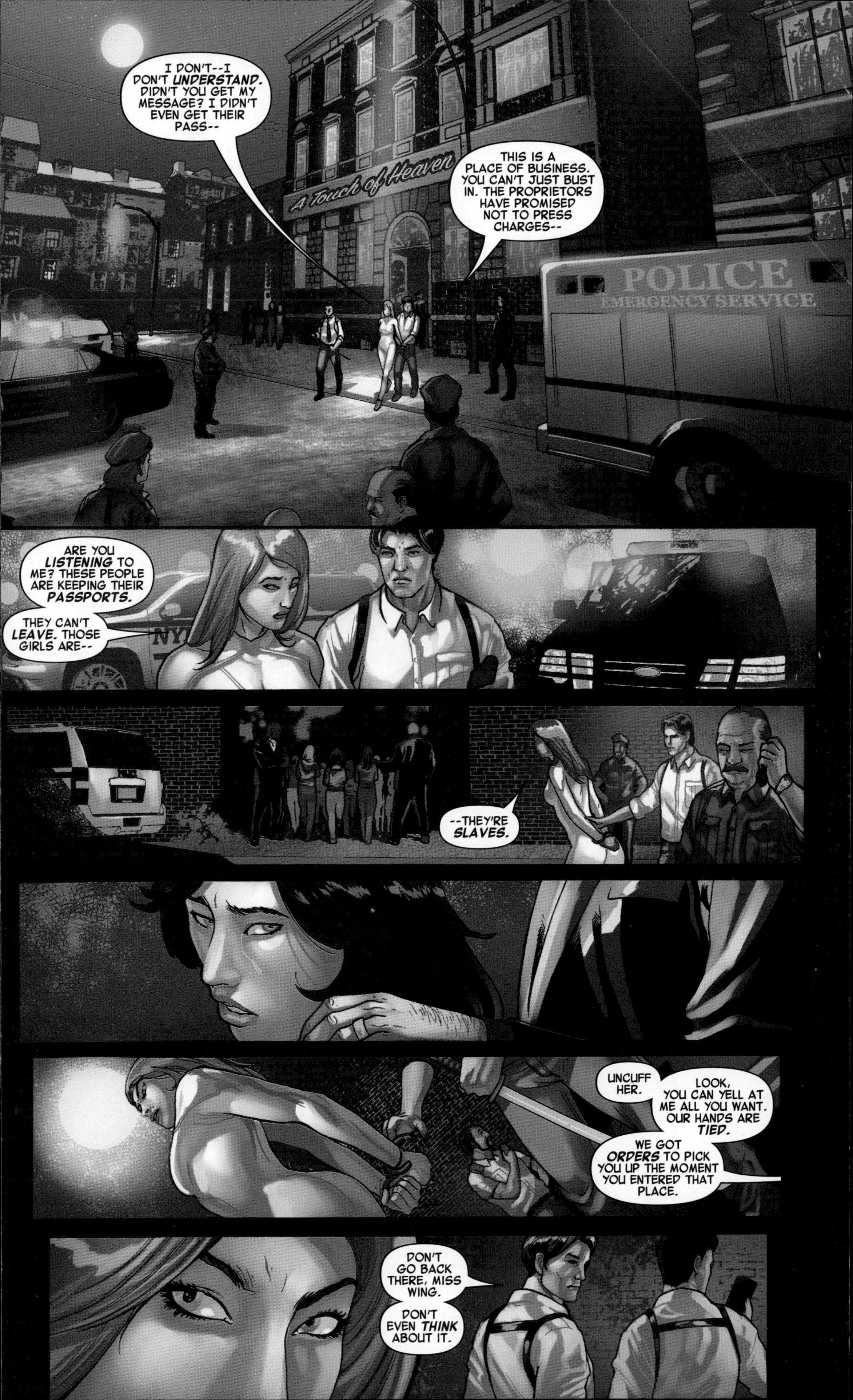
I DON'T--I DON'T UNDERSTAND. DIDN'T YOU GET MY MESSAGE? I DIDN'T EVEN GET THEIR PASS--
A Touch of Heaven
THIS IS A PLACE OF BUSINESS. YOU CAN'T JUST BUST IN. THE PROPRIETORS HAVE PROMISED NOT TO PRESS CHARGES--
POLICE
EMERGENCY SERVICE
ARE YOU LISTENING TO ME? THESE PEOPLE ARE KEEPING THEIR PASSPORTS.
THEY CAN'T LEAVE. THOSE GIRLS ARE--
--THEY'RE SLAVES.
UNCUFF HER.
LOOK, YOU CAN YELL AT ME ALL YOU WANT. OUR HANDS ARE TIED.
WE GOT ORDERS TO PICK YOU UP THE MOMENT YOU ENTERED THAT PLACE.
DON'T GO BACK THERE, MISS WING.
DON'T EVEN THINK ABOUT IT.

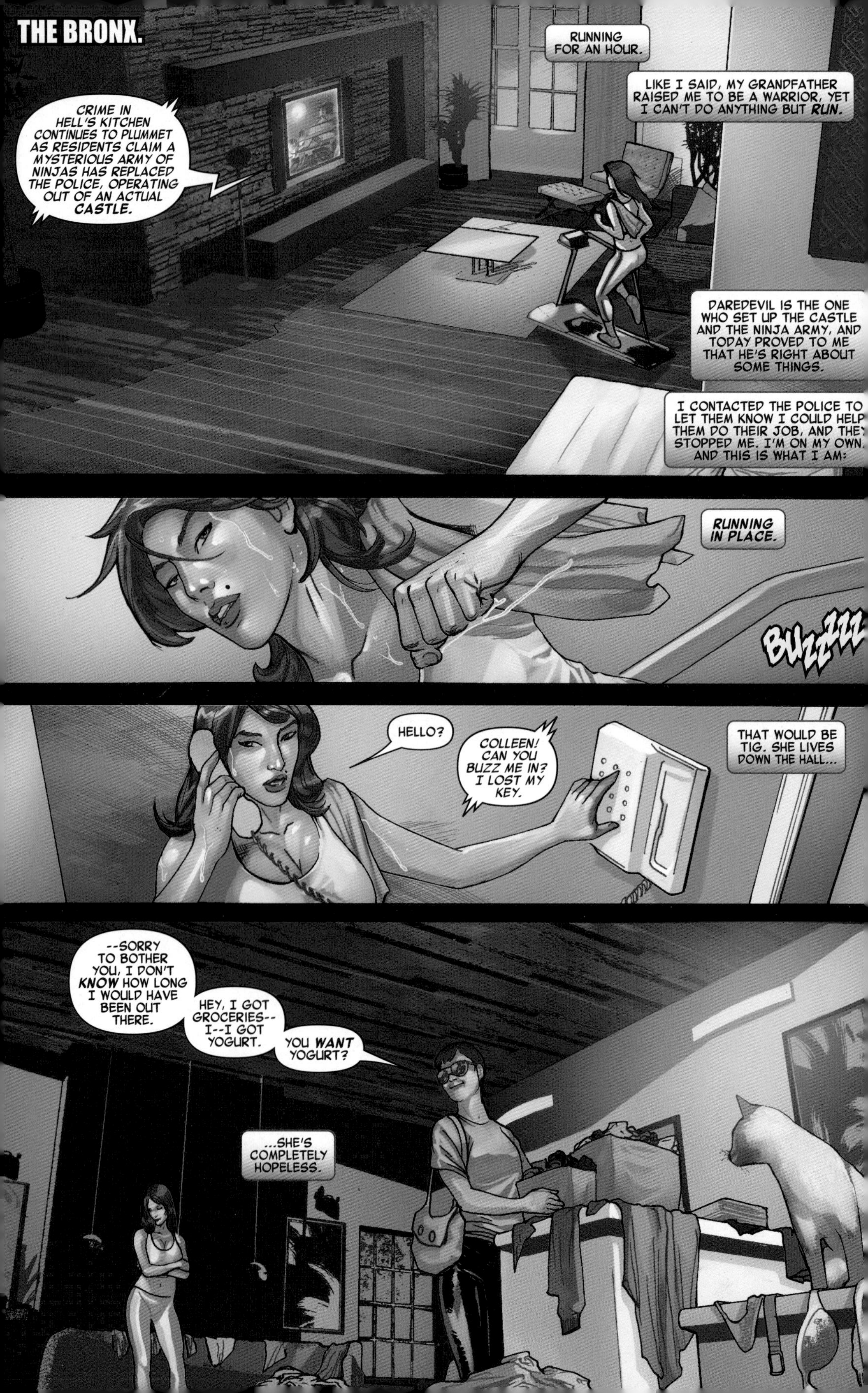
THE BRONX.
CRIME IN HELL'S KITCHEN CONTINUES TO PLUMMET AS RESIDENTS CLAIM A MYSTERIOUS ARMY OF NINJAS HAS REPLACED THE POLICE, OPERATING OUT OF AN ACTUAL CASTLE.
RUNNING FOR AN HOUR.
LIKE I SAID, MY GRANDFATHER RAISED ME TO BE A WARRIOR, YET I CAN'T DO ANYTHING BUT RUN.
DAREDEVIL IS THE ONE WHO SET UP THE CASTLE AND THE NINJA ARMY, AND TODAY PROVED TO ME THAT HE'S RIGHT ABOUT SOME THINGS.
I CONTACTED THE POLICE TO LET THEM KNOW I COULD HELP THEM DO THEIR JOB, AND THEY STOPPED ME. I'M ON MY OWN. AND THIS IS WHAT I AM:
RUNNING IN PLACE.
BUZZZZZ
HELLO?
COLLEEN! CAN YOU BUZZ ME IN? I LOST MY KEY.
THAT WOULD BE TIG. SHE LIVES DOWN THE HALL...
--SORRY TO BOTHER YOU, I DON'T KNOW HOW LONG I WOULD HAVE BEEN OUT THERE.
HEY, I GOT GROCERIES-- I--I GOT YOGURT.
YOU WANT YOGURT?
...SHE'S COMPLETELY HOPELESS.

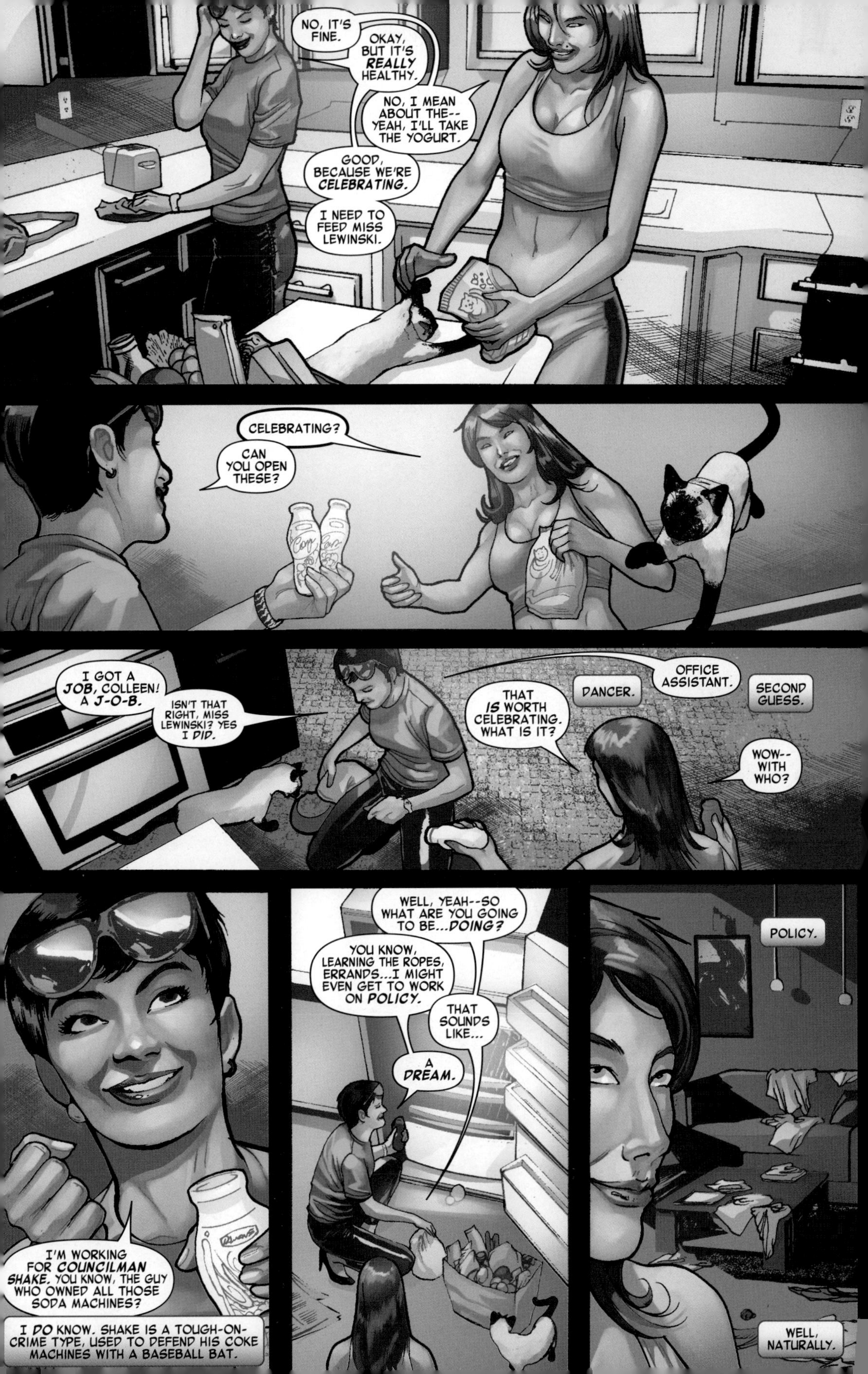
NO, IT'S FINE.
OKAY, BUT IT'S REALLY HEALTHY.
NO, I MEAN ABOUT THE-- YEAH, I'LL TAKE THE YOGURT.
GOOD, BECAUSE WE'RE CELEBRATING.
I NEED TO FEED MISS LEWINSKI.
CELEBRATING?
CAN YOU OPEN THESE?
I GOT A JOB, COLLEEN! A J-O-B.
ISN'T THAT RIGHT, MISS LEWINSKI? YES I DID.
THAT IS WORTH CELEBRATING. WHAT IS IT?
DANCER.
OFFICE ASSISTANT.
SECOND GUESS.
WOW-- WITH WHO?
I'M WORKING FOR COUNCILMAN SHAKE. YOU KNOW, THE GUY WHO OWNED ALL THOSE SODA MACHINES?
I DO KNOW. SHAKE IS A TOUGH-ON-CRIME TYPE, USED TO DEFEND HIS COKE MACHINES WITH A BASEBALL BAT.
WELL, YEAH--SO WHAT ARE YOU GOING TO BE...DOING?
YOU KNOW, LEARNING THE ROPES, ERRANDS...I MIGHT EVEN GET TO WORK ON POLICY.
THAT SOUNDS LIKE...
A DREAM.
POLICY.
WELL, NATURALLY.

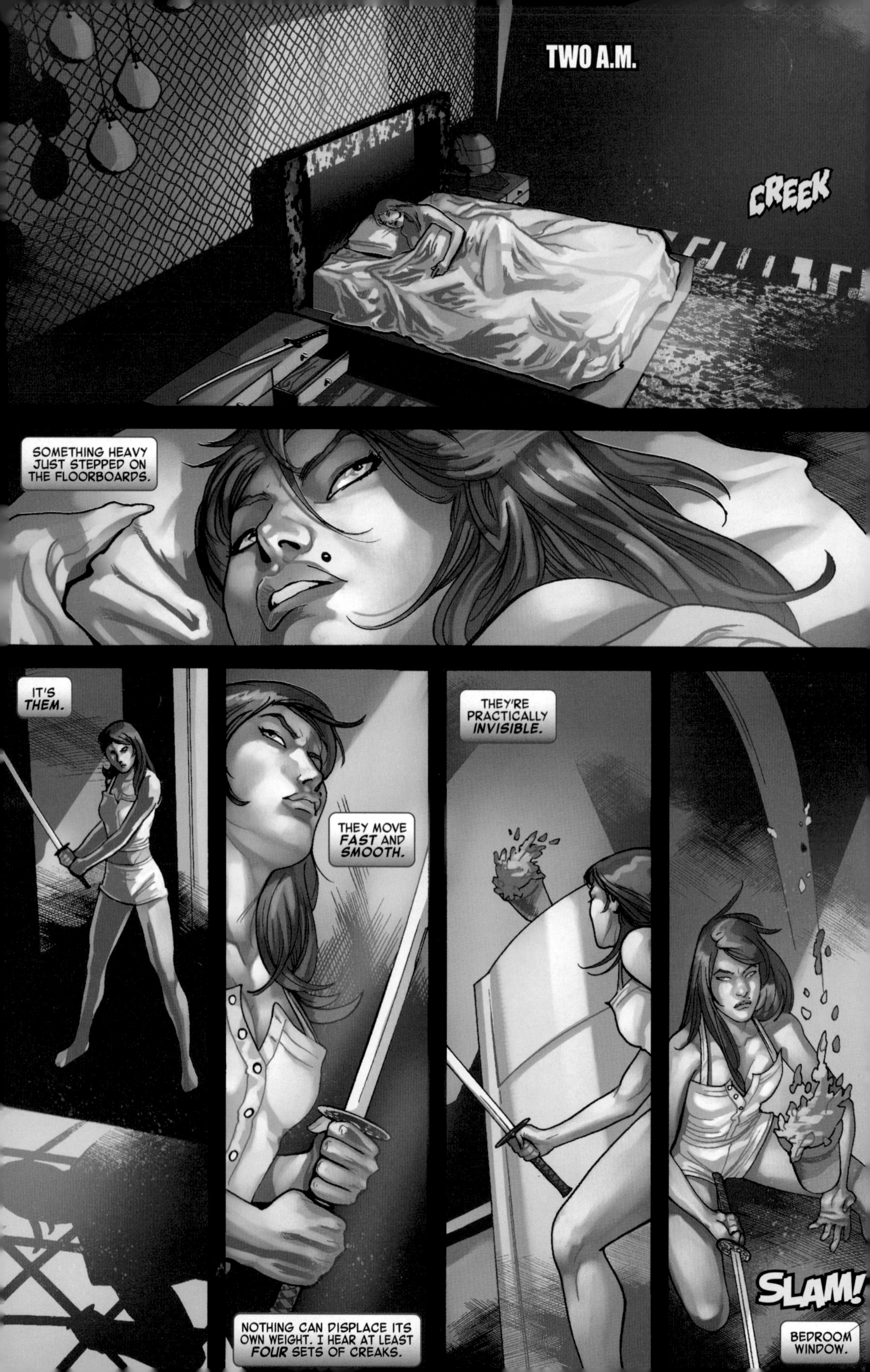
TWO A.M.
CREEK
SOMETHING HEAVY JUST STEPPED ON THE FLOORBOARDS.
IT'S *THEM*.
THEY MOVE *FAST* AND *SMOOTH*.
NOTHING CAN DISPLACE ITS OWN WEIGHT. I HEAR AT LEAST *FOUR* SETS OF CREAKS.
THEY'RE PRACTICALLY *INVISIBLE*.
SLAM!
BEDROOM WINDOW.

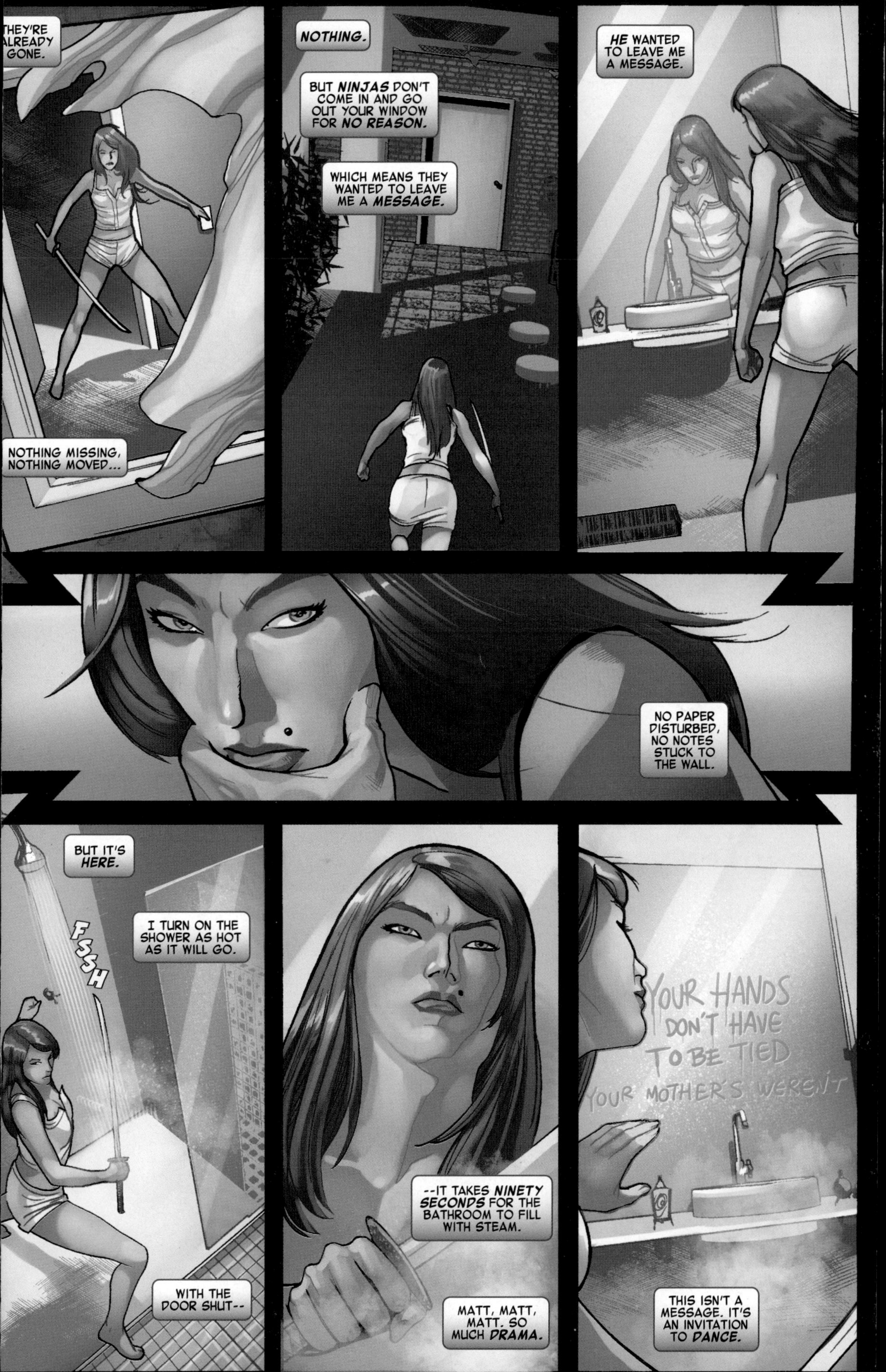

THEY'RE ALREADY GONE.
NOTHING MISSING, NOTHING MOVED...
NOTHING.
BUT NINJAS DON'T COME IN AND GO OUT YOUR WINDOW FOR NO REASON.
WHICH MEANS THEY WANTED TO LEAVE ME A MESSAGE.
HE WANTED TO LEAVE ME A MESSAGE.
NO PAPER DISTURBED, NO NOTES STUCK TO THE WALL.
BUT IT'S HERE.
I TURN ON THE SHOWER AS HOT AS IT WILL GO.
FSSH
WITH THE DOOR SHUT--
--IT TAKES NINETY SECONDS FOR THE BATHROOM TO FILL WITH STEAM.
MATT, MATT, MATT. SO MUCH DRAMA.
YOUR HANDS DON'T HAVE TO BE TIED
YOUR MOTHER'S WEREN'T
THIS ISN'T A MESSAGE. IT'S AN INVITATION TO DANCE.

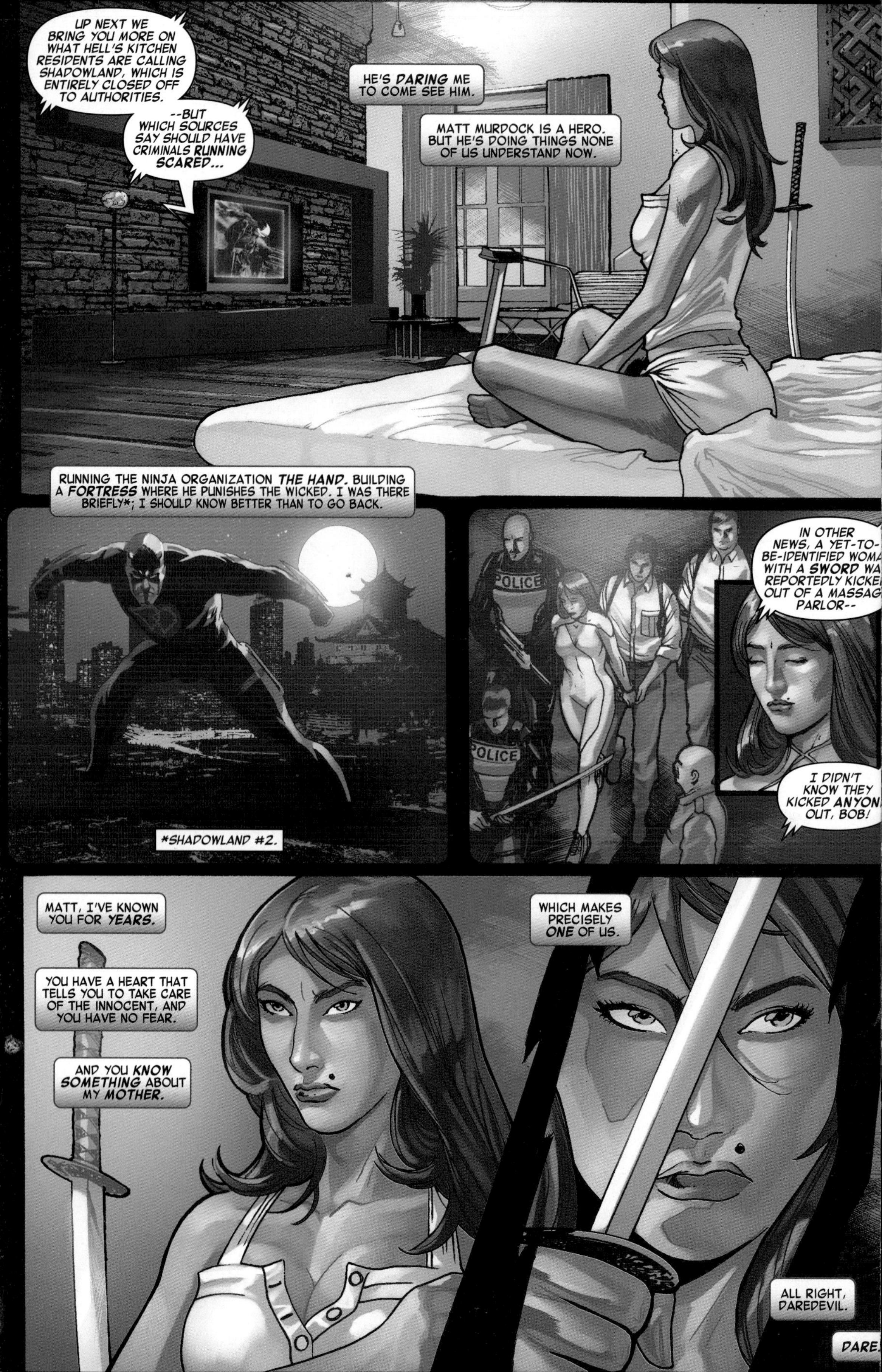
UP NEXT WE BRING YOU MORE ON WHAT HELL'S KITCHEN RESIDENTS ARE CALLING SHADOWLAND, WHICH IS ENTIRELY CLOSED OFF TO AUTHORITIES.
--BUT WHICH SOURCES SAY SHOULD HAVE CRIMINALS RUNNING SCARED...
HE'S DARING ME TO COME SEE HIM.
MATT MURDOCK IS A HERO. BUT HE'S DOING THINGS NONE OF US UNDERSTAND NOW.
RUNNING THE NINJA ORGANIZATION THE HAND. BUILDING A FORTRESS WHERE HE PUNISHES THE WICKED. I WAS THERE BRIEFLY*; I SHOULD KNOW BETTER THAN TO GO BACK.
*SHADOWLAND #2.
POLICE
IN OTHER NEWS, A YET-TO-BE-IDENTIFIED WOMA WITH A SWORD WA REPORTEDLY KICKE OUT OF A MASSAG PARLOR--
POLICE
I DIDN'T KNOW THEY KICKED ANYON OUT, BOB!
MATT, I'VE KNOWN YOU FOR YEARS.
YOU HAVE A HEART THAT TELLS YOU TO TAKE CARE OF THE INNOCENT, AND YOU HAVE NO FEAR.
AND YOU KNOW SOMETHING ABOUT MY MOTHER.
WHICH MAKES PRECISELY ONE OF US.
ALL RIGHT, DAREDEVIL.
DARE.

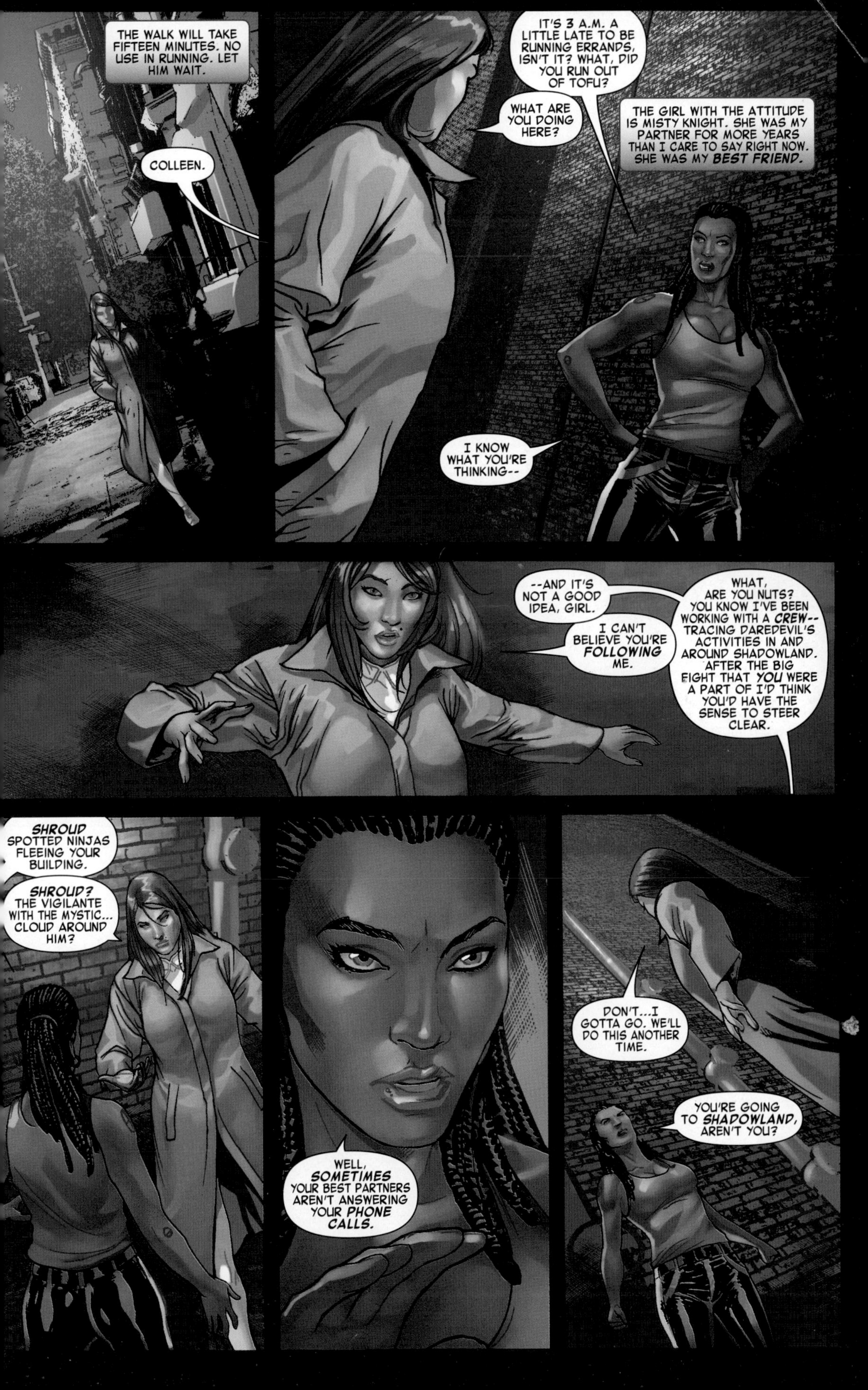
THE WALK WILL TAKE FIFTEEN MINUTES. NO USE IN RUNNING. LET HIM WAIT.
COLLEEN.
WHAT ARE YOU DOING HERE?
IT'S 3 A.M. A LITTLE LATE TO BE RUNNING ERRANDS, ISN'T IT? WHAT, DID YOU RUN OUT OF TOFU?
THE GIRL WITH THE ATTITUDE IS MISTY KNIGHT. SHE WAS MY PARTNER FOR MORE YEARS THAN I CARE TO SAY RIGHT NOW. SHE WAS MY BEST FRIEND.
I KNOW WHAT YOU'RE THINKING--
--AND IT'S NOT A GOOD IDEA, GIRL.
I CAN'T BELIEVE YOU'RE FOLLOWING ME.
WHAT, ARE YOU NUTS? YOU KNOW I'VE BEEN WORKING WITH A CREW-- TRACING DAREDEVIL'S ACTIVITIES IN AND AROUND SHADOWLAND. AFTER THE BIG FIGHT THAT YOU WERE A PART OF I'D THINK YOU'D HAVE THE SENSE TO STEER CLEAR.
SHROUD SPOTTED NINJAS FLEEING YOUR BUILDING.
SHROUD? THE VIGILANTE WITH THE MYSTIC... CLOUD AROUND HIM?
WELL, SOMETIMES YOUR BEST PARTNERS AREN'T ANSWERING YOUR PHONE CALLS.
DON'T...I GOTTA GO. WE'LL DO THIS ANOTHER TIME.
YOU'RE GOING TO SHADOWLAND, AREN'T YOU?

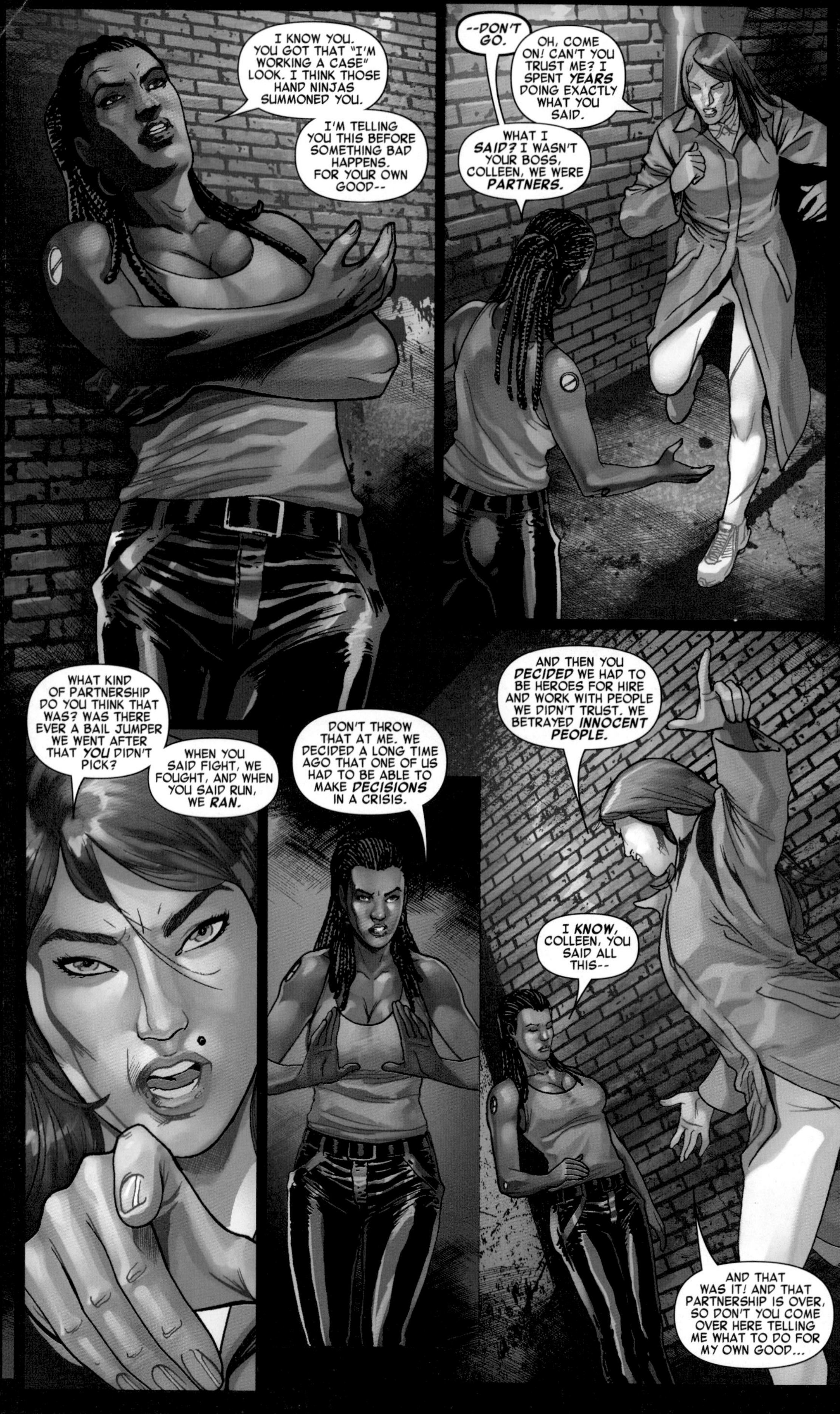
I KNOW YOU. YOU GOT THAT "I'M WORKING A CASE" LOOK. I THINK THOSE HAND NINJAS SUMMONED YOU.
I'M TELLING YOU THIS BEFORE SOMETHING BAD HAPPENS. FOR YOUR OWN GOOD--
--DON'T GO.
OH, COME ON! CAN'T YOU TRUST ME? I SPENT YEARS DOING EXACTLY WHAT YOU SAID.
WHAT I SAID? I WASN'T YOUR BOSS, COLLEEN, WE WERE PARTNERS.
WHAT KIND OF PARTNERSHIP DO YOU THINK THAT WAS? WAS THERE EVER A BAIL JUMPER WE WENT AFTER THAT YOU DIDN'T PICK?
WHEN YOU SAID FIGHT, WE FOUGHT, AND WHEN YOU SAID RUN, WE RAN.
DON'T THROW THAT AT ME. WE DECIDED A LONG TIME AGO THAT ONE OF US HAD TO BE ABLE TO MAKE DECISIONS IN A CRISIS.
AND THEN YOU DECIDED WE HAD TO BE HEROES FOR HIRE AND WORK WITH PEOPLE WE DIDN'T TRUST. WE BETRAYED INNOCENT PEOPLE.
I KNOW, COLLEEN, YOU SAID ALL THIS--
AND THAT WAS IT! AND THAT PARTNERSHIP IS OVER, SO DON'T YOU COME OVER HERE TELLING ME WHAT TO DO FOR MY OWN GOOD...

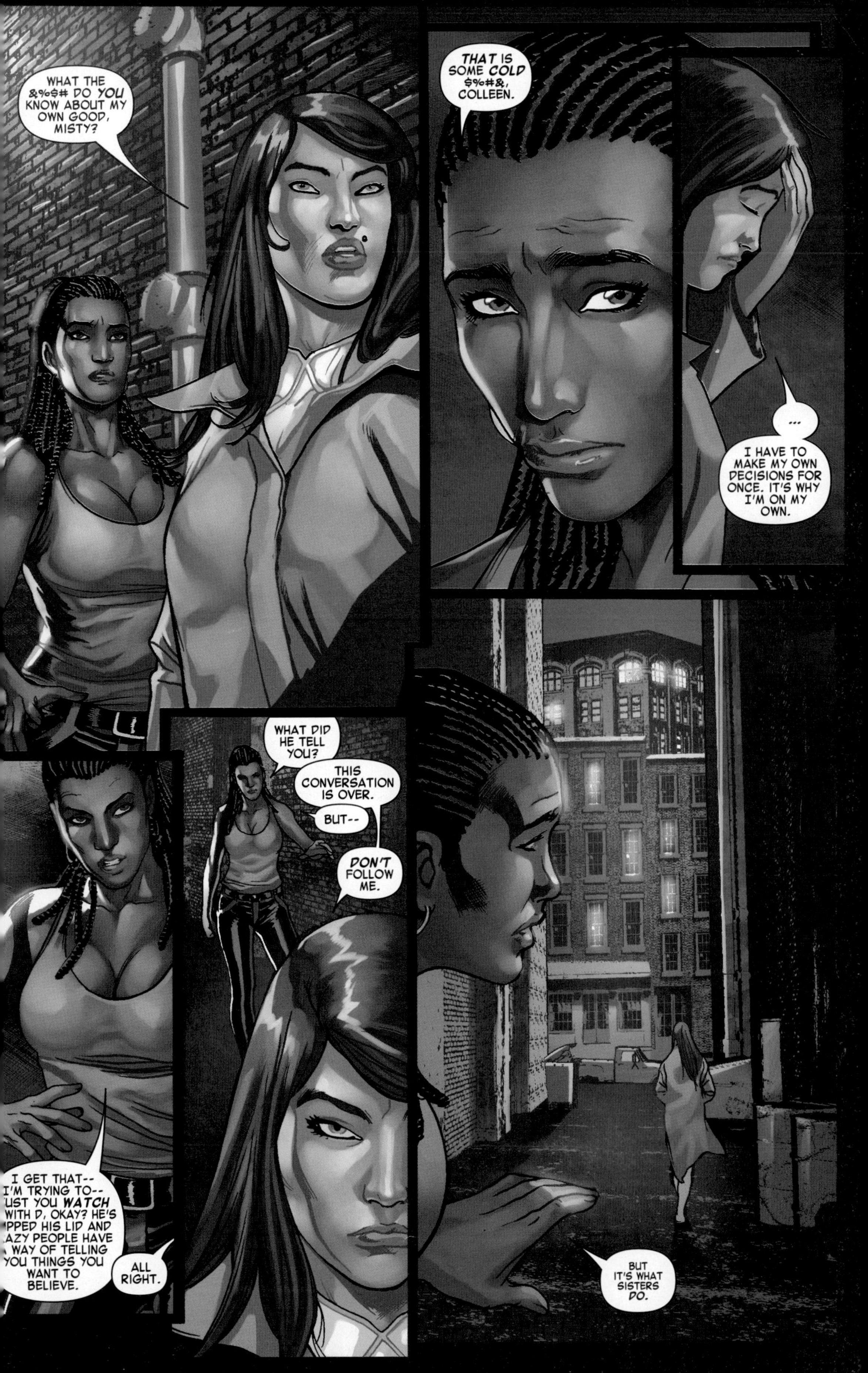
WHAT THE &%$# DO YOU KNOW ABOUT MY OWN GOOD, MISTY?
THAT IS SOME COLD $%#&, COLLEEN.
...
I HAVE TO MAKE MY OWN DECISIONS FOR ONCE. IT'S WHY I'M ON MY OWN.
I GET THAT-- I'M TRYING TO-- UST YOU WATCH WITH D, OKAY? HE'S PPED HIS LID AND AZY PEOPLE HAVE WAY OF TELLING YOU THINGS YOU WANT TO BELIEVE.
ALL RIGHT.
WHAT DID HE TELL YOU?
THIS CONVERSATION IS OVER.
BUT--
DON'T FOLLOW ME.
BUT IT'S WHAT SISTERS DO.

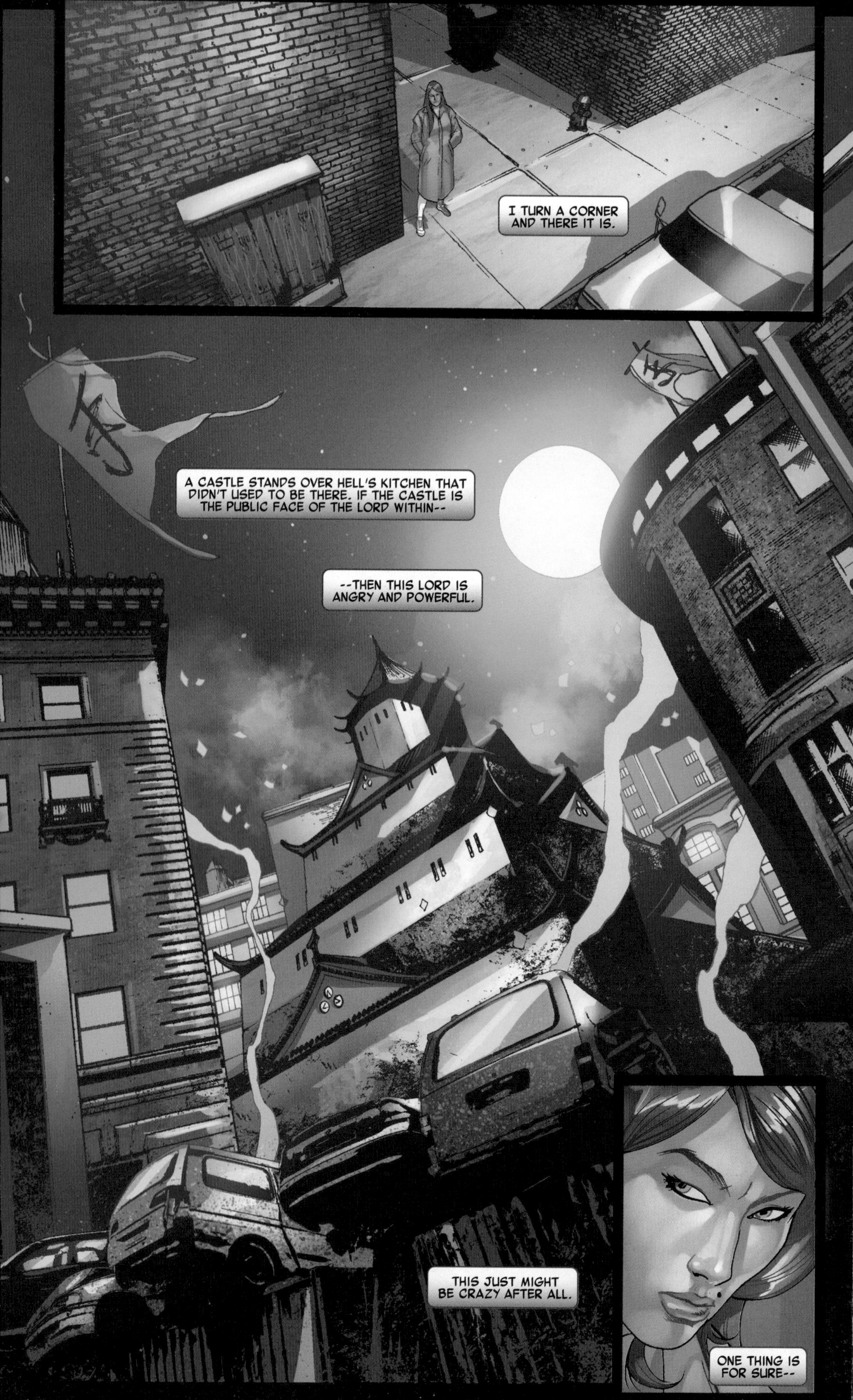
I TURN A CORNER AND THERE IT IS.
A CASTLE STANDS OVER HELL'S KITCHEN THAT DIDN'T USED TO BE THERE. IF THE CASTLE IS THE PUBLIC FACE OF THE LORD WITHIN--
--THEN THIS LORD IS ANGRY AND POWERFUL.
THIS JUST MIGHT BE CRAZY AFTER ALL.
ONE THING IS FOR SURE--

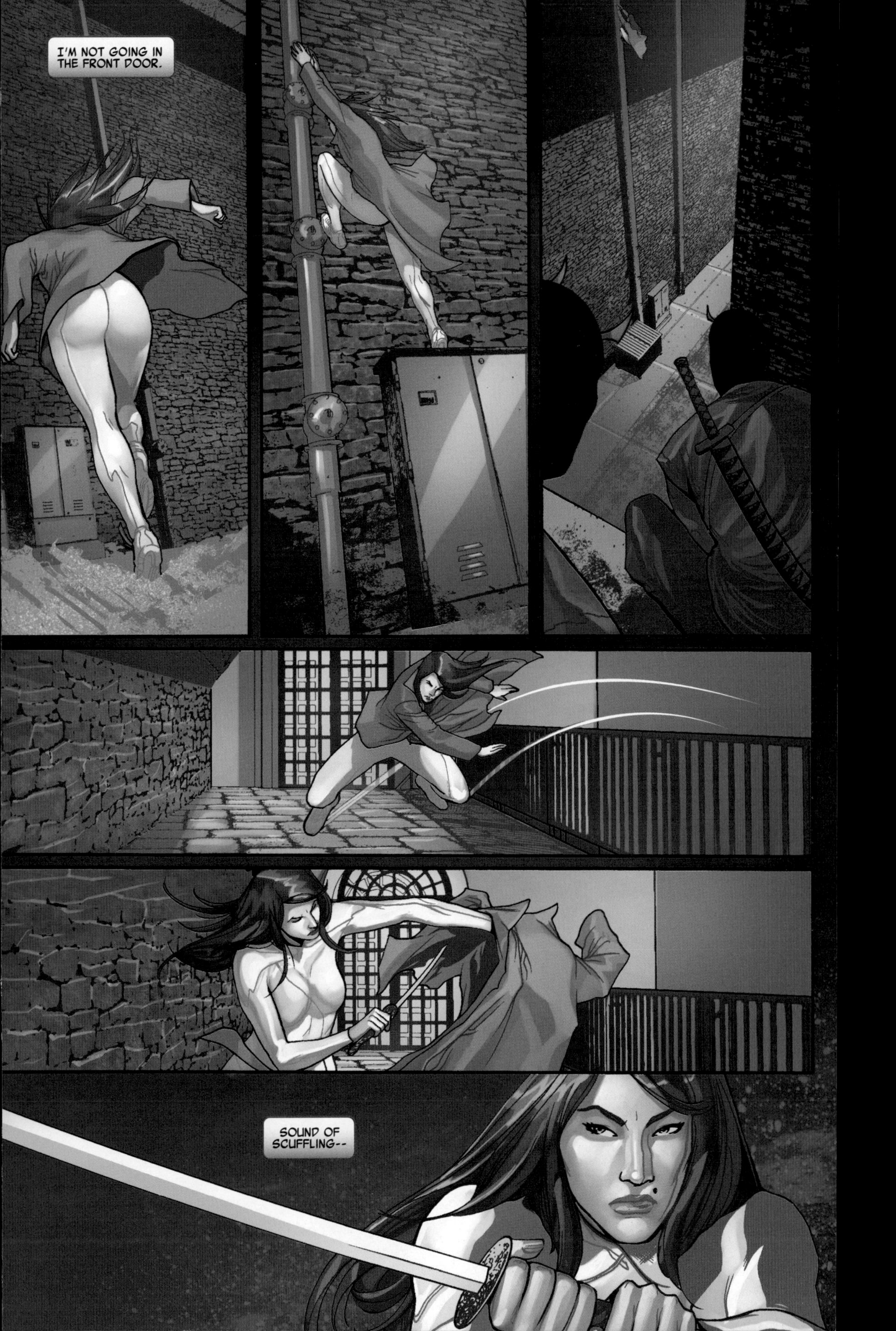
I'M NOT GOING IN THE FRONT DOOR.
SOUND OF SCUFFLING--

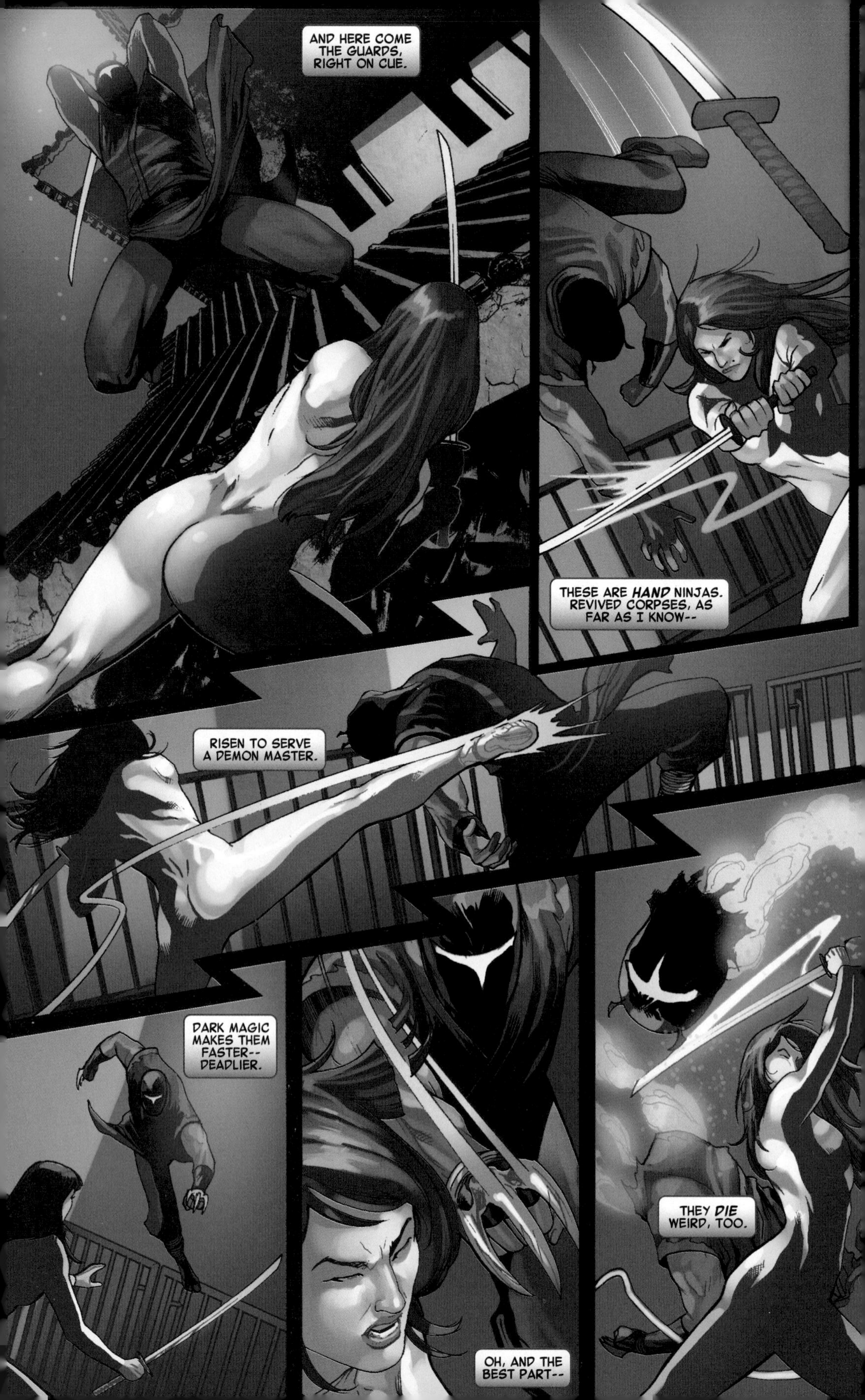
AND HERE COME THE GUARDS, RIGHT ON CUE.
THESE ARE HAND NINJAS. REVIVED CORPSES, AS FAR AS I KNOW--
RISEN TO SERVE A DEMON MASTER.
DARK MAGIC MAKES THEM FASTER--DEADLIER.
OH, AND THE BEST PART--
THEY DIE WEIRD, TOO.

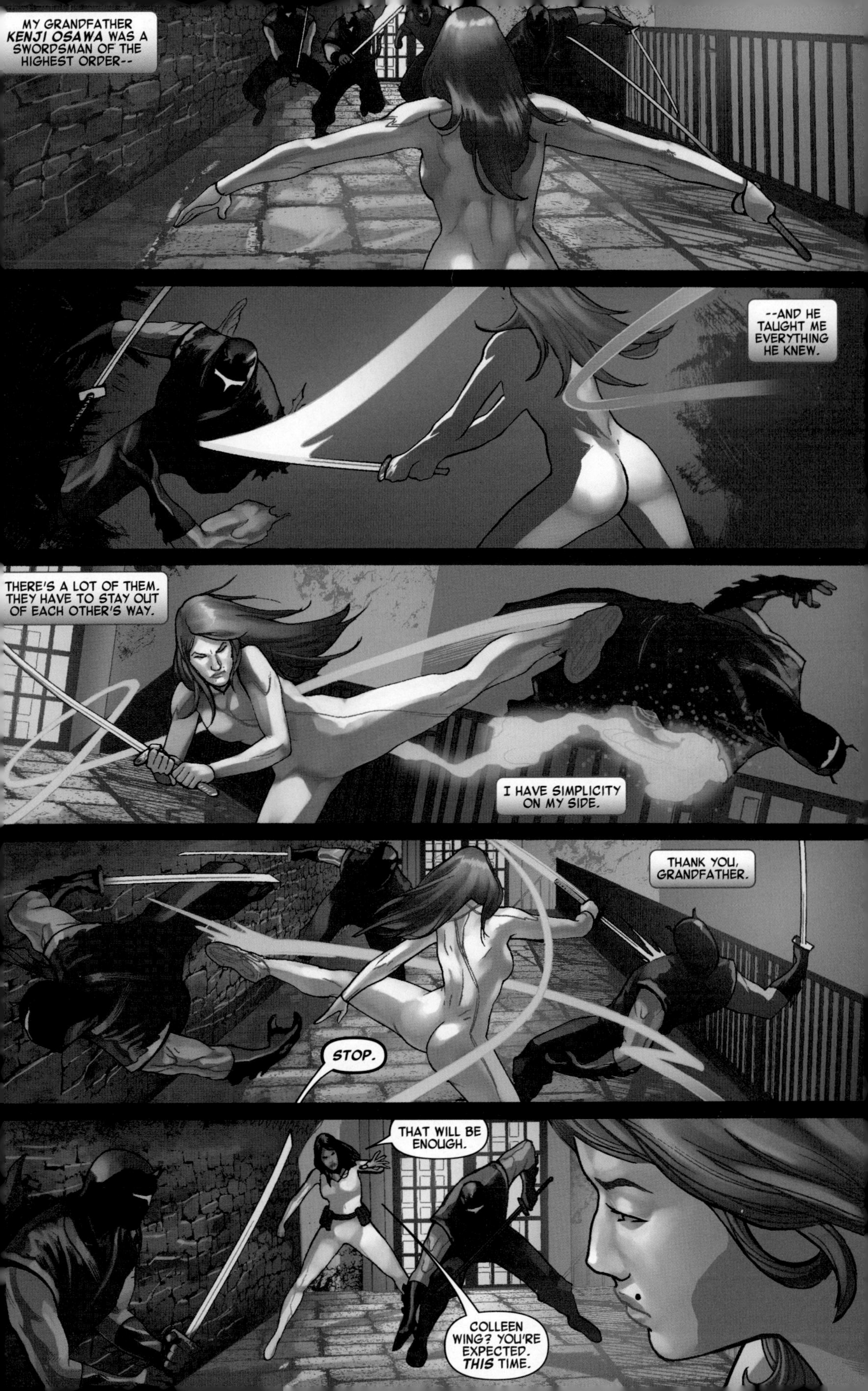
MY GRANDFATHER KENJI OSAWA WAS A SWORDSMAN OF THE HIGHEST ORDER--
--AND HE TAUGHT ME EVERYTHING HE KNEW.
THERE'S A LOT OF THEM. THEY HAVE TO STAY OUT OF EACH OTHER'S WAY.
I HAVE SIMPLICITY ON MY SIDE.
THANK YOU, GRANDFATHER.
STOP.
THAT WILL BE ENOUGH.
COLLEEN WING? YOU'RE EXPECTED. THIS TIME.

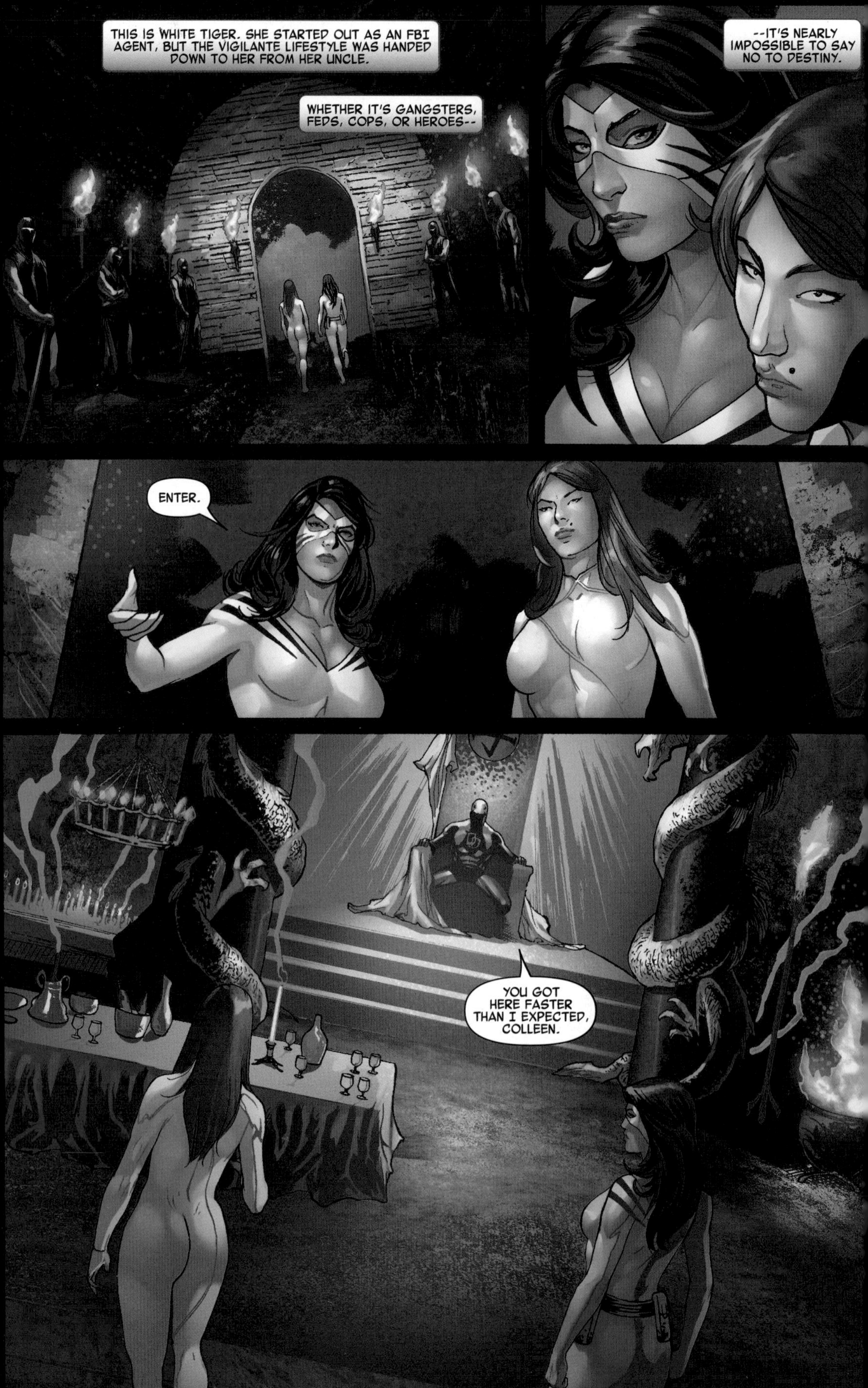
THIS IS WHITE TIGER. SHE STARTED OUT AS AN FBI AGENT, BUT THE VIGILANTE LIFESTYLE WAS HANDED DOWN TO HER FROM HER UNCLE.
WHETHER IT'S GANGSTERS, FEDS, COPS, OR HEROES--
--IT'S NEARLY IMPOSSIBLE TO SAY NO TO DESTINY.
ENTER.
YOU GOT HERE FASTER THAN I EXPECTED, COLLEEN.

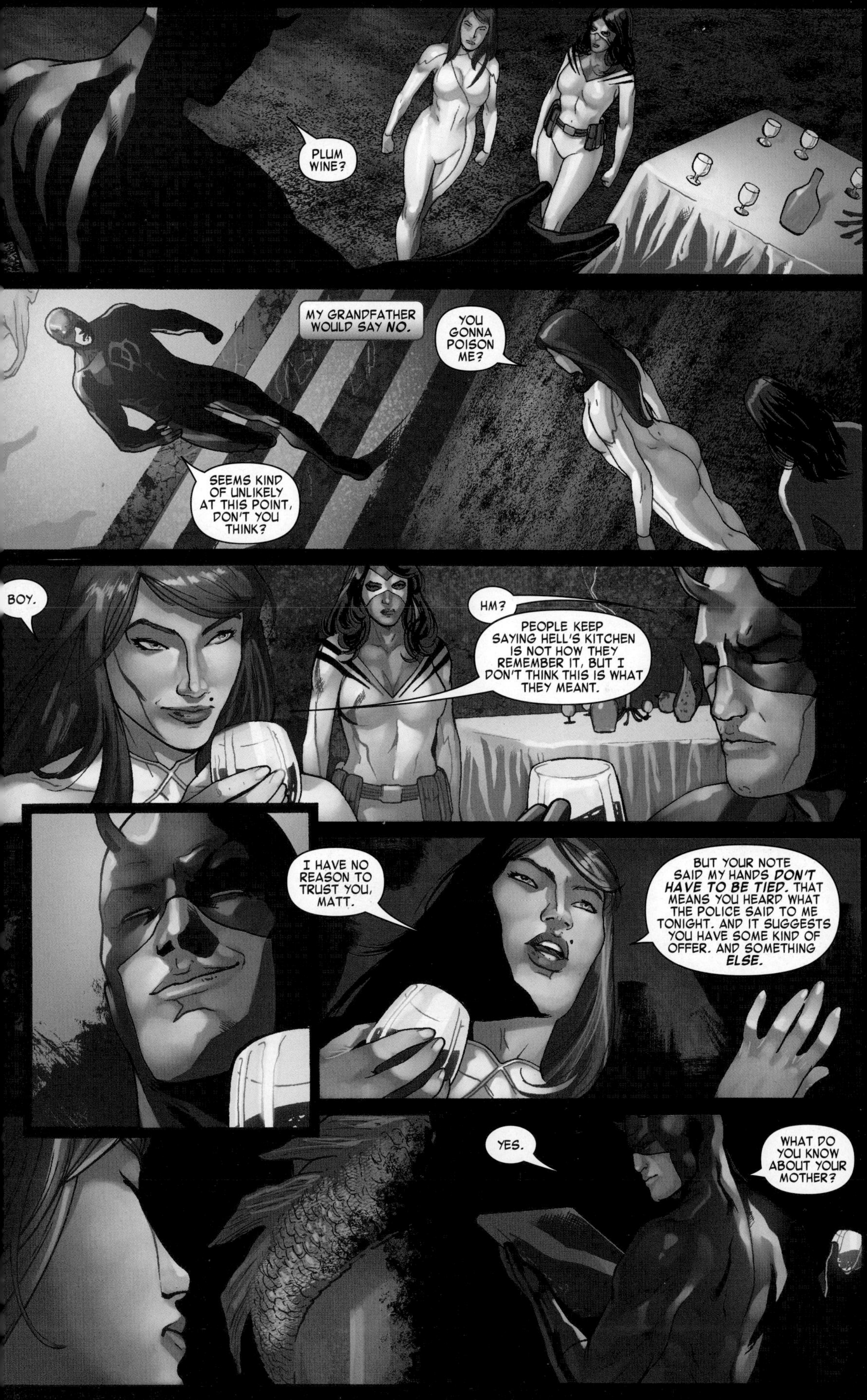
PLUM WINE?
MY GRANDFATHER WOULD SAY NO.
YOU GONNA POISON ME?
SEEMS KIND OF UNLIKELY AT THIS POINT, DON'T YOU THINK?
BOY.
HM?
PEOPLE KEEP SAYING HELL'S KITCHEN IS NOT HOW THEY REMEMBER IT, BUT I DON'T THINK THIS IS WHAT THEY MEANT.
I HAVE NO REASON TO TRUST YOU, MATT.
BUT YOUR NOTE SAID MY HANDS DON'T HAVE TO BE TIED. THAT MEANS YOU HEARD WHAT THE POLICE SAID TO ME TONIGHT. AND IT SUGGESTS YOU HAVE SOME KIND OF OFFER. AND SOMETHING ELSE.
YES.
WHAT DO YOU KNOW ABOUT YOUR MOTHER?

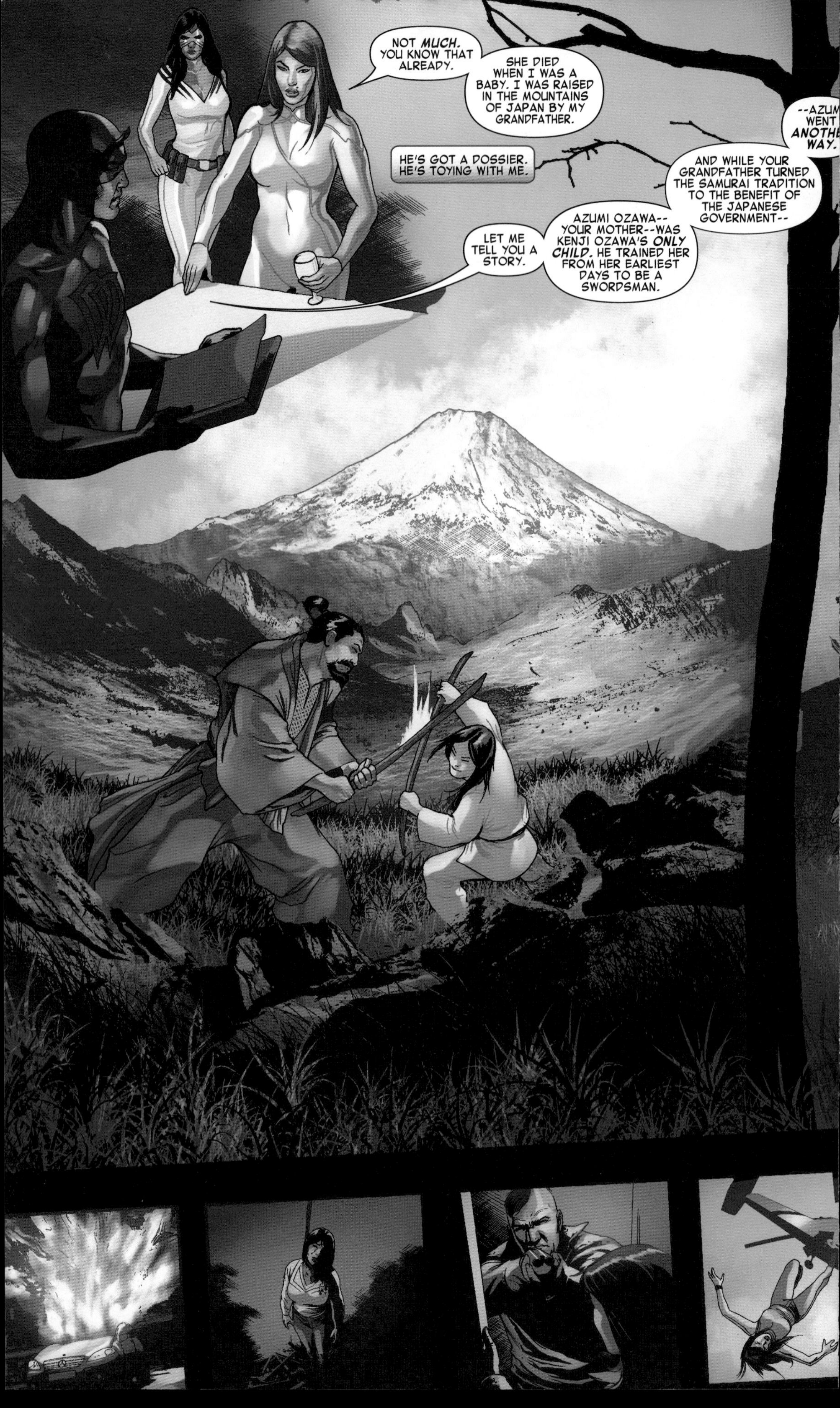
NOT MUCH. YOU KNOW THAT ALREADY.
SHE DIED WHEN I WAS A BABY. I WAS RAISED IN THE MOUNTAINS OF JAPAN BY MY GRANDFATHER.
HE'S GOT A DOSSIER. HE'S TOYING WITH ME.
LET ME TELL YOU A STORY.
AZUMI OZAWA--YOUR MOTHER--WAS KENJI OZAWA'S ONLY CHILD. HE TRAINED HER FROM HER EARLIEST DAYS TO BE A SWORDSMAN.
AND WHILE YOUR GRANDFATHER TURNED THE SAMURAI TRADITION TO THE BENEFIT OF THE JAPANESE GOVERNMENT--
--AZUM WENT ANOTHE WAY.

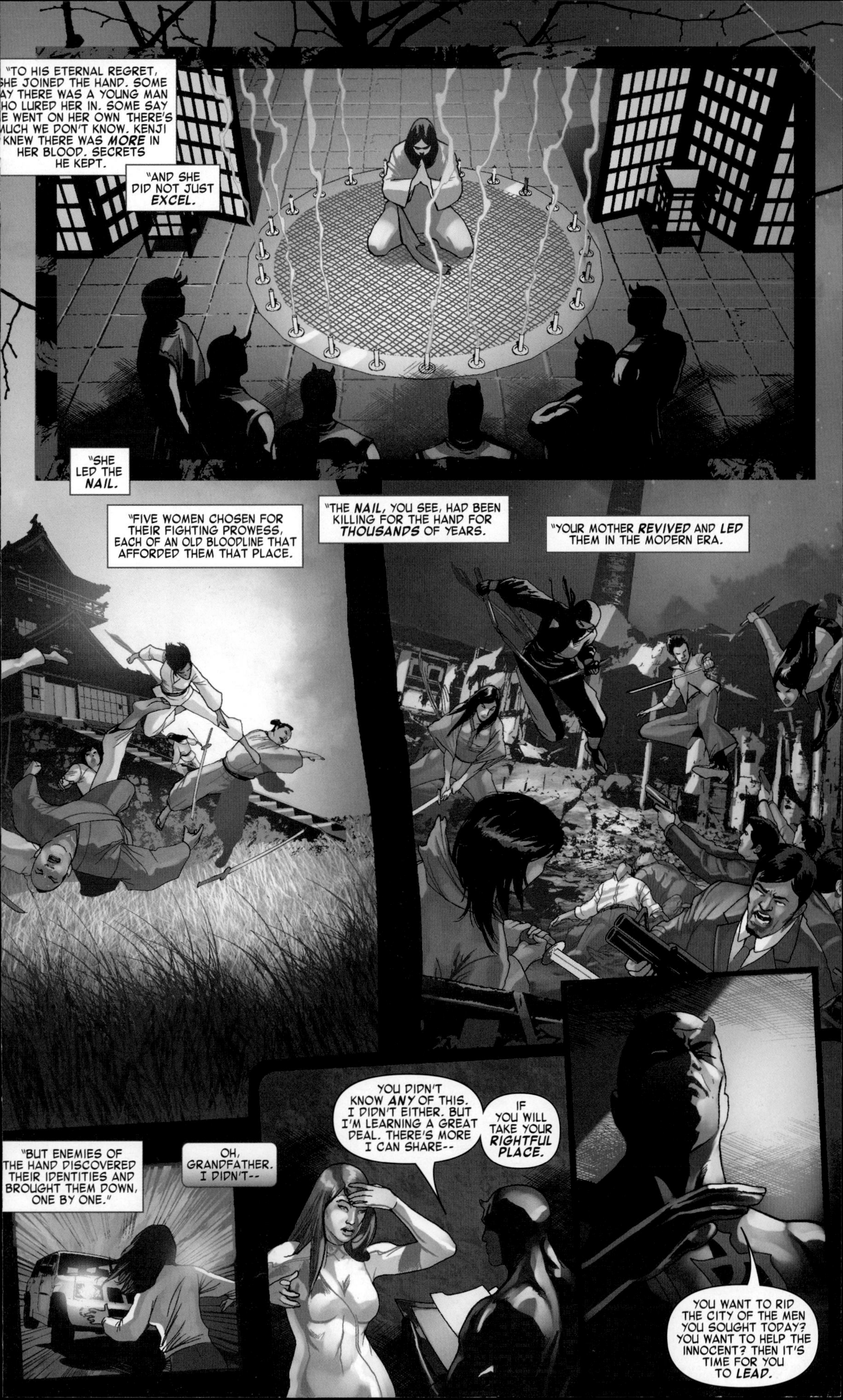
"TO HIS ETERNAL REGRET, SHE JOINED THE HAND. SOME SAY THERE WAS A YOUNG MAN WHO LURED HER IN. SOME SAY SHE WENT ON HER OWN. THERE'S MUCH WE DON'T KNOW. KENJI KNEW THERE WAS MORE IN HER BLOOD. SECRETS HE KEPT.
"AND SHE DID NOT JUST EXCEL.
"SHE LED THE NAIL.
"FIVE WOMEN CHOSEN FOR THEIR FIGHTING PROWESS, EACH OF AN OLD BLOODLINE THAT AFFORDED THEM THAT PLACE.
"THE NAIL, YOU SEE, HAD BEEN KILLING FOR THE HAND FOR THOUSANDS OF YEARS.
"YOUR MOTHER REVIVED AND LED THEM IN THE MODERN ERA.
"BUT ENEMIES OF THE HAND DISCOVERED THEIR IDENTITIES AND BROUGHT THEM DOWN, ONE BY ONE."
OH, GRANDFATHER. I DIDN'T--
YOU DIDN'T KNOW ANY OF THIS. I DIDN'T EITHER. BUT I'M LEARNING A GREAT DEAL. THERE'S MORE I CAN SHARE--
IF YOU WILL TAKE YOUR RIGHTFUL PLACE.
YOU WANT TO RID THE CITY OF THE MEN YOU SOUGHT TODAY? YOU WANT TO HELP THE INNOCENT? THEN IT'S TIME FOR YOU TO LEAD.

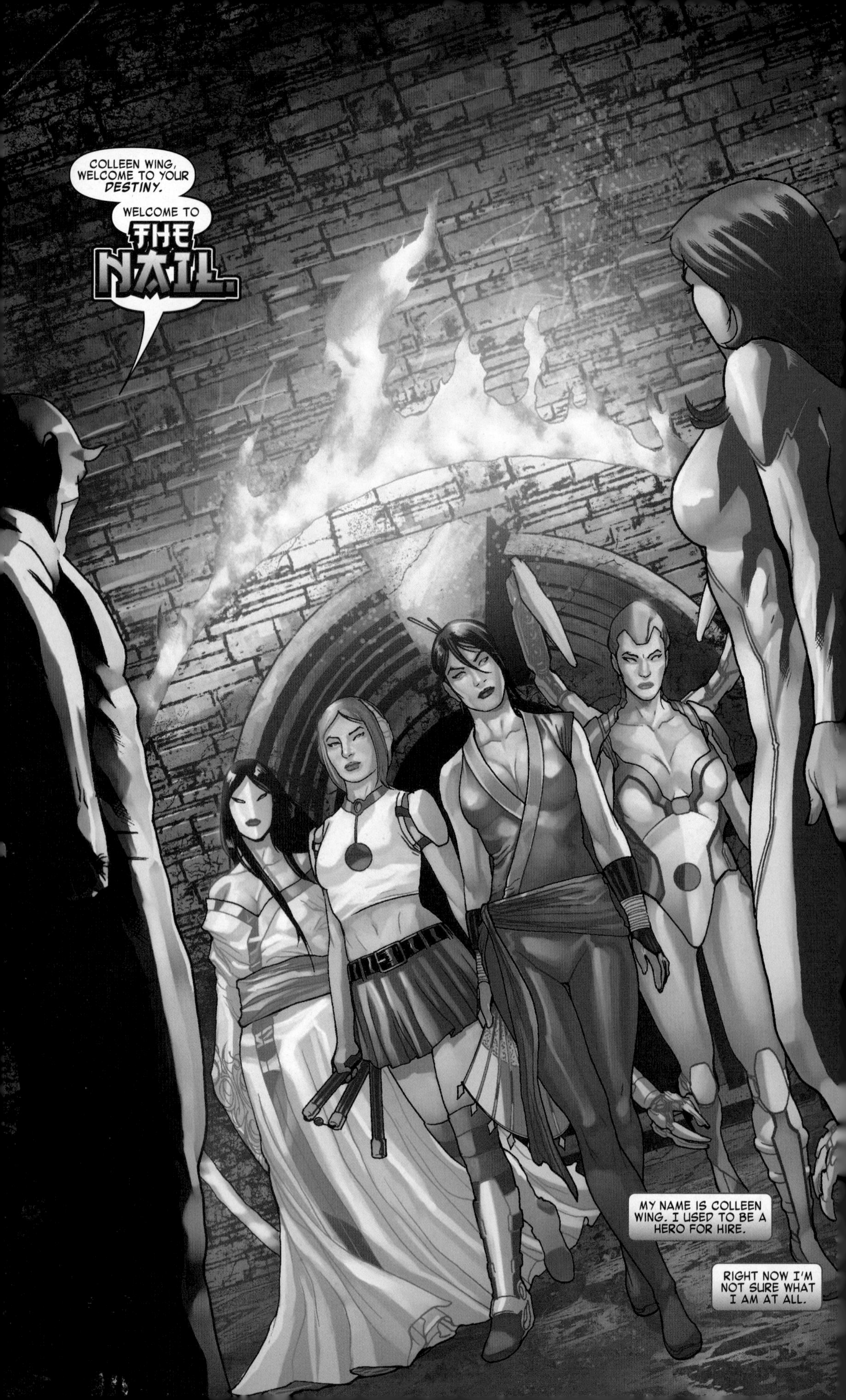

COLLEEN WING, WELCOME TO YOUR DESTINY.
WELCOME TO
THE NAIL.
MY NAME IS COLLEEN WING. I USED TO BE A HERO FOR HIRE.
RIGHT NOW I'M NOT SURE WHAT I AM AT ALL.

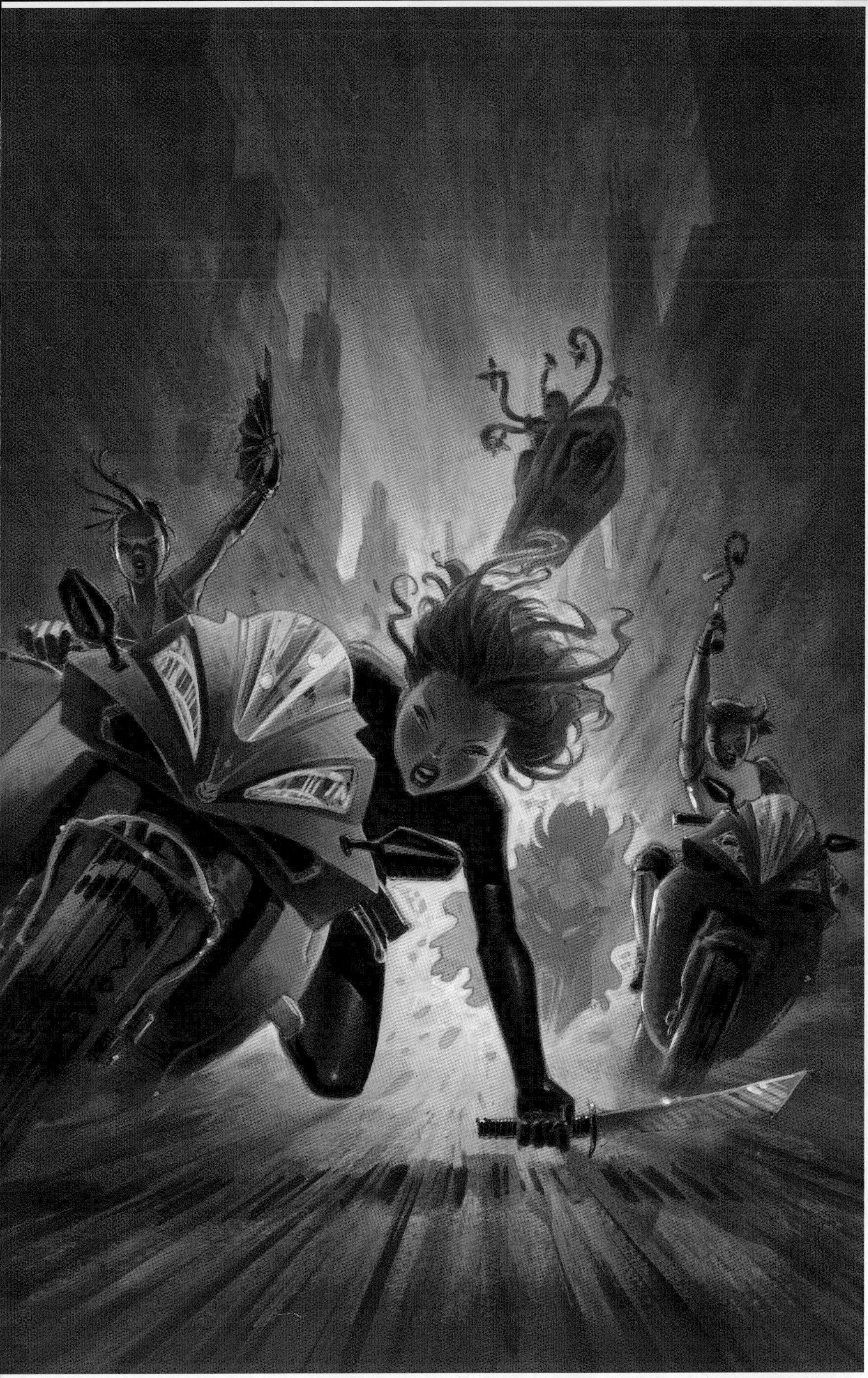

SHADOWLAND: DAUGHTERS OF THE SHADOW **#2**

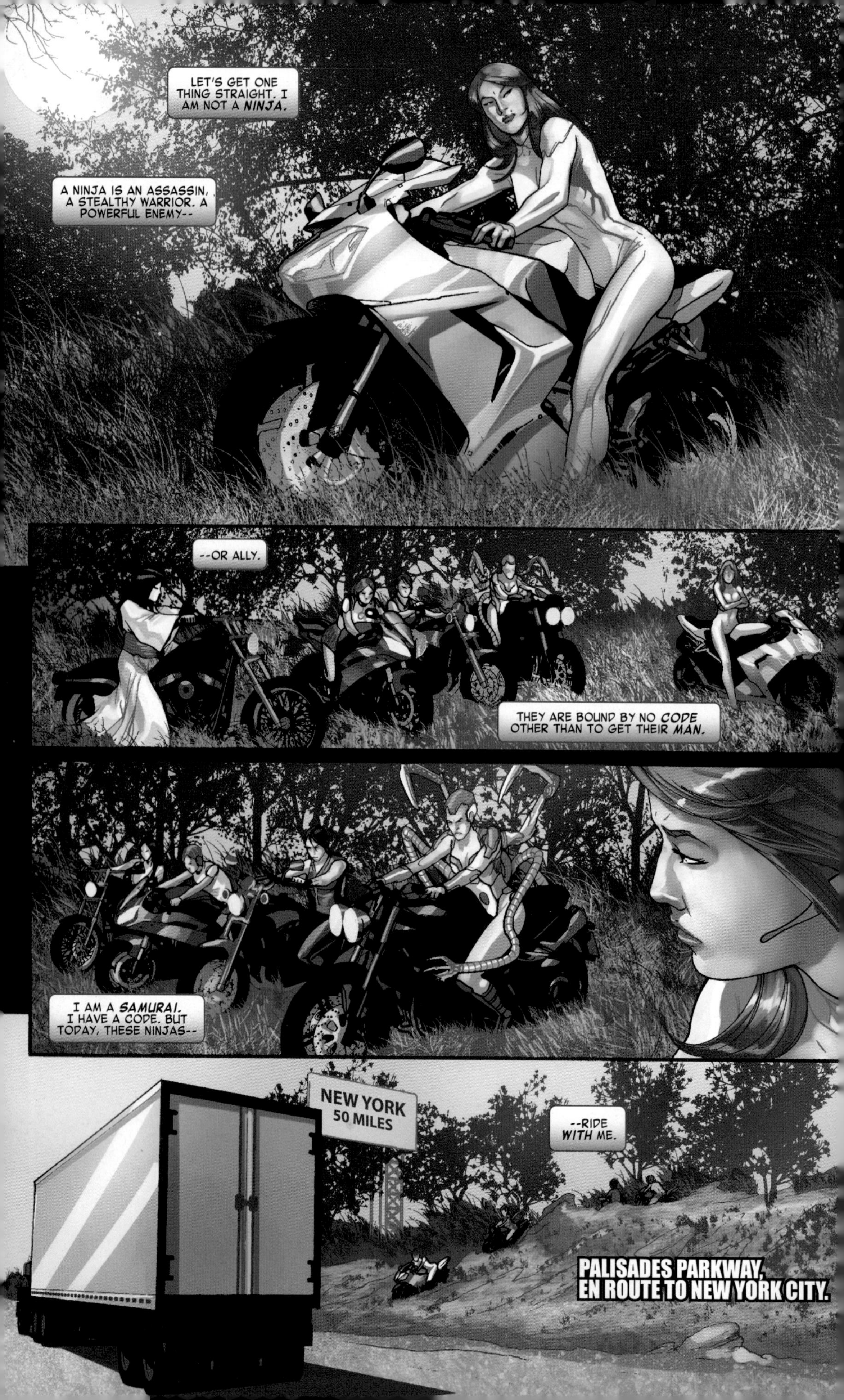
LET'S GET ONE THING STRAIGHT. I AM NOT A *NINJA.*
A NINJA IS AN ASSASSIN, A STEALTHY WARRIOR. A POWERFUL ENEMY--
--OR ALLY.
THEY ARE BOUND BY NO *CODE* OTHER THAN TO GET THEIR *MAN.*
I AM A *SAMURAI.* I HAVE A CODE. BUT TODAY, THESE NINJAS--
NEW YORK
50 MILES
--RIDE *WITH* ME.
PALISADES PARKWAY,
EN ROUTE TO NEW YORK CITY.

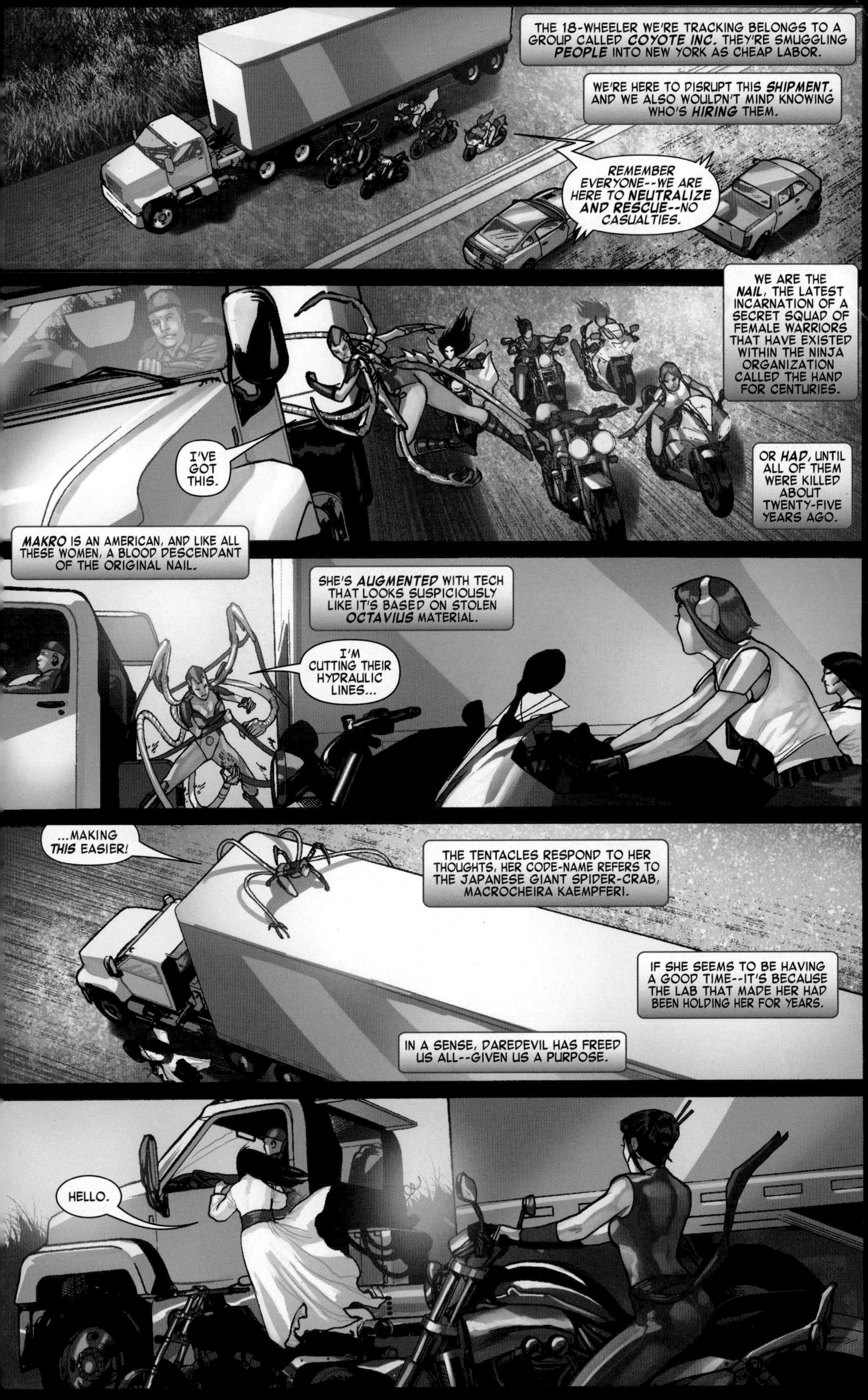
THE 18-WHEELER WE'RE TRACKING BELONGS TO A GROUP CALLED COYOTE INC. THEY'RE SMUGGLING PEOPLE INTO NEW YORK AS CHEAP LABOR.
WE'RE HERE TO DISRUPT THIS SHIPMENT. AND WE ALSO WOULDN'T MIND KNOWING WHO'S HIRING THEM.
REMEMBER EVERYONE--WE ARE HERE TO NEUTRALIZE AND RESCUE--NO CASUALTIES.
WE ARE THE NAIL, THE LATEST INCARNATION OF A SECRET SQUAD OF FEMALE WARRIORS THAT HAVE EXISTED WITHIN THE NINJA ORGANIZATION CALLED THE HAND FOR CENTURIES.
I'VE GOT THIS.
OR HAD, UNTIL ALL OF THEM WERE KILLED ABOUT TWENTY-FIVE YEARS AGO.
MAKRO IS AN AMERICAN, AND LIKE ALL THESE WOMEN, A BLOOD DESCENDANT OF THE ORIGINAL NAIL.
SHE'S AUGMENTED WITH TECH THAT LOOKS SUSPICIOUSLY LIKE IT'S BASED ON STOLEN OCTAVIUS MATERIAL.
I'M CUTTING THEIR HYDRAULIC LINES...
...MAKING THIS EASIER!
THE TENTACLES RESPOND TO HER THOUGHTS, HER CODE-NAME REFERS TO THE JAPANESE GIANT SPIDER-CRAB, MACROCHEIRA KAEMPFERI.
IF SHE SEEMS TO BE HAVING A GOOD TIME--IT'S BECAUSE THE LAB THAT MADE HER HAD BEEN HOLDING HER FOR YEARS.
IN A SENSE, DAREDEVIL HAS FREED US ALL--GIVEN US A PURPOSE.
HELLO.

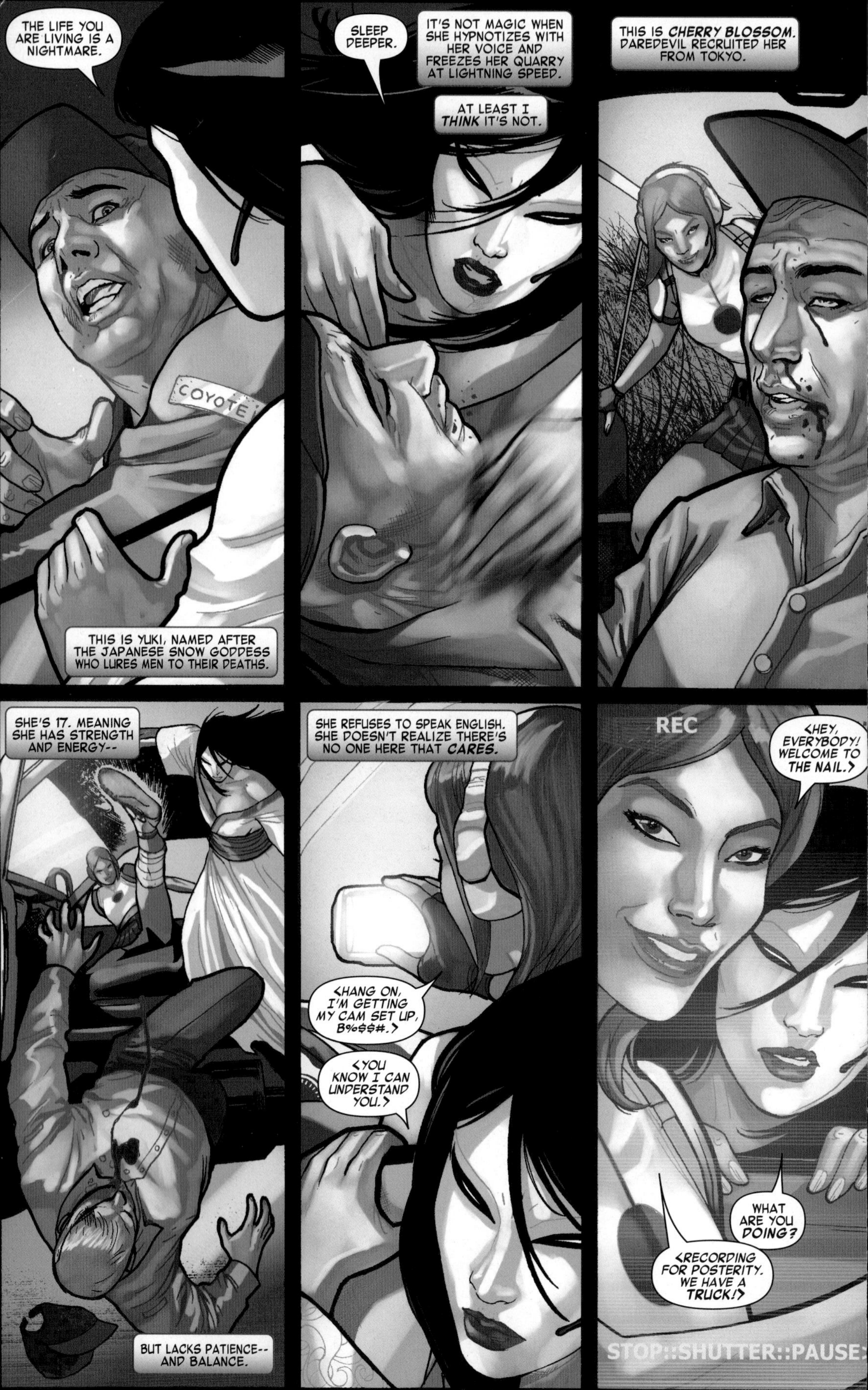
THE LIFE YOU ARE LIVING IS A NIGHTMARE.
COYOTE
THIS IS YUKI, NAMED AFTER THE JAPANESE SNOW GODDESS WHO LURES MEN TO THEIR DEATHS.
SLEEP DEEPER.
IT'S NOT MAGIC WHEN SHE HYPNOTIZES WITH HER VOICE AND FREEZES HER QUARRY AT LIGHTNING SPEED.
AT LEAST I THINK IT'S NOT.
THIS IS CHERRY BLOSSOM. DAREDEVIL RECRUITED HER FROM TOKYO.
SHE'S 17. MEANING SHE HAS STRENGTH AND ENERGY--
BUT LACKS PATIENCE--AND BALANCE.
SHE REFUSES TO SPEAK ENGLISH. SHE DOESN'T REALIZE THERE'S NO ONE HERE THAT CARES.
<HANG ON, I'M GETTING MY CAM SET UP, B%$$#.>
<YOU KNOW I CAN UNDERSTAND YOU.>
REC
<HEY, EVERYBODY! WELCOME TO THE NAIL.>
WHAT ARE YOU DOING?
<RECORDING FOR POSTERITY. WE HAVE A TRUCK!>
STOP::SHUTTER::PAUSE:

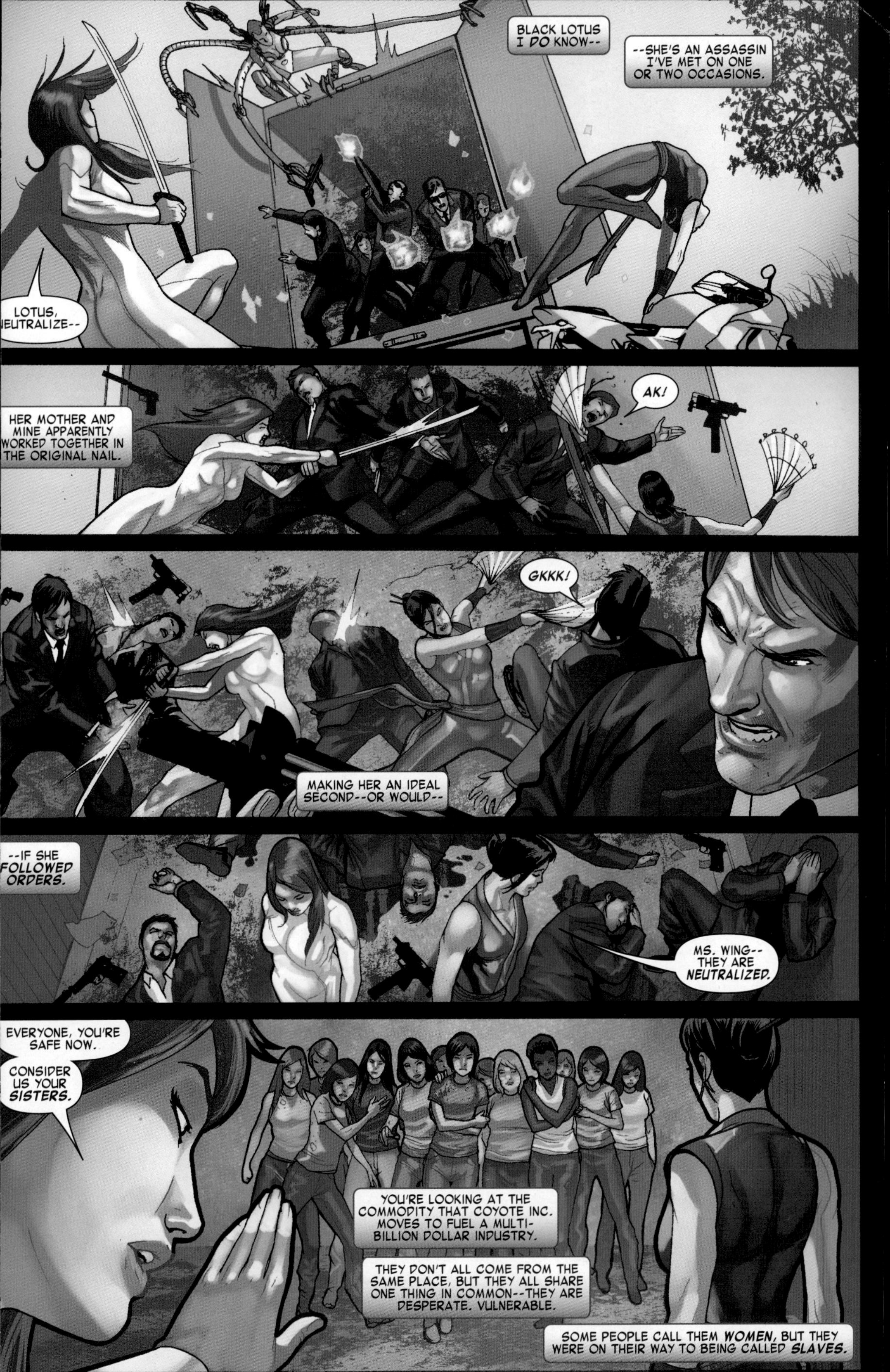
BLACK LOTUS I DO KNOW--
--SHE'S AN ASSASSIN I'VE MET ON ONE OR TWO OCCASIONS.
LOTUS, NEUTRALIZE--
HER MOTHER AND MINE APPARENTLY WORKED TOGETHER IN THE ORIGINAL NAIL.
AK!
GKKK!
MAKING HER AN IDEAL SECOND--OR WOULD--
--IF SHE FOLLOWED ORDERS.
MS. WING-- THEY ARE NEUTRALIZED.
EVERYONE, YOU'RE SAFE NOW.
CONSIDER US YOUR SISTERS.
YOU'RE LOOKING AT THE COMMODITY THAT COYOTE INC. MOVES TO FUEL A MULTI-BILLION DOLLAR INDUSTRY.
THEY DON'T ALL COME FROM THE SAME PLACE, BUT THEY ALL SHARE ONE THING IN COMMON--THEY ARE DESPERATE. VULNERABLE.
SOME PEOPLE CALL THEM WOMEN, BUT THEY WERE ON THEIR WAY TO BEING CALLED SLAVES.

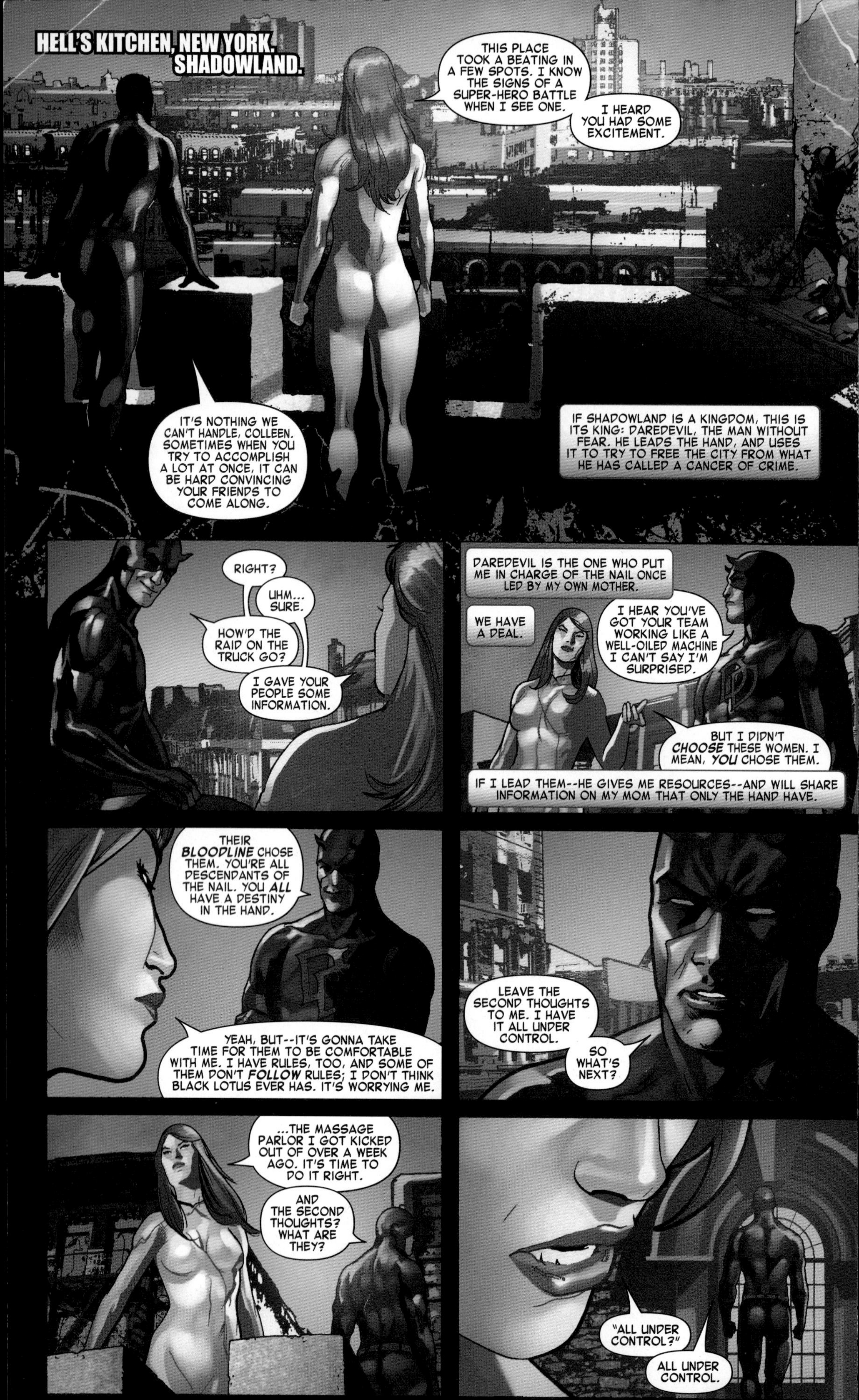
HELL'S KITCHEN, NEW YORK. SHADOWLAND.
THIS PLACE TOOK A BEATING IN A FEW SPOTS. I KNOW THE SIGNS OF A SUPER-HERO BATTLE WHEN I SEE ONE.
I HEARD YOU HAD SOME EXCITEMENT.
IT'S NOTHING WE CAN'T HANDLE, COLLEEN. SOMETIMES WHEN YOU TRY TO ACCOMPLISH A LOT AT ONCE, IT CAN BE HARD CONVINCING YOUR FRIENDS TO COME ALONG.
IF SHADOWLAND IS A KINGDOM, THIS IS ITS KING: DAREDEVIL, THE MAN WITHOUT FEAR. HE LEADS THE HAND, AND USES IT TO TRY TO FREE THE CITY FROM WHAT HE HAS CALLED A CANCER OF CRIME.
RIGHT?
UHM... SURE.
HOW'D THE RAID ON THE TRUCK GO?
I GAVE YOUR PEOPLE SOME INFORMATION.
DAREDEVIL IS THE ONE WHO PUT ME IN CHARGE OF THE NAIL ONCE LED BY MY OWN MOTHER.
WE HAVE A DEAL.
I HEAR YOU'VE GOT YOUR TEAM WORKING LIKE A WELL-OILED MACHINE I CAN'T SAY I'M SURPRISED.
BUT I DIDN'T CHOOSE THESE WOMEN. I MEAN, YOU CHOSE THEM.
IF I LEAD THEM--HE GIVES ME RESOURCES--AND WILL SHARE INFORMATION ON MY MOM THAT ONLY THE HAND HAVE.
THEIR BLOODLINE CHOSE THEM. YOU'RE ALL DESCENDANTS OF THE NAIL. YOU ALL HAVE A DESTINY IN THE HAND.
YEAH, BUT--IT'S GONNA TAKE TIME FOR THEM TO BE COMFORTABLE WITH ME. I HAVE RULES, TOO, AND SOME OF THEM DON'T FOLLOW RULES; I DON'T THINK BLACK LOTUS EVER HAS. IT'S WORRYING ME.
LEAVE THE SECOND THOUGHTS TO ME. I HAVE IT ALL UNDER CONTROL.
SO WHAT'S NEXT?
...THE MASSAGE PARLOR I GOT KICKED OUT OF OVER A WEEK AGO. IT'S TIME TO DO IT RIGHT.
AND THE SECOND THOUGHTS? WHAT ARE THEY?
"ALL UNDER CONTROL?"
ALL UNDER CONTROL.

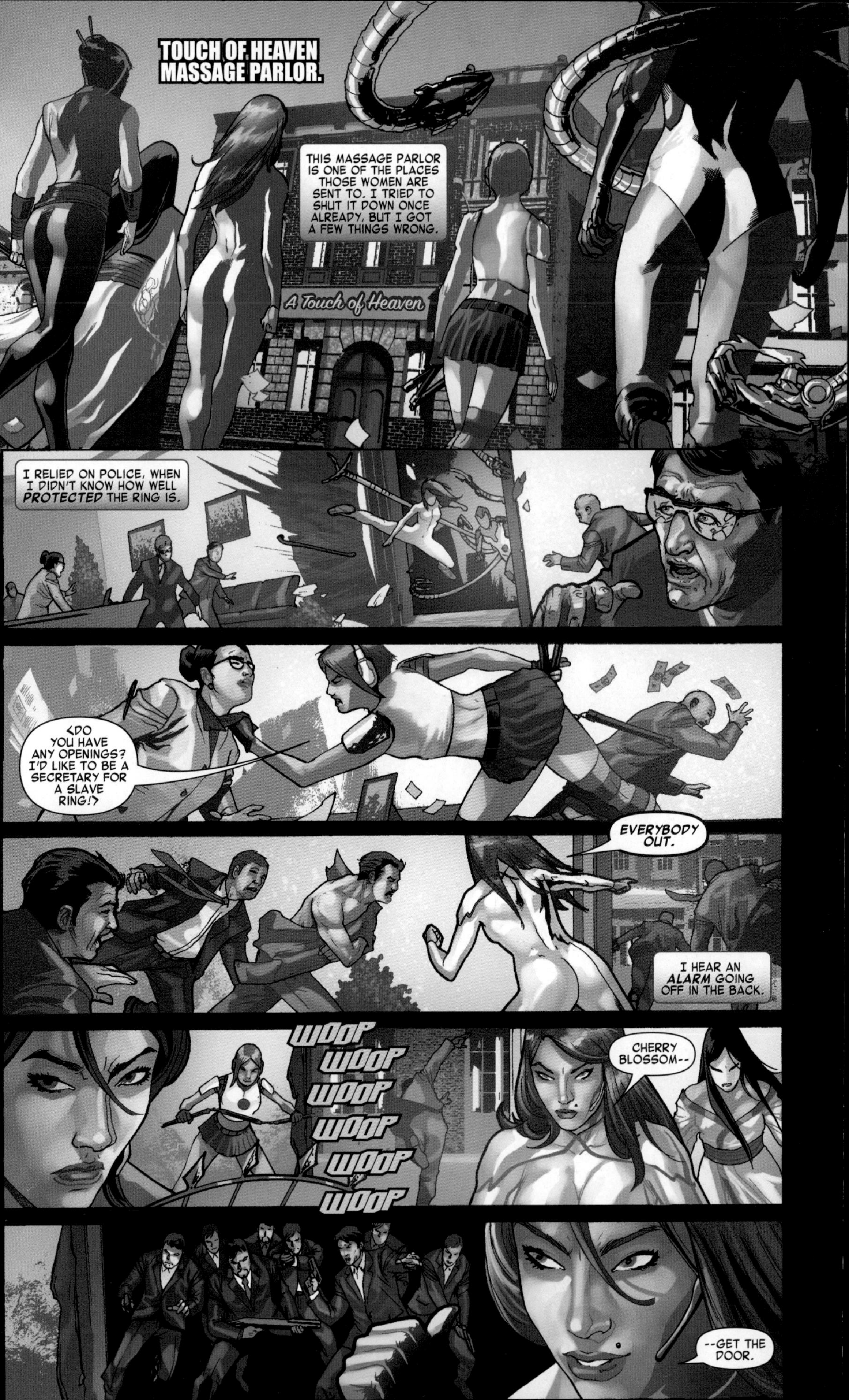
TOUCH OF HEAVEN MASSAGE PARLOR.
THIS MASSAGE PARLOR IS ONE OF THE PLACES THOSE WOMEN ARE SENT TO. I TRIED TO SHUT IT DOWN ONCE ALREADY, BUT I GOT A FEW THINGS WRONG.
A Touch of Heaven
I RELIED ON POLICE, WHEN I DIDN'T KNOW HOW WELL PROTECTED THE RING IS.
<DO YOU HAVE ANY OPENINGS? I'D LIKE TO BE A SECRETARY FOR A SLAVE RING!>
EVERYBODY OUT.
I HEAR AN ALARM GOING OFF IN THE BACK.
WOOP WOOP WOOP WOOP WOOP WOOP
CHERRY BLOSSOM--
--GET THE DOOR.

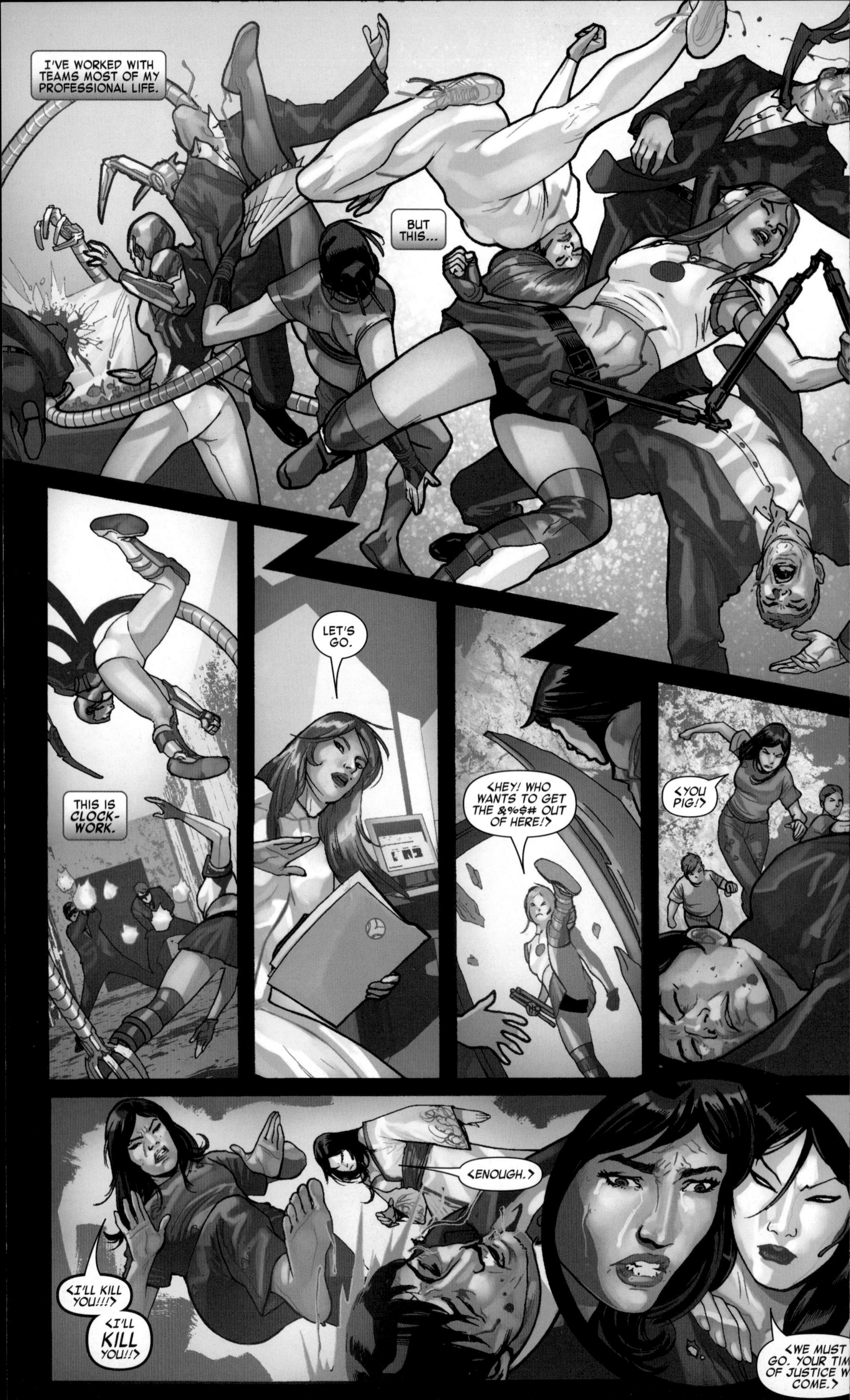
I'VE WORKED WITH TEAMS MOST OF MY PROFESSIONAL LIFE.
BUT THIS...
THIS IS CLOCK-WORK.
LET'S GO.
<HEY! WHO WANTS TO GET THE &%$# OUT OF HERE!>
<YOU PIG!>
<ENOUGH.>
<I'LL KILL YOU!!!>
<I'LL KILL YOU!!>

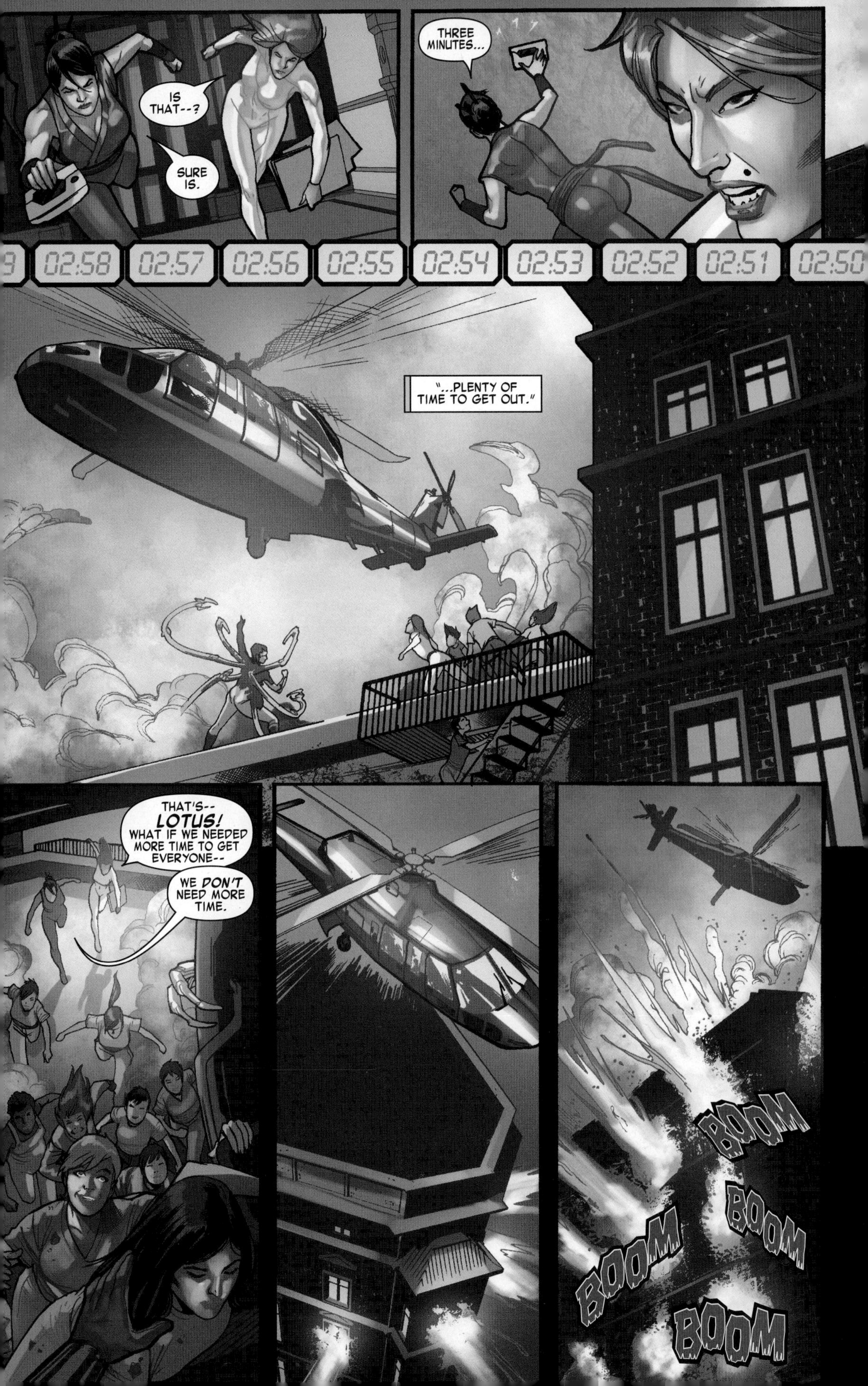
IS THAT--?
SURE IS.
THREE MINUTES...
02:58
02:57
02:56
02:55
02:54
02:53
02:52
02:51
02:50
"...PLENTY OF TIME TO GET OUT."
THAT'S-- LOTUS! WHAT IF WE NEEDED MORE TIME TO GET EVERYONE--
WE DON'T NEED MORE TIME.
BOOM
BOOM
BOOM
BOOM

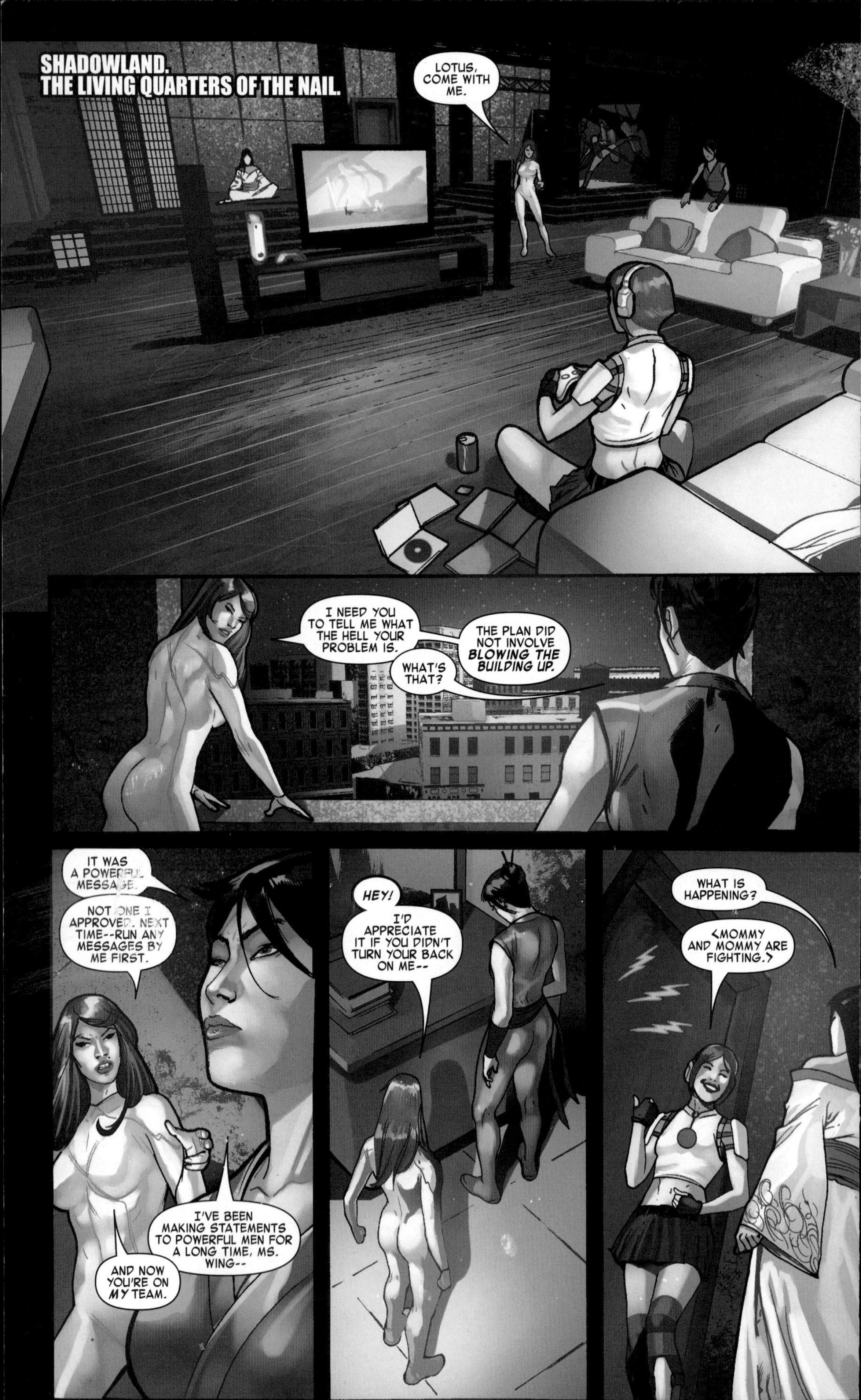
SHADOWLAND.
THE LIVING QUARTERS OF THE NAIL.
LOTUS, COME WITH ME.
I NEED YOU TO TELL ME WHAT THE HELL YOUR PROBLEM IS.
WHAT'S THAT?
THE PLAN DID NOT INVOLVE BLOWING THE BUILDING UP.
IT WAS A POWERFUL MESSAGE.
NOT ONE I APPROVED. NEXT TIME--RUN ANY MESSAGES BY ME FIRST.
I'VE BEEN MAKING STATEMENTS TO POWERFUL MEN FOR A LONG TIME, MS. WING--
AND NOW YOU'RE ON MY TEAM.
HEY!
I'D APPRECIATE IT IF YOU DIDN'T TURN YOUR BACK ON ME--
WHAT IS HAPPENING?
<MOMMY AND MOMMY ARE FIGHTING.>

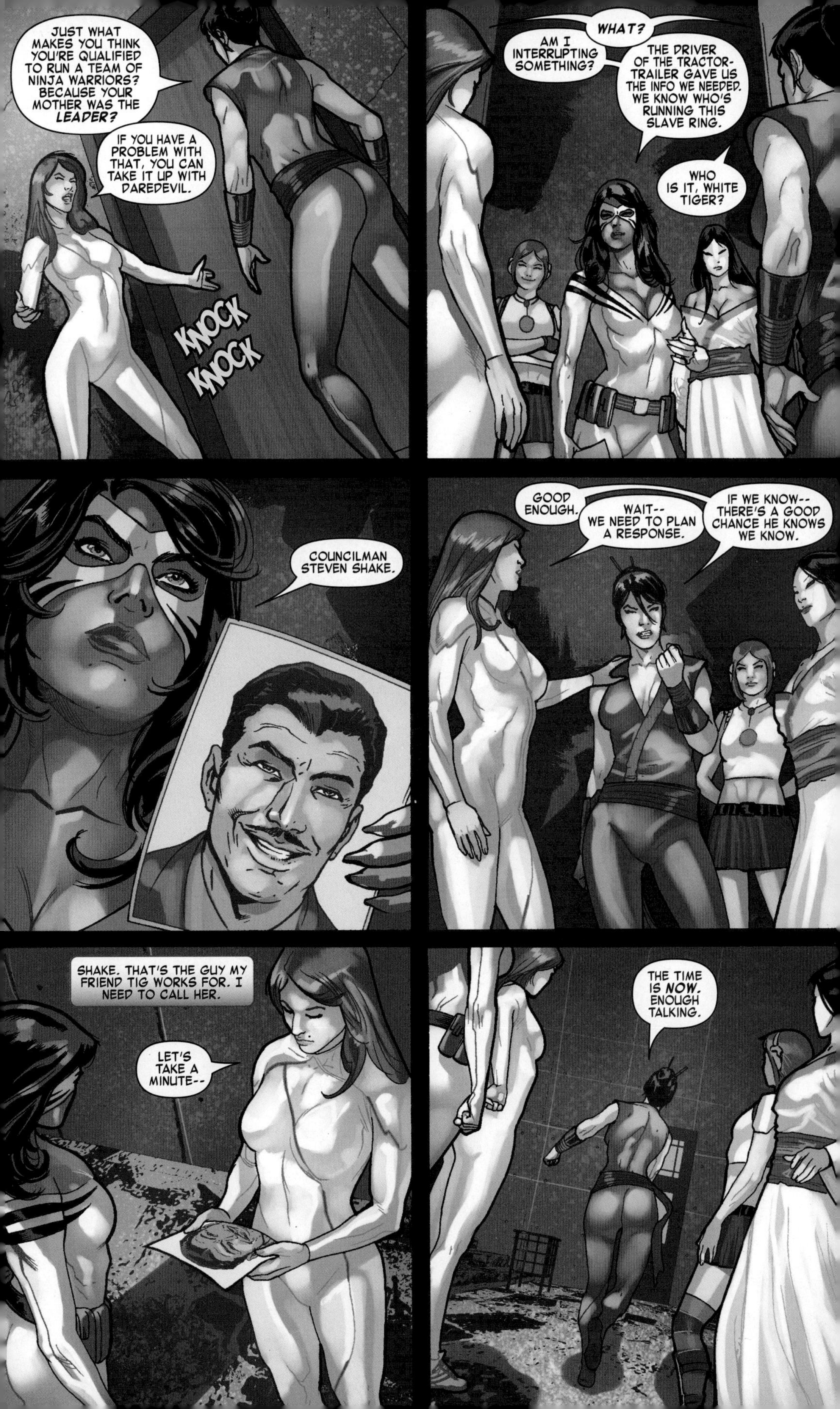

JUST WHAT MAKES YOU THINK YOU'RE QUALIFIED TO RUN A TEAM OF NINJA WARRIORS? BECAUSE YOUR MOTHER WAS THE *LEADER*?
IF YOU HAVE A PROBLEM WITH THAT, YOU CAN TAKE IT UP WITH DAREDEVIL.
KNOCK KNOCK
WHAT?
AM I INTERRUPTING SOMETHING?
THE DRIVER OF THE TRACTOR-TRAILER GAVE US THE INFO WE NEEDED. WE KNOW WHO'S RUNNING THIS SLAVE RING.
WHO IS IT, WHITE TIGER?
COUNCILMAN STEVEN SHAKE.
GOOD ENOUGH.
WAIT-- WE NEED TO PLAN A RESPONSE.
IF WE KNOW-- THERE'S A GOOD CHANCE HE KNOWS WE KNOW.
SHAKE. THAT'S THE GUY MY FRIEND TIG WORKS FOR. I NEED TO CALL HER.
LET'S TAKE A MINUTE--
THE TIME IS *NOW*. ENOUGH TALKING.

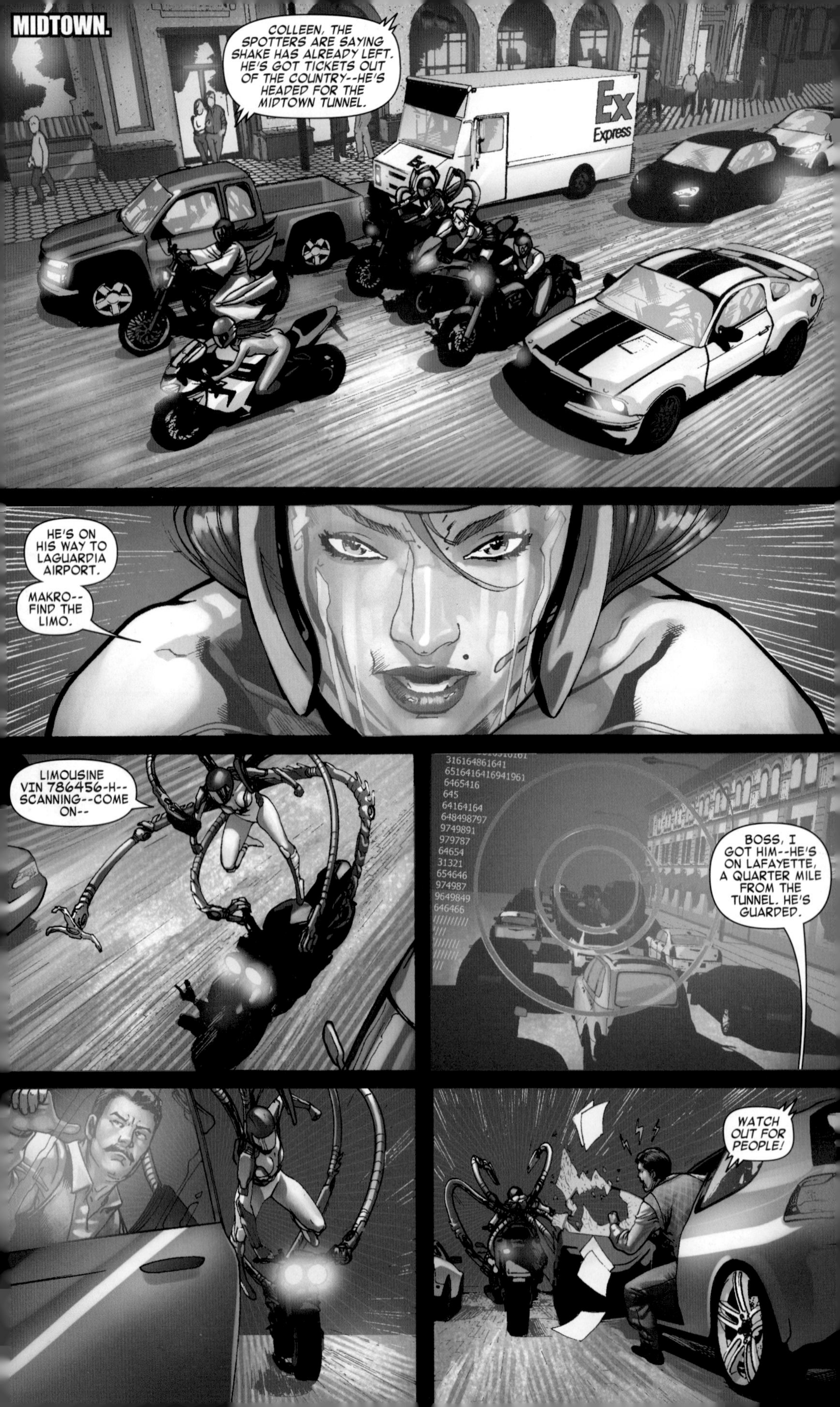
MIDTOWN.
COLLEEN, THE SPOTTERS ARE SAYING SHAKE HAS ALREADY LEFT. HE'S GOT TICKETS OUT OF THE COUNTRY--HE'S HEADED FOR THE MIDTOWN TUNNEL.
Ex Express
HE'S ON HIS WAY TO LAGUARDIA AIRPORT.
MAKRO-- FIND THE LIMO.
LIMOUSINE VIN 786456-H-- SCANNING--COME ON--
BOSS, I GOT HIM--HE'S ON LAFAYETTE, A QUARTER MILE FROM THE TUNNEL. HE'S GUARDED.
WATCH OUT FOR PEOPLE!

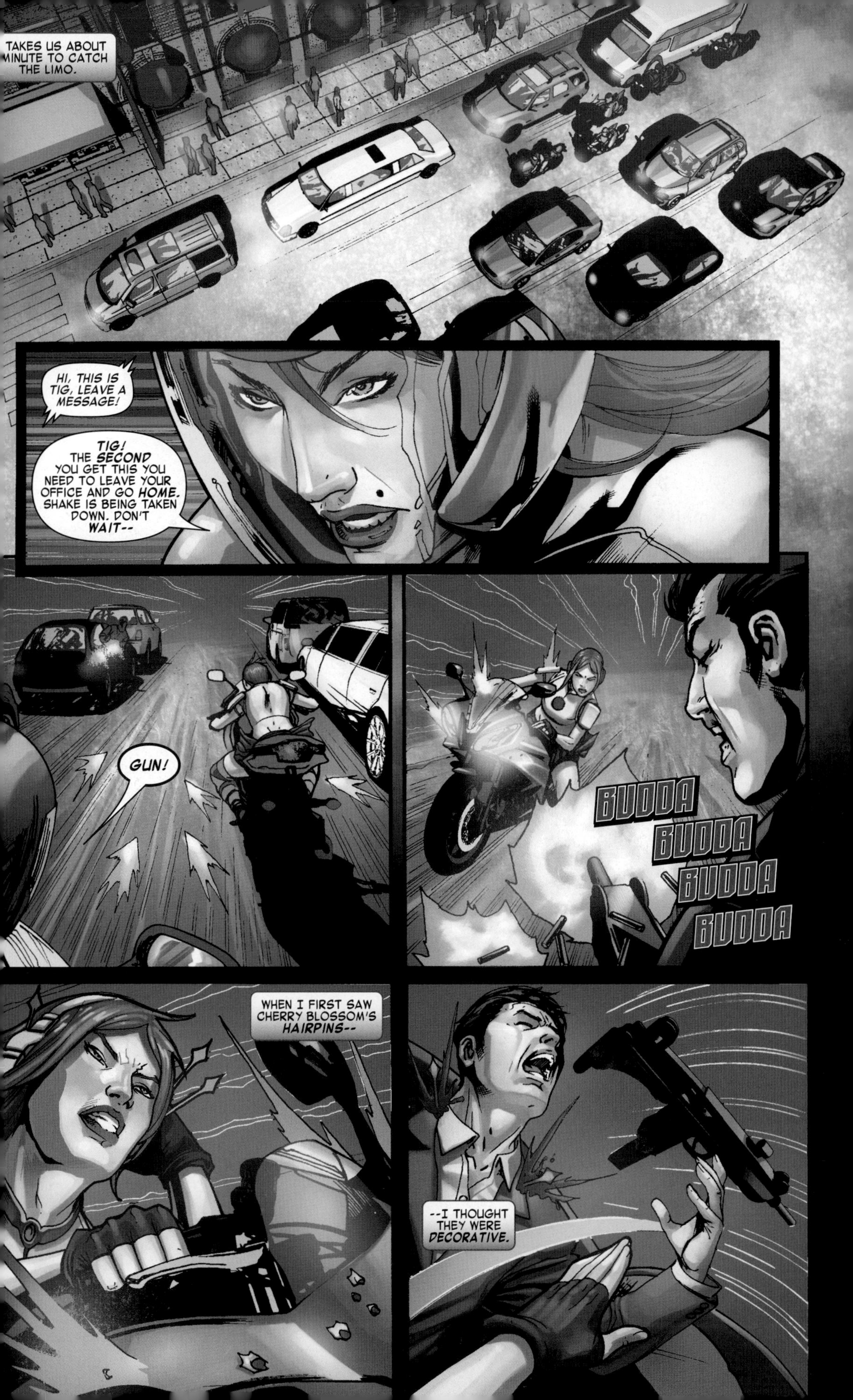
TAKES US ABOUT
MINUTE TO CATCH
THE LIMO.
HI, THIS IS
TIG, LEAVE A
MESSAGE!
TIG!
THE SECOND
YOU GET THIS YOU
NEED TO LEAVE YOUR
OFFICE AND GO HOME.
SHAKE IS BEING TAKEN
DOWN. DON'T
WAIT--
GUN!
BUDDA
BUDDA
BUDDA
BUDDA
WHEN I FIRST SAW
CHERRY BLOSSOM'S
HAIRPINS--
--I THOUGHT
THEY WERE
DECORATIVE.

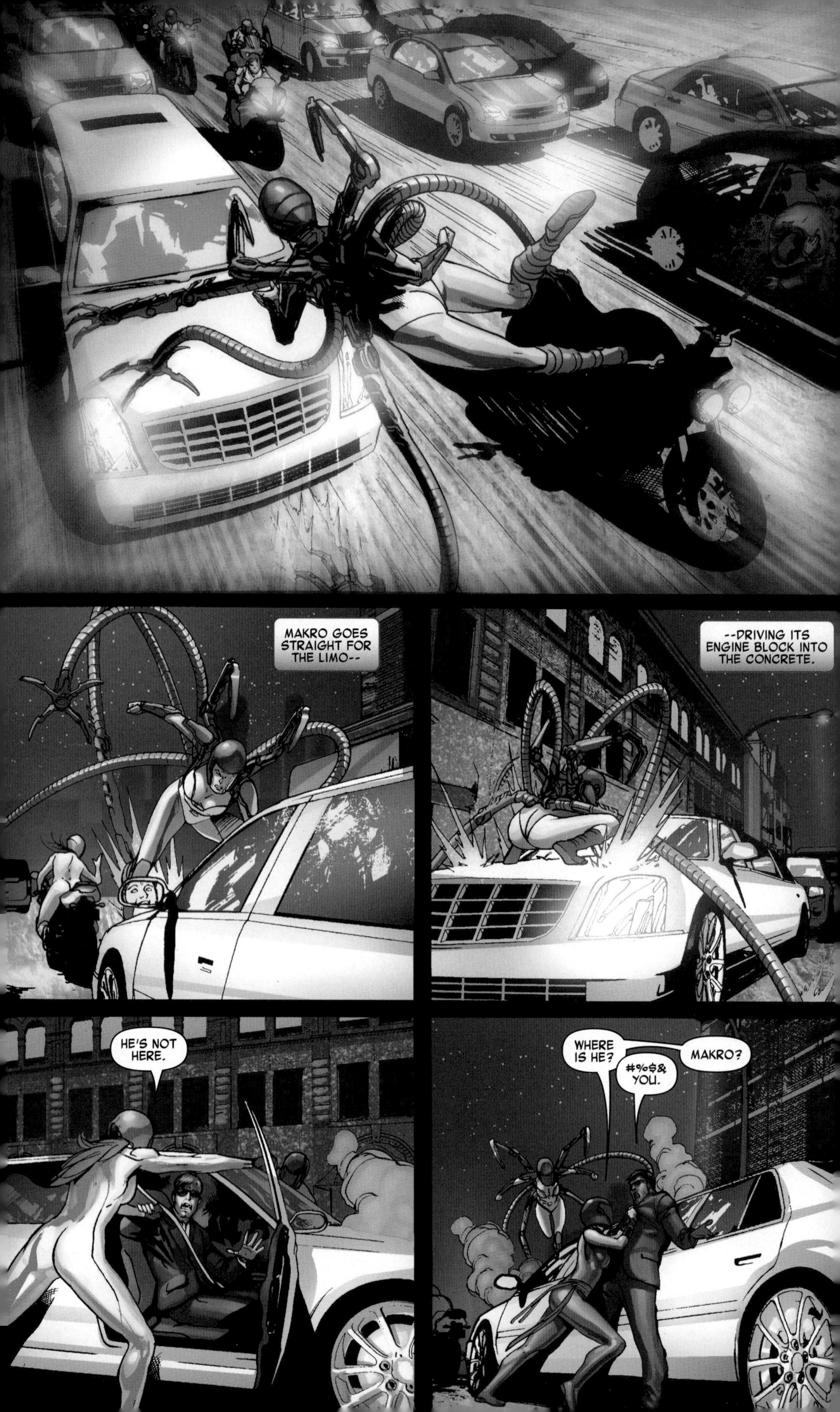

MAKRO GOES STRAIGHT FOR THE LIMO--
--DRIVING ITS ENGINE BLOCK INTO THE CONCRETE.
HE'S NOT HERE.
WHERE IS HE?
MAKRO?
#%$& YOU.

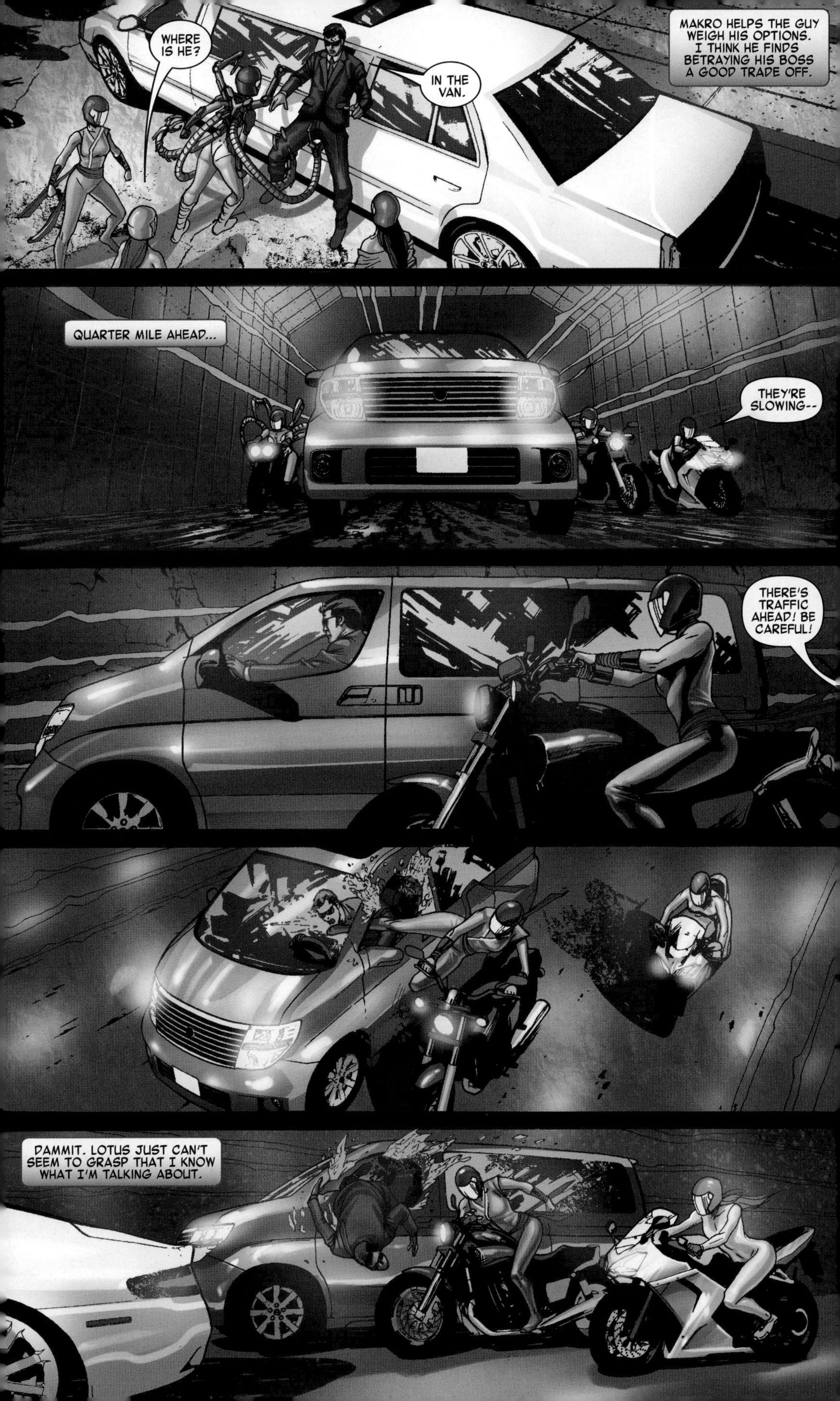

MAKRO HELPS THE GUY WEIGH HIS OPTIONS. I THINK HE FINDS BETRAYING HIS BOSS A GOOD TRADE OFF.
WHERE IS HE?
IN THE VAN.
QUARTER MILE AHEAD...
THEY'RE SLOWING--
THERE'S TRAFFIC AHEAD! BE CAREFUL!
DAMMIT. LOTUS JUST CAN'T SEEM TO GRASP THAT I KNOW WHAT I'M TALKING ABOUT.

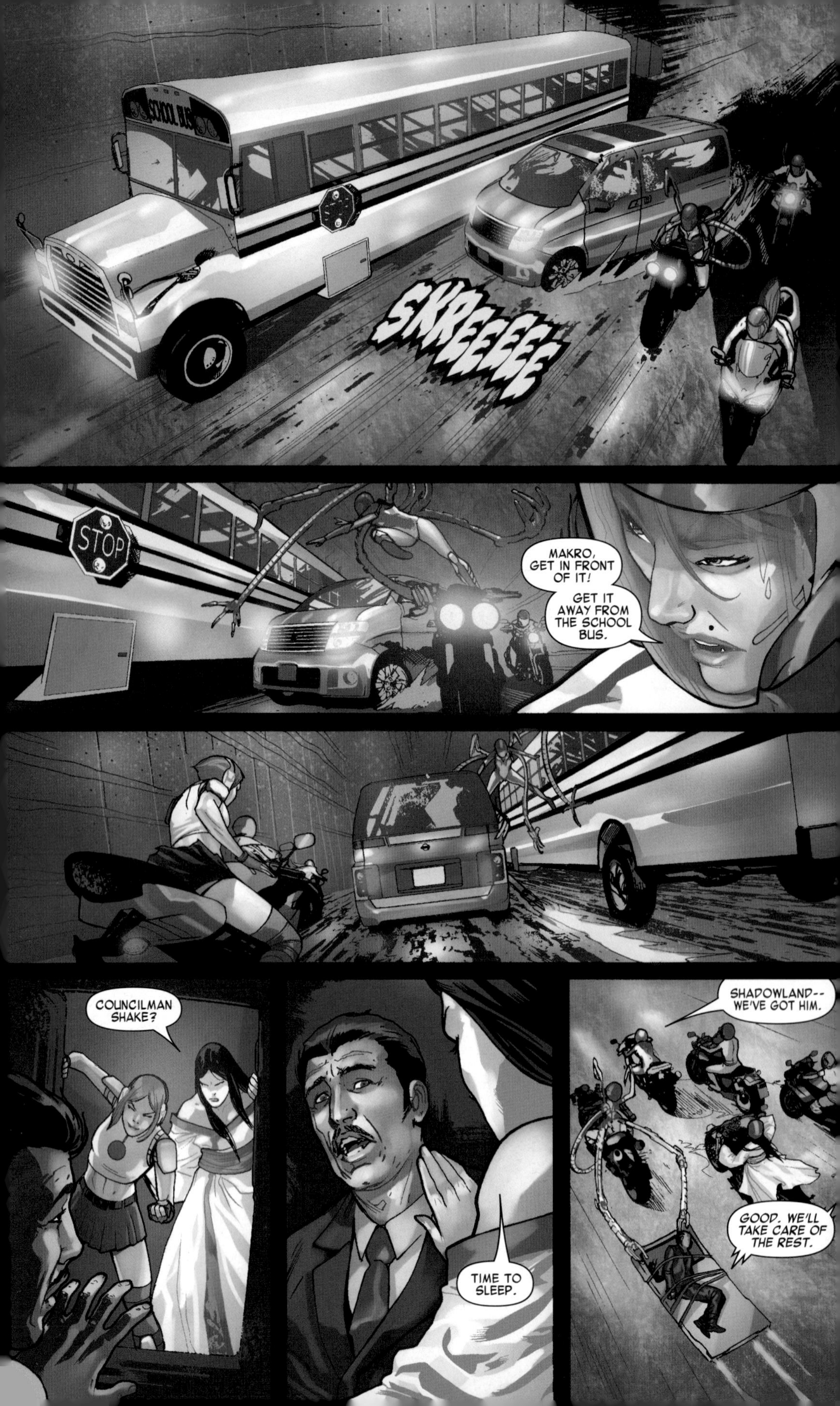
SKREEEEEE
STOP
MAKRO, GET IN FRONT OF IT!
GET IT AWAY FROM THE SCHOOL BUS.
COUNCILMAN SHAKE?
TIME TO SLEEP.
SHADOWLAND-- WE'VE GOT HIM.
GOOD. WE'LL TAKE CARE OF THE REST.

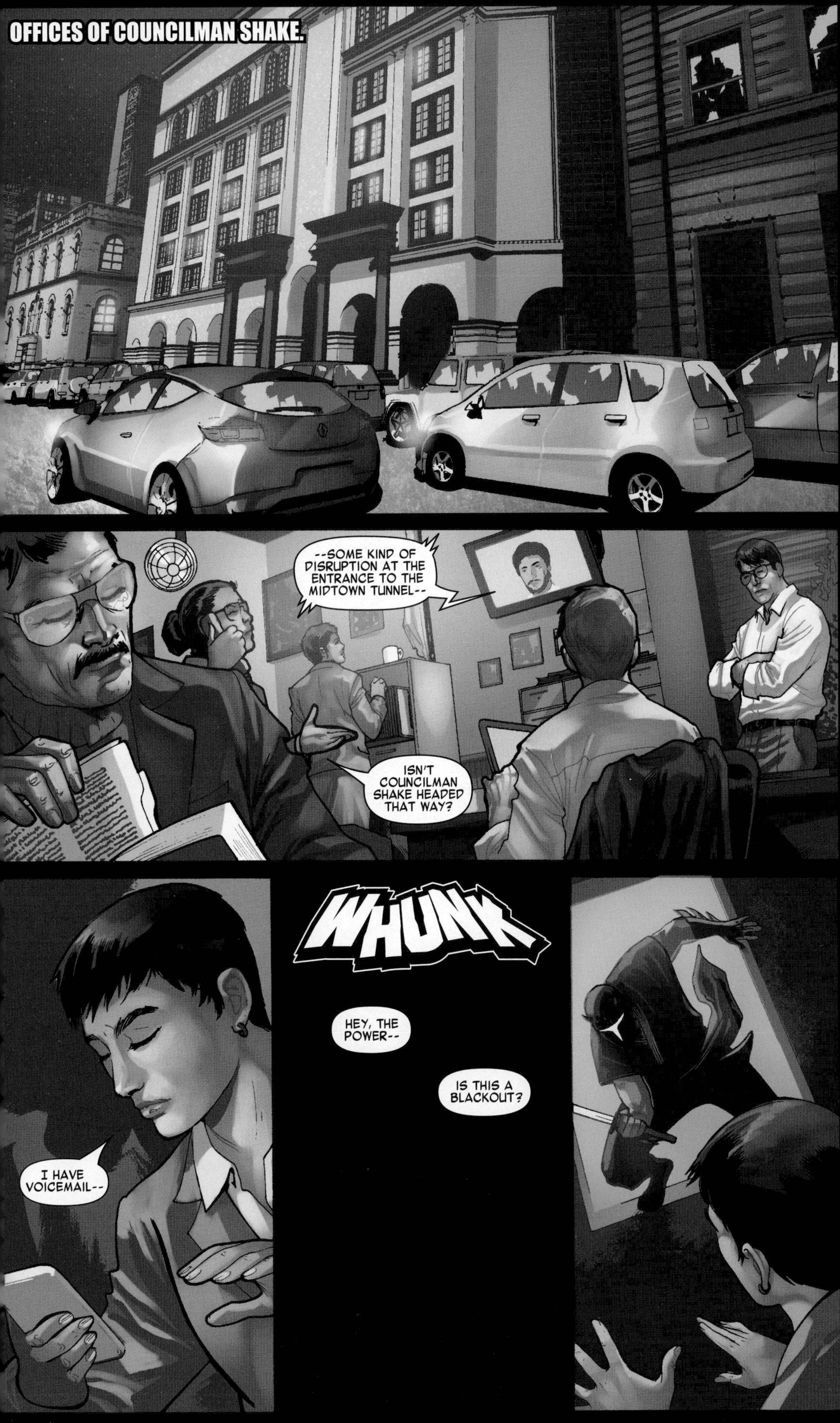

OFFICES OF COUNCILMAN SHAKE.
--SOME KIND OF DISRUPTION AT THE ENTRANCE TO THE MIDTOWN TUNNEL--
ISN'T COUNCILMAN SHAKE HEADED THAT WAY?
I HAVE VOICEMAIL--
WHUNK
HEY, THE POWER--
IS THIS A BLACKOUT?

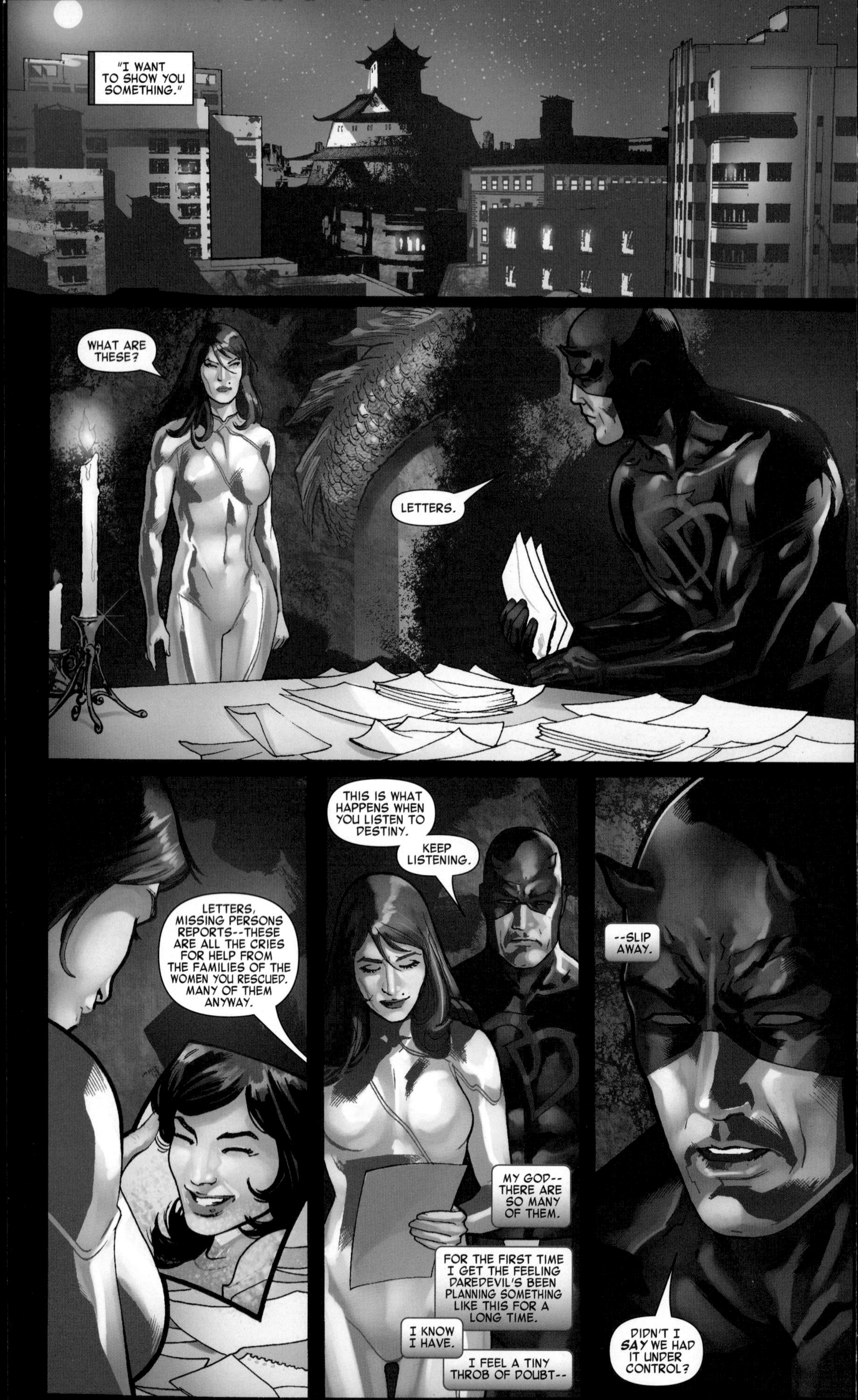
"I WANT TO SHOW YOU SOMETHING."
WHAT ARE THESE?
LETTERS.
LETTERS, MISSING PERSONS REPORTS--THESE ARE ALL THE CRIES FOR HELP FROM THE FAMILIES OF THE WOMEN YOU RESCUED. MANY OF THEM ANYWAY.
THIS IS WHAT HAPPENS WHEN YOU LISTEN TO DESTINY.
KEEP LISTENING.
MY GOD-- THERE ARE SO MANY OF THEM.
FOR THE FIRST TIME I GET THE FEELING DAREDEVIL'S BEEN PLANNING SOMETHING LIKE THIS FOR A LONG TIME.
I KNOW I HAVE.
I FEEL A TINY THROB OF DOUBT--
--SLIP AWAY.
DIDN'T I SAY WE HAD IT UNDER CONTROL?

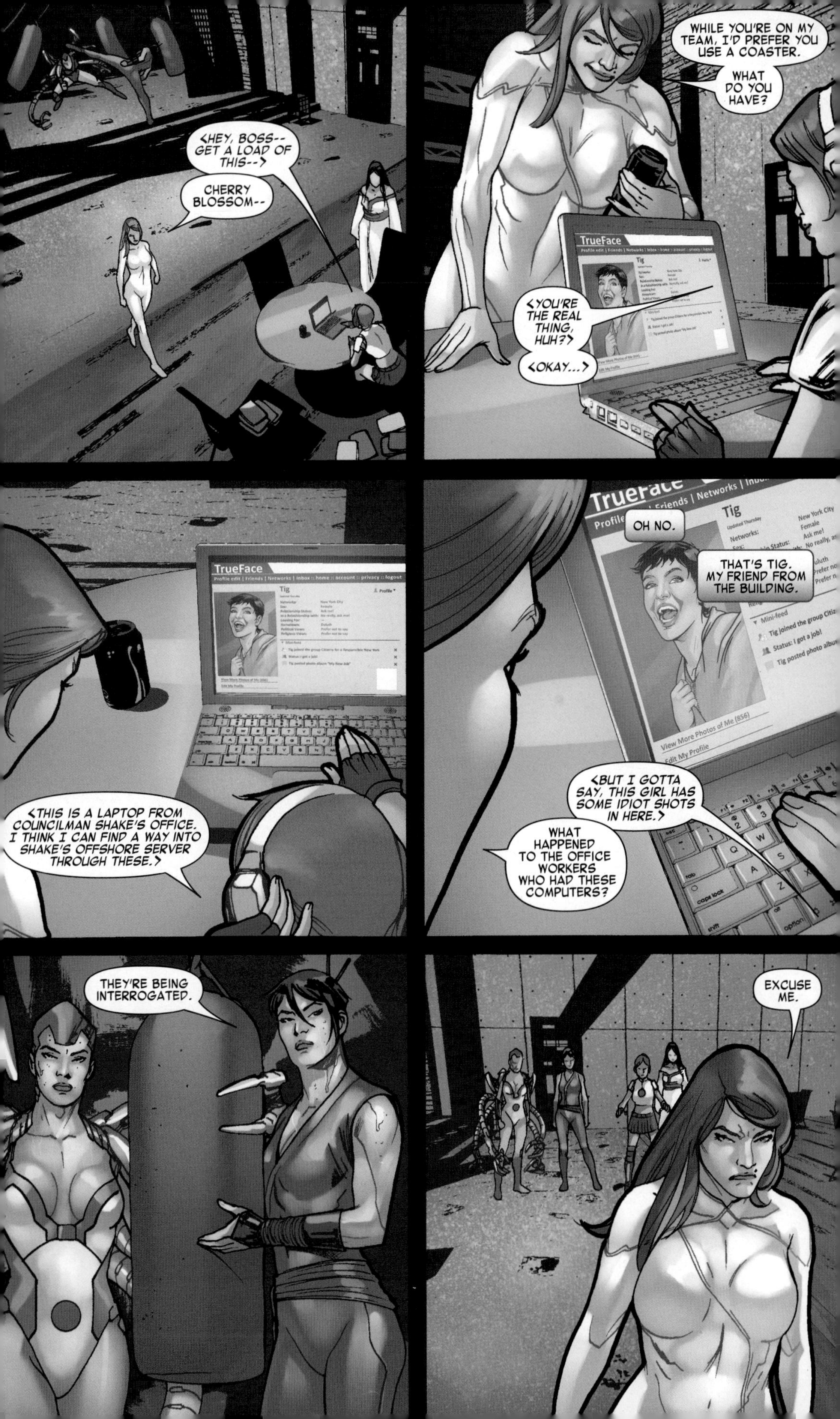

CHERRY BLOSSOM--
<HEY, BOSS-- GET A LOAD OF THIS-->
WHILE YOU'RE ON MY TEAM, I'D PREFER YOU USE A COASTER.
WHAT DO YOU HAVE?
TrueFace
<YOU'RE THE REAL THING, HUH?>
<OKAY...>
TrueFace
Tig
<THIS IS A LAPTOP FROM COUNCILMAN SHAKE'S OFFICE. I THINK I CAN FIND A WAY INTO SHAKE'S OFFSHORE SERVER THROUGH THESE.>
TrueFace
Tig
OH NO.
THAT'S TIG. MY FRIEND FROM THE BUILDING.
Mini-feed
Status: I got a job!
View More Photos of Me (856)
Edit My Profile
<BUT I GOTTA SAY, THIS GIRL HAS SOME IDIOT SHOTS IN HERE.>
WHAT HAPPENED TO THE OFFICE WORKERS WHO HAD THESE COMPUTERS?
THEY'RE BEING INTERROGATED.
EXCUSE ME.

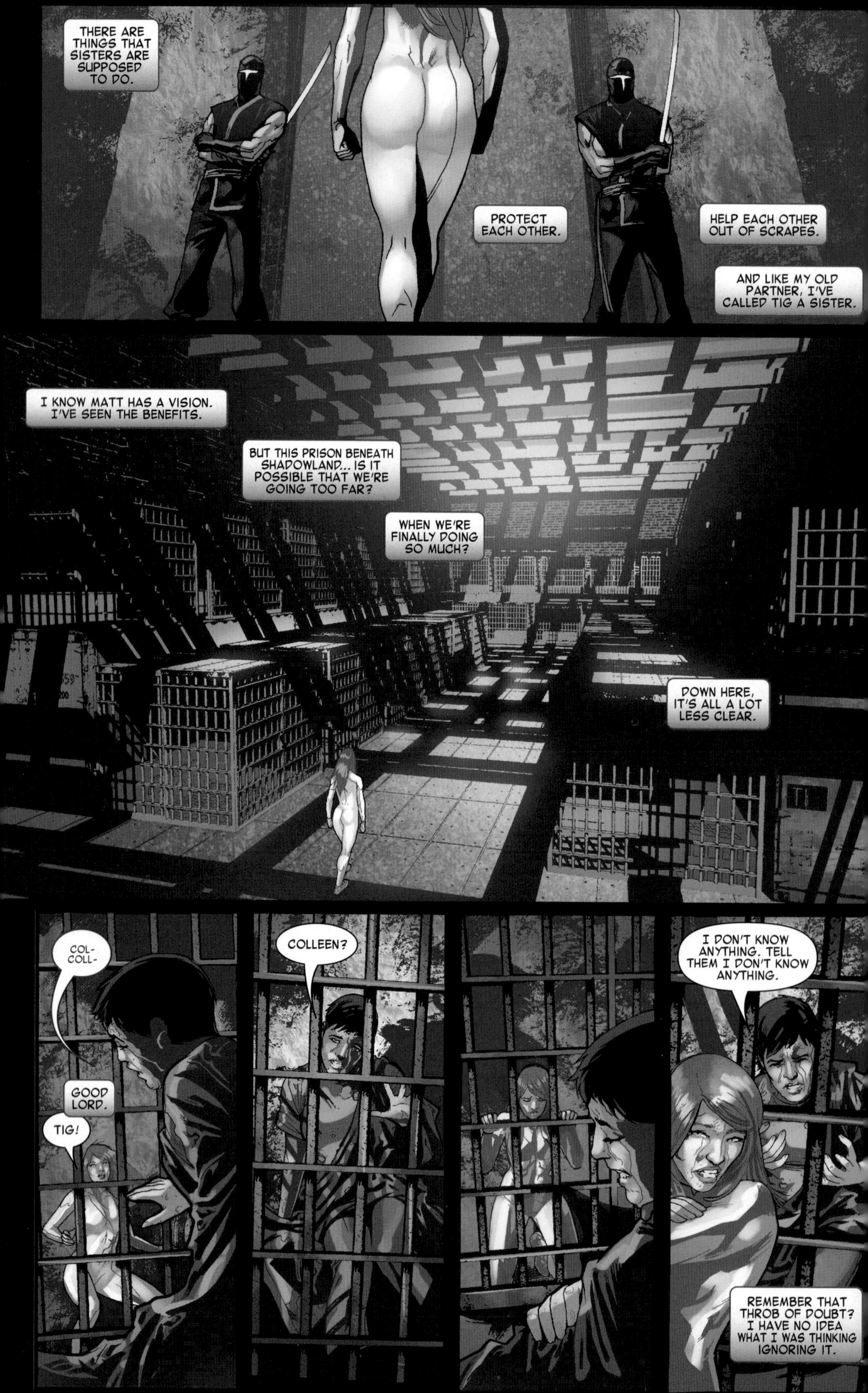
THERE ARE THINGS THAT SISTERS ARE SUPPOSED TO DO.
PROTECT EACH OTHER.
HELP EACH OTHER OUT OF SCRAPES.
AND LIKE MY OLD PARTNER, I'VE CALLED TIG A SISTER.
I KNOW MATT HAS A VISION. I'VE SEEN THE BENEFITS.
BUT THIS PRISON BENEATH SHADOWLAND... IS IT POSSIBLE THAT WE'RE GOING TOO FAR?
WHEN WE'RE FINALLY DOING SO MUCH?
DOWN HERE, IT'S ALL A LOT LESS CLEAR.
COL- COLL-
GOOD LORD.
TIG!
COLLEEN?
I DON'T KNOW ANYTHING. TELL THEM I DON'T KNOW ANYTHING.
REMEMBER THAT THROB OF DOUBT? I HAVE NO IDEA WHAT I WAS THINKING IGNORING IT.

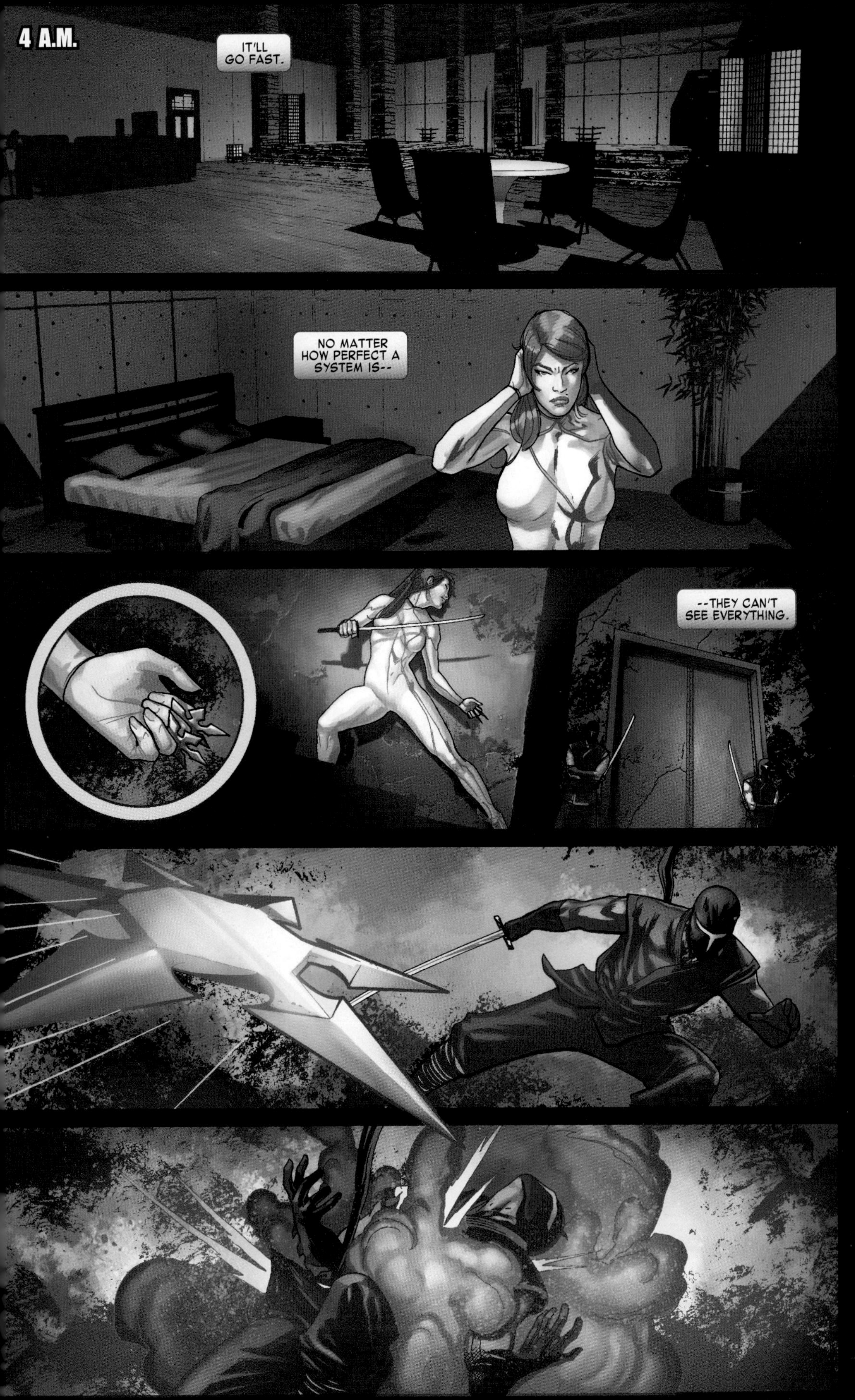
4 A.M.
IT'LL GO FAST.
NO MATTER HOW PERFECT A SYSTEM IS--
--THEY CAN'T SEE EVERYTHING.

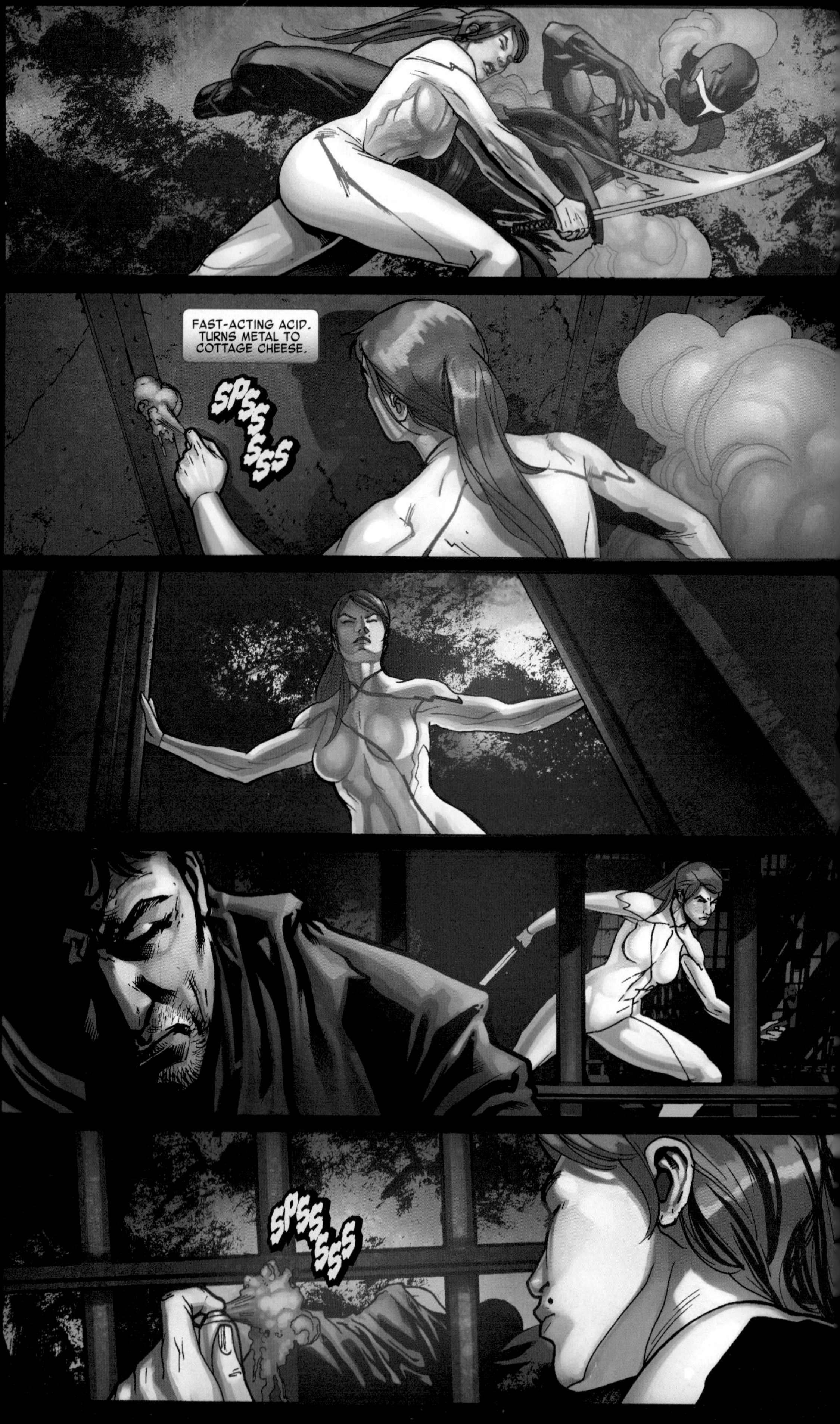
FAST-ACTING ACID. TURNS METAL TO COTTAGE CHEESE.
SPSSSSS
SPSSSSS

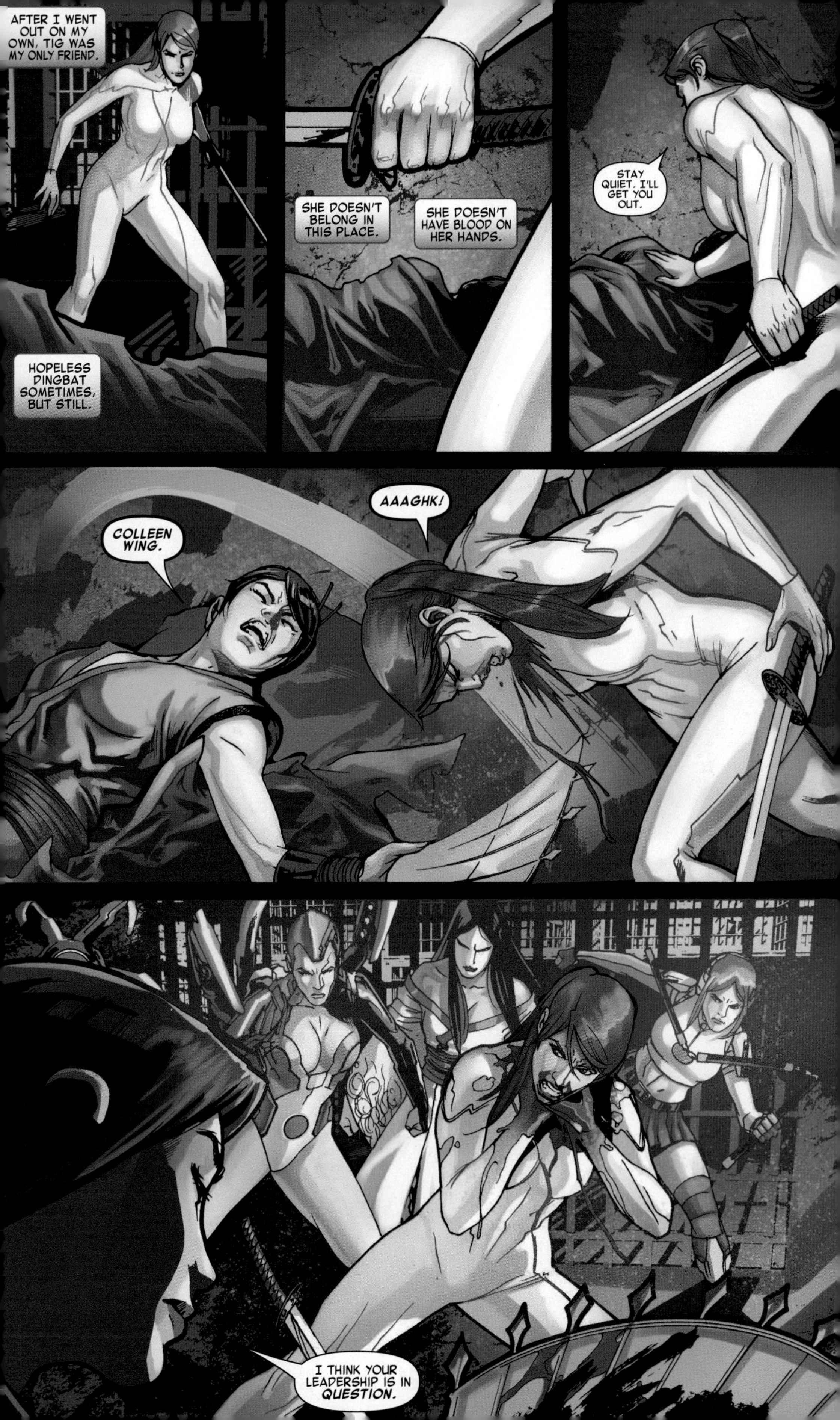
AFTER I WENT OUT ON MY OWN, TIG WAS MY ONLY FRIEND.
HOPELESS DINGBAT SOMETIMES, BUT STILL.
SHE DOESN'T BELONG IN THIS PLACE.
SHE DOESN'T HAVE BLOOD ON HER HANDS.
STAY QUIET. I'LL GET YOU OUT.
COLLEEN WING.
AAAGHK!
I THINK YOUR LEADERSHIP IS IN QUESTION.

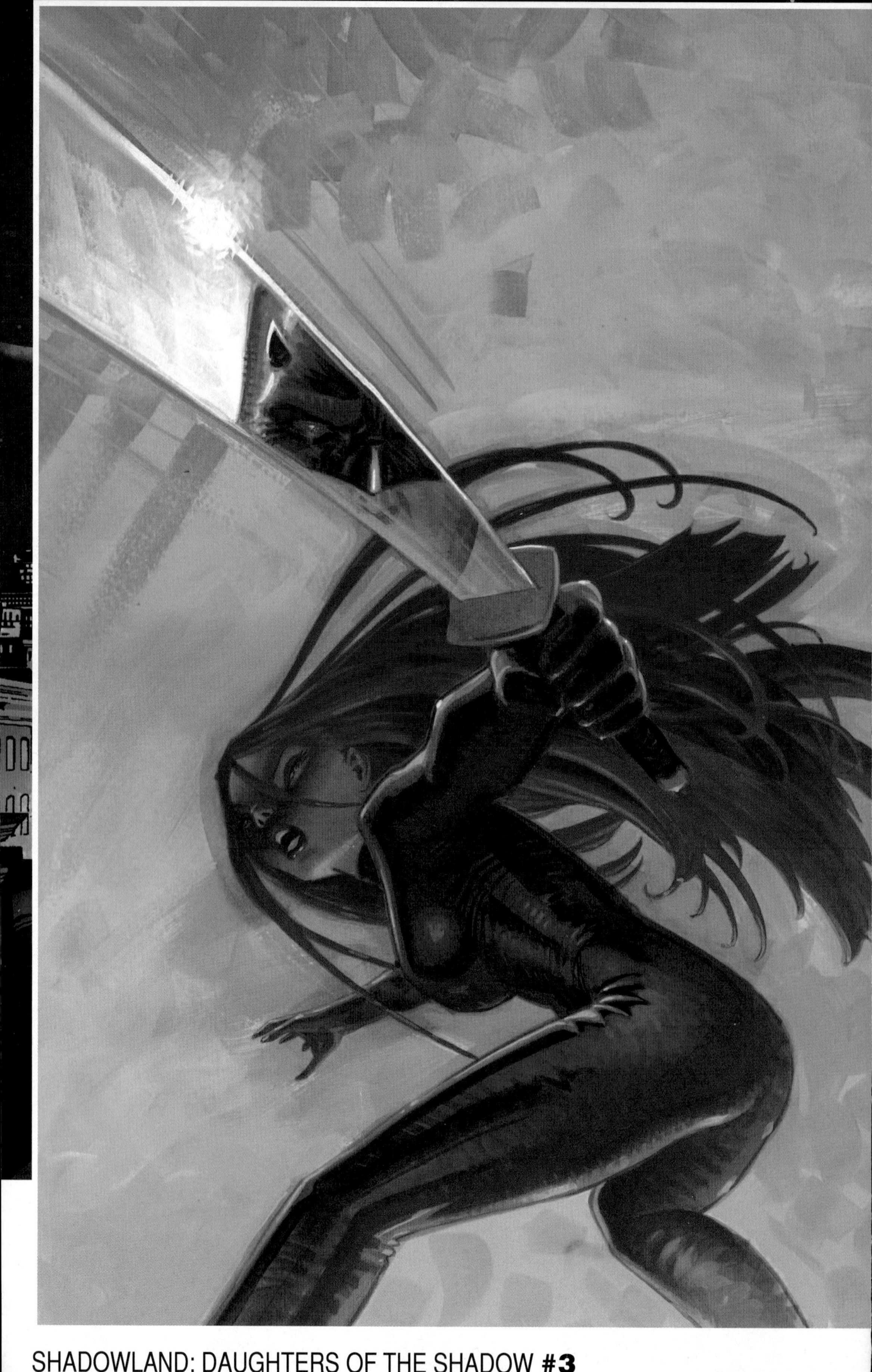

SHADOWLAND: DAUGHTERS OF THE SHADOW **#3**

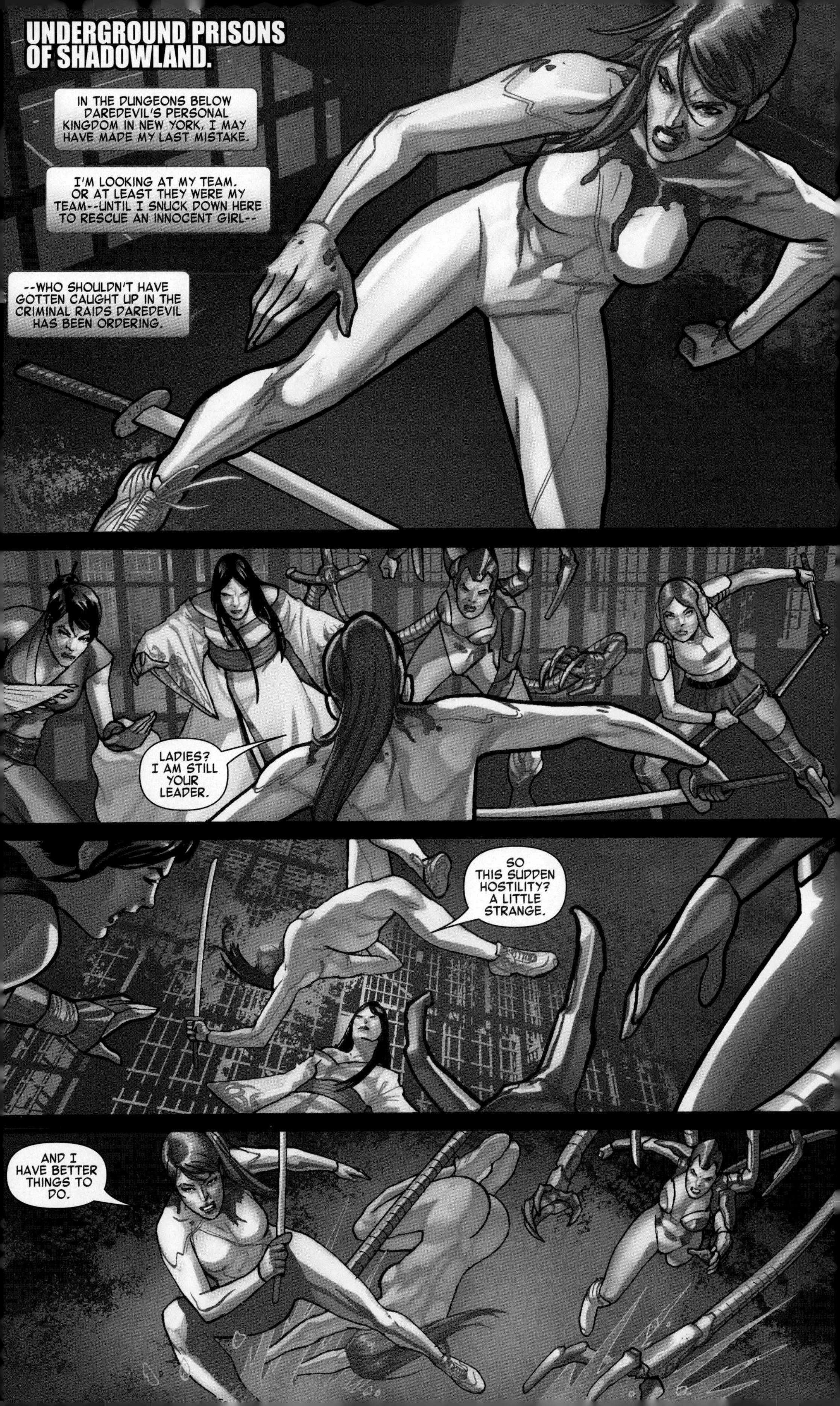
UNDERGROUND PRISONS OF SHADOWLAND.
IN THE DUNGEONS BELOW DAREDEVIL'S PERSONAL KINGDOM IN NEW YORK, I MAY HAVE MADE MY LAST MISTAKE.
I'M LOOKING AT MY TEAM. OR AT LEAST THEY WERE MY TEAM--UNTIL I SNUCK DOWN HERE TO RESCUE AN INNOCENT GIRL--
--WHO SHOULDN'T HAVE GOTTEN CAUGHT UP IN THE CRIMINAL RAIDS DAREDEVIL HAS BEEN ORDERING.
LADIES? I AM STILL YOUR LEADER.
SO THIS SUDDEN HOSTILITY? A LITTLE STRANGE.
AND I HAVE BETTER THINGS TO DO.

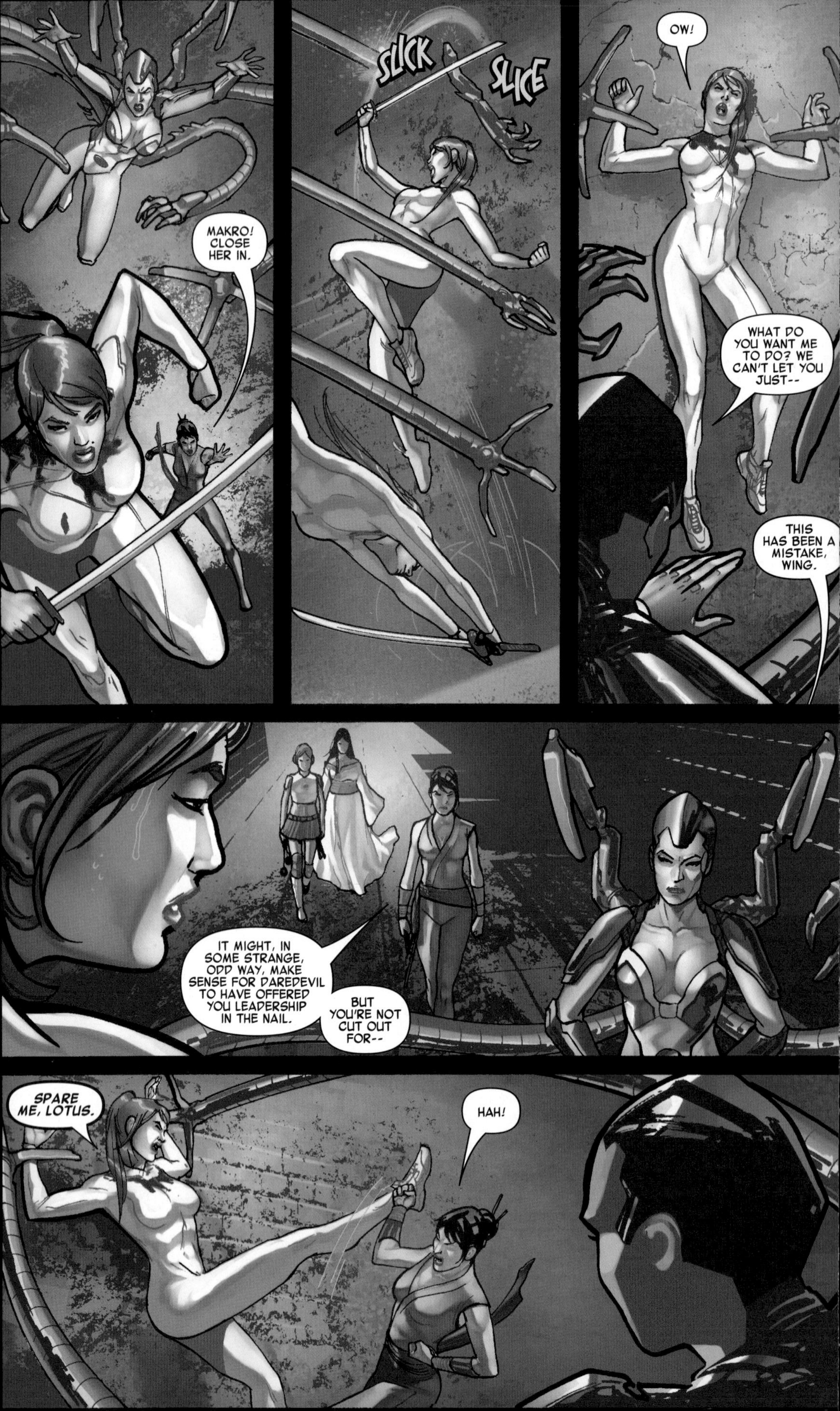
MAKRO! CLOSE HER IN.
SLICK
SLICE
OW!
WHAT DO YOU WANT ME TO DO? WE CAN'T LET YOU JUST--
THIS HAS BEEN A MISTAKE, WING.
IT MIGHT, IN SOME STRANGE, ODD WAY, MAKE SENSE FOR DAREDEVIL TO HAVE OFFERED YOU LEADERSHIP IN THE NAIL.
BUT YOU'RE NOT CUT OUT FOR--
SPARE ME, LOTUS.
HAH!

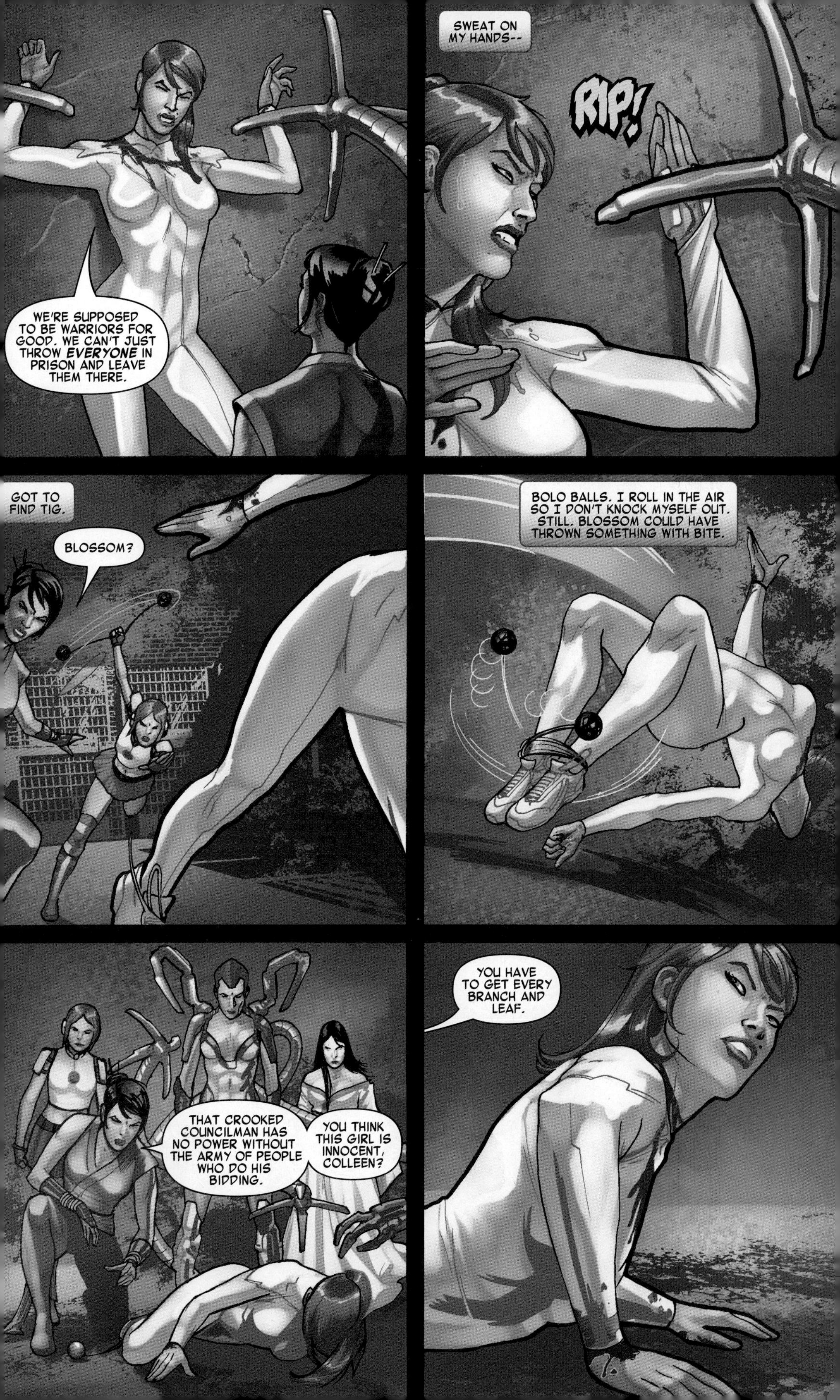

WE'RE SUPPOSED TO BE WARRIORS FOR GOOD. WE CAN'T JUST THROW *EVERYONE* IN PRISON AND LEAVE THEM THERE.
SWEAT ON MY HANDS--
RIP!
GOT TO FIND TIG.
BLOSSOM?
BOLO BALLS. I ROLL IN THE AIR SO I DON'T KNOCK MYSELF OUT. STILL. BLOSSOM COULD HAVE THROWN SOMETHING WITH BITE.
THAT CROOKED COUNCILMAN HAS NO POWER WITHOUT THE ARMY OF PEOPLE WHO DO HIS BIDDING.
YOU THINK THIS GIRL IS INNOCENT, COLLEEN?
YOU HAVE TO GET EVERY BRANCH AND LEAF.

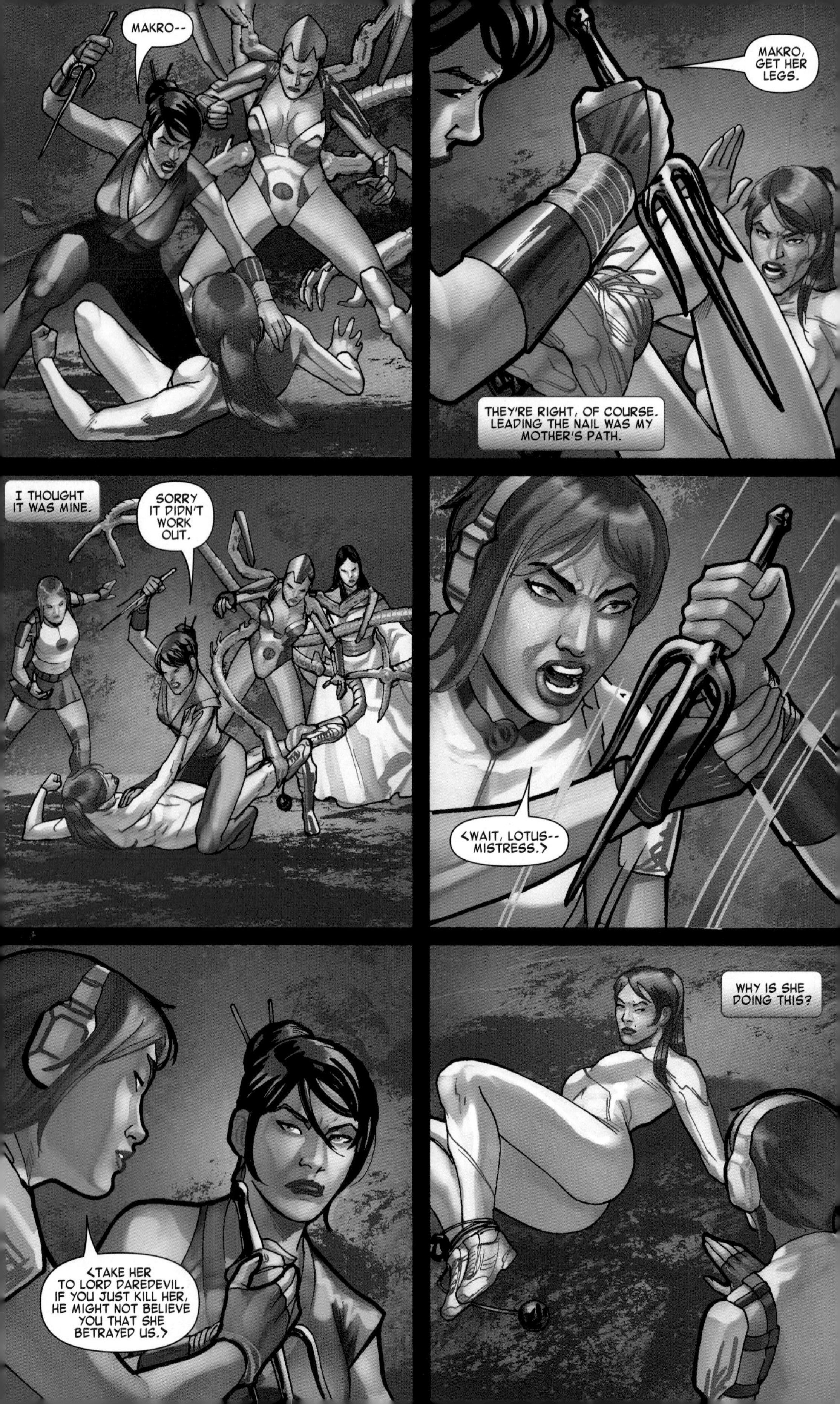
MAKRO--
MAKRO, GET HER LEGS.
THEY'RE RIGHT, OF COURSE. LEADING THE NAIL WAS MY MOTHER'S PATH.
I THOUGHT IT WAS MINE.
SORRY IT DIDN'T WORK OUT.
<WAIT, LOTUS-- MISTRESS.>
<TAKE HER TO LORD DAREDEVIL. IF YOU JUST KILL HER, HE MIGHT NOT BELIEVE YOU THAT SHE BETRAYED US.>
WHY IS SHE DOING THIS?

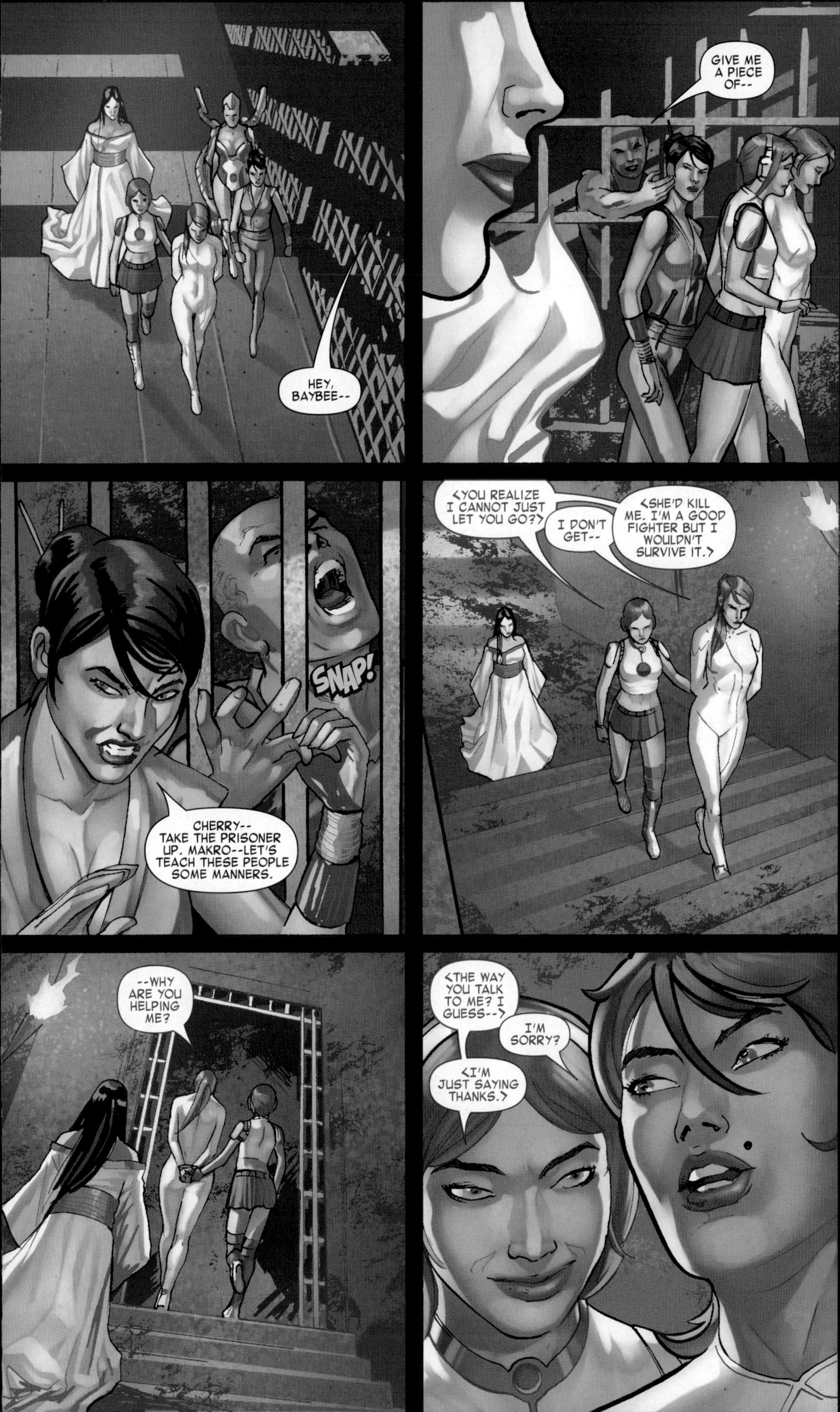
HEY, BAYBEE--
GIVE ME A PIECE OF--
SNAP!
CHERRY-- TAKE THE PRISONER UP. MAKRO--LET'S TEACH THESE PEOPLE SOME MANNERS.
<YOU REALIZE I CANNOT JUST LET YOU GO?>
I DON'T GET--
<SHE'D KILL ME. I'M A GOOD FIGHTER BUT I WOULDN'T SURVIVE IT.>
--WHY ARE YOU HELPING ME?
<THE WAY YOU TALK TO ME? I GUESS-->
I'M SORRY?
<I'M JUST SAYING THANKS.>

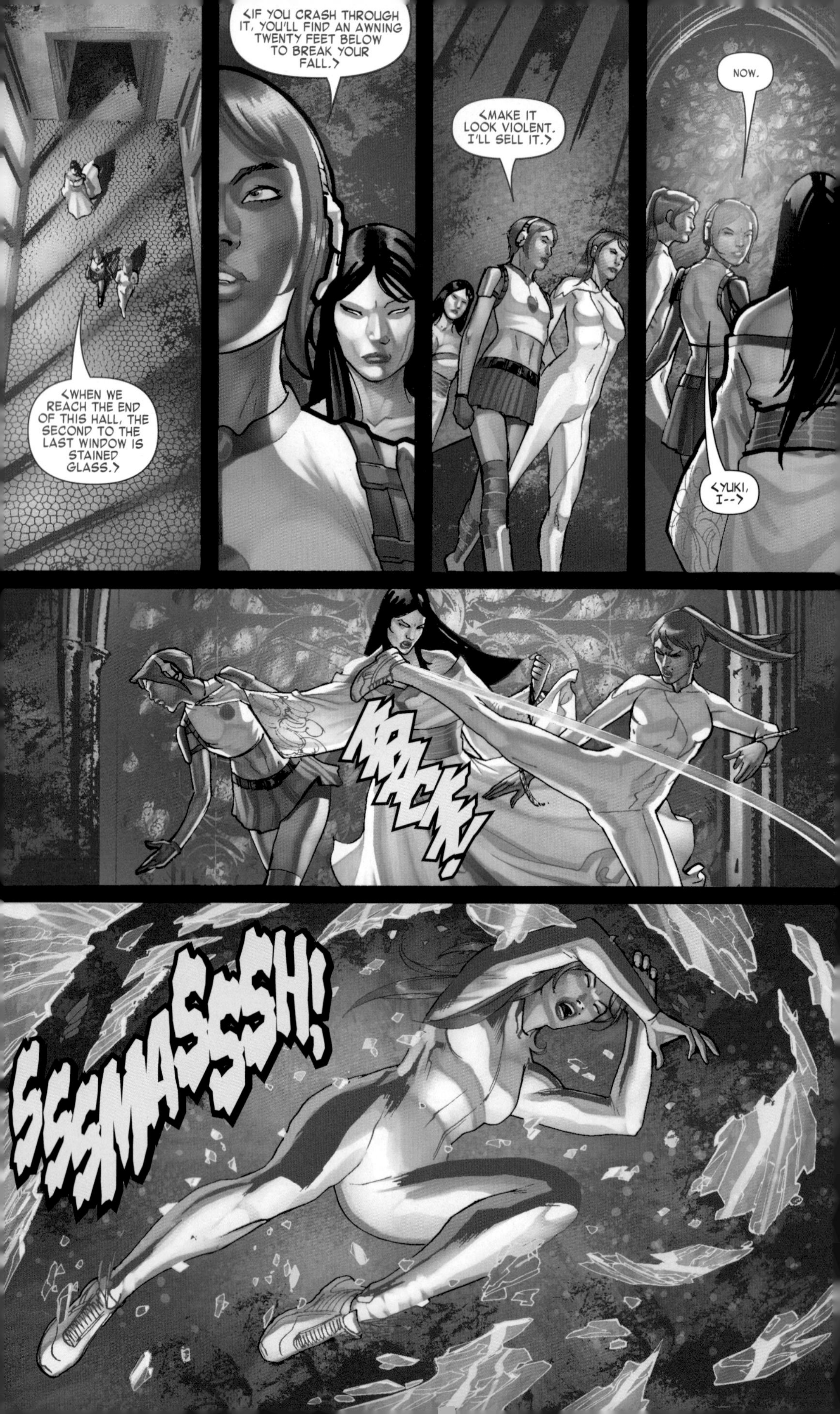

<WHEN WE REACH THE END OF THIS HALL, THE SECOND TO THE LAST WINDOW IS STAINED GLASS.>
<IF YOU CRASH THROUGH IT, YOU'LL FIND AN AWNING TWENTY FEET BELOW TO BREAK YOUR FALL.>
<MAKE IT LOOK VIOLENT. I'LL SELL IT.>
NOW.
<YUKI, I-->
KRACK!
SSSMASSSH!

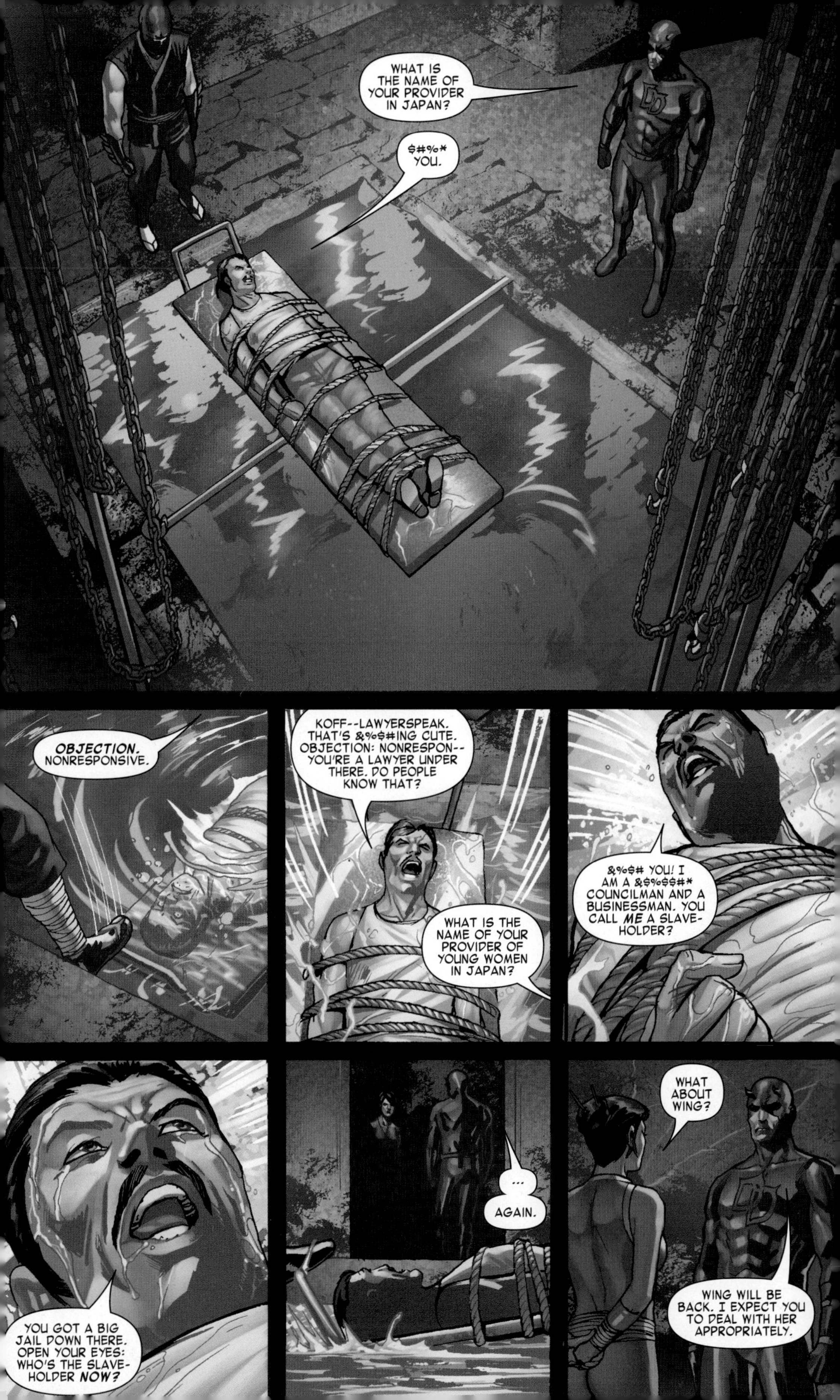
WHAT IS THE NAME OF YOUR PROVIDER IN JAPAN?
$#%* YOU.
OBJECTION. NONRESPONSIVE.
KOFF--LAWYERSPEAK. THAT'S &%$#ING CUTE. OBJECTION: NONRESPON-- YOU'RE A LAWYER UNDER THERE. DO PEOPLE KNOW THAT?
WHAT IS THE NAME OF YOUR PROVIDER OF YOUNG WOMEN IN JAPAN?
&%$# YOU! I AM A &$%$$#* COUNCILMAN AND A BUSINESSMAN. YOU CALL ME A SLAVE-HOLDER?
YOU GOT A BIG JAIL DOWN THERE. OPEN YOUR EYES: WHO'S THE SLAVE-HOLDER NOW?
...
AGAIN.
WHAT ABOUT WING?
WING WILL BE BACK. I EXPECT YOU TO DEAL WITH HER APPROPRIATELY.

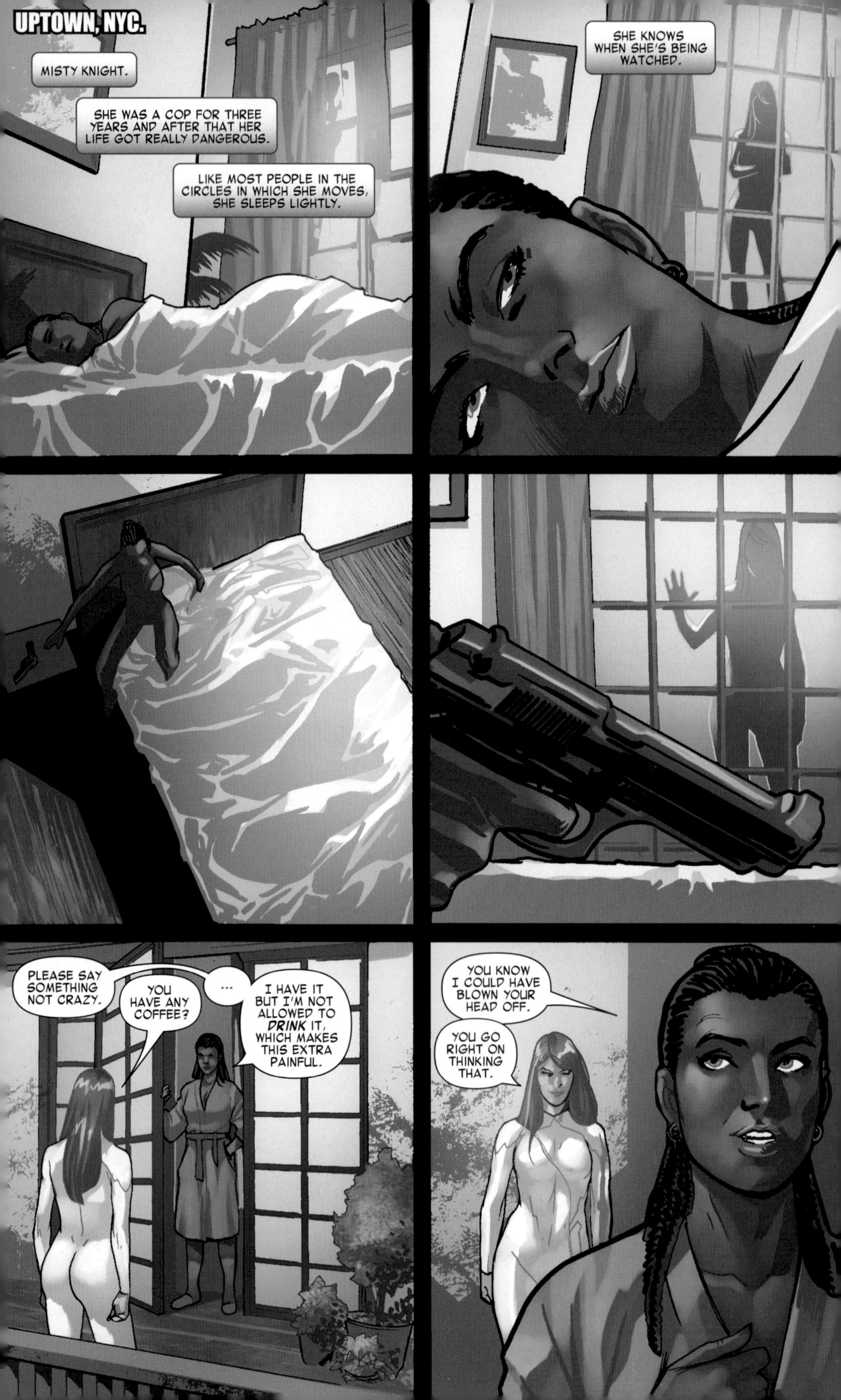

UPTOWN, NYC.
MISTY KNIGHT.
SHE WAS A COP FOR THREE YEARS AND AFTER THAT HER LIFE GOT REALLY DANGEROUS.
LIKE MOST PEOPLE IN THE CIRCLES IN WHICH SHE MOVES, SHE SLEEPS LIGHTLY.
SHE KNOWS WHEN SHE'S BEING WATCHED.
PLEASE SAY SOMETHING NOT CRAZY.
YOU HAVE ANY COFFEE?
...
I HAVE IT BUT I'M NOT ALLOWED TO DRINK IT, WHICH MAKES THIS EXTRA PAINFUL.
YOU KNOW I COULD HAVE BLOWN YOUR HEAD OFF.
YOU GO RIGHT ON THINKING THAT.

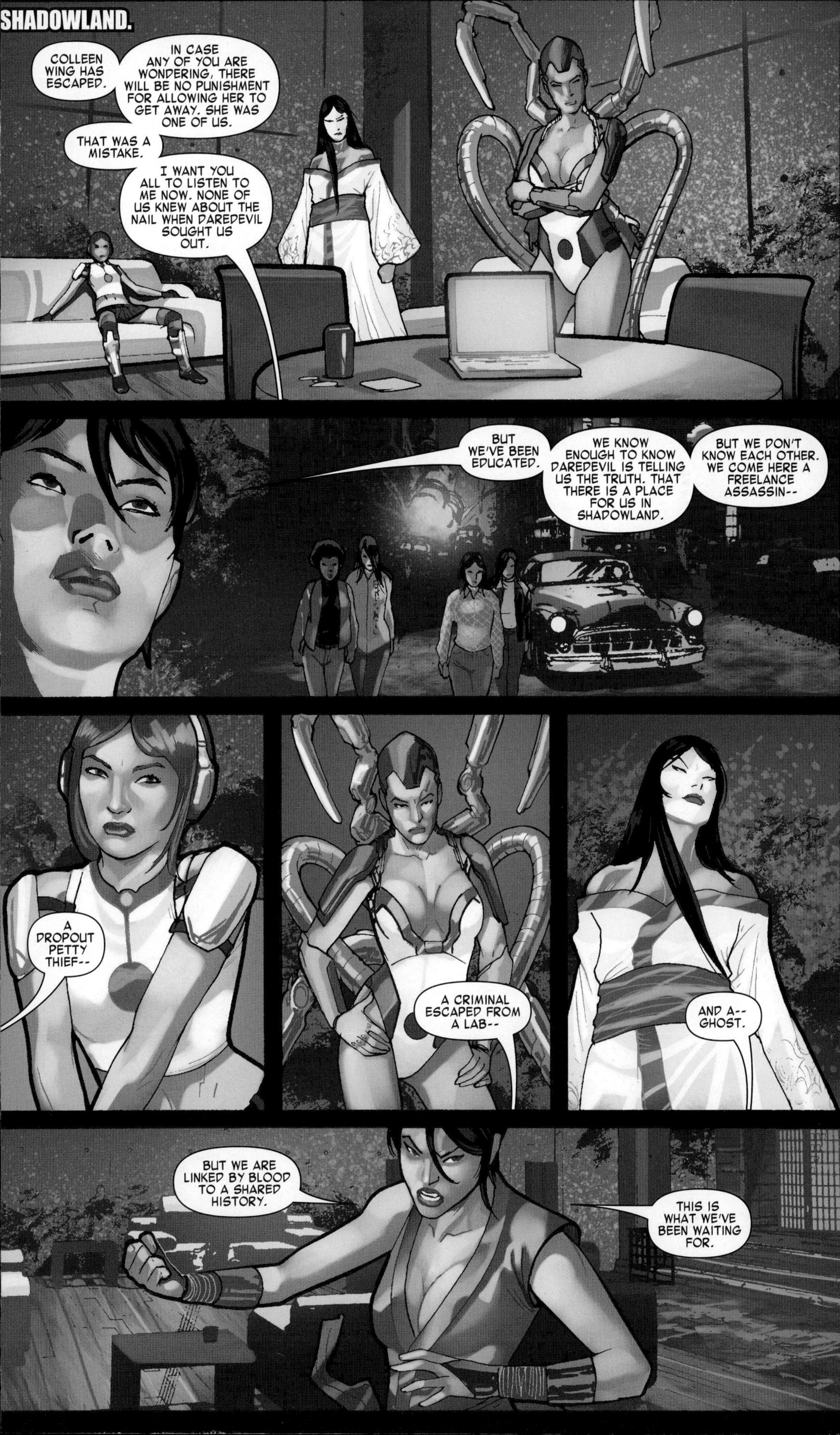
SHADOWLAND.
COLLEEN WING HAS ESCAPED.
IN CASE ANY OF YOU ARE WONDERING, THERE WILL BE NO PUNISHMENT FOR ALLOWING HER TO GET AWAY. SHE WAS ONE OF US.
THAT WAS A MISTAKE.
I WANT YOU ALL TO LISTEN TO ME NOW. NONE OF US KNEW ABOUT THE NAIL WHEN DAREDEVIL SOUGHT US OUT.
BUT WE'VE BEEN EDUCATED.
WE KNOW ENOUGH TO KNOW DAREDEVIL IS TELLING US THE TRUTH. THAT THERE IS A PLACE FOR US IN SHADOWLAND.
BUT WE DON'T KNOW EACH OTHER. WE COME HERE A FREELANCE ASSASSIN--
A DROPOUT PETTY THIEF--
A CRIMINAL ESCAPED FROM A LAB--
AND A-- GHOST.
BUT WE ARE LINKED BY BLOOD TO A SHARED HISTORY.
THIS IS WHAT WE'VE BEEN WAITING FOR.

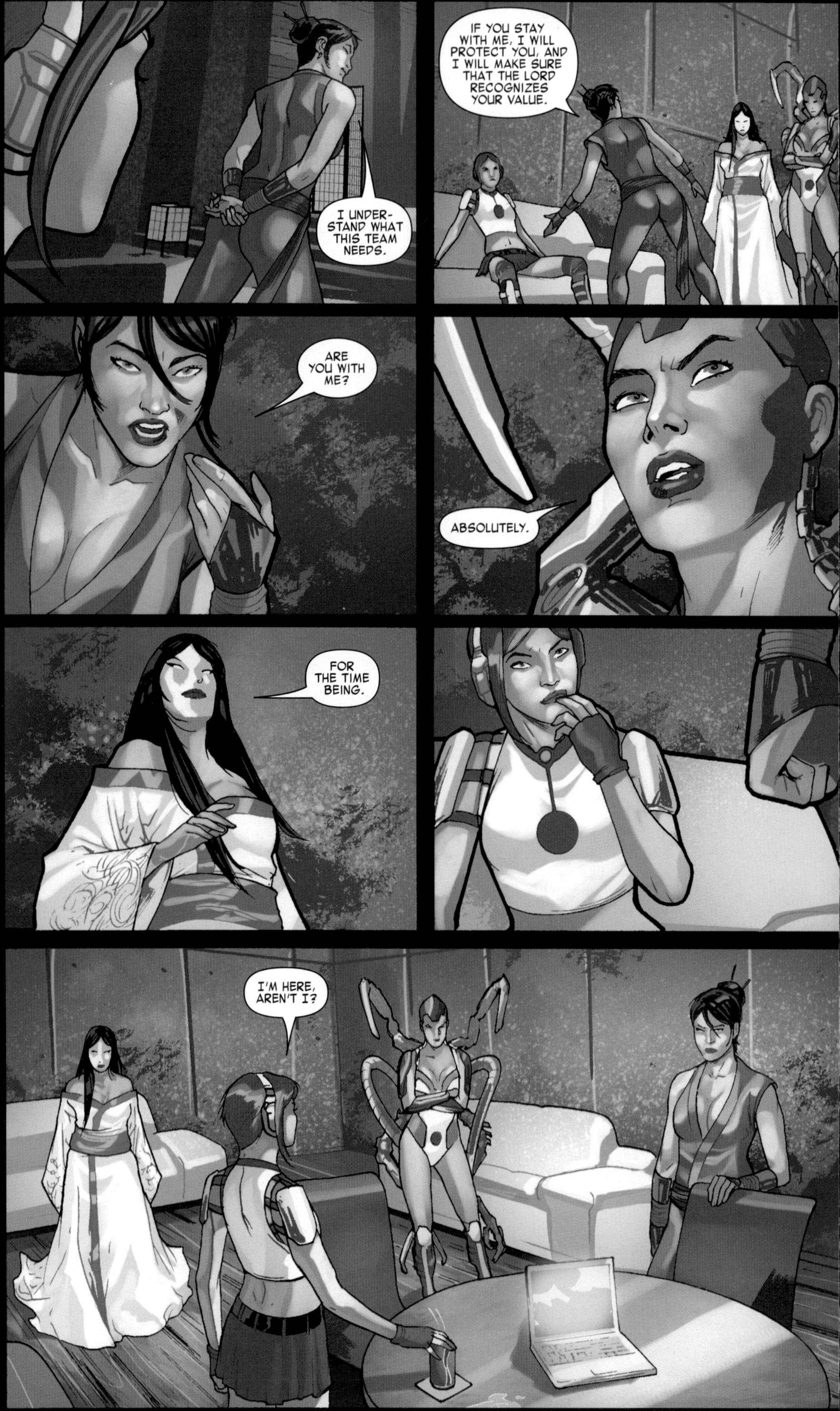
I UNDER-STAND WHAT THIS TEAM NEEDS.
IF YOU STAY WITH ME, I WILL PROTECT YOU, AND I WILL MAKE SURE THAT THE LORD RECOGNIZES YOUR VALUE.
ARE YOU WITH ME?
ABSOLUTELY.
FOR THE TIME BEING.
I'M HERE, AREN'T I?

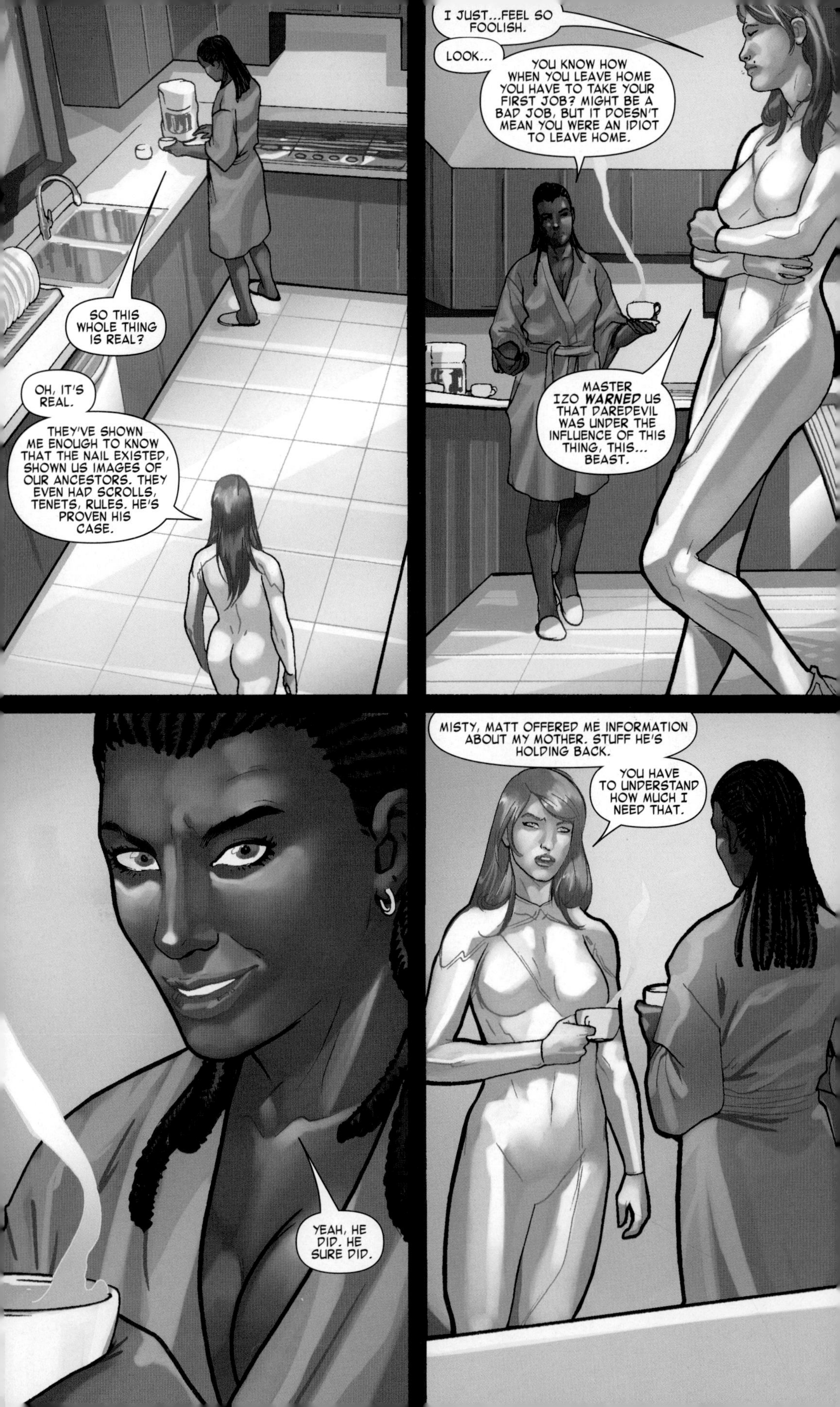
SO THIS WHOLE THING IS REAL?
OH, IT'S REAL.
THEY'VE SHOWN ME ENOUGH TO KNOW THAT THE NAIL EXISTED, SHOWN US IMAGES OF OUR ANCESTORS. THEY EVEN HAD SCROLLS, TENETS, RULES. HE'S PROVEN HIS CASE.
I JUST...FEEL SO FOOLISH.
LOOK...
YOU KNOW HOW WHEN YOU LEAVE HOME YOU HAVE TO TAKE YOUR FIRST JOB? MIGHT BE A BAD JOB, BUT IT DOESN'T MEAN YOU WERE AN IDIOT TO LEAVE HOME.
MASTER IZO WARNED US THAT DAREDEVIL WAS UNDER THE INFLUENCE OF THIS THING, THIS... BEAST.
YEAH, HE DID. HE SURE DID.
MISTY, MATT OFFERED ME INFORMATION ABOUT MY MOTHER. STUFF HE'S HOLDING BACK.
YOU HAVE TO UNDERSTAND HOW MUCH I NEED THAT.

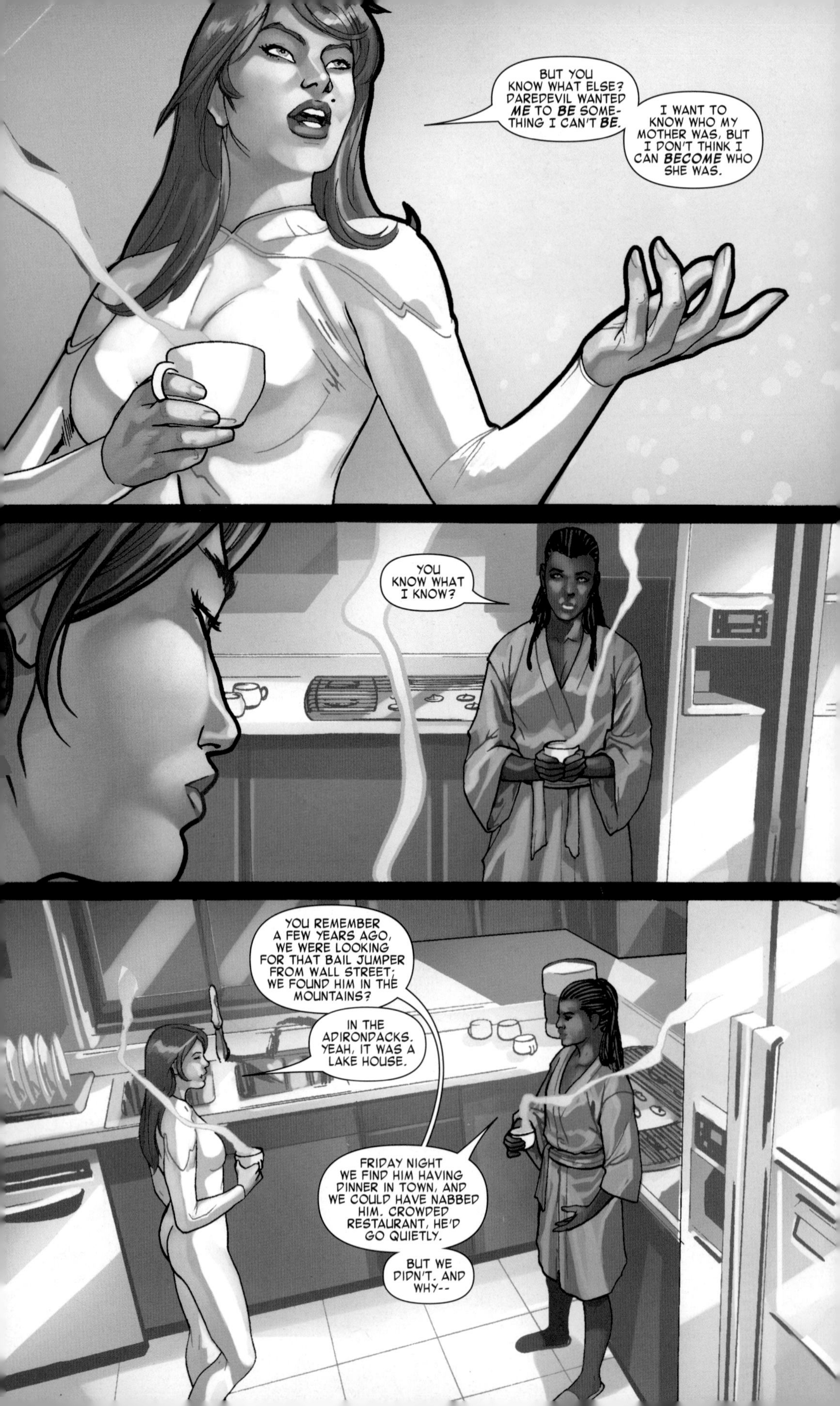

BUT YOU KNOW WHAT ELSE? DAREDEVIL WANTED ME TO BE SOME-THING I CAN'T BE.
I WANT TO KNOW WHO MY MOTHER WAS, BUT I DON'T THINK I CAN BECOME WHO SHE WAS.
YOU KNOW WHAT I KNOW?
YOU REMEMBER A FEW YEARS AGO, WE WERE LOOKING FOR THAT BAIL JUMPER FROM WALL STREET; WE FOUND HIM IN THE MOUNTAINS?
IN THE ADIRONDACKS. YEAH, IT WAS A LAKE HOUSE.
FRIDAY NIGHT WE FIND HIM HAVING DINNER IN TOWN, AND WE COULD HAVE NABBED HIM. CROWDED RESTAURANT, HE'D GO QUIETLY.
BUT WE DIDN'T. AND WHY--

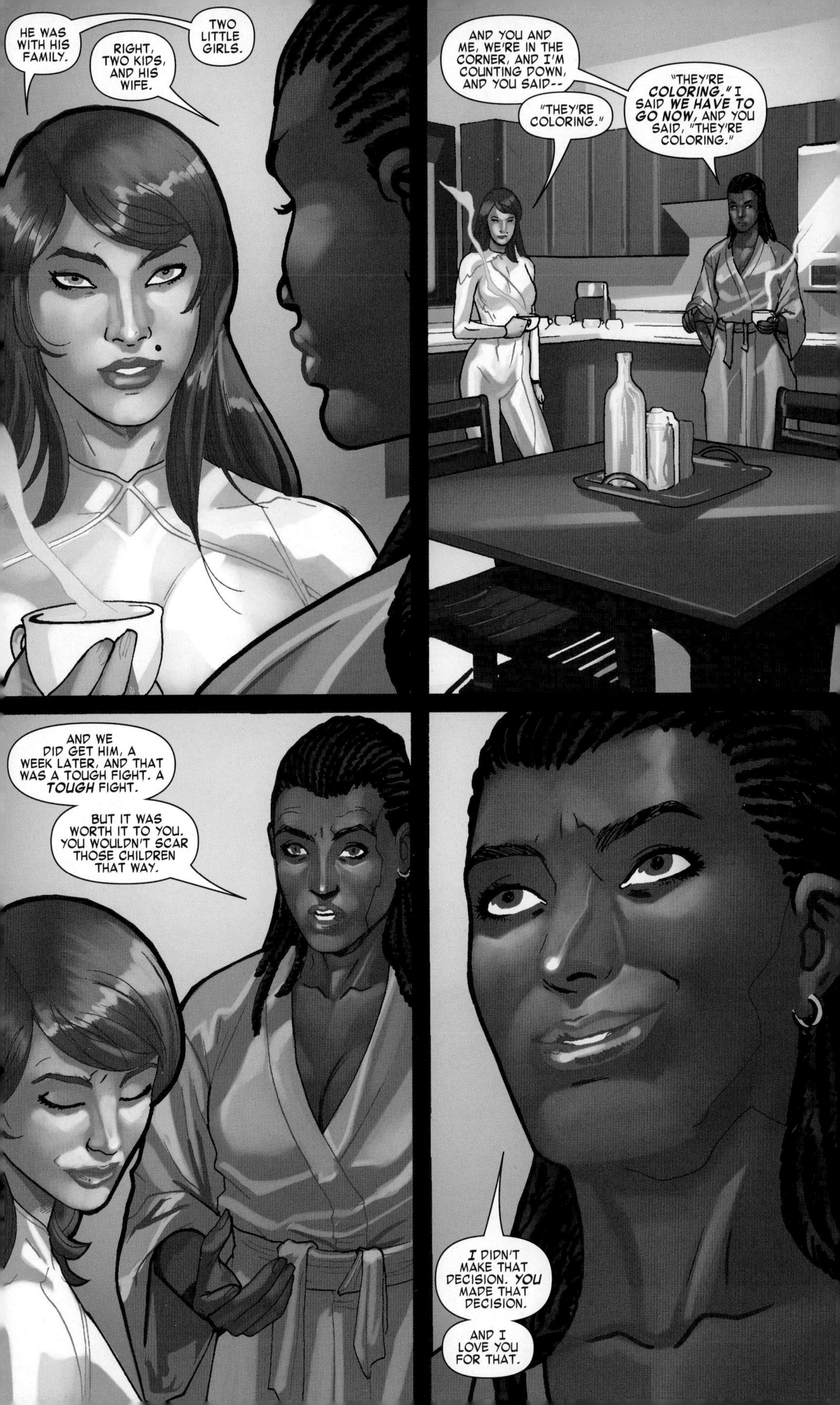
HE WAS WITH HIS FAMILY.
TWO LITTLE GIRLS.
RIGHT, TWO KIDS, AND HIS WIFE.
AND YOU AND ME, WE'RE IN THE CORNER, AND I'M COUNTING DOWN, AND YOU SAID--
"THEY'RE COLORING."
"THEY'RE COLORING." I SAID WE HAVE TO GO NOW, AND YOU SAID, "THEY'RE COLORING."
AND WE DID GET HIM, A WEEK LATER, AND THAT WAS A TOUGH FIGHT. A TOUGH FIGHT.
BUT IT WAS WORTH IT TO YOU. YOU WOULDN'T SCAR THOSE CHILDREN THAT WAY.
I DIDN'T MAKE THAT DECISION. YOU MADE THAT DECISION.
AND I LOVE YOU FOR THAT.

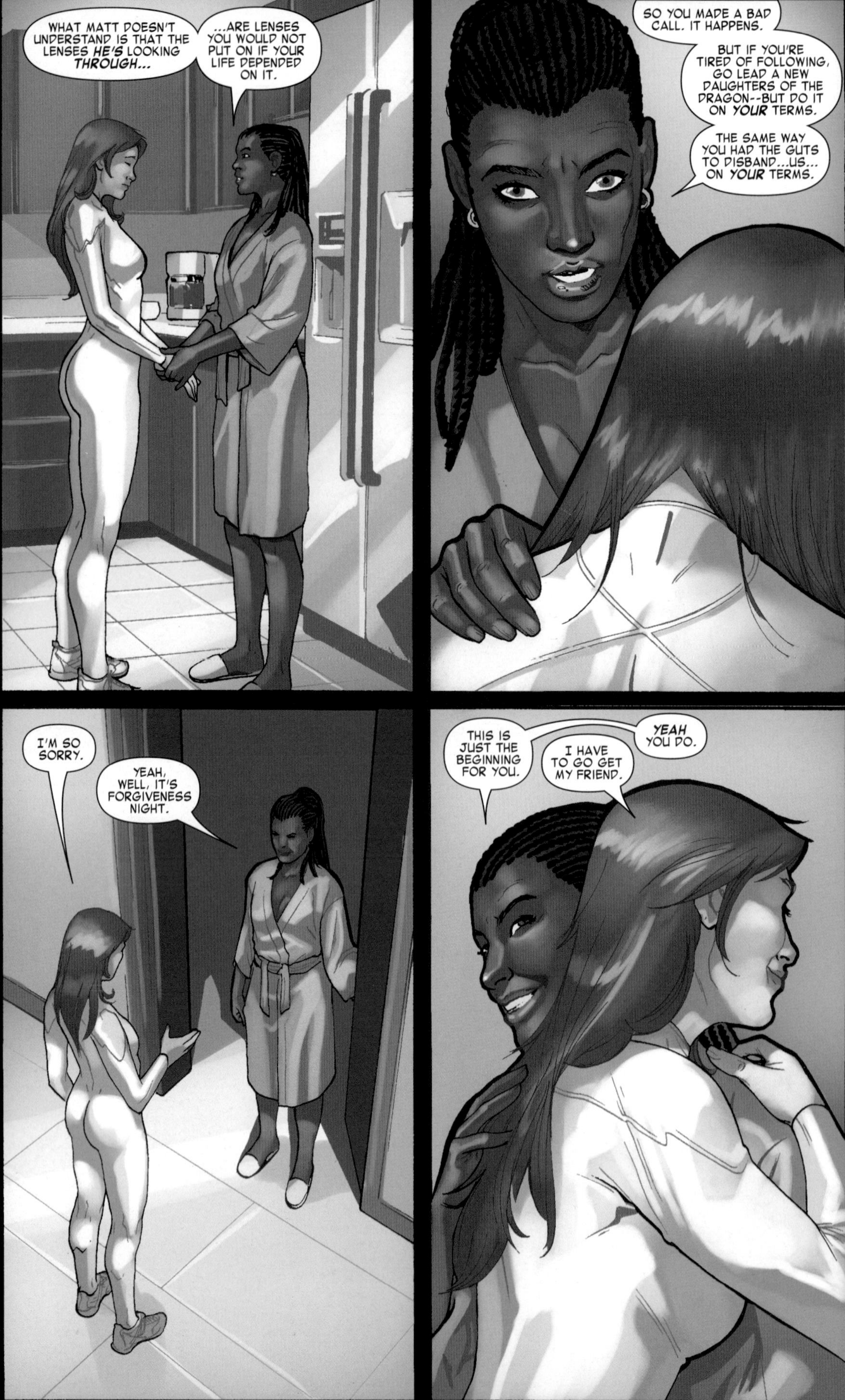
WHAT MATT DOESN'T UNDERSTAND IS THAT THE LENSES *HE'S* LOOKING *THROUGH...*
...ARE LENSES YOU WOULD NOT PUT ON IF YOUR LIFE DEPENDED ON IT.
SO YOU MADE A BAD CALL. IT HAPPENS.
BUT IF YOU'RE TIRED OF FOLLOWING, GO LEAD A NEW DAUGHTERS OF THE DRAGON--BUT DO IT ON *YOUR* TERMS.
THE SAME WAY YOU HAD THE GUTS TO DISBAND...US... ON *YOUR* TERMS.
I'M SO SORRY.
YEAH, WELL, IT'S FORGIVENESS NIGHT.
THIS IS JUST THE BEGINNING FOR YOU.
I HAVE TO GO GET MY FRIEND.
YEAH YOU DO.

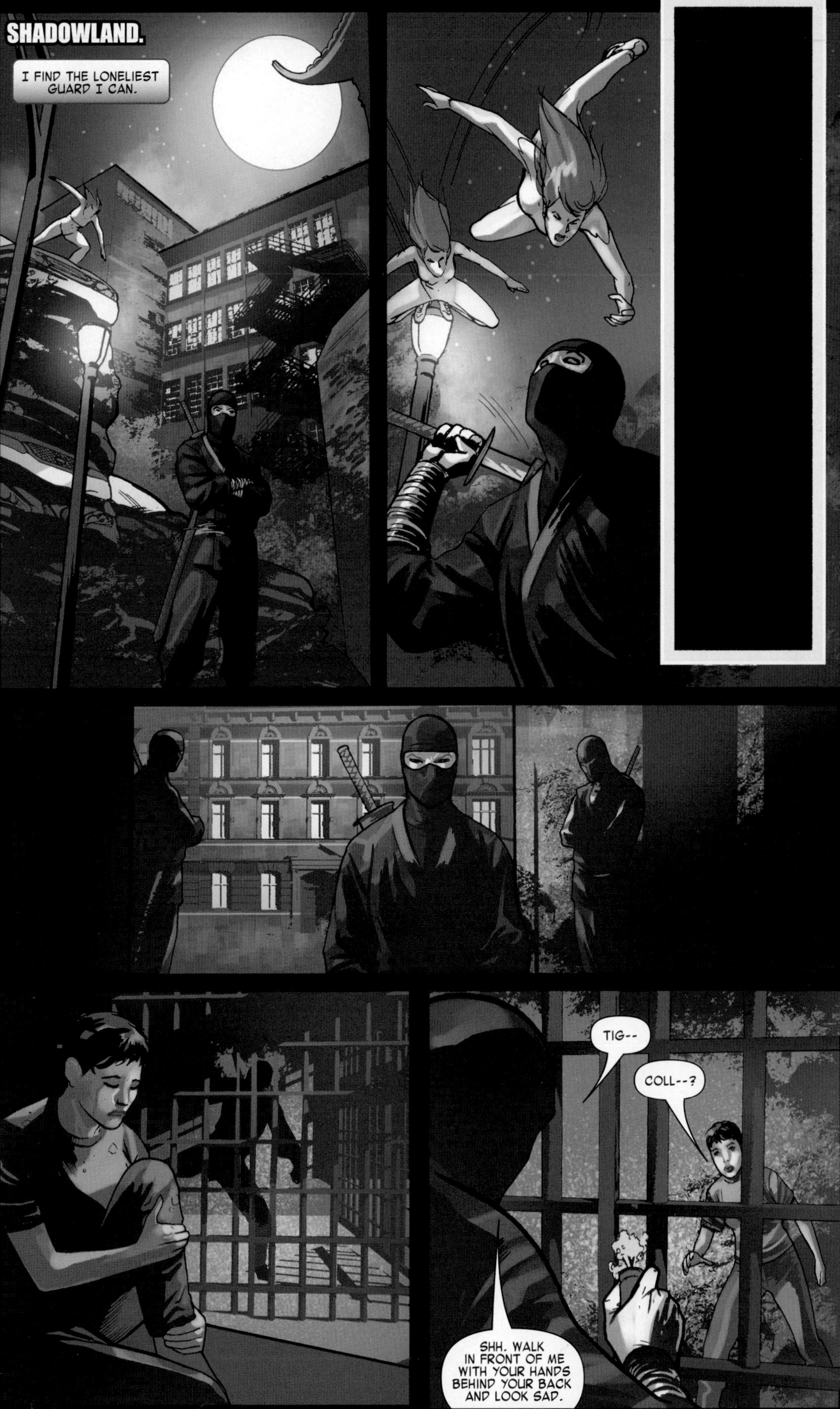
SHADOWLAND.
I FIND THE LONELIEST GUARD I CAN.
TIG--
COLL--?
SHH. WALK IN FRONT OF ME WITH YOUR HANDS BEHIND YOUR BACK AND LOOK SAD.

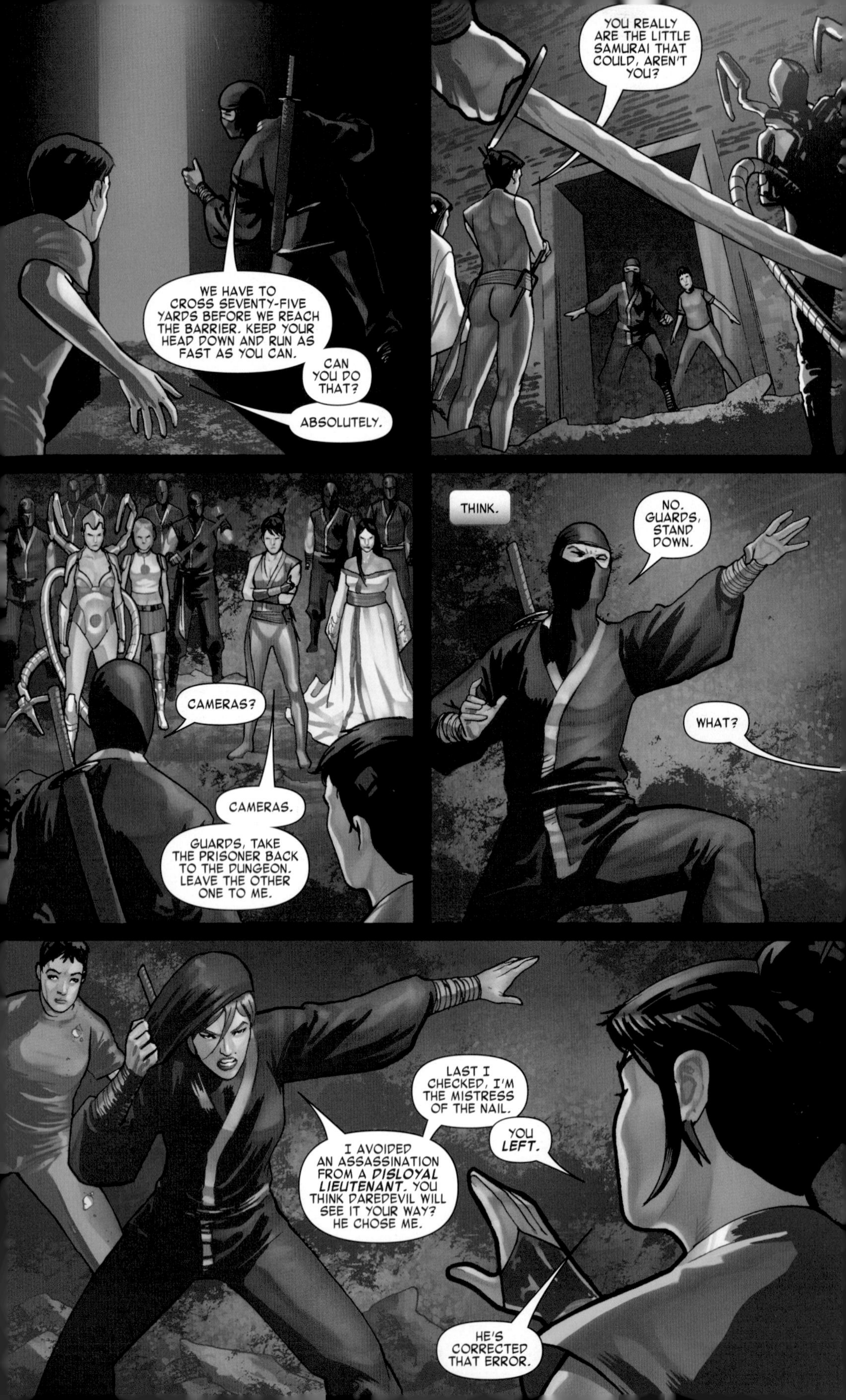
WE HAVE TO CROSS SEVENTY-FIVE YARDS BEFORE WE REACH THE BARRIER. KEEP YOUR HEAD DOWN AND RUN AS FAST AS YOU CAN.
CAN YOU DO THAT?
ABSOLUTELY.
YOU REALLY ARE THE LITTLE SAMURAI THAT COULD, AREN'T YOU?
CAMERAS?
CAMERAS.
GUARDS, TAKE THE PRISONER BACK TO THE DUNGEON. LEAVE THE OTHER ONE TO ME.
THINK.
NO. GUARDS, STAND DOWN.
WHAT?
LAST I CHECKED, I'M THE MISTRESS OF THE NAIL.
YOU LEFT.
I AVOIDED AN ASSASSINATION FROM A DISLOYAL LIEUTENANT. YOU THINK DAREDEVIL WILL SEE IT YOUR WAY? HE CHOSE ME.
HE'S CORRECTED THAT ERROR.

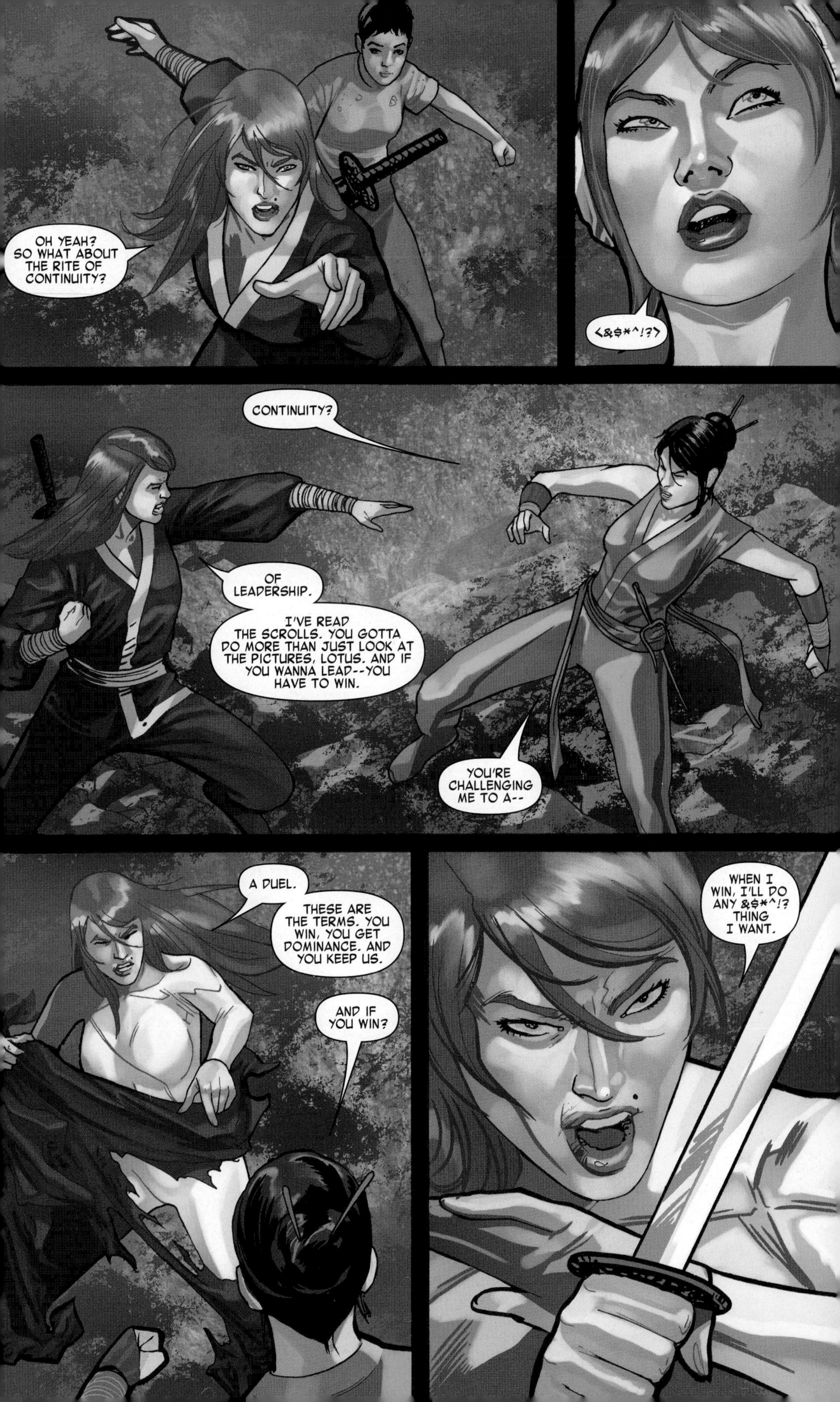
OH YEAH? SO WHAT ABOUT THE RITE OF CONTINUITY?
<&$*^!?>
CONTINUITY?
OF LEADERSHIP.
I'VE READ THE SCROLLS. YOU GOTTA DO MORE THAN JUST LOOK AT THE PICTURES, LOTUS. AND IF YOU WANNA LEAD--YOU HAVE TO WIN.
YOU'RE CHALLENGING ME TO A--
A DUEL.
THESE ARE THE TERMS. YOU WIN, YOU GET DOMINANCE. AND YOU KEEP US.
AND IF YOU WIN?
WHEN I WIN, I'LL DO ANY &$*^!? THING I WANT.

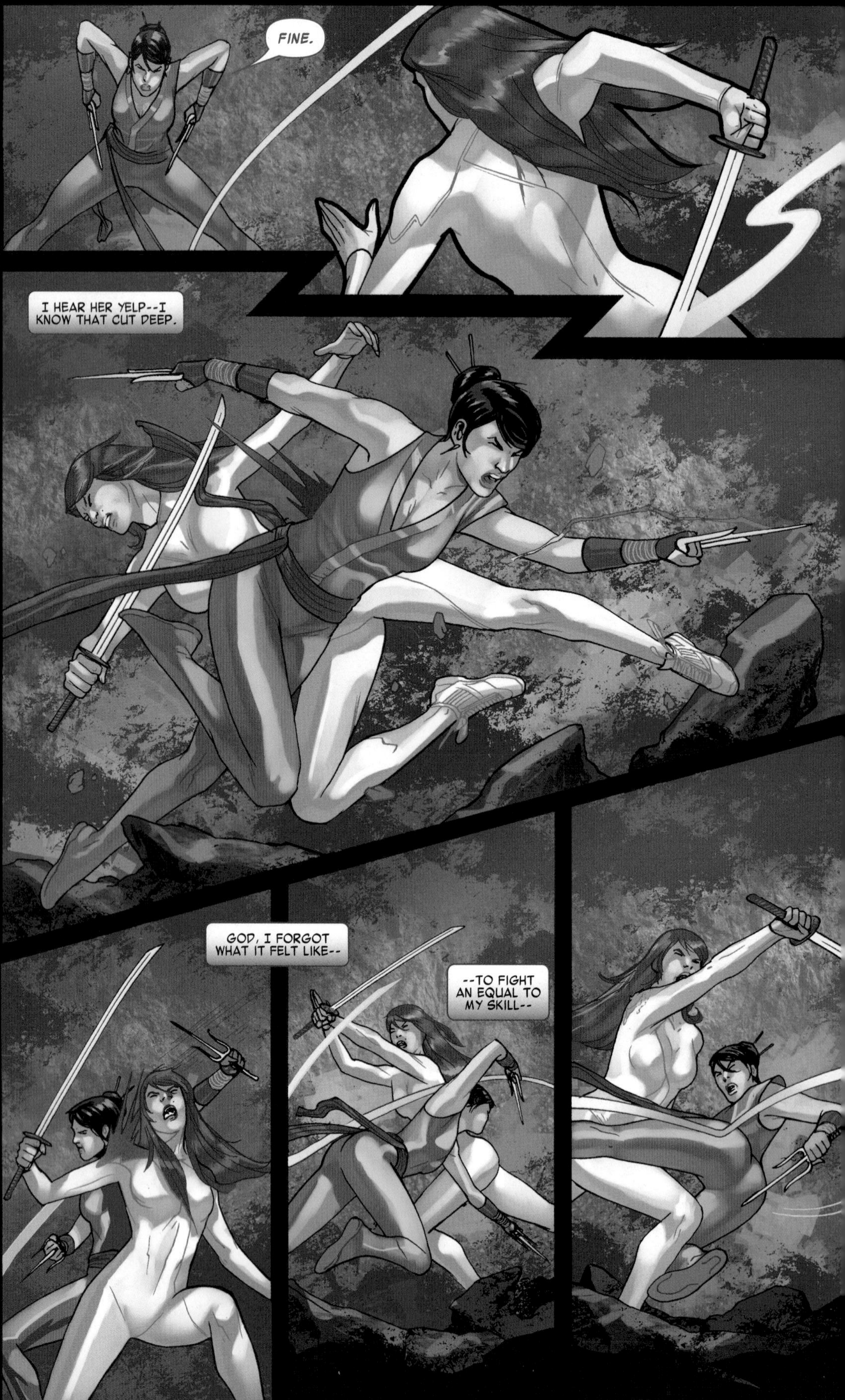

FINE.
I HEAR HER YELP--I KNOW THAT CUT DEEP.
GOD, I FORGOT WHAT IT FELT LIKE--
--TO FIGHT AN EQUAL TO MY SKILL--

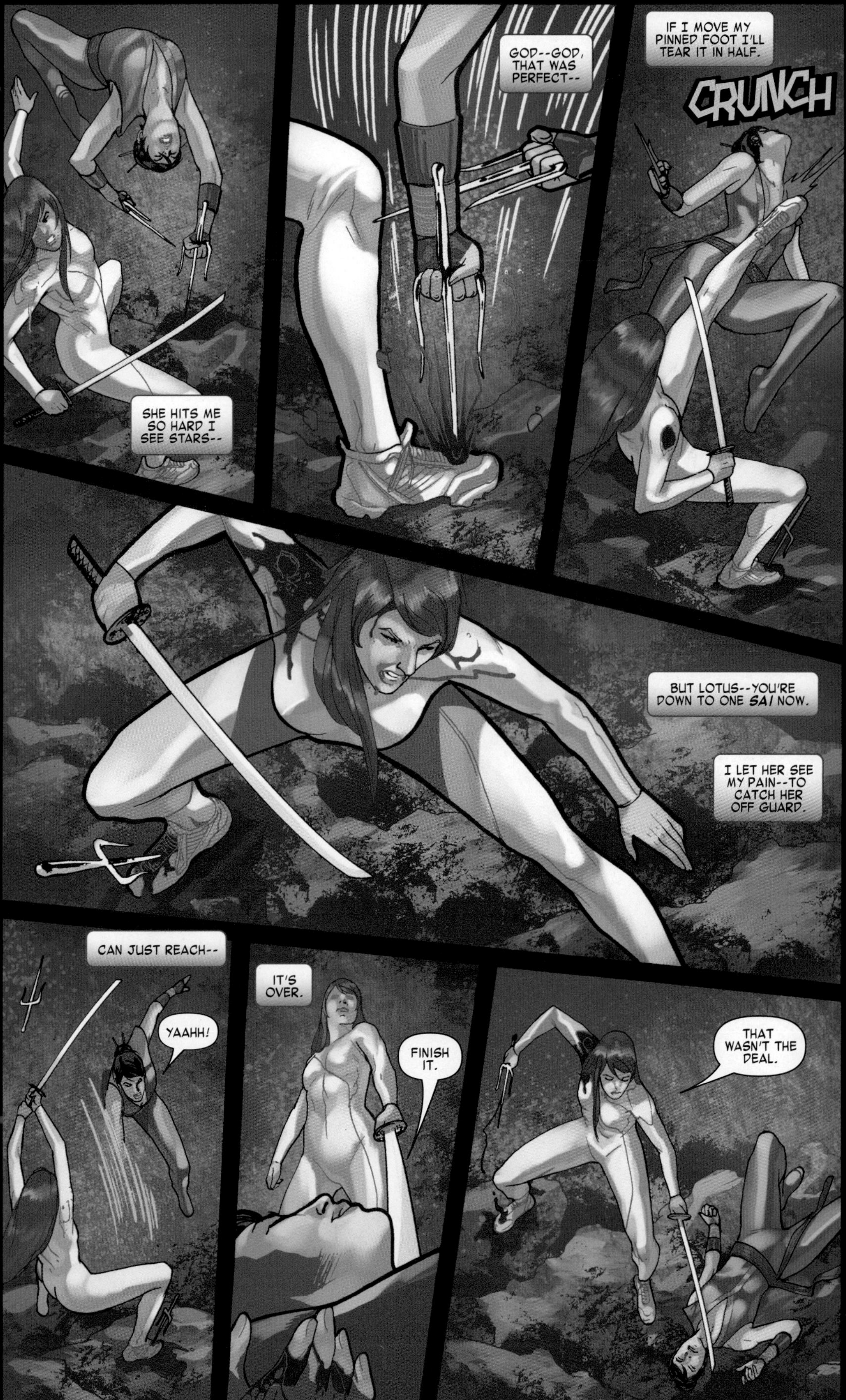
SHE HITS ME SO HARD I SEE STARS--
GOD--GOD, THAT WAS PERFECT--
IF I MOVE MY PINNED FOOT I'LL TEAR IT IN HALF.
CRUNCH
BUT LOTUS--YOU'RE DOWN TO ONE SAI NOW.
I LET HER SEE MY PAIN--TO CATCH HER OFF GUARD.
CAN JUST REACH--
YAAHH!
IT'S OVER.
FINISH IT.
THAT WASN'T THE DEAL.

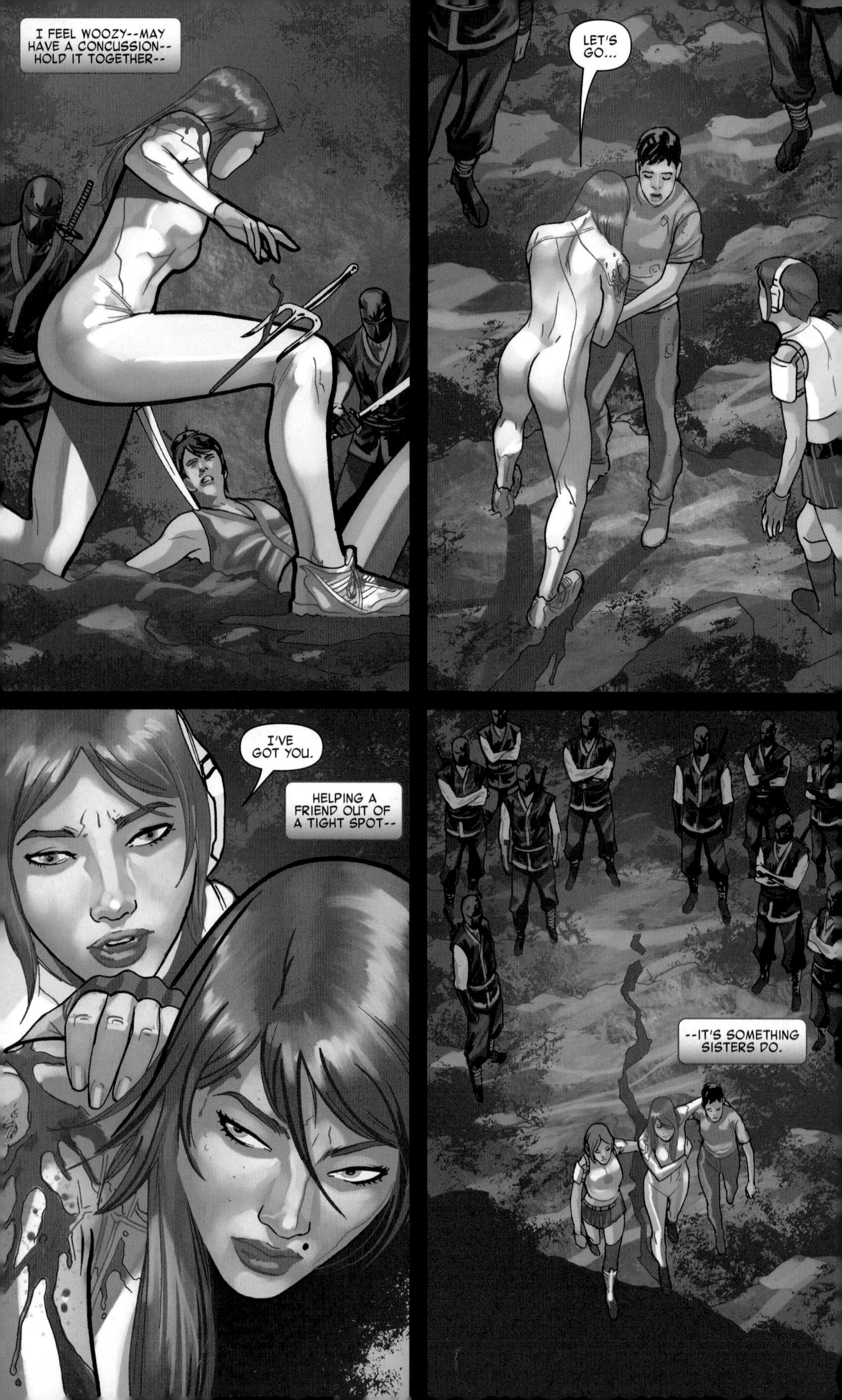
I FEEL WOOZY--MAY HAVE A CONCUSSION--HOLD IT TOGETHER--
LET'S GO...
I'VE GOT YOU.
HELPING A FRIEND OUT OF A TIGHT SPOT--
--IT'S SOMETHING SISTERS DO.

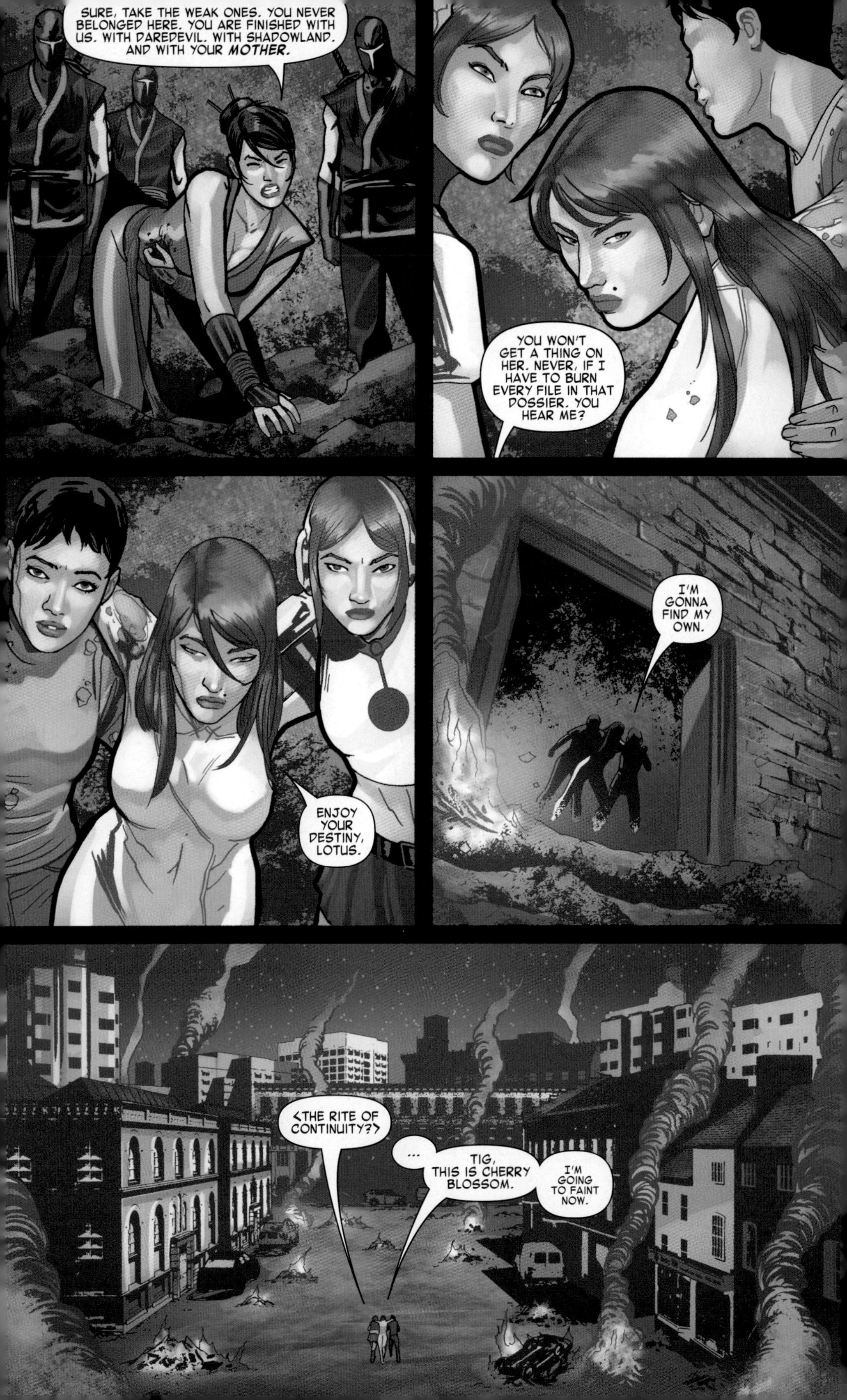
SURE, TAKE THE WEAK ONES. YOU NEVER BELONGED HERE. YOU ARE FINISHED WITH US. WITH DAREDEVIL. WITH SHADOWLAND. AND WITH YOUR MOTHER.
YOU WON'T GET A THING ON HER. NEVER, IF I HAVE TO BURN EVERY FILE IN THAT DOSSIER. YOU HEAR ME?
ENJOY YOUR DESTINY, LOTUS.
I'M GONNA FIND MY OWN.
<THE RITE OF CONTINUITY?>
...
TIG, THIS IS CHERRY BLOSSOM.
I'M GOING TO FAINT NOW.

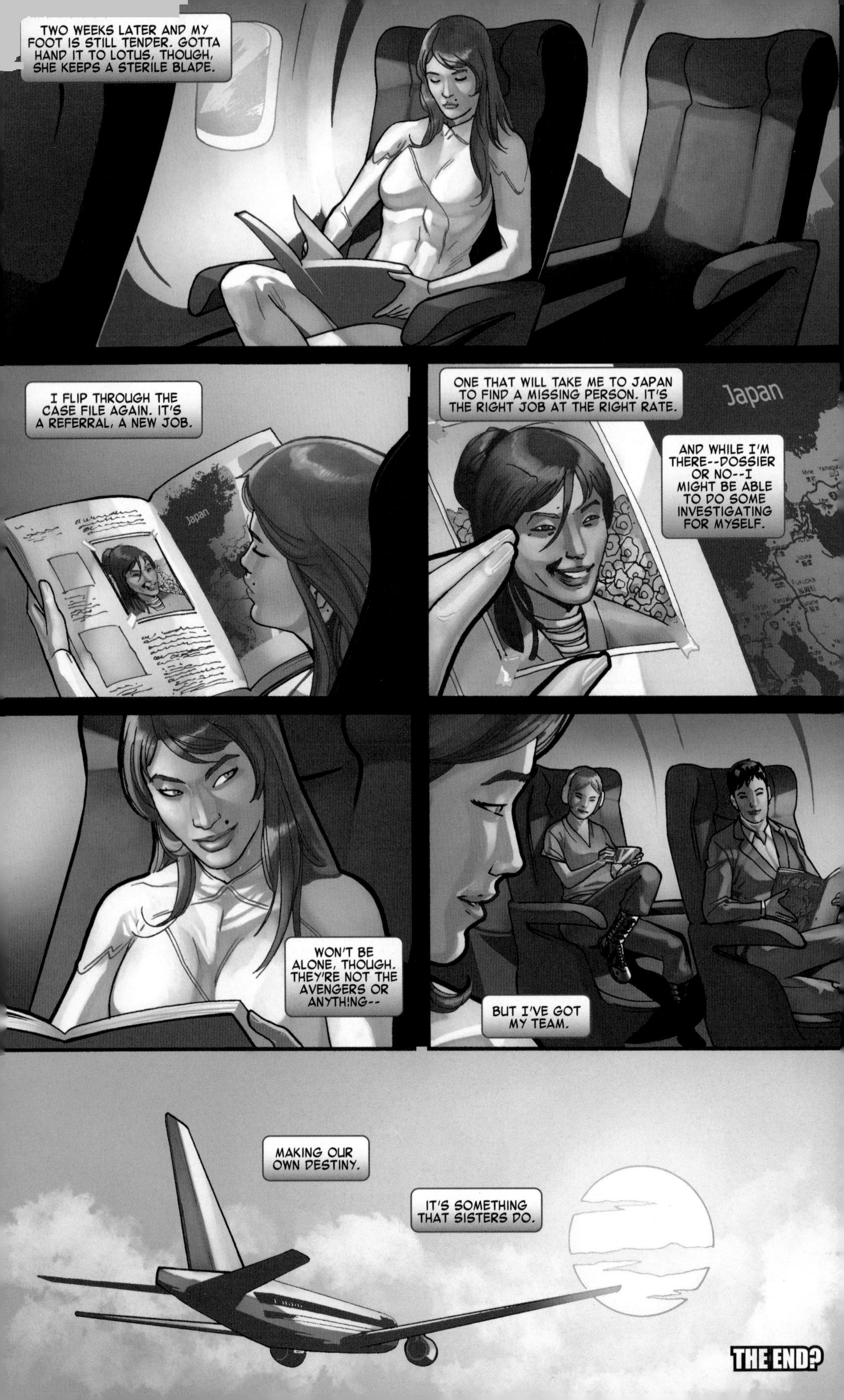
TWO WEEKS LATER AND MY FOOT IS STILL TENDER. GOTTA HAND IT TO LOTUS, THOUGH. SHE KEEPS A STERILE BLADE.
I FLIP THROUGH THE CASE FILE AGAIN. IT'S A REFERRAL, A NEW JOB.
Japan
ONE THAT WILL TAKE ME TO JAPAN TO FIND A MISSING PERSON. IT'S THE RIGHT JOB AT THE RIGHT RATE.
Japan
AND WHILE I'M THERE--DOSSIER OR NO--I MIGHT BE ABLE TO DO SOME INVESTIGATING FOR MYSELF.
WON'T BE ALONE, THOUGH. THEY'RE NOT THE AVENGERS OR ANYTHING--
BUT I'VE GOT MY TEAM.
MAKING OUR OWN DESTINY.
IT'S SOMETHING THAT SISTERS DO.
THE END?

Who are the Nail? The mystery behind the Hand's all-lovely, all-dangerous cadre of female killers unfolds in the pages of *Shadowland: Daughters of the Shadow*, but careful-eyed readers can spy a few clues in superstar artist Carlo Pagulayan's brilliant character designs. Taken from writer Jason Henderson's initial concepts, Pagulayan's detail rich impressions are seeped in a long-time love of anime and Japanese pop-culture. Take a gander at these gorgeous sketches, along with Carlo and Jason's thoughts...

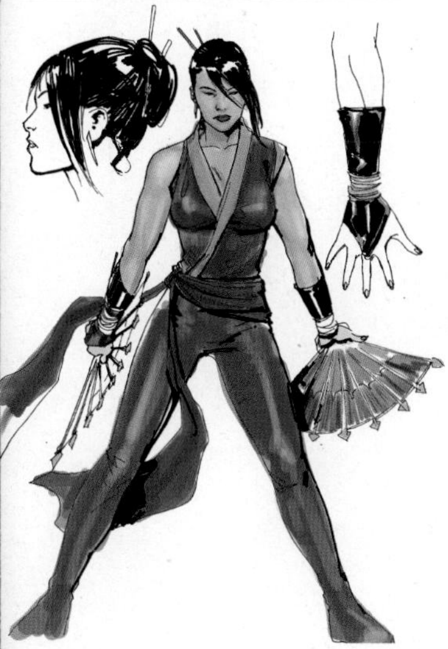

BLACK LOTUS

JASON: She is the only one of these characters who has appeared before in Marvel. She's always been seen as a quiet, cool killer who's done everything right.

CARLO: I went for a more Female Ninja get up, and grabbed the color scheme from the original but made it darker. On her right she has metal spikes and her hairpins can be used as throwing weapons. Her fans have projectile darts, similar to Monica Belluci's in "Brotherhood of the Wolf".

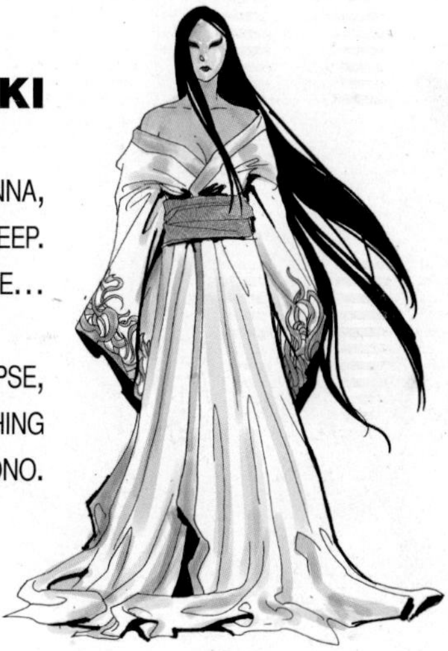

YUKI

JASON: Yuki is named after Yuki-Onna, the snow goddess who lulls men to sleep. She's dreamy and strange...

CARLO: Her skin color looks almost like a frozen corpse, very long hair, which she may choose to use as a whip. Everything about her should look fluid since she has an oversized kimono.

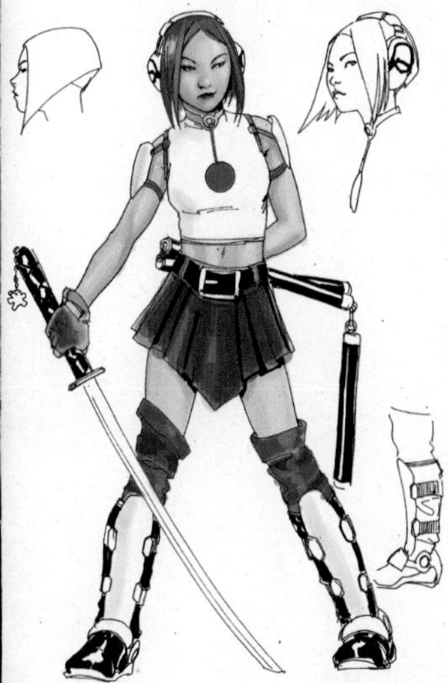

CHERRY BLOSSOM

CARLO: I thought I'd give her headphones. I see her killing people while listening through her favorite playlist. I also leaned towards a J-rock look and took inspiration from Japanese fashion. For her palette I tried to go near cherry blossom colors.

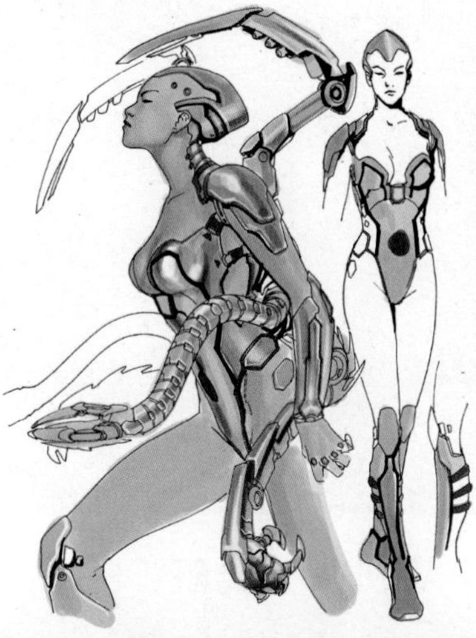

MAKRO

JASON: Makro is the weirdest, a jumpy, violent woman who's been augmented by some powerful forces to have mechanical arms a la Doctor Octopus. She can do more things than we've seen Doc Ock do, though...

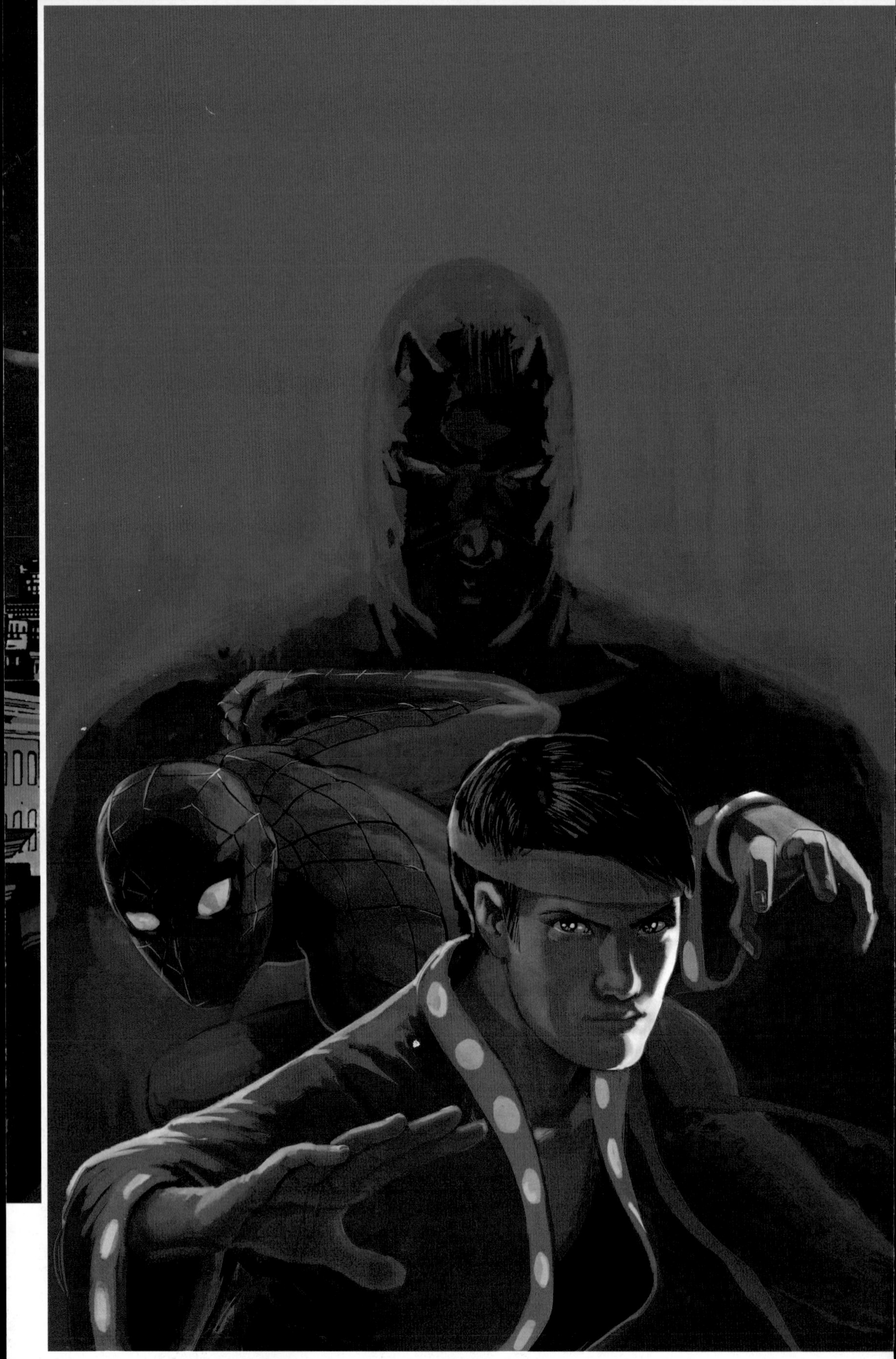

SHADOWLAND: SPIDER-MAN

When the ancient order of the Hand — an organization of Ninjas, thieves and assassins — sought Daredevil out to become their new leader, he plotted to use the organization as a force for good. When his archenemy Bullseye destroyed a city block — and killed 107 people in the process — Murdock was pushed over the edge. He killed Bullseye, and on the site of the decimated city block, built his fortress, Shadowland.

A handful of his oldest friends, including the high-flying super hero known as the Amazing Spider-Man and the noble Shang Chi, master of Kung-Fu, attempted to appeal to whatever humanity might remain in the Man Without Fear. They discovered that the Daredevil they knew was possessed by something evil, powerful and unflinching — something even the superhuman Spider-Man wasn't tough enough to fight. He is not their ally anymore, and it may take drastic measures to stop him.

In recent months, Spider-Man has fought Mr. Negative, crime lord of Chinatown. Negative has sought to take control of the city's criminal underworld — a plan that Daredevil's new power base has greatly impeded...

SHADOWLAND
SPIDER-MAN

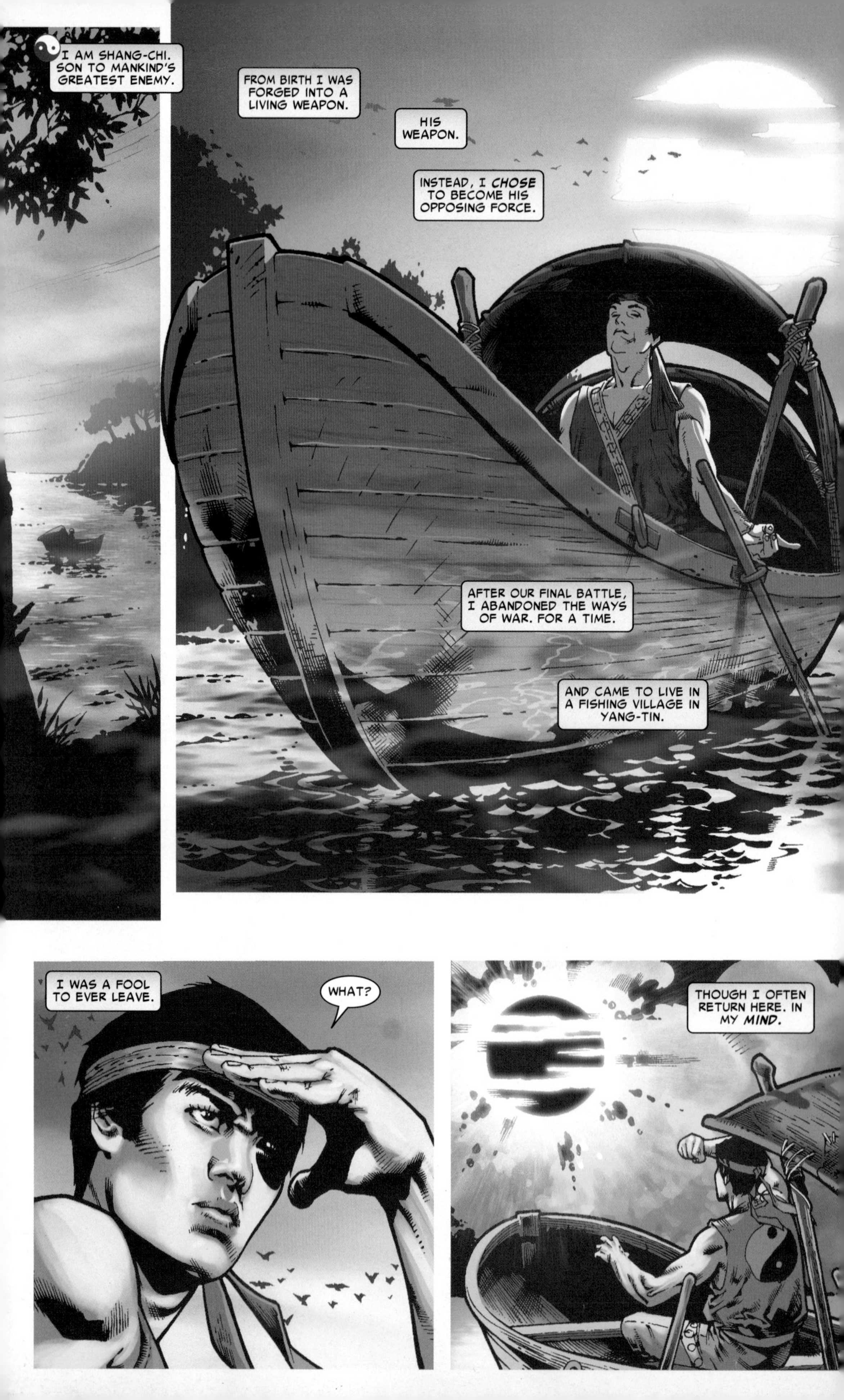
I AM SHANG-CHI. SON TO MANKIND'S GREATEST ENEMY.
FROM BIRTH I WAS FORGED INTO A LIVING WEAPON.
HIS WEAPON.
INSTEAD, I CHOSE TO BECOME HIS OPPOSING FORCE.
AFTER OUR FINAL BATTLE, I ABANDONED THE WAYS OF WAR. FOR A TIME.
AND CAME TO LIVE IN A FISHING VILLAGE IN YANG-TIN.
I WAS A FOOL TO EVER LEAVE.
WHAT?
THOUGH I OFTEN RETURN HERE. IN MY MIND.

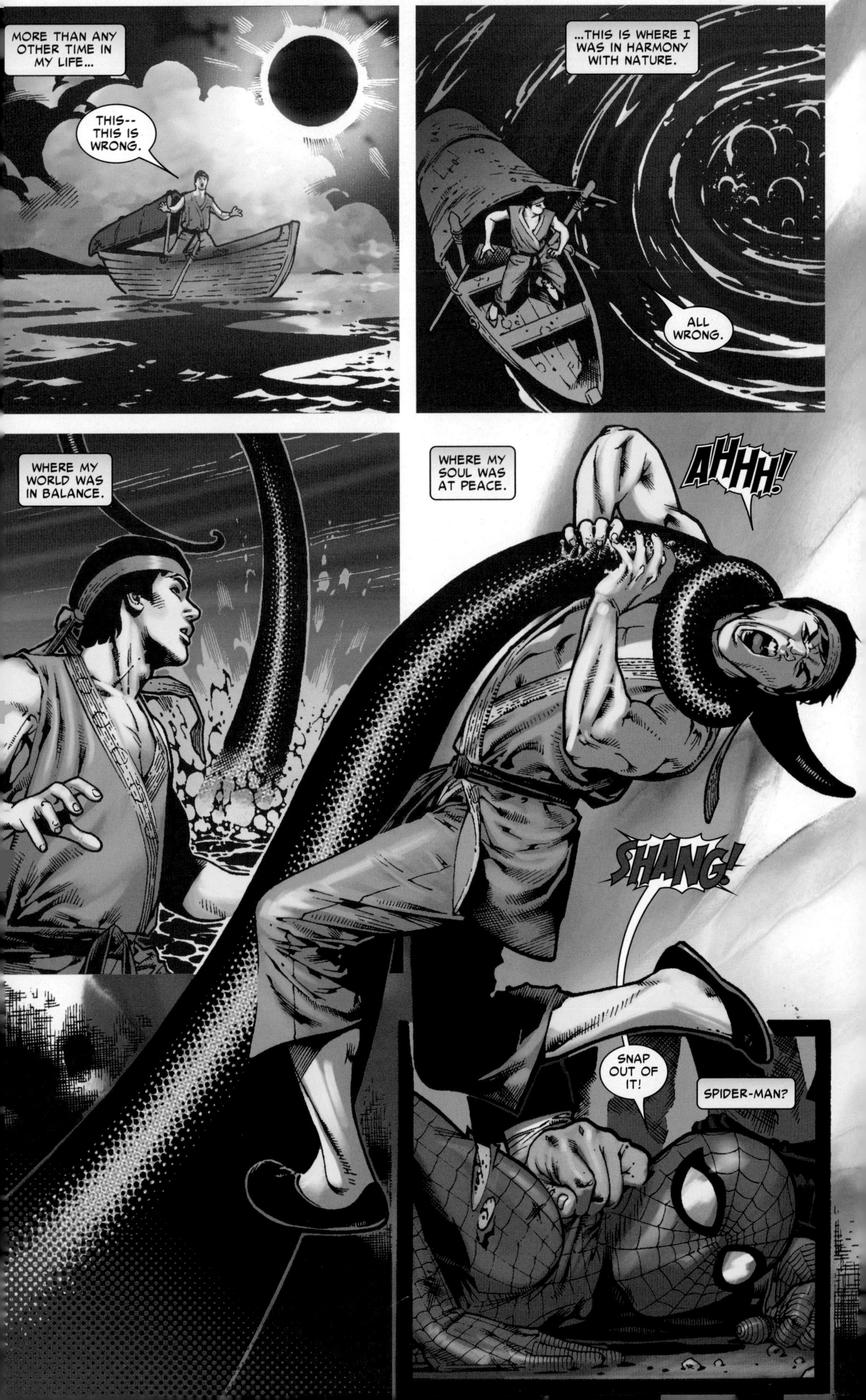
MORE THAN ANY OTHER TIME IN MY LIFE...
THIS-- THIS IS WRONG.
...THIS IS WHERE I WAS IN HARMONY WITH NATURE.
ALL WRONG.
WHERE MY WORLD WAS IN BALANCE.
WHERE MY SOUL WAS AT PEACE.
AHHH!
SHANG!
SNAP OUT OF IT!
SPIDER-MAN?

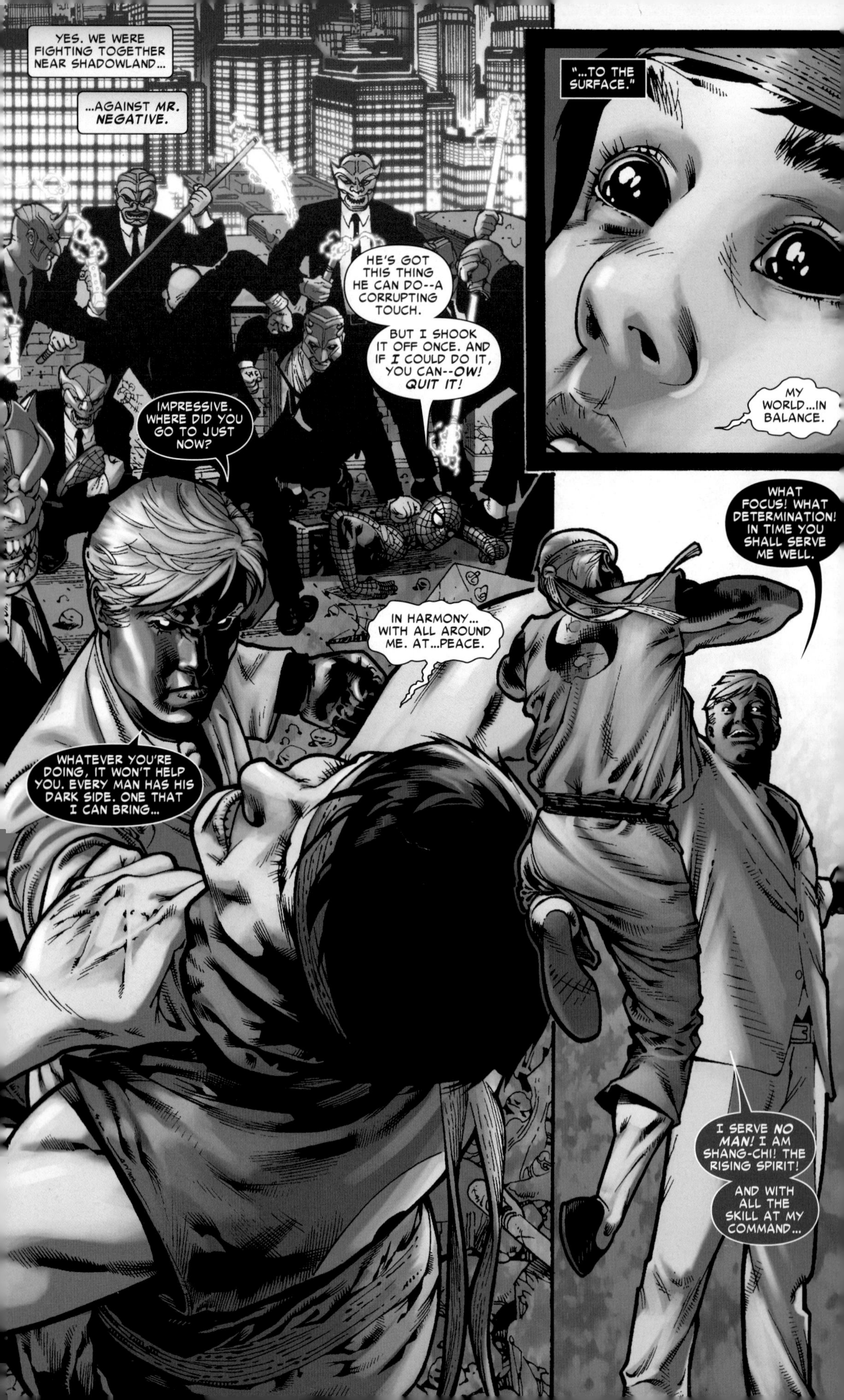
YES. WE WERE FIGHTING TOGETHER NEAR SHADOWLAND...
...AGAINST MR. NEGATIVE.
HE'S GOT THIS THING HE CAN DO--A CORRUPTING TOUCH.
BUT I SHOOK IT OFF ONCE. AND IF I COULD DO IT, YOU CAN--OW! QUIT IT!
"...TO THE SURFACE."
MY WORLD...IN BALANCE.
IMPRESSIVE. WHERE DID YOU GO TO JUST NOW?
IN HARMONY... WITH ALL AROUND ME. AT...PEACE.
WHATEVER YOU'RE DOING, IT WON'T HELP YOU. EVERY MAN HAS HIS DARK SIDE. ONE THAT I CAN BRING...
WHAT FOCUS! WHAT DETERMINATION! IN TIME YOU SHALL SERVE ME WELL.
I SERVE NO MAN! I AM SHANG-CHI! THE RISING SPIRIT!
AND WITH ALL THE SKILL AT MY COMMAND...

MBALANCED

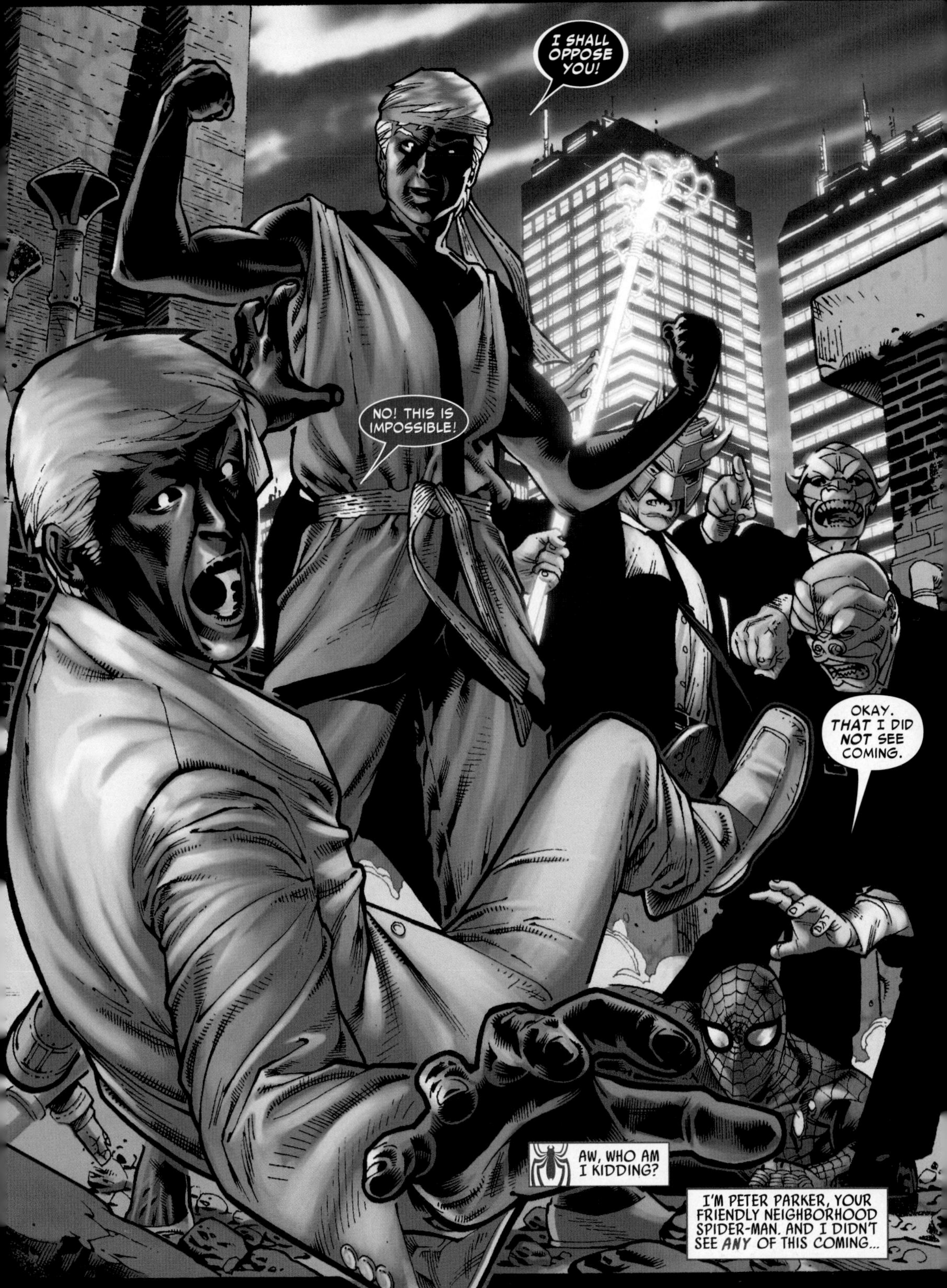

I SHALL OPPOSE YOU!
NO! THIS IS IMPOSSIBLE!
OKAY. THAT I DID NOT SEE COMING.
AW, WHO AM I KIDDING?
I'M PETER PARKER, YOUR FRIENDLY NEIGHBORHOOD SPIDER-MAN. AND I DIDN'T SEE ANY OF THIS COMING...

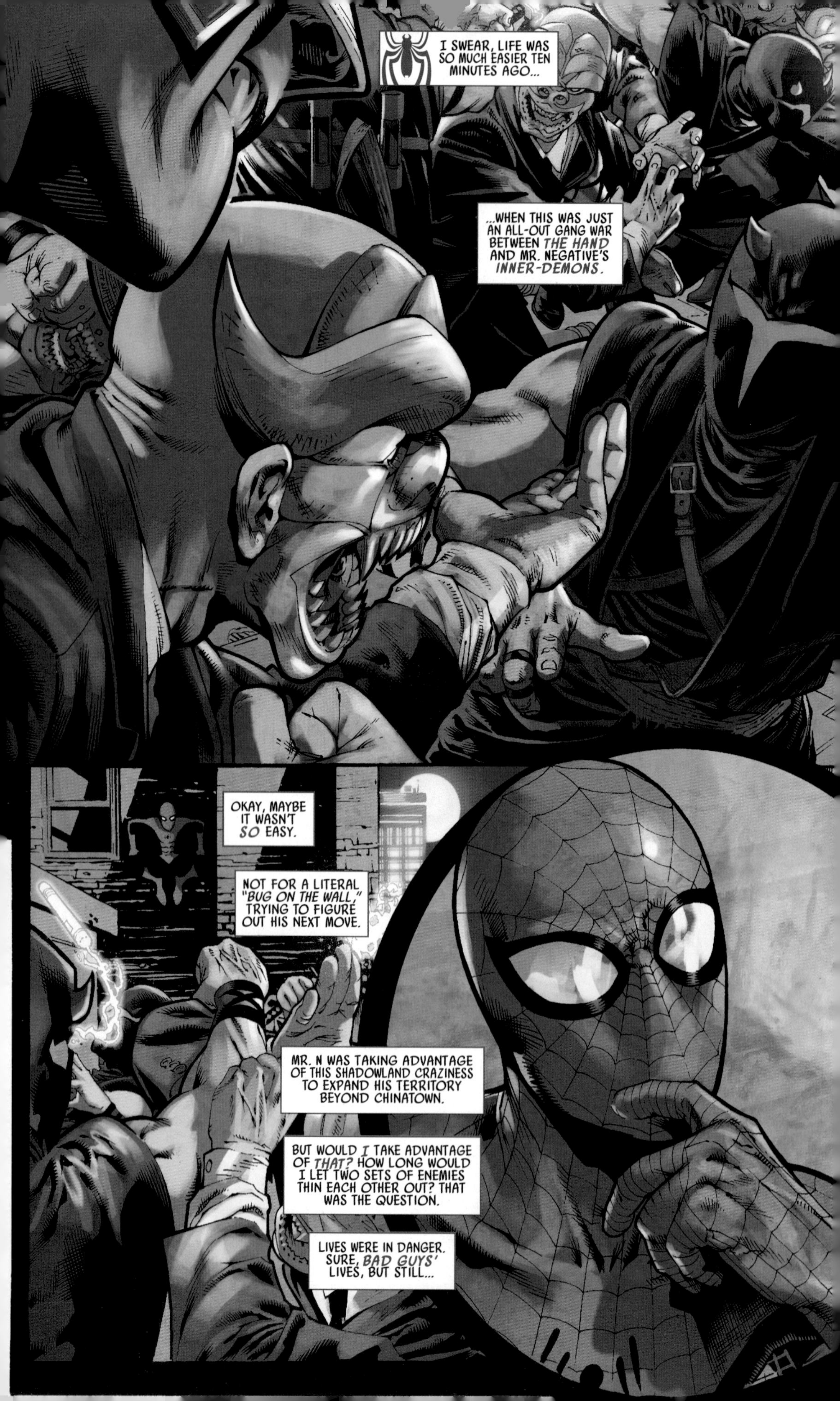
I SWEAR, LIFE WAS SO MUCH EASIER TEN MINUTES AGO...
...WHEN THIS WAS JUST AN ALL-OUT GANG WAR BETWEEN THE HAND AND MR. NEGATIVE'S INNER-DEMONS.
OKAY, MAYBE IT WASN'T SO EASY.
NOT FOR A LITERAL "BUG ON THE WALL," TRYING TO FIGURE OUT HIS NEXT MOVE.
MR. N WAS TAKING ADVANTAGE OF THIS SHADOWLAND CRAZINESS TO EXPAND HIS TERRITORY BEYOND CHINATOWN.
BUT WOULD I TAKE ADVANTAGE OF THAT? HOW LONG WOULD I LET TWO SETS OF ENEMIES THIN EACH OTHER OUT? THAT WAS THE QUESTION.
LIVES WERE IN DANGER. SURE, BAD GUYS' LIVES, BUT STILL...

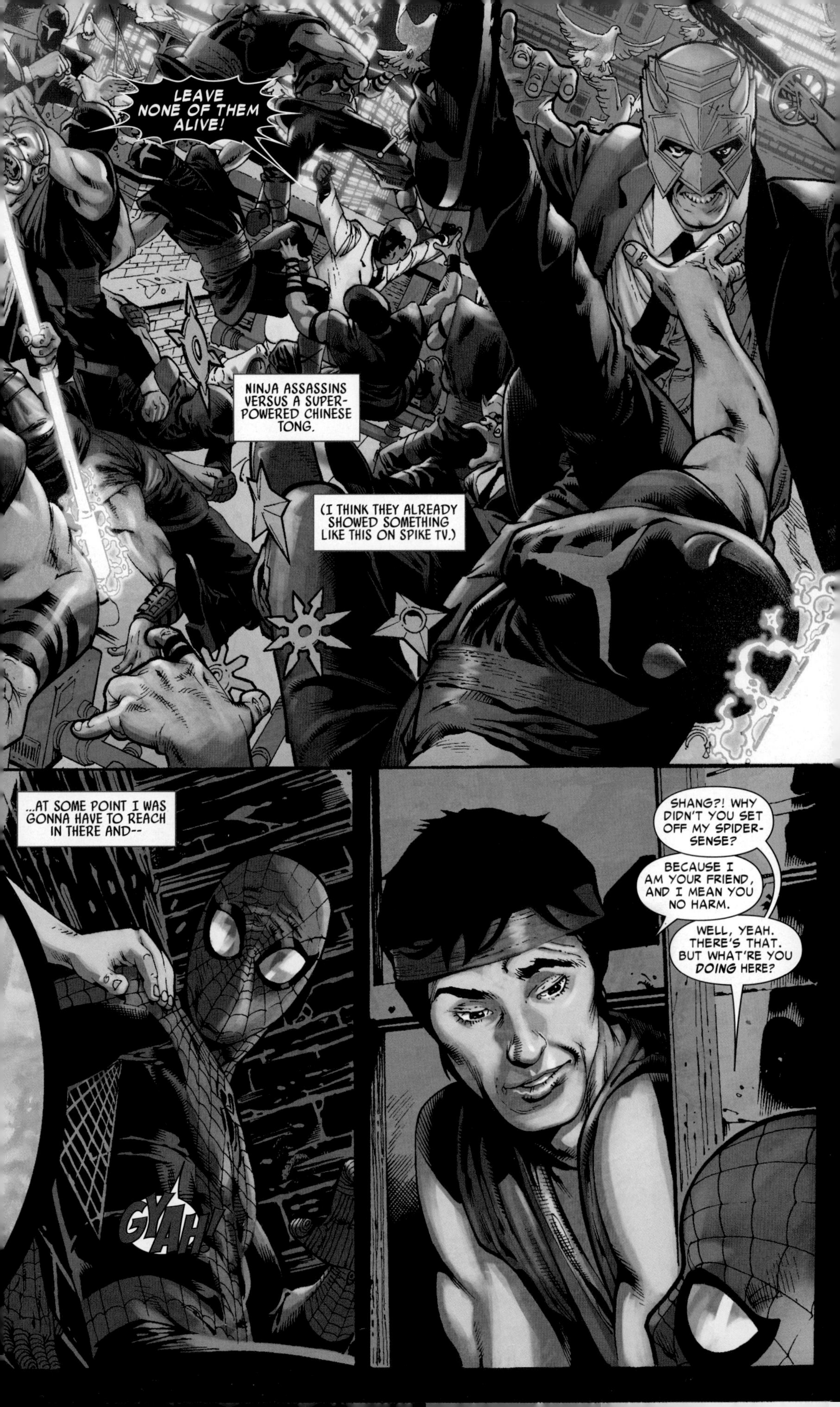
LEAVE NONE OF THEM ALIVE!
NINJA ASSASSINS VERSUS A SUPER-POWERED CHINESE TONG.
(I THINK THEY ALREADY SHOWED SOMETHING LIKE THIS ON SPIKE TV.)
...AT SOME POINT I WAS GONNA HAVE TO REACH IN THERE AND--
GYAH!
SHANG?! WHY DIDN'T YOU SET OFF MY SPIDER-SENSE?
BECAUSE I AM YOUR FRIEND, AND I MEAN YOU NO HARM.
WELL, YEAH. THERE'S THAT. BUT WHAT'RE YOU DOING HERE?

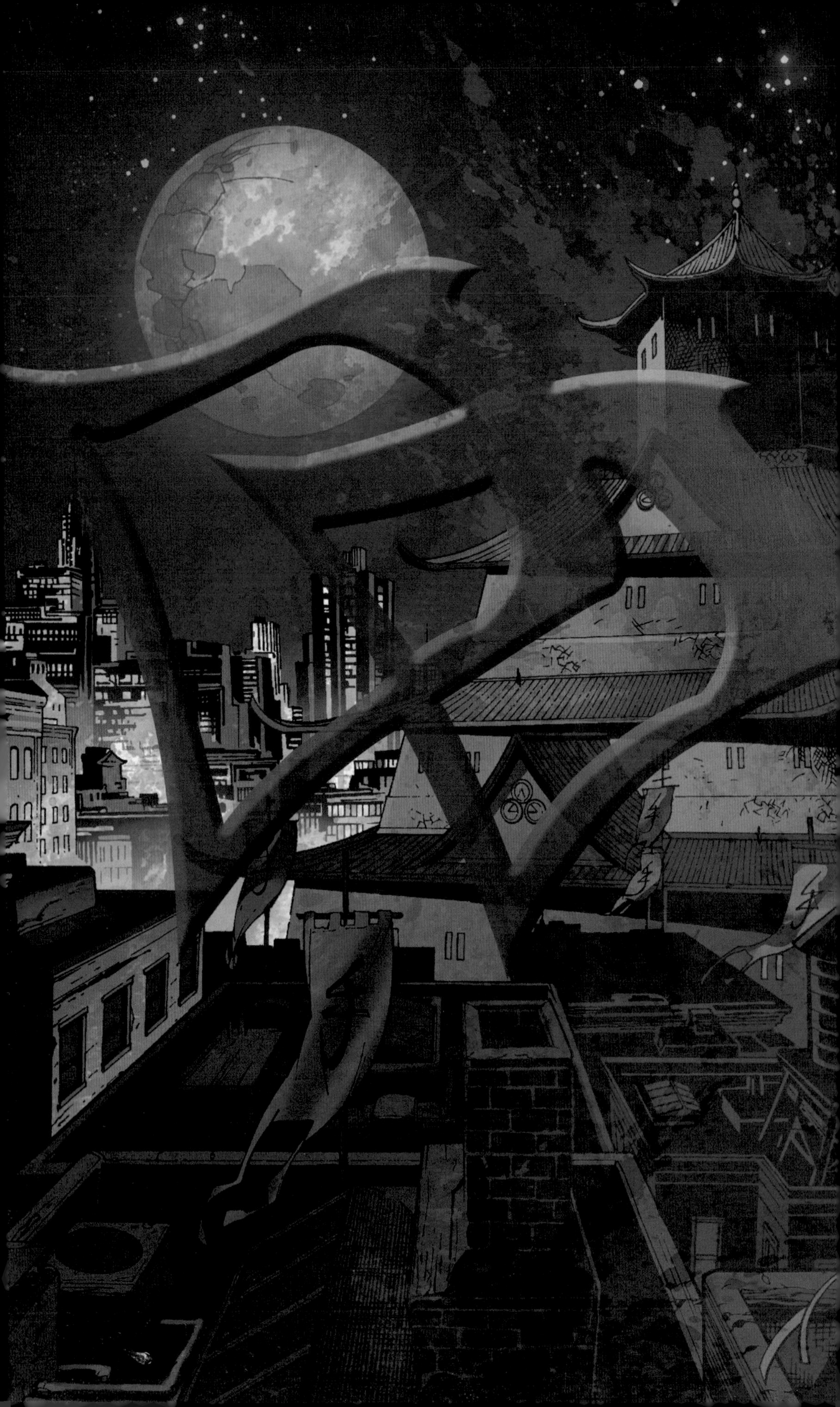

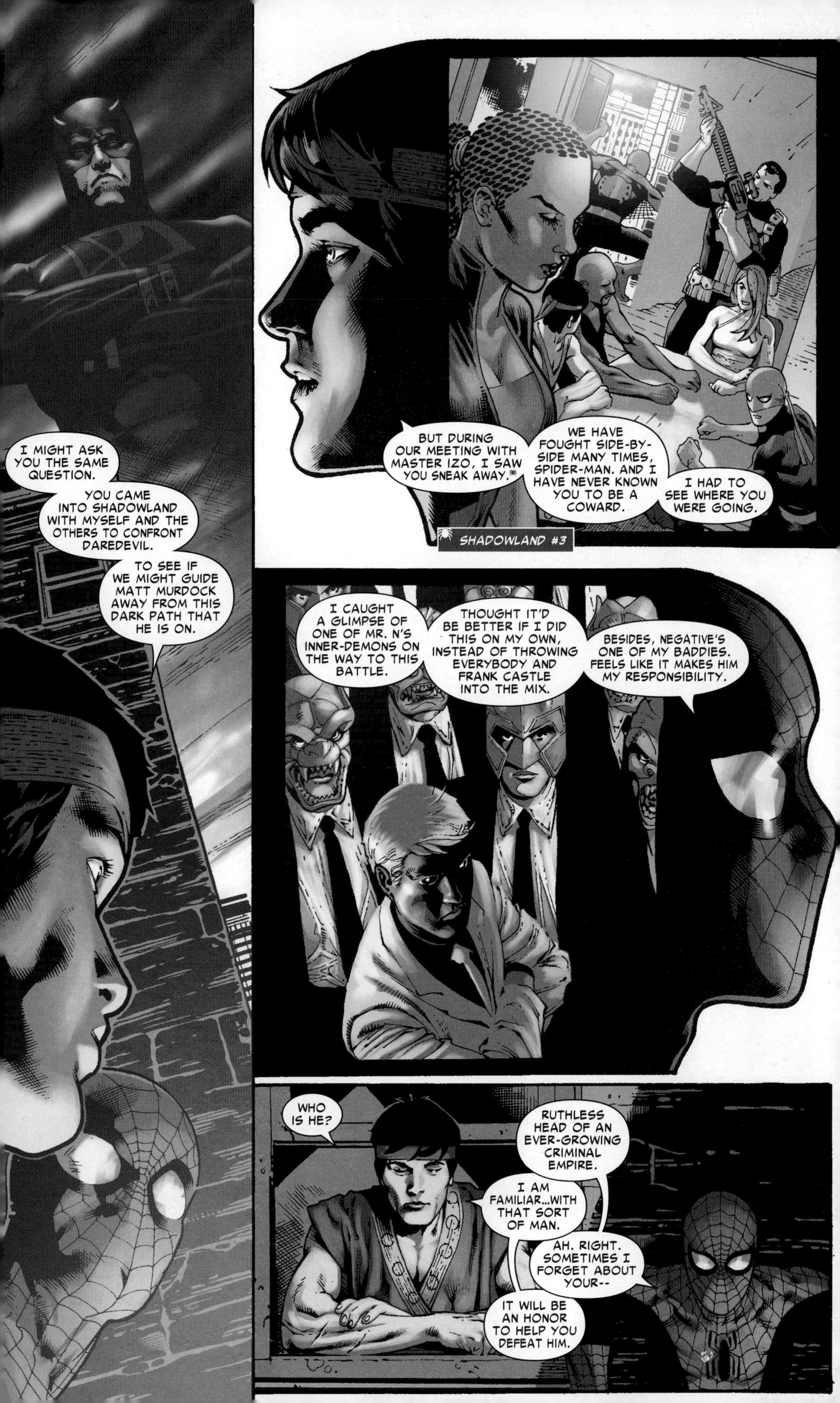
I MIGHT ASK YOU THE SAME QUESTION.
YOU CAME INTO SHADOWLAND WITH MYSELF AND THE OTHERS TO CONFRONT DAREDEVIL.
TO SEE IF WE MIGHT GUIDE MATT MURDOCK AWAY FROM THIS DARK PATH THAT HE IS ON.
BUT DURING OUR MEETING WITH MASTER IZO, I SAW YOU SNEAK AWAY.
WE HAVE FOUGHT SIDE-BY-SIDE MANY TIMES, SPIDER-MAN. AND I HAVE NEVER KNOWN YOU TO BE A COWARD.
I HAD TO SEE WHERE YOU WERE GOING.
SHADOWLAND #3
I CAUGHT A GLIMPSE OF ONE OF MR. N'S INNER-DEMONS ON THE WAY TO THIS BATTLE.
THOUGHT IT'D BE BETTER IF I DID THIS ON MY OWN, INSTEAD OF THROWING EVERYBODY AND FRANK CASTLE INTO THE MIX.
BESIDES, NEGATIVE'S ONE OF MY BADDIES. FEELS LIKE IT MAKES HIM MY RESPONSIBILITY.
WHO IS HE?
RUTHLESS HEAD OF AN EVER-GROWING CRIMINAL EMPIRE.
I AM FAMILIAR...WITH THAT SORT OF MAN.
AH. RIGHT. SOMETIMES I FORGET ABOUT YOUR--
IT WILL BE AN HONOR TO HELP YOU DEFEAT HIM.

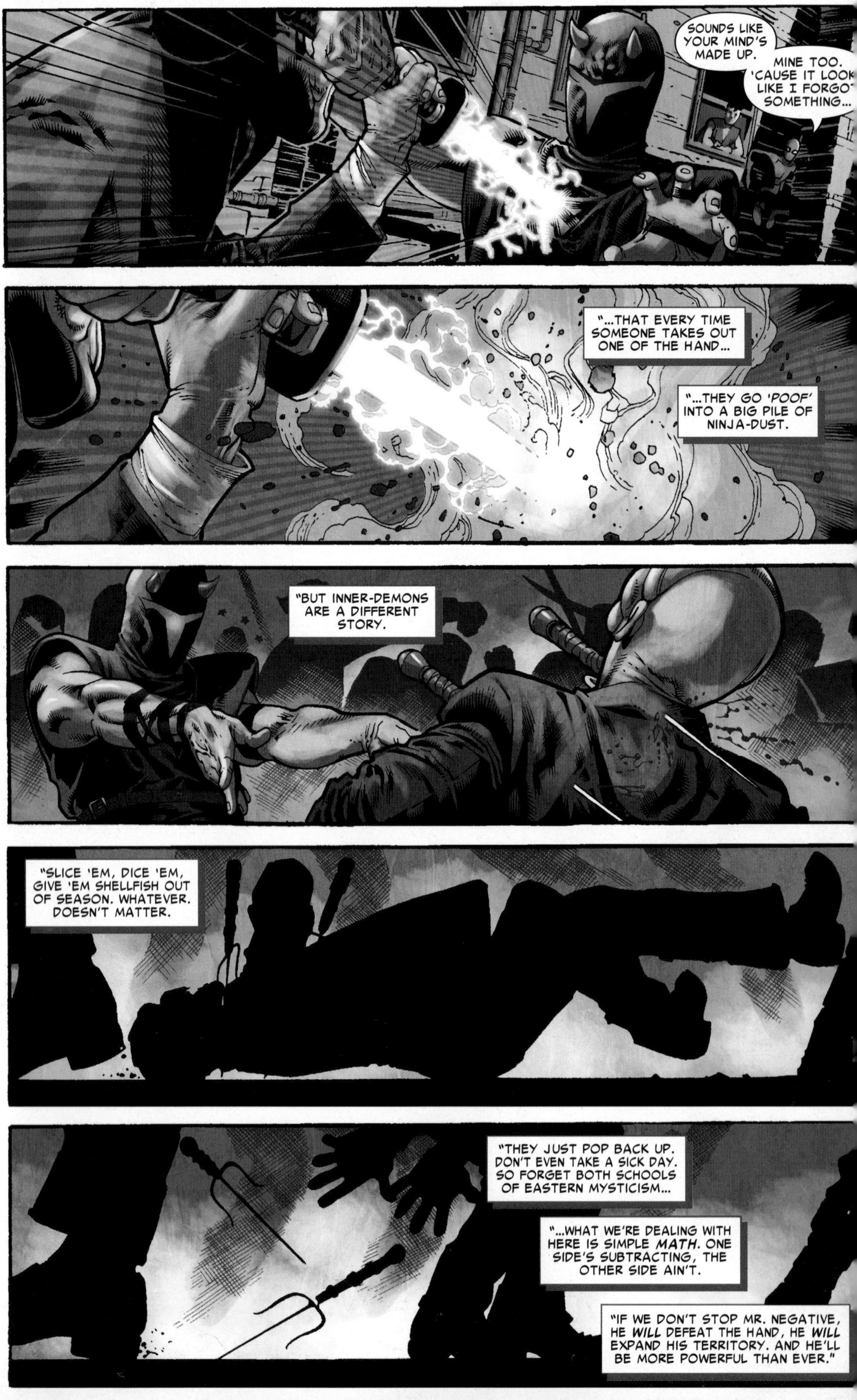
SOUNDS LIKE YOUR MIND'S MADE UP.
MINE TOO. 'CAUSE IT LOOK LIKE I FORGO SOMETHING...
"...THAT EVERY TIME SOMEONE TAKES OUT ONE OF THE HAND...
"...THEY GO 'POOF' INTO A BIG PILE OF NINJA-DUST.
"BUT INNER-DEMONS ARE A DIFFERENT STORY.
"SLICE 'EM, DICE 'EM, GIVE 'EM SHELLFISH OUT OF SEASON. WHATEVER. DOESN'T MATTER.
"THEY JUST POP BACK UP. DON'T EVEN TAKE A SICK DAY. SO FORGET BOTH SCHOOLS OF EASTERN MYSTICISM...
"...WHAT WE'RE DEALING WITH HERE IS SIMPLE MATH. ONE SIDE'S SUBTRACTING, THE OTHER SIDE AIN'T.
"IF WE DON'T STOP MR. NEGATIVE, HE WILL DEFEAT THE HAND, HE WILL EXPAND HIS TERRITORY. AND HE'LL BE MORE POWERFUL THAN EVER."

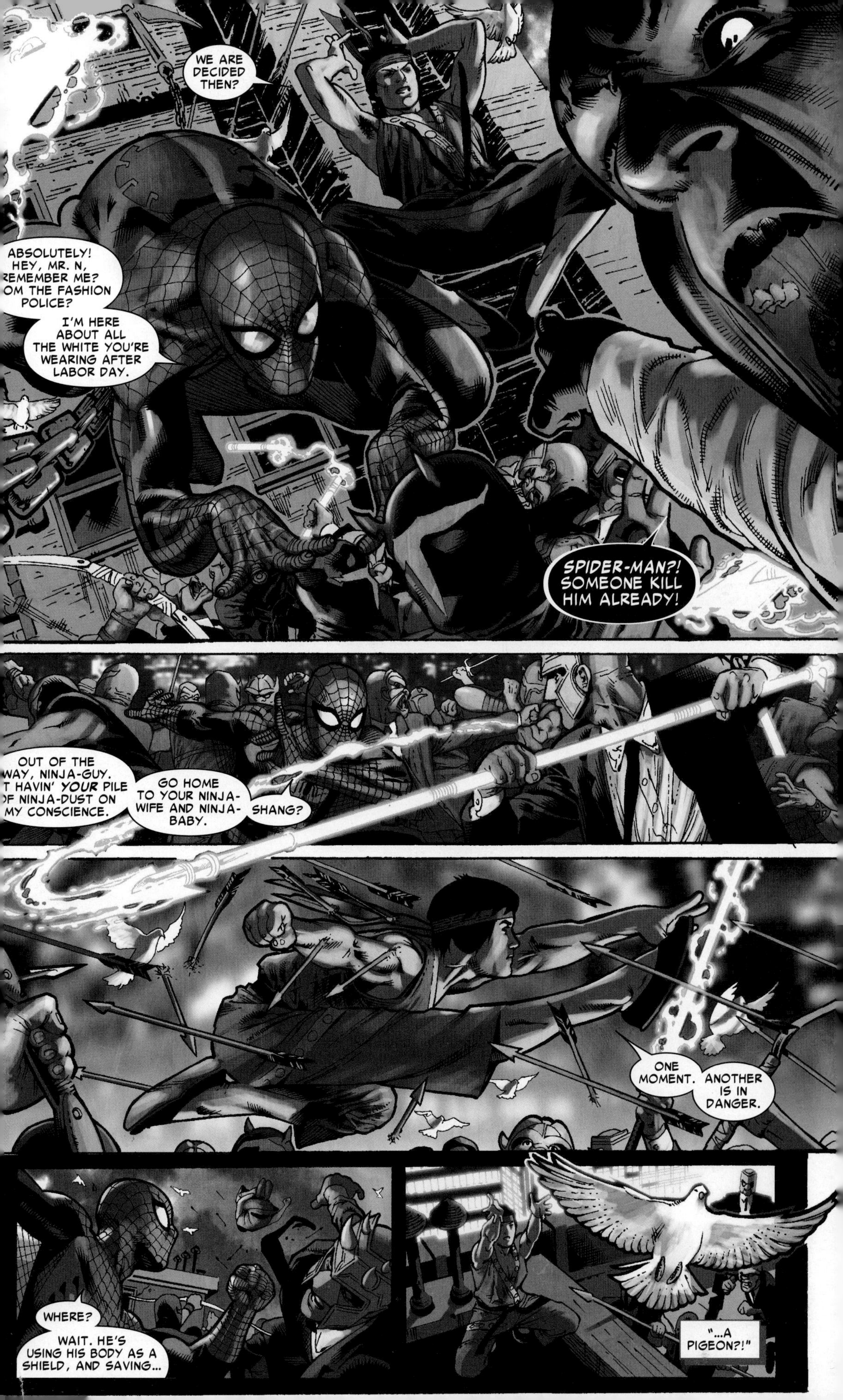
WE ARE DECIDED THEN?
ABSOLUTELY! HEY, MR. N, REMEMBER ME? OM THE FASHION POLICE?
I'M HERE ABOUT ALL THE WHITE YOU'RE WEARING AFTER LABOR DAY.
SPIDER-MAN?! SOMEONE KILL HIM ALREADY!
OUT OF THE WAY, NINJA-GUY. T HAVIN' YOUR PILE OF NINJA-DUST ON MY CONSCIENCE.
GO HOME TO YOUR NINJA-WIFE AND NINJA-BABY.
SHANG?
ONE MOMENT.
ANOTHER IS IN DANGER.
WHERE?
WAIT. HE'S USING HIS BODY AS A SHIELD, AND SAVING...
"...A PIGEON?!"

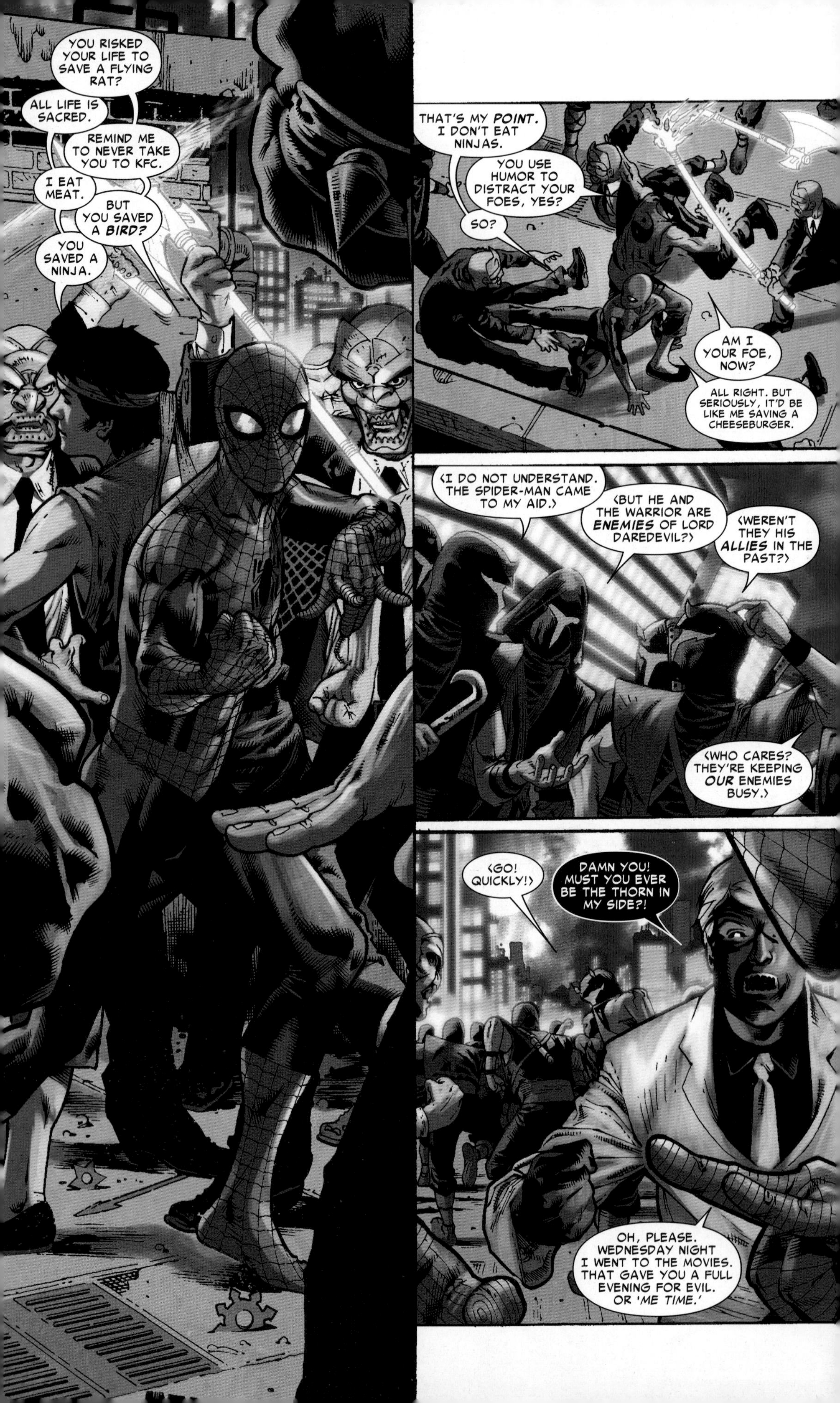

YOU RISKED YOUR LIFE TO SAVE A FLYING RAT?
ALL LIFE IS SACRED.
REMIND ME TO NEVER TAKE YOU TO KFC.
I EAT MEAT.
BUT YOU SAVED A *BIRD?*
YOU SAVED A NINJA.
THAT'S MY *POINT.* I DON'T EAT NINJAS.
YOU USE HUMOR TO DISTRACT YOUR FOES, YES?
SO?
AM I YOUR FOE, NOW?
ALL RIGHT. BUT SERIOUSLY, IT'D BE LIKE ME SAVING A CHEESEBURGER.
‹I DO NOT UNDERSTAND. THE SPIDER-MAN CAME TO MY AID.›
‹BUT HE AND THE WARRIOR ARE *ENEMIES* OF LORD DAREDEVIL?›
‹WEREN'T THEY HIS *ALLIES* IN THE PAST?›
‹WHO CARES? THEY'RE KEEPING *OUR* ENEMIES BUSY.›
‹GO! QUICKLY!›
DAMN YOU! MUST YOU EVER BE THE THORN IN MY SIDE?!
OH, PLEASE. WEDNESDAY NIGHT I WENT TO THE MOVIES. THAT GAVE YOU A FULL EVENING FOR EVIL. OR '*ME TIME.*'

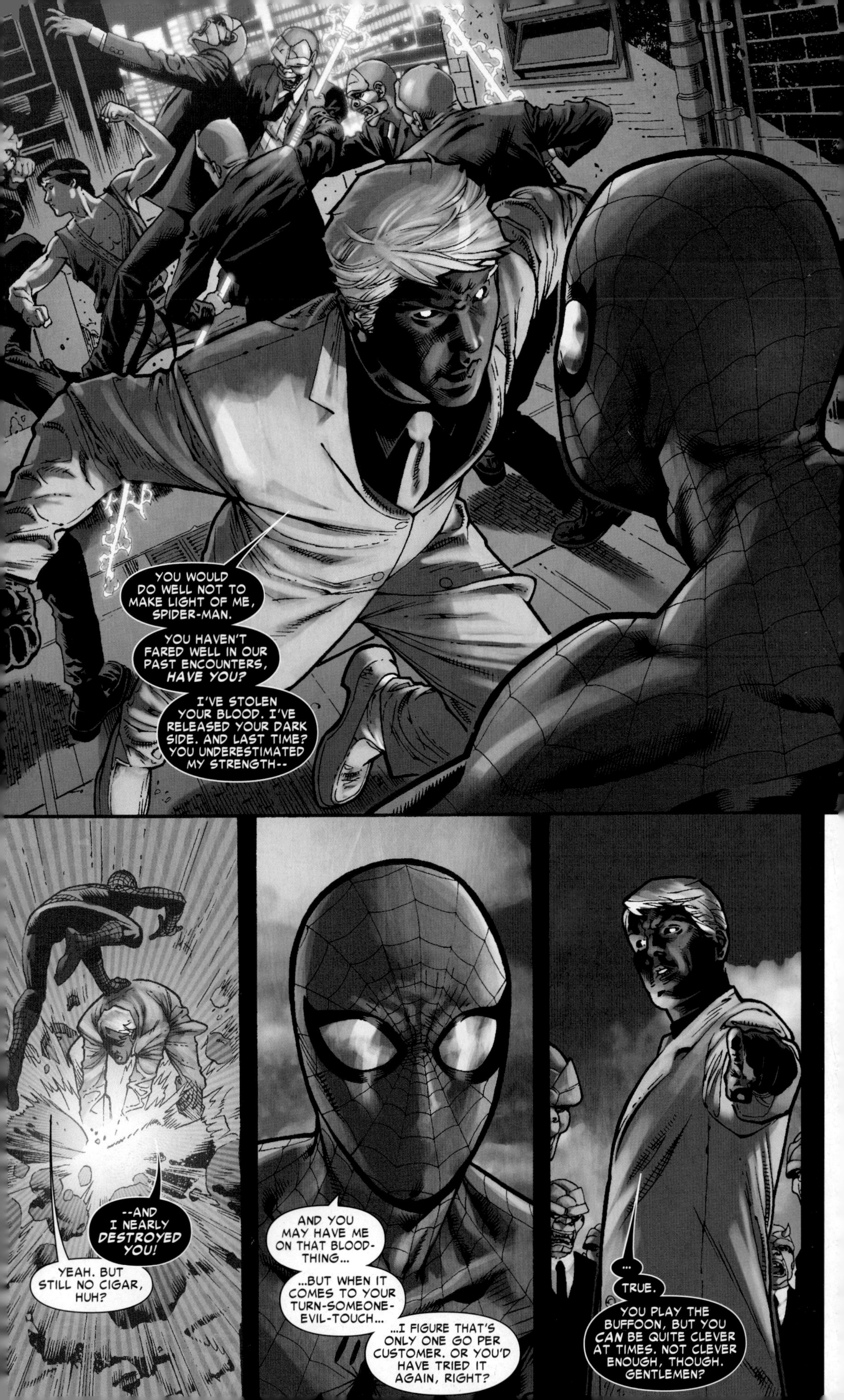
YOU WOULD DO WELL NOT TO MAKE LIGHT OF ME, SPIDER-MAN.
YOU HAVEN'T FARED WELL IN OUR PAST ENCOUNTERS, HAVE YOU?
I'VE STOLEN YOUR BLOOD. I'VE RELEASED YOUR DARK SIDE. AND LAST TIME? YOU UNDERESTIMATED MY STRENGTH--
--AND I NEARLY DESTROYED YOU!
YEAH. BUT STILL NO CIGAR, HUH?
AND YOU MAY HAVE ME ON THAT BLOOD-THING...
...BUT WHEN IT COMES TO YOUR TURN-SOMEONE-EVIL-TOUCH...
...I FIGURE THAT'S ONLY ONE GO PER CUSTOMER. OR YOU'D HAVE TRIED IT AGAIN, RIGHT?
...
TRUE.
YOU PLAY THE BUFFOON, BUT YOU CAN BE QUITE CLEVER AT TIMES. NOT CLEVER ENOUGH, THOUGH. GENTLEMEN?

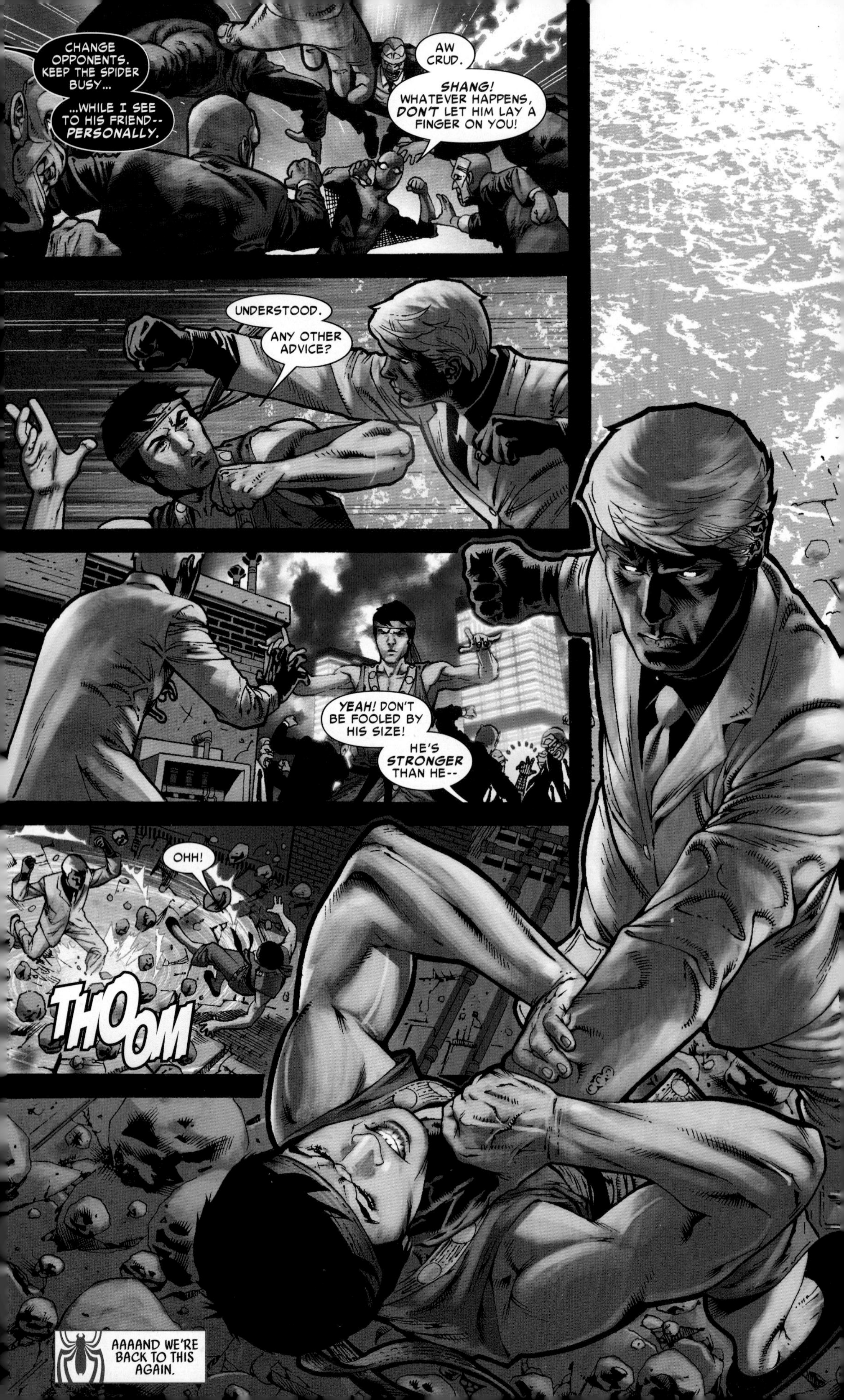
CHANGE OPPONENTS. KEEP THE SPIDER BUSY...
...WHILE I SEE TO HIS FRIEND-- PERSONALLY.
AW CRUD.
SHANG! WHATEVER HAPPENS, DON'T LET HIM LAY A FINGER ON YOU!
UNDERSTOOD.
ANY OTHER ADVICE?
YEAH! DON'T BE FOOLED BY HIS SIZE!
HE'S STRONGER THAN HE--
OHH!
THOOM
AAAAND WE'RE BACK TO THIS AGAIN.

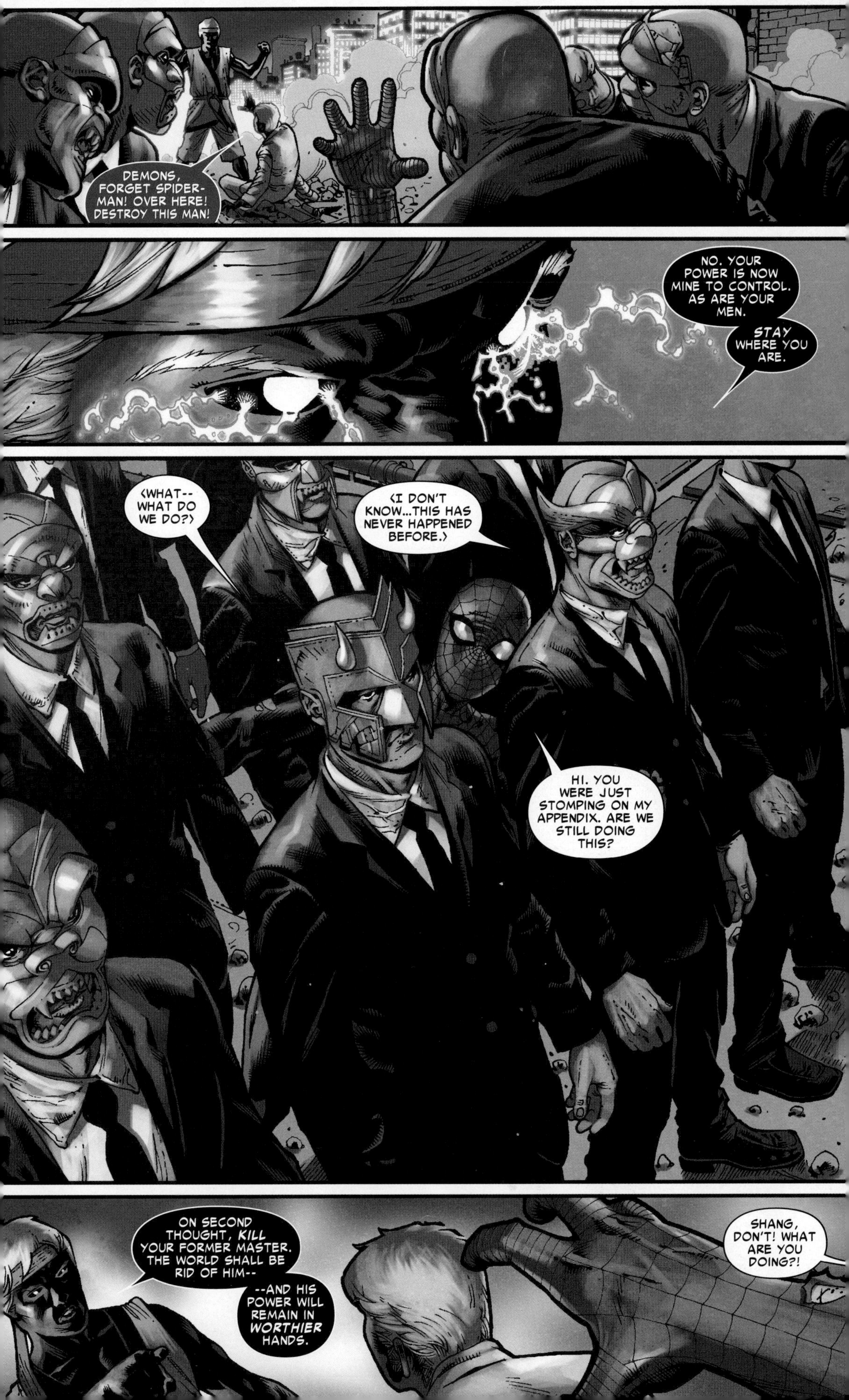

DEMONS, FORGET SPIDER-MAN! OVER HERE! DESTROY THIS MAN!
NO. YOUR POWER IS NOW MINE TO CONTROL. AS ARE YOUR MEN.
STAY WHERE YOU ARE.
<WHAT-- WHAT DO WE DO?>
<I DON'T KNOW...THIS HAS NEVER HAPPENED BEFORE.>
HI. YOU WERE JUST STOMPING ON MY APPENDIX. ARE WE STILL DOING THIS?
ON SECOND THOUGHT, KILL YOUR FORMER MASTER. THE WORLD SHALL BE RID OF HIM--
--AND HIS POWER WILL REMAIN IN WORTHIER HANDS.
SHANG, DON'T! WHAT ARE YOU DOING?!

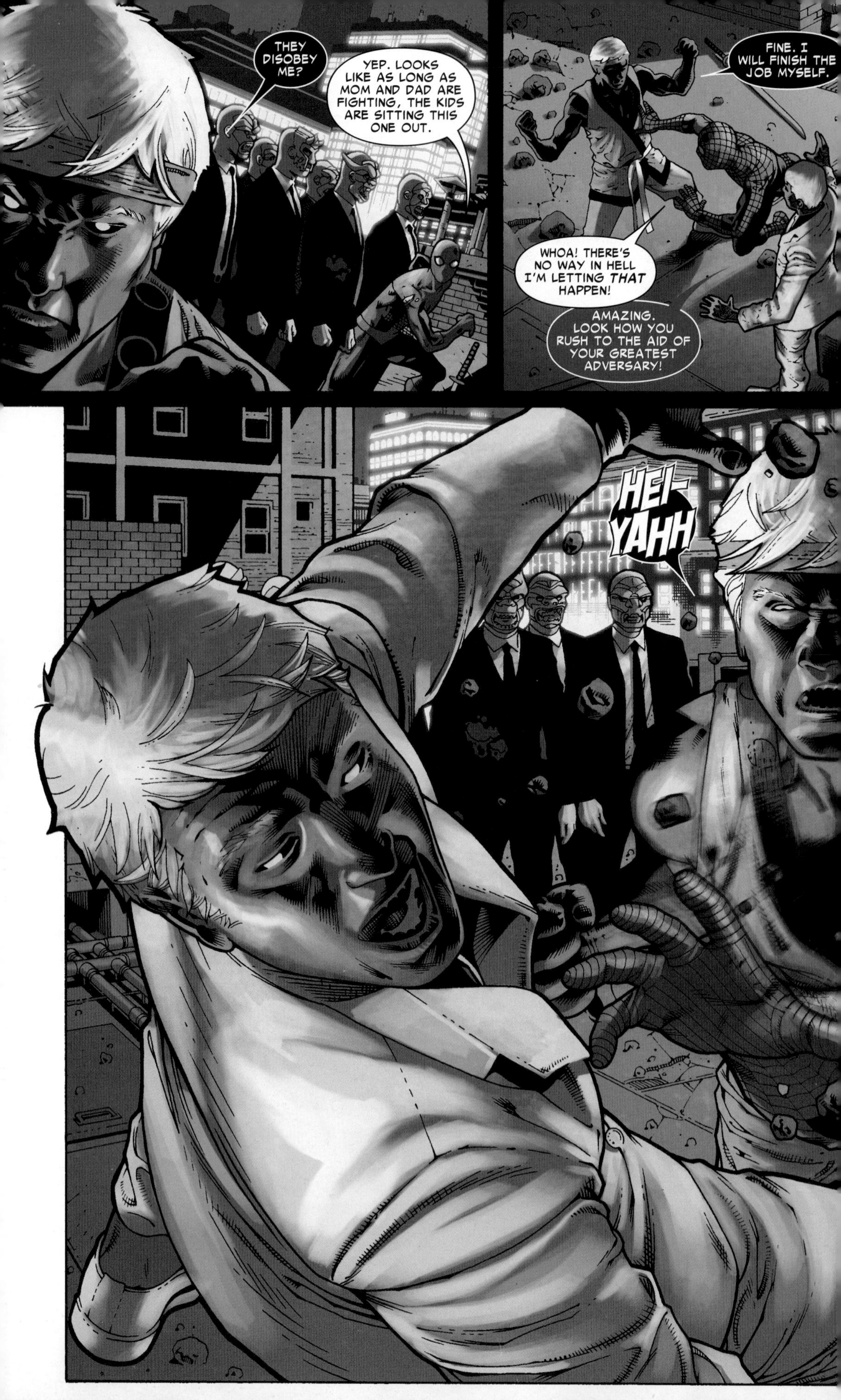
THEY DISOBEY ME?
YEP. LOOKS LIKE AS LONG AS MOM AND DAD ARE FIGHTING, THE KIDS ARE SITTING THIS ONE OUT.
FINE. I WILL FINISH THE JOB MYSELF.
WHOA! THERE'S NO WAY IN HELL I'M LETTING *THAT* HAPPEN!
AMAZING. LOOK HOW YOU RUSH TO THE AID OF YOUR GREATEST ADVERSARY!
HEI-YAHH

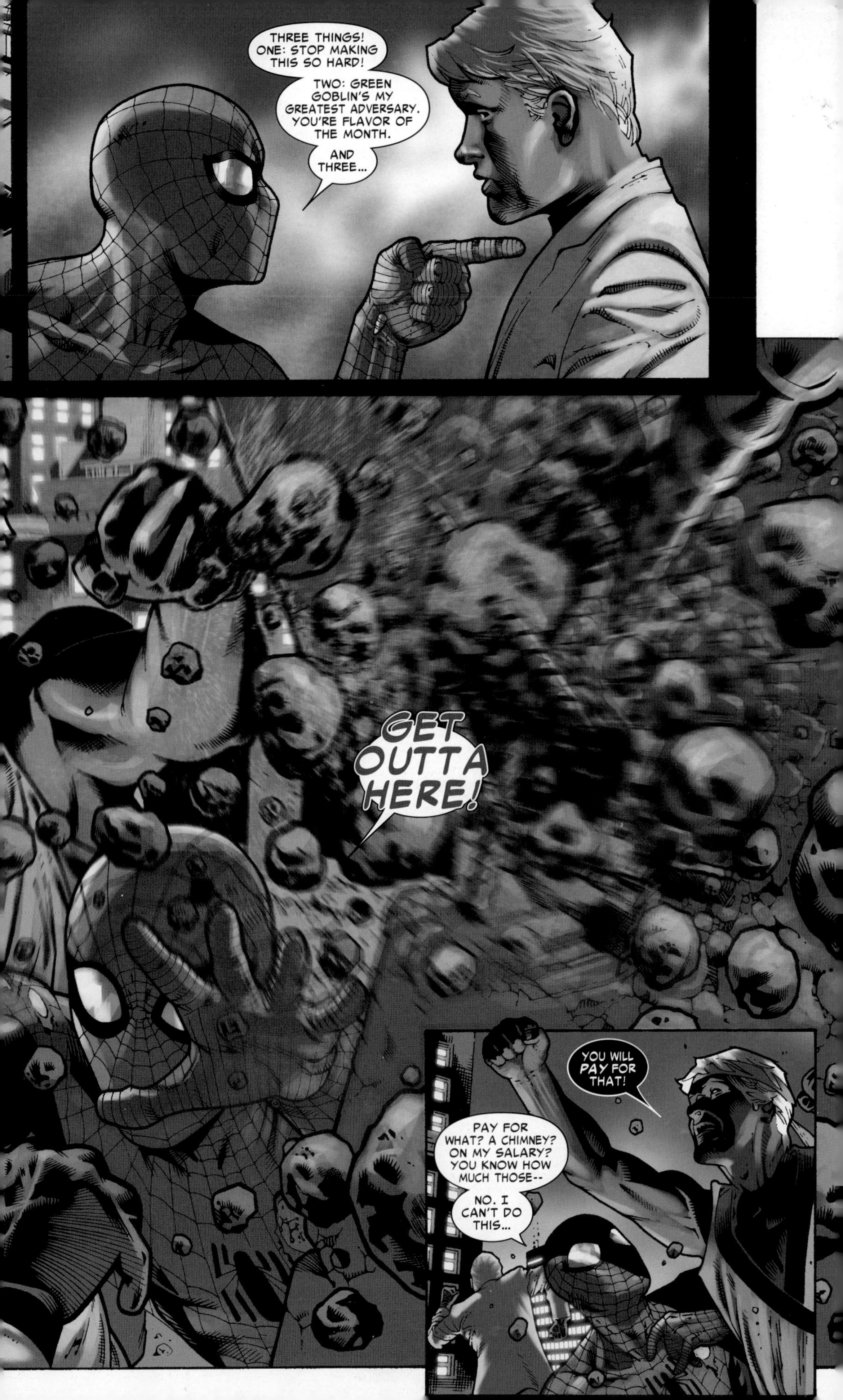
THREE THINGS! ONE: STOP MAKING THIS SO HARD!
TWO: GREEN GOBLIN'S MY GREATEST ADVERSARY. YOU'RE FLAVOR OF THE MONTH.
AND THREE...
GET OUTTA HERE!
YOU WILL PAY FOR THAT!
PAY FOR WHAT? A CHIMNEY? ON MY SALARY? YOU KNOW HOW MUCH THOSE--
NO. I CAN'T DO THIS...

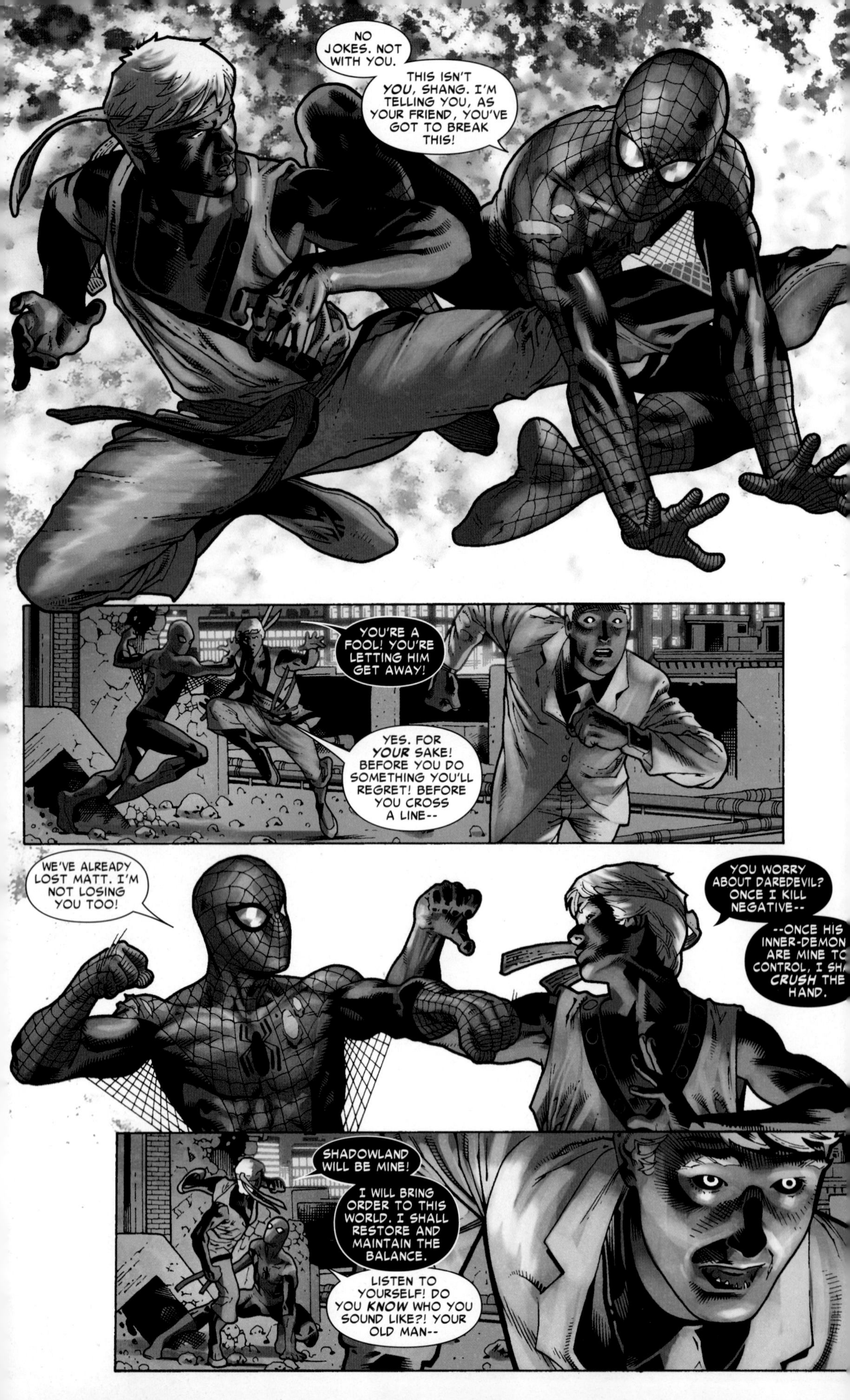
NO JOKES. NOT WITH YOU.
THIS ISN'T YOU, SHANG. I'M TELLING YOU, AS YOUR FRIEND, YOU'VE GOT TO BREAK THIS!
YOU'RE A FOOL! YOU'RE LETTING HIM GET AWAY!
YES. FOR YOUR SAKE! BEFORE YOU DO SOMETHING YOU'LL REGRET! BEFORE YOU CROSS A LINE--
WE'VE ALREADY LOST MATT. I'M NOT LOSING YOU TOO!
YOU WORRY ABOUT DAREDEVIL? ONCE I KILL NEGATIVE--
--ONCE HIS INNER-DEMON ARE MINE TO CONTROL, I SHA CRUSH THE HAND.
SHADOWLAND WILL BE MINE!
I WILL BRING ORDER TO THIS WORLD. I SHALL RESTORE AND MAINTAIN THE BALANCE.
LISTEN TO YOURSELF! DO YOU KNOW WHO YOU SOUND LIKE?! YOUR OLD MAN--

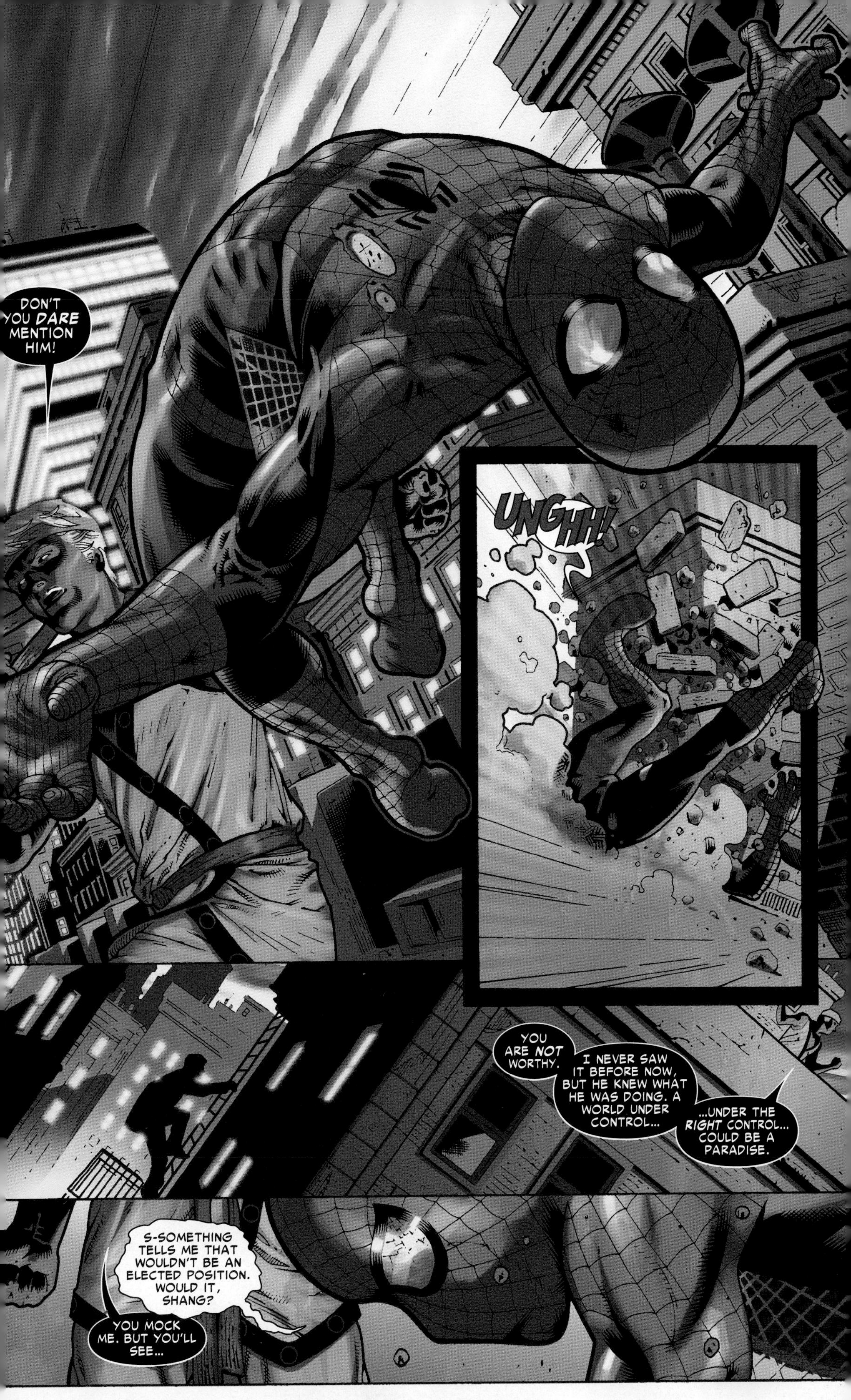
DON'T YOU DARE MENTION HIM!
UNGHH!
YOU ARE NOT WORTHY.
I NEVER SAW IT BEFORE NOW, BUT HE KNEW WHAT HE WAS DOING. A WORLD UNDER CONTROL...
...UNDER THE RIGHT CONTROL... COULD BE A PARADISE.
S-SOMETHING TELLS ME THAT WOULDN'T BE AN ELECTED POSITION. WOULD IT, SHANG?
YOU MOCK ME. BUT YOU'LL SEE...

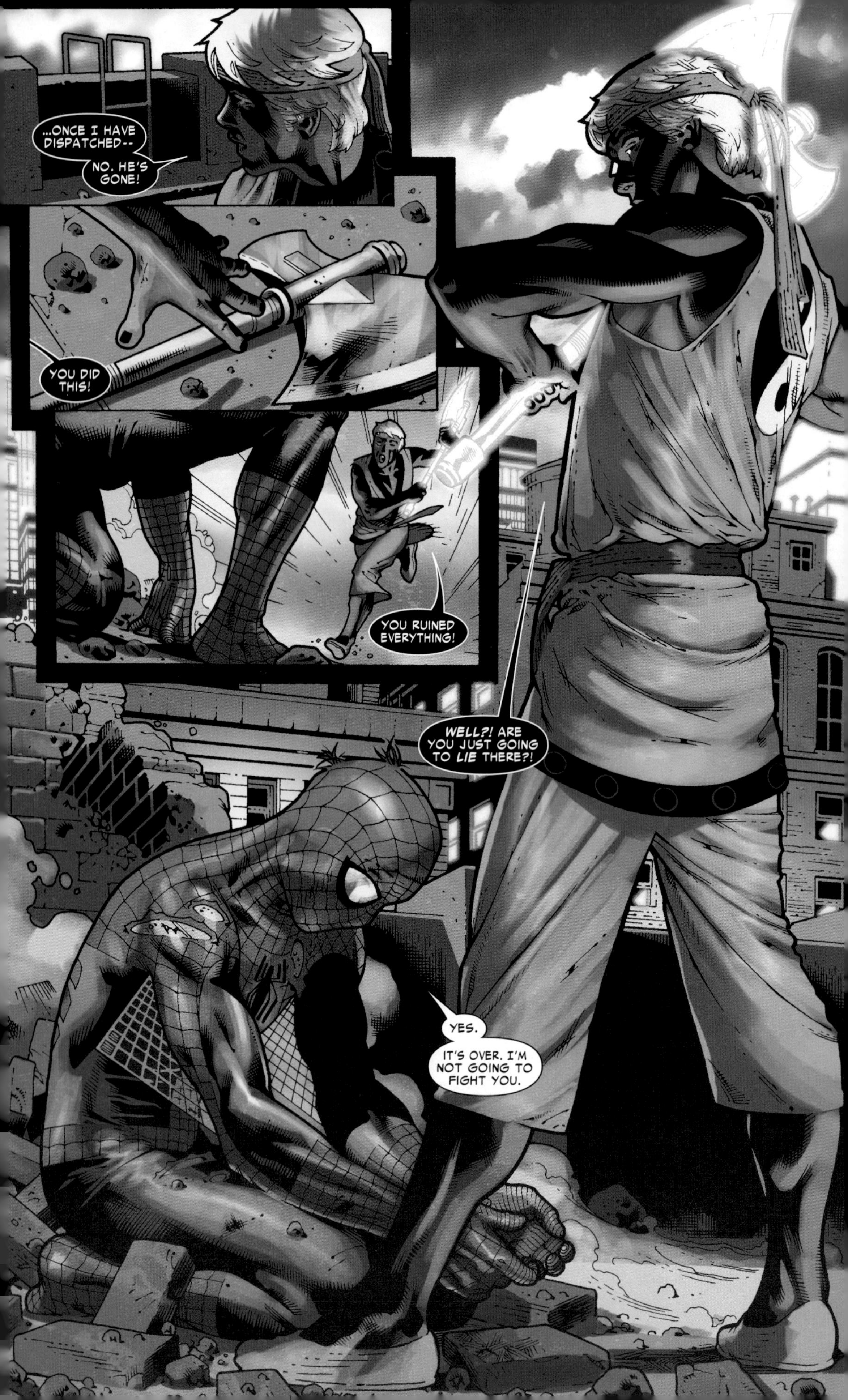
...ONCE I HAVE DISPATCHED--
NO. HE'S GONE!
YOU DID THIS!
YOU RUINED EVERYTHING!
WELL?! ARE YOU JUST GOING TO LIE THERE?!
YES.
IT'S OVER. I'M NOT GOING TO FIGHT YOU.

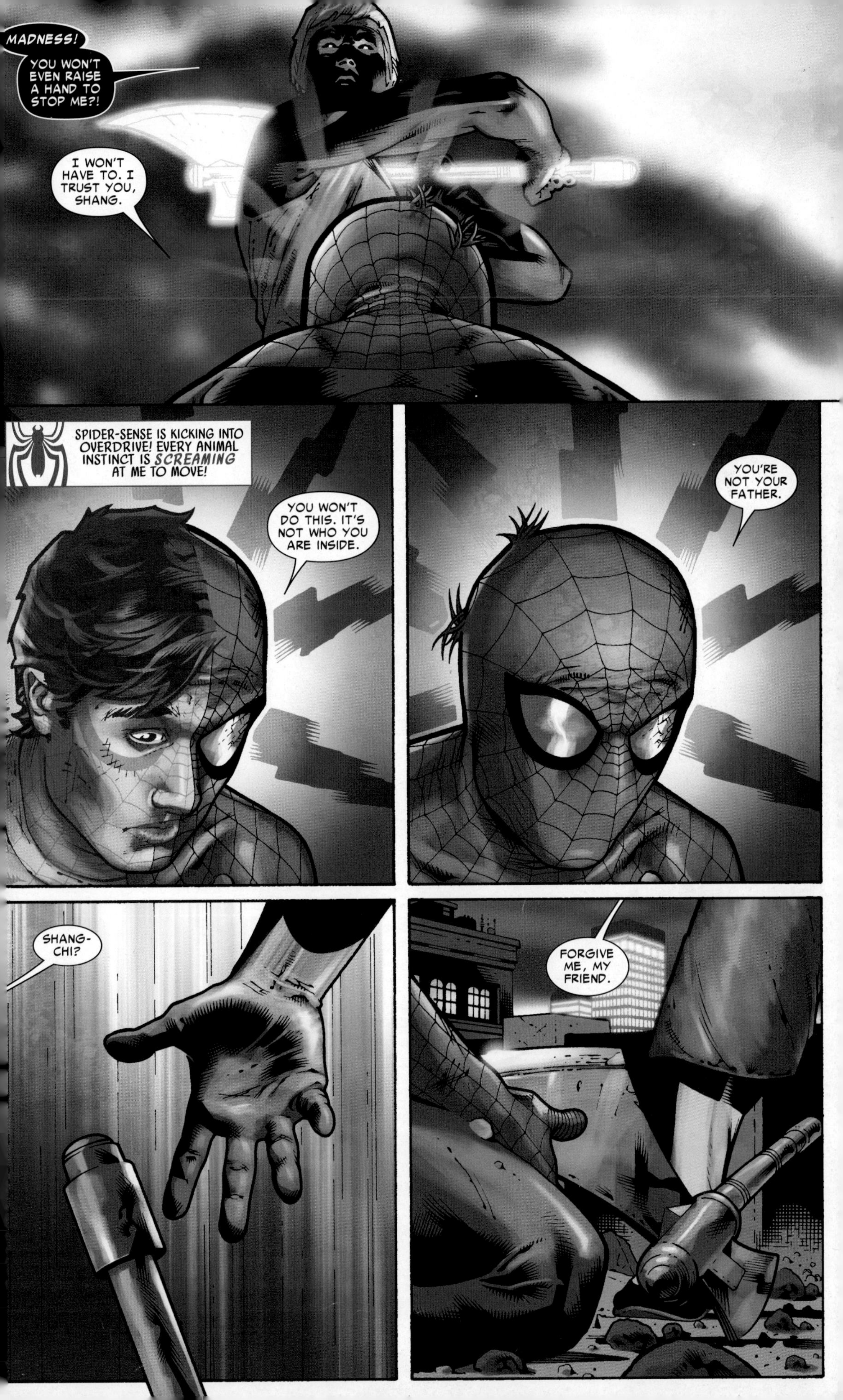
MADNESS!
YOU WON'T EVEN RAISE A HAND TO STOP ME?!
I WON'T HAVE TO. I TRUST YOU, SHANG.
SPIDER-SENSE IS KICKING INTO OVERDRIVE! EVERY ANIMAL INSTINCT IS SCREAMING AT ME TO MOVE!
YOU WON'T DO THIS. IT'S NOT WHO YOU ARE INSIDE.
YOU'RE NOT YOUR FATHER.
SHANG-CHI?
FORGIVE ME, MY FRIEND.

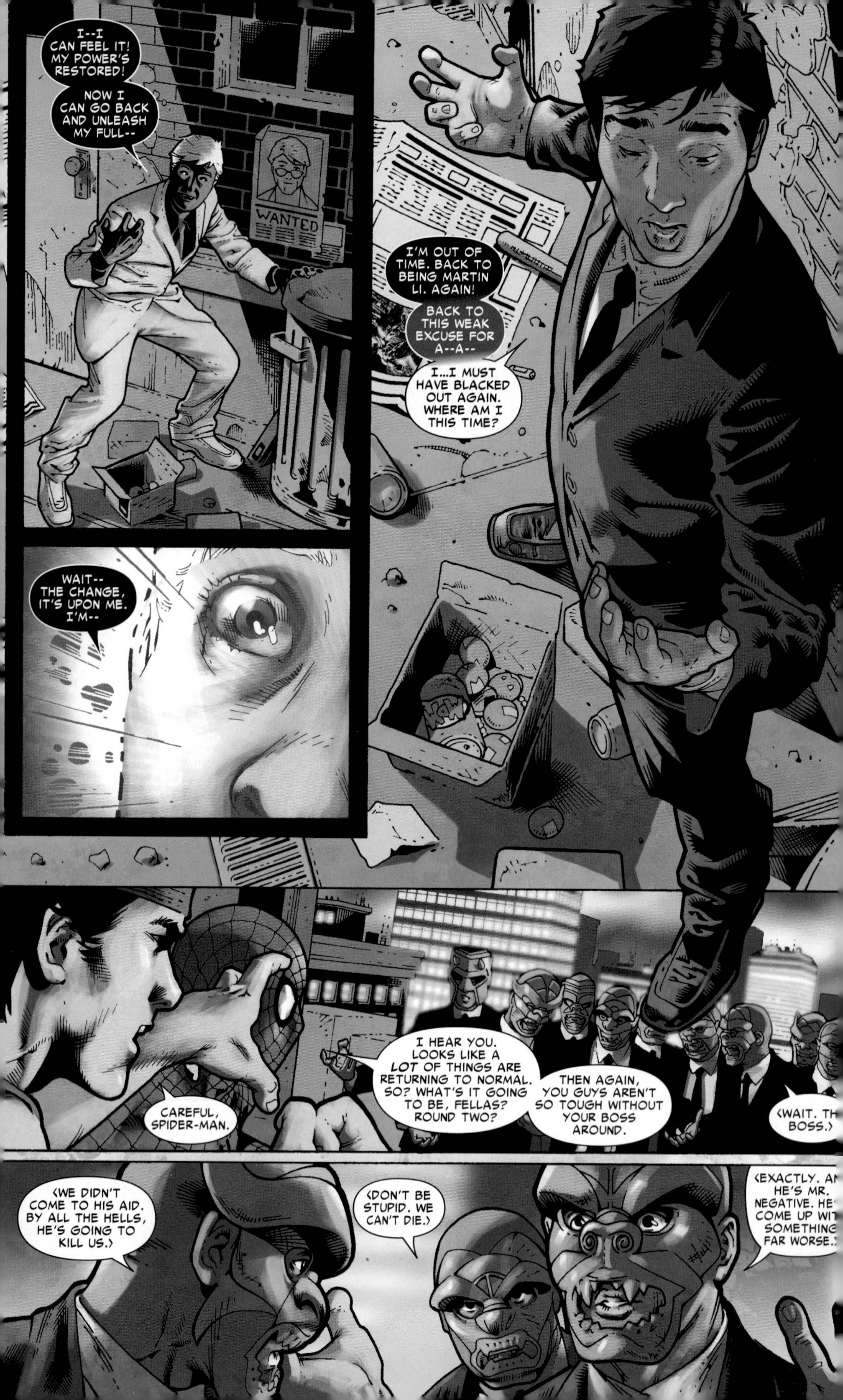

I--I CAN FEEL IT! MY POWER'S RESTORED!
NOW I CAN GO BACK AND UNLEASH MY FULL--
WANTED
WAIT-- THE CHANGE, IT'S UPON ME. I'M--
I'M OUT OF TIME. BACK TO BEING MARTIN LI. AGAIN!
BACK TO THIS WEAK EXCUSE FOR A--A--
I...I MUST HAVE BLACKED OUT AGAIN. WHERE AM I THIS TIME?
CAREFUL, SPIDER-MAN.
I HEAR YOU. LOOKS LIKE A *LOT* OF THINGS ARE RETURNING TO NORMAL. SO? WHAT'S IT GOING TO BE, FELLAS? ROUND TWO?
THEN AGAIN, YOU GUYS AREN'T SO TOUGH WITHOUT YOUR BOSS AROUND.
‹WAIT. TH BOSS.›
‹WE DIDN'T COME TO HIS AID. BY ALL THE HELLS, HE'S GOING TO KILL US.›
‹DON'T BE STUPID. WE CAN'T DIE.›
‹EXACTLY. AN HE'S MR. NEGATIVE. HE' COME UP WIT SOMETHING FAR WORSE.›

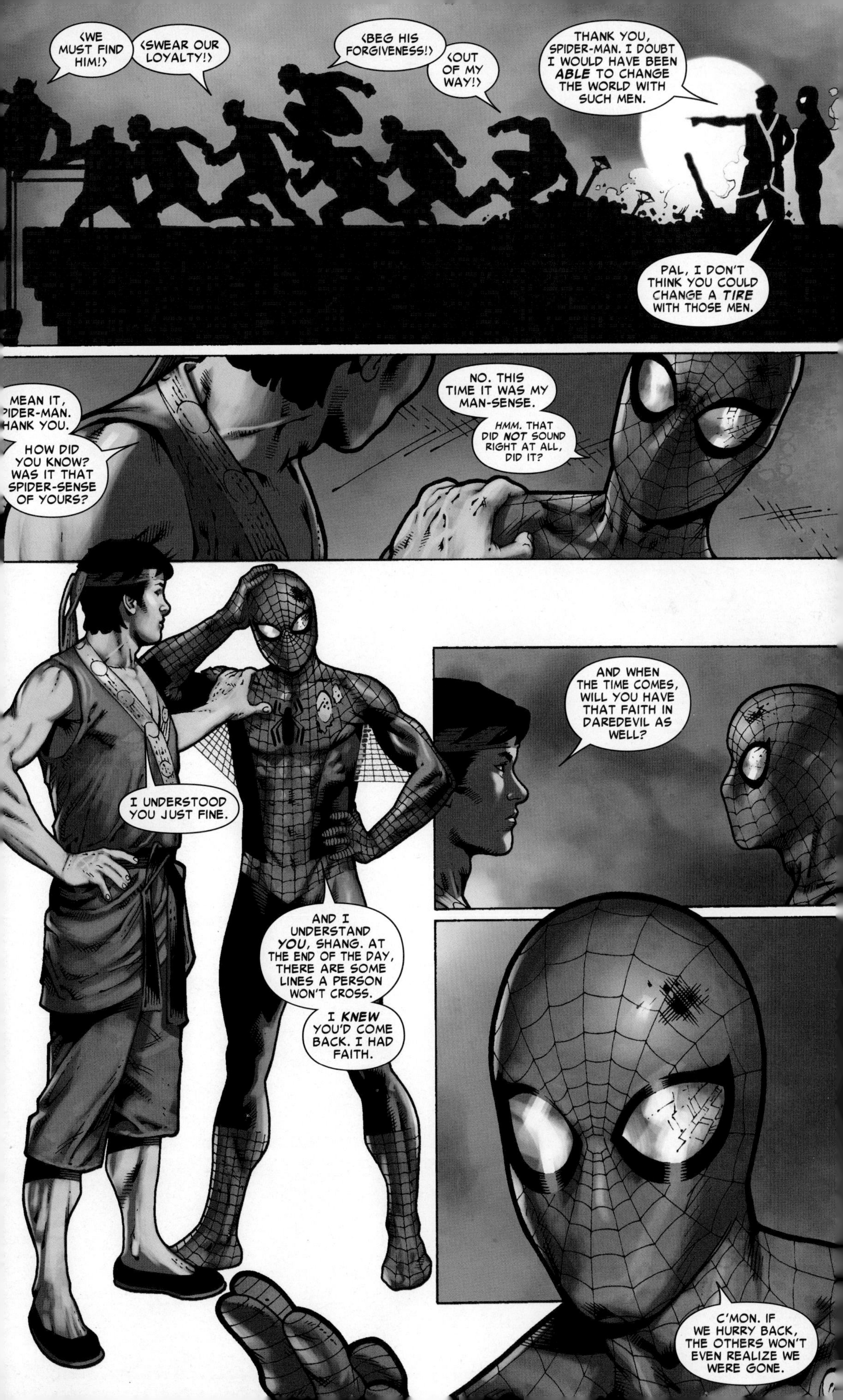
‹WE MUST FIND HIM!›
‹SWEAR OUR LOYALTY!›
‹BEG HIS FORGIVENESS!›
‹OUT OF MY WAY!›
THANK YOU, SPIDER-MAN. I DOUBT I WOULD HAVE BEEN *ABLE* TO CHANGE THE WORLD WITH SUCH MEN.
PAL, I DON'T THINK YOU COULD CHANGE A *TIRE* WITH THOSE MEN.
MEAN IT, PIDER-MAN. HANK YOU.
HOW DID YOU KNOW? WAS IT THAT SPIDER-SENSE OF YOURS?
NO. THIS TIME IT WAS MY MAN-SENSE.
HMM. THAT DID *NOT* SOUND RIGHT AT ALL, DID IT?
I UNDERSTOOD YOU JUST FINE.
AND I UNDERSTAND *YOU*, SHANG. AT THE END OF THE DAY, THERE ARE SOME LINES A PERSON WON'T CROSS.
I *KNEW* YOU'D COME BACK. I HAD FAITH.
AND WHEN THE TIME COMES, WILL YOU HAVE THAT FAITH IN DAREDEVIL AS WELL?
C'MON. IF WE HURRY BACK, THE OTHERS WON'T EVEN REALIZE WE WERE GONE.

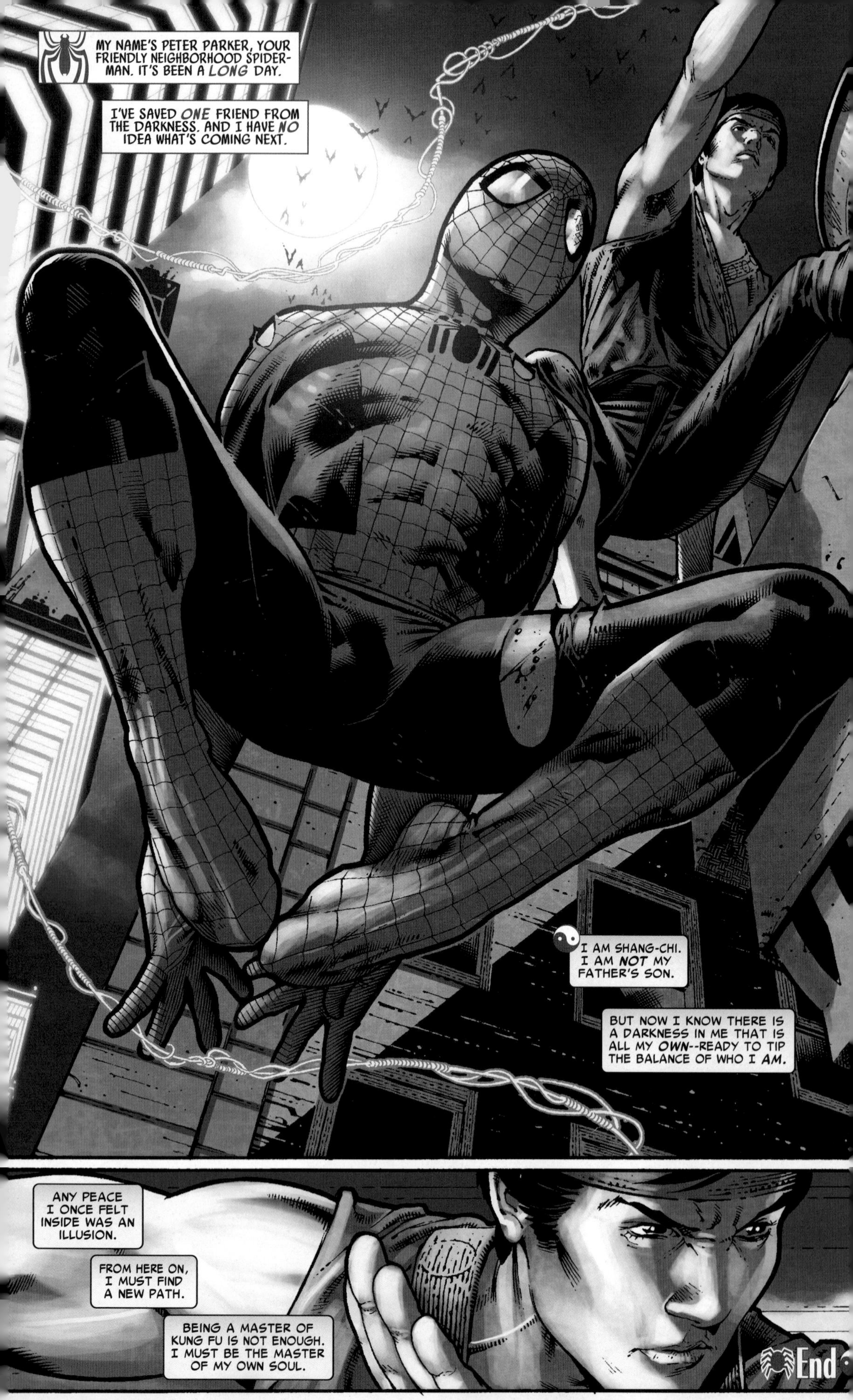
MY NAME'S PETER PARKER, YOUR FRIENDLY NEIGHBORHOOD SPIDER-MAN. IT'S BEEN A *LONG* DAY.
I'VE SAVED *ONE* FRIEND FROM THE DARKNESS. AND I HAVE *NO* IDEA WHAT'S COMING NEXT.
I AM SHANG-CHI. I AM ***NOT*** MY FATHER'S SON.
BUT NOW I KNOW THERE IS A DARKNESS IN ME THAT IS ALL MY *OWN*--READY TO TIP THE BALANCE OF WHO I *AM*.
ANY PEACE I ONCE FELT INSIDE WAS AN ILLUSION.
FROM HERE ON, I MUST FIND A NEW PATH.
BEING A MASTER OF KUNG FU IS NOT ENOUGH. I MUST BE THE MASTER OF MY OWN SOUL.
End

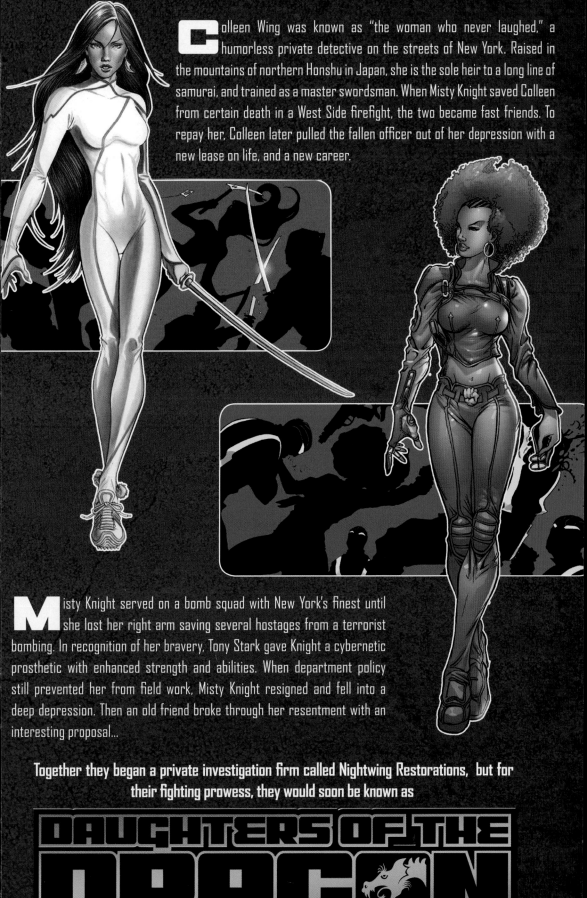

Colleen Wing was known as "the woman who never laughed," a humorless private detective on the streets of New York. Raised in the mountains of northern Honshu in Japan, she is the sole heir to a long line of samurai, and trained as a master swordsman. When Misty Knight saved Colleen from certain death in a West Side firefight, the two became fast friends. To repay her, Colleen later pulled the fallen officer out of her depression with a new lease on life, and a new career.

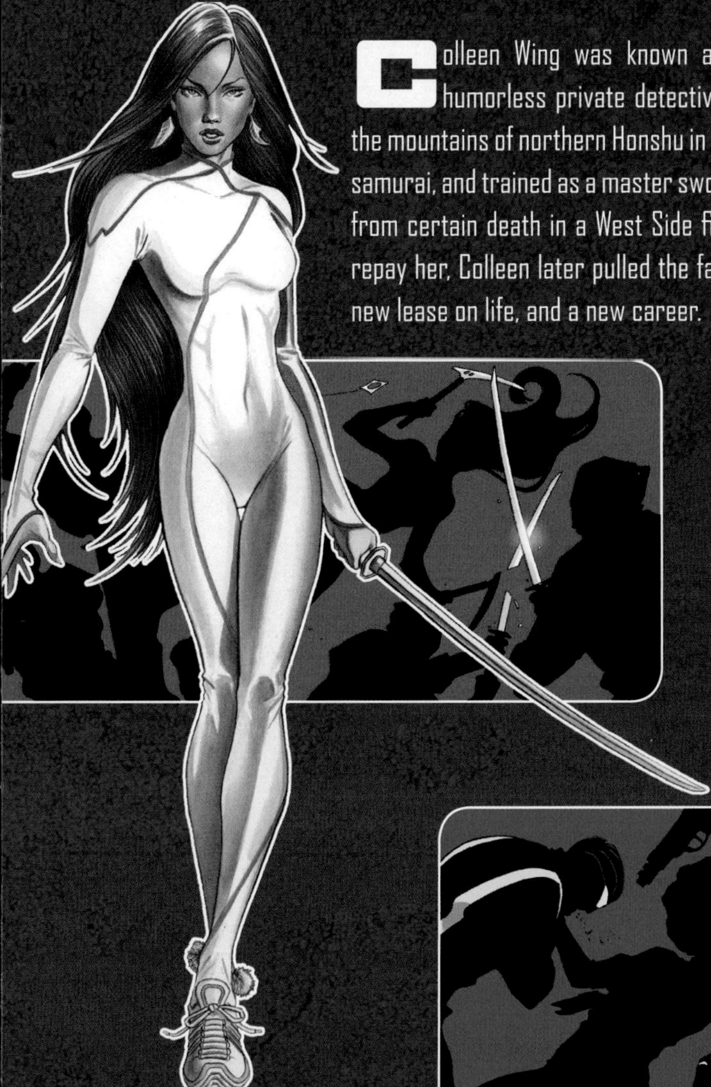

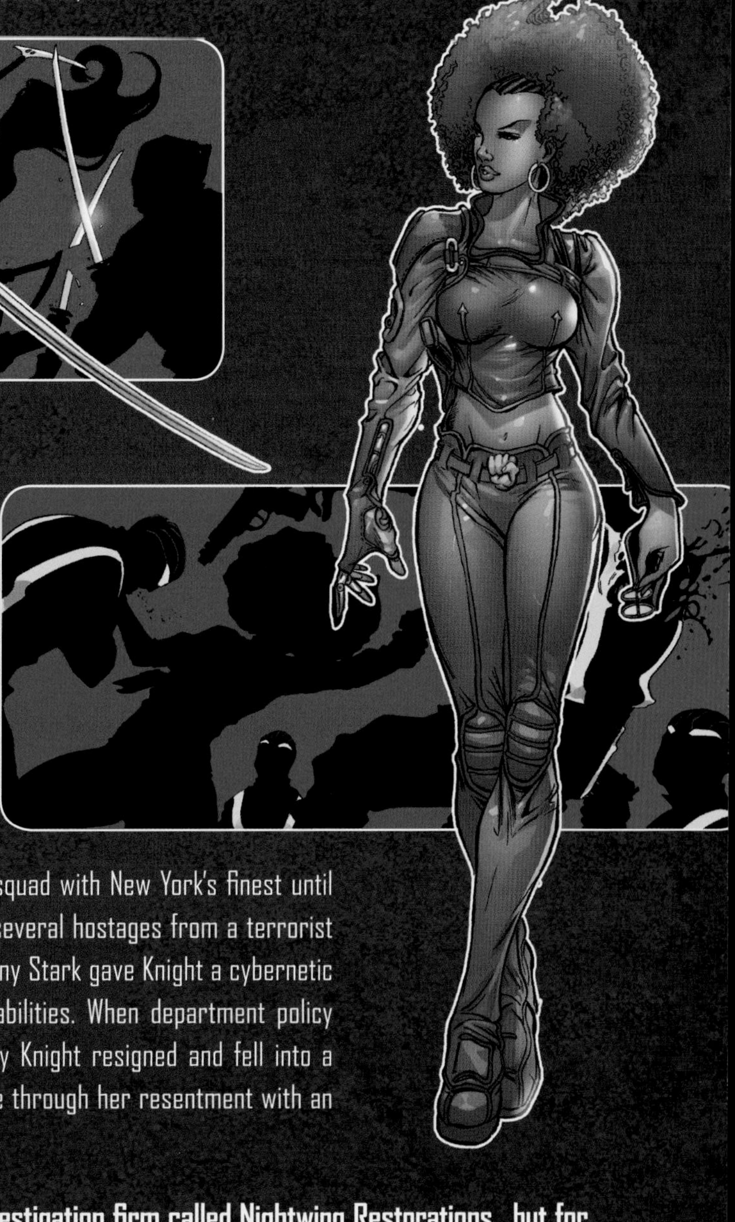

Misty Knight served on a bomb squad with New York's finest until she lost her right arm saving several hostages from a terrorist bombing. In recognition of her bravery, Tony Stark gave Knight a cybernetic prosthetic with enhanced strength and abilities. When department policy still prevented her from field work, Misty Knight resigned and fell into a deep depression. Then an old friend broke through her resentment with an interesting proposal...

Together they began a private investigation firm called Nightwing Restorations, but for their fighting prowess, they would soon be known as

DAUGHTERS OF THE DRAGON

Colleen and Misty made many allies in the early days of Nightwing Restorations:

Daniel Rand, the Immortal Iron Fist, was hired to protect Colleen's father Lee Wing, Professor of Oriental Studies at Columbia University. He had discovered the Book of Many Things, written by sorceror Master Khan, sought by the death cult of Kali to use in the destruction of Danny's home, the mystic city of K'un Lun.

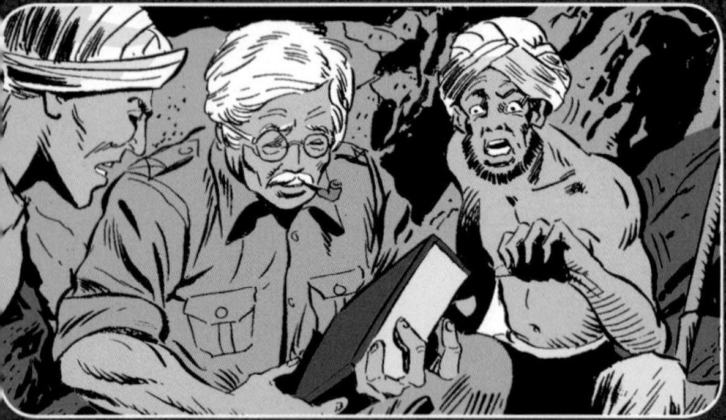

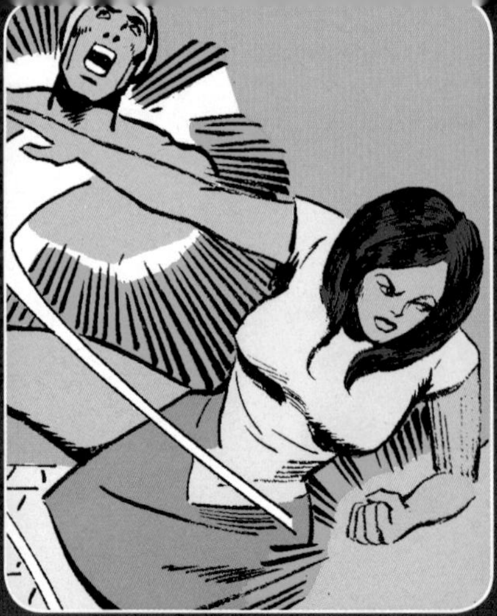

Though abducted by the cult, Colleen and her fathe were later rescued by Iron Fist and fought thei way to freedom. From then on, Danny Rand becam Colleen's closest friend after Misty.

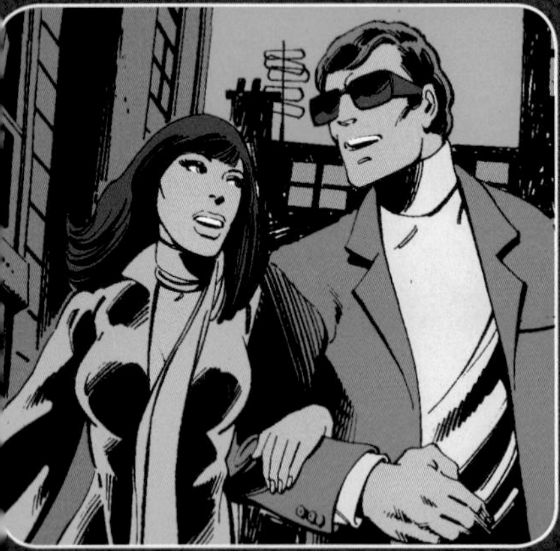

Searching for a new apartment to match her new life, Misty Knight became roommates with Jean Grey a.k.a. Phoenix of the X-Men. While working for Colleen's uncle, Prime Minister Fukada, Colleen and Misty went on to help the X-Men stop Moses Magnum from taking over Japan. Colleen became involved with Cyclops (Scott Summers) for a short time after this encounter, until he abruptly ended the relationship, returning to Jean Grey.

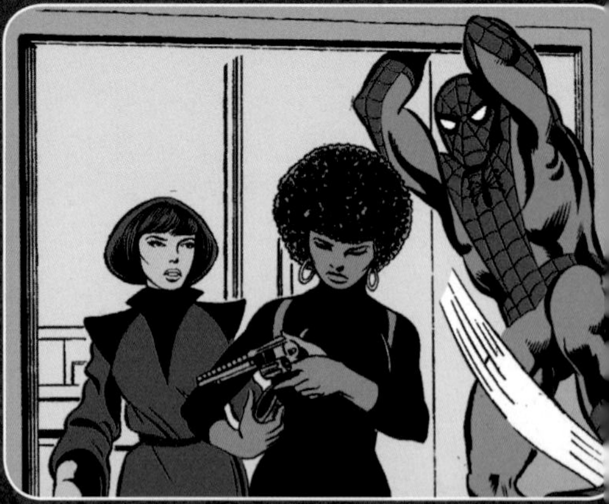

Even Spider-Man crossed their paths a time or two, when the three teamed up to help Iron Fist face the K'un-Lun exile Steel Serpent, bent on stealing the power of the Iron Fist from Danny.

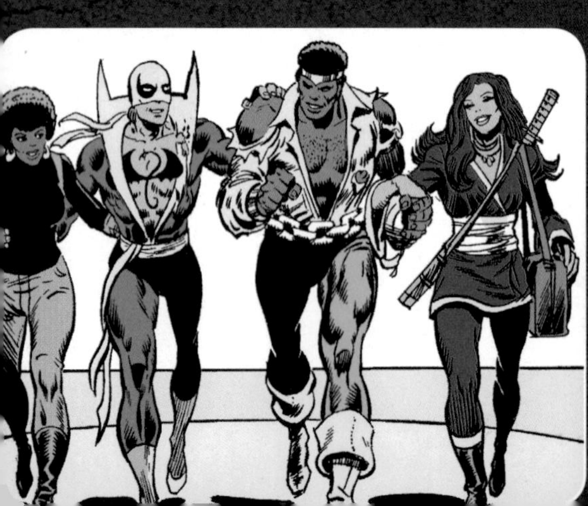

The duo's longest and greatest partnershi however, was with the organization whose monike they would one day adopt for themselves. With Luk Cage framed for crimes he didn't commit, Collee and Misty helped Iron Fist clear his name, afte which Cage and Iron Fist formed the bodyguard/ investigation firm Heroes for Hire.

When many superheroes disappeared during the Onslaught crisis, Colleen helped Misty, Luke Cage and Iron Fist to organize a new Heroes for Hire to pick up the slack. The roster included a wide range of heroes from mission-to-mission, including Ant-Man, Black Knight, Brother Voodoo, Deadpool, Shang-Chi, She-Hulk and the original Human Torch. The new team would last only a few months before the lost heroes' return.

Free to rebuild Nightwing Restorations, Colleen and Misty expanded to bail bond work and bounty hunting. Their most notable assignment foiled mafiosa princess, Celia Ricadonna's auction of a computer chip capable of creating worldwide economic collapse.

Following passage of the Superhuman Registration Act, Colleen and Misty formed a new Heroes for Hire at the behest of Tony Stark, complete with federal funding. Under the condition that they would only pursue unregistered villains, not heroes, Misty chose a questionable team including ex-villains Humbug and Orka, the mercenary Paladin, and martial experts Shang-Chi and Tarantula. With Paladin betraying them in a failed attempt to capture anti-Registration leader Captain America, the team repeatedly displayed moral and ethical ambiguity. Finally, Colleen split from Misty, wondering if heroes who have a price can truly be heroes at all.

he two set aside their differences to aid Luke Cage and Iron
ist in defeating agents of Hydra intent on entering the immortal
ity of K'un-Lun and destroying it. Later, they saved Iron Fist
rom death at the hands of Zhou Cheng, servent of Ch'i-Lin, the
east which devours the dragon of K'un-Lun. But though they
ontinued to work with mutual friends, the future of Colleen and
isty's friendship remains unknown...

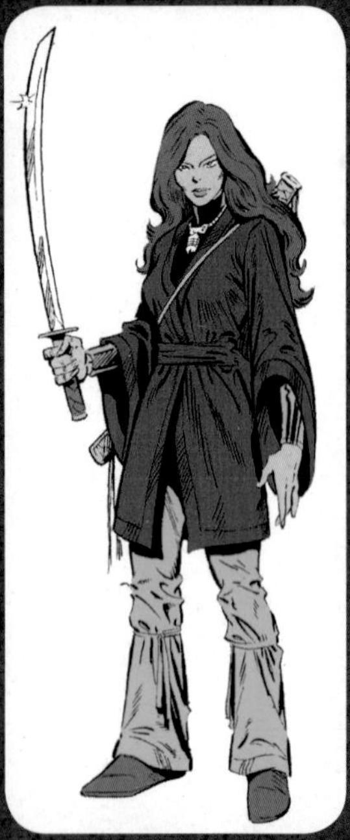

Colleen was raised in the mountains of northern Honshu, Japan, by her maternal grandfather Kenji Ozawa, Chief of the Japanese Secret Service. Being the sole heir to a long line of samurai and Daimyo, Colleen was pushed to her limits, running ten miles barefoot through the mountains each day and learning to focus her chi for feats of strength.

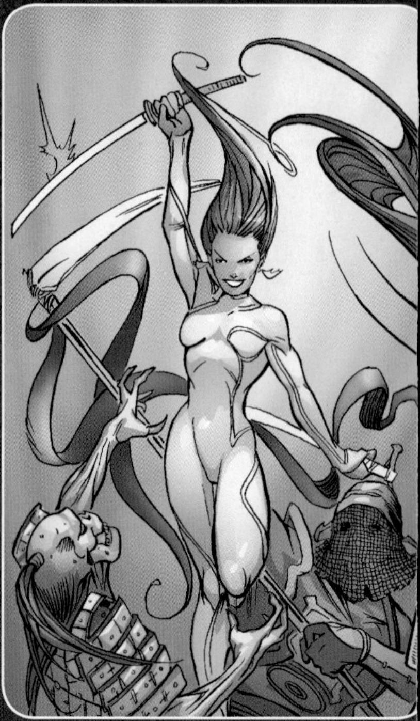

Once brainwashed as a living weapon by Iron Fist's long-time enemy Master Khan, Colleen was freed from his control by melding her mind with Iron Fist, sharing their innermost thoughts and memories. As a result, Colleen gained knowledge of K'un-Lun martial arts, and greater chi abilities. She can now focus her chi to enhance her strength, accelerate healing, reduce body functions to near zero to survive extreme cold or feign death, or burn foreign substances out of her system.

When her grandfather was killed by Hon Kong crimelord Emil Vachon, Collee inherited his katana, a 1,000-year-ol Meitou ("noted sword"). Colleen follow the samurai tradition which states that warrior's blade should only be resheathe once drawn if it has taken an enemy's lif and tasted his blood.

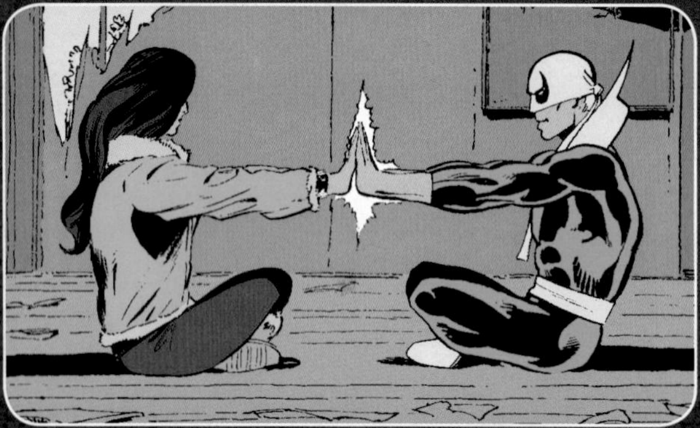

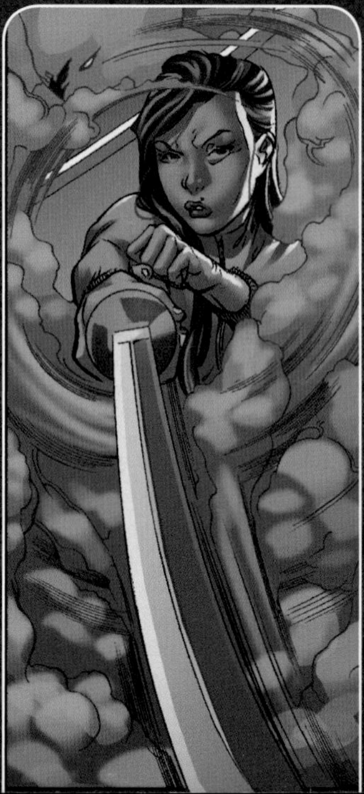

Colleen maintains peak physical condition at all times. She is an exceptional acrobat, a third-dan Karate black belt, and world-class Kenjutsu swordswoman.

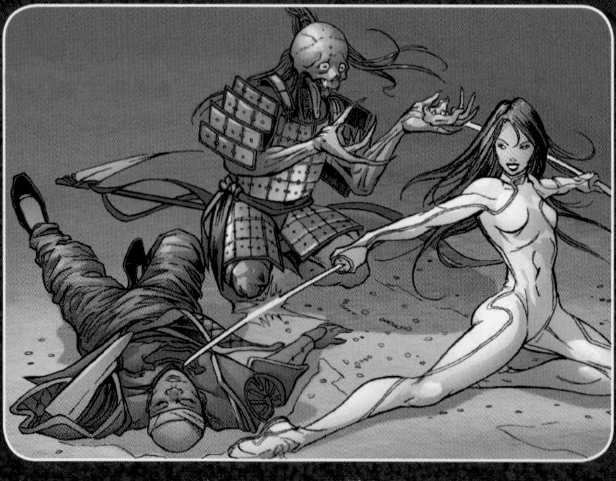